The Way the Modern World Works

The Way the Modern World Works

World Hegemony to World Impasse

Peter J. Taylor
Department of Geography, Loughborough University, UK

JOHN WILEY & SONS
Chichester · New York · Brisbane · Toronto · Singapore

Copyright © 1996 by John Wiley & Sons Ltd,
Baffins Lane, Chichester,
West Sussex PO19 1UD, England

National   01243 779777
International   (+44) 1243 779777

Other Wiley Editorial Offices

John Wiley & Sons, Inc., 605 Third Avenue,
New York, NY 10158-0012, USA

Jacaranda Wiley Ltd, 33 Park Road, Milton,
Queensland 4064, Australia

John Wiley & Sons (Canada) Ltd, 22 Worcester Road,
Rexdale, Ontario M9W 1L1, Canada

John Wiley & Sons (Asia) Pte Ltd, 2 Clementi Loop #02-01,
Jin Xing Distripark, Singapore 0512

British Library Cataloguing in Publication Data

A catalogue record for this book is available from the British Library

ISBN 0 471 96586 3

Typeset in 10/12pt Palatino by Dorwyn Ltd, Rowlands Castle, Hants
Printed and bound in Great Britain by Bookcraft (Bath) Ltd, Midsomer Norton
This book is printed on acid-free paper responsibly manufactured from sustainable
forestation, for which at least two trees are planted for each one used for paper production.

FOR CALVERTON

Contents

Contents

Preface

Postage stamps say more than simply 'delivery tariff paid': every country uses them to convey their national identity. Small countries, in particular, relish the fact that through stamps they are able to proclaim their independence to the rest of the world. But irrespective of size, great national heroes, famous national events, distinctive national flora and fauna abound on stamps proudly bearing the name of the country of issue. But there is one interesting exception concerning the name: all British stamps have no country of origin printed on them. From the original 'penny black' issued in 1840 to the contemporary 'special issues' of the Royal Mail, there is no concession to the rest of the world: no name on a stamp means it must be British. This does not cause confusion precisely because every other country names its stamps. There is a long-term informal convention that allows Britain to produce its nameless stamps, and every one else falls into line. A strictly formal convention which similarly treats Britain as special was signed in 1884 at Washington DC where it was agreed that the starting point for measuring longitude, 0 degrees, would be located through Greenwich in London. Unlike latitude, where the poles and equator physically define a measuring system, longitude has no natural points or lines of reference so that numbering of lines can begin anywhere. For many years different countries had different systems of longitude with zero degrees located through their territory. The 1883 conference in Washington DC was called to overcome this confusion and provide a single international longitude system. The result was that the British provided the 'prime meridian', meaning that the rest of the world measured their relative location east or west of the Greenwich meridian and their time before or after Greenwich Mean Time. Both literally and figuratively, Britain was located at the centre of the world in the 19th century.

In the 20th century Britain has lost this position. Today letters bearing stamps are being replaced by electronic mail. This requires the recipient to have a precise electronic address to which messages can be sent. Given that my job has involved working in two countries, I have had two such addresses in recent years. These are:

'p.j.taylor@vtvm1.ac.edu' and
'p.j.taylor@newcastle.ac.uk'.

The latter has a clear country identification for the United Kingdom, but to which country does the first address refer? There is no country label, 'edu' stands for the education network originally set up in the USA; in e-mail there is no country label for the United States. The similarity with Britain a century ago can be extended to international phone calls. There is no 'natural' place to start in coding countries for calls but it comes as no surprise that the USA international code is 1 — and no other country even has a single digit code. Both literally and figuratively this is one area where the United States is indisputably Number One in the world.

These are minor manifestations of British and American pre-eminence over the last two centuries, examples of what we might call hegemonic trivia. Assuming we can agree that these are trivial illustrations, why call them 'hegemonic'? I use this word in this case because of the subtle nature of the power being wielded by the British and the Americans. There is a sense of power taken for granted: certainly neither country was coercing others to accept these outcomes. For much of the 19th century there was a general expectation of British leadership across many fields of social activity and the same can be said for the USA for a good deal of this century. In their heydays, Britain and the USA were not just great powers, not even just the greatest power of the era, they were different in kind from their contemporary rivals. As well as possessing some of the traditional characteristics of military–political power, these two countries had a range of additional attributes that marked them out as conspicuously different. A combination of political, economic and cultural features made Britain and America world leaders, made them 'hegemons'.

Beginning with hegemonic trivia is a crafty way to introduce a book that will develop a serious argument about hegemony. The original project from which this book grew started with a fascination with the concept of hegemony and proceeded as an exercise to see how far its range of relevance could be extended. The problem, as I saw it, was that of the two main schools of thought where the idea of hegemony was central, one employed the concept at an international scale but with a very narrow focus, while the other had a more rounded and fuller concept but failed to apply it beyond the confines of particular states. My ambition was to combine the best of these schools by avoiding each one's particular narrow limitations. It is not for me to say to what degree I have been successful, but I can admit to being frequently surprised while writing this book by how easily the concept of world hegemony could be extended into areas I had had no initial expectation of entering. The end result is that any merit the book may have is due to the myriad of connections I make between seemingly disparate topics that can all be traced back to hegemony. Here is a random check-list of some of the items I deal with below: world wars and long peaces, Orientalism and communism, the Crystal Palace and the Apollo Moon shots, Dutch windmills and American highways, republicanism and liberalism, utopias and progress, development and world cities, Dutch paintings and English novels, Doris Day and Jane Austen, Grotius and Richard Cobden, social science and political economy, Manchester and Los Angeles, Chippendale chairs and suburbia and finally, eco-Fascists and deep greens. I have nothing original to add to any of these subjects or the many others I deal with and have relied upon secondary sources, others' research. But I have made what I believe to be a unique amalgam of connections that show the power of hegemony as a concept for understanding our modern world. The breakthrough for me came about half-way through writing the book, when I realized that what it all added up to was a particular insight into modernity or, rather, modernities. As the writing finally came to an end, I found that my concept of ordinary modernity had come to rival world hegemony as the core idea of the book — but they were not really rivals — ordinary modernity provides the vital link between world hegemony and the ending of my story, world impasse.

The prime stimulus to begin this work came from Immanuel Wallerstein who invited me to visit the Fernand Braudel Center at the University of Binghamton, New York, in 1990 to act as a research associate on a MacArthur Foundation research project on comparative hegemonies. Although my research has diverged somewhat from that of the working group led by Wallerstein, Giovanni Arrighi and Terence Hopkins at Binghamton, there is no doubt about the great benefit I derived from that visit and subsequent contacts on the project. However the great opportunity to have a sustained and concentrated immersion in things hegemonic was provided by Virginia Tech who invited me to be the C. C. Garvin Visiting Professor for 1992–3. The Department of Geography at Blacksburg became the convivial base from which to explore my hegemonic themes, and I left Virginia with half a book. It has taken me about a year and a half back at Newcastle University finally to complete the book. I must thank my Head of Department in Geography, Tony Stephenson, for his support and understanding in providing time in the crucial final six months when the completion seemed always so near yet so far away. Also at Newcastle, Malcolm Newson has been a most accommodating tutor on things green, allowing my open access to his bookshelves. Thanks also to those attentive audiences with their often revealing questions to whom I have presented parts of this book over the past two or three years: at the University of Miami, the University of Kentucky, the University of South Carolina, Johns Hopkins University, the University of California at Davis, Virginia Tech, the University of Delaware, the College of William and Mary, the University of North Carolina, Newcastle University, Cambridge University, the University of Westville-Durban, the University of Natal, the University of Port Elizabeth, Rhodes University, Stellenbosch University, the University of Cape Town, the University of Pretoria and the University of Amsterdam plus conferences at Washington, DC (ISA), Prague (IGU), Rio de Janeiro (IGU), Nottingham Trent and Ghent.

In addition, many friends and colleagues have taken the time to read all or part of the penultimate version of the book and have been lavish with both encouragement and critical suggestions. These are Edward Weisband, Paul Knox and Gerard O'Tuathail of the Blacksburg critical social science reading group, Pieter Saey and the Ghent World-Systems Analysis study group, Immanuel Wallerstein and his post-doctoral students at the Maison des Sciences de l'Homme, Richard Johnson and John Tomlinson of CRICC at Nottingham Trent University and Ash Amin and Ronen Palan of RIPE at Newcastle University. I would also like to record my thanks to Iain Stevenson and Katrina Sinclair for seeing the manuscript through John Wiley's Scottish office in London. Only when the book has been read will it be appreciated how much I owe to my son Carl and daughter Clare; familial osmosis is difficult to detect but no less real for all that. Thanks 'kids'.

Finally, I have dedicated this book to the place where I grew up. Calverton is a mining village to the north-east of Nottingham where I spent a very happy childhood. Half-way through writing this book Calverton Colliery was closed and it reminded me that if things had turned out differently, I would have been one of those made redundant. One of the reasons that was not so was because my father, with the strong encouragement of my mother, took me down the pit when I was twelve to frighten me into working harder at school! A major theme of this book is Americanization and although I grew up in a council house in an English pit village I did not escape its hegemonic intrusion. One of my earliest recollections of the British state was when I realized at a young age that somewhere in my distant future I would have to do national service in the armed forces. Cheered up by the fact that you had a choice of which one of the forces to join, I thought this choice extended to five sets of fighting men — army, navy, air force, cowboys and Indians. Needless to say, I wanted to spend my national service as a cowboy. A life on the open range . . . and this was when McWorld, that is to say, McDonalds was still unheard of in England.

Some prefaces include an outline of the book but not this one. Instead I begin my text with a prologue that provides the skeleton argument of the book as a story of hegemonies and modernities. This is intended as a sort of map so that the reader knows where the argument is eventually leading. This book is a simple tale of a particular social organization, the modern world-system, not a whodunit about the end of the world.

Tynemouth, August 1995

Prologue: A tale of three hegemons and more

Once upon a time there was a modern world-system. We are still living in that time but perhaps not for too much longer. Given that this particular social system has been in existence for about half a millennium, there are innumerable stories that can be told about it. This book tells one of those stories, arguably the most important, the story of its hegemons. The three main social actors in this tale of political power, economic eminence and cultural arrogance are the 17th-century Dutch, the 19th-century British and 20th-century Americans. We will argue that the three countries housing these people, the United Provinces, Kingdom and States respectively, were, in their 'centuries', very special places. They were more than just great powers, more even than the contemporary number one among their peers: these three were hegemonic states. Each had 'something extra' that marked it out as a unique type of state in the modern world-system. Hegemony is a complex power phenomenon that uses consensus just as much as coercion in a mix that is very difficult to define. Through much of our story we will be trying to capture exactly what is that 'extra' dimension that great powers such as Spain, France, Germany and the USSR never possessed but which can be found in the Netherlands, Great Britain and the USA at their peaks.

Our story is about long-term and large-scale social change. It is prefaced by the demise of European feudalism from its peak as a social system around 1250. The 'crisis' of feudalism is a long strung-out affair, but sometime in the period after 1450 there emerged a new form of social organization which we call 'the modern world-system'. Coinciding with the first major geographical expansion of Europe into the Americas, this new system embodied several features that had not been combined in quite the same way before. Two contrary tendencies that mark our modern world were set in train producing, on the one hand, a unified economic space and, on the other, a divided political space. The earlier economic organization of localized agricultural production plus a little long-distance trade in luxury items was replaced by a more integrated economic system based upon new agricultural production for a world market. Sugar production in the Caribbean using slave labour from Africa to supply demand for sweeteners by European consumers is a classic example of this new capitalist world-economy. It is capitalist because the dominant logic in these new economic ventures tying the system together is the goal of capital accumulation. At the same time the very complex political legacy of feudalism, premised upon an hierarchical pattern of authority, was being undermined by the rise of modern states with sole sovereign control over their territories: the medieval political order from the universal (papacy and empire) to the local (manor and town) was being replaced by an inter-state system of independent polities. This was facilitated by the Reformation and Counter-Reformation, the disruption of the single Catholic church producing religious divisions upon which the states could build. The end result was that religiously unified 'Christendom' became transmuted into politically divided 'Europe'.

Europe is a peculiar world region that has had a uniquely important role in world history: it is Europeans who have taken over the whole world and reconstructed it in their own image politically, economically and even culturally. Given that today's 'one world' is a European-created world, the big historical question is: when did Europe become so decisively different from other regions that it had the potential capability for such momentous expansion? There is no doubt that the origins of the modern world-system can be traced to the 'long 16th century' (c. 1450–1650) in Europe, but it does not follow that these roots would inevitably grow into a global system. Taking a long-term view we have to say that initially the Europe that emerged from Christendom was not that unusual. It was certainly not unknown for a civilization to be divided into many political units. In fact for most regions that have housed major civilizations, there has been a discernible cycle from political unity to disunity and back again. This cycle reflects competition between states that is resolved militarily. Wars produce winners and losers until eventually a really big winner emerges to become a new empire. There is no reason to think that the early rise of capitalism in 16th-century Europe would provide a formidable obstacle to this general process. Divisions of labour for production requiring long-distance bulk trade was by no means unknown previously. The problem had always been that the major participants in such activities had never been able to protect their capital from political elites. To do so required a new social arrangement where the needs of economic elites would be taken into account alongside traditional political imperatives. The prospects for such an innovative change did not look good in 16th-century Europe. Despite the import of vast amounts of bullion from newly conquered America, the major states of Europe still managed to go bankrupt regularly: even new sources of wealth could not keep pace with an ever-increasingly expensive war machine. For instance, after years of rivalry, the two most powerful states, Hapsburg Spain and Valois France, both went bankrupt in the same year, 1557. In short, the states were great consumers of capital, using it to make war and thereby to destroy other capital through the ravishing of land and sacking of cities. All this came to a head in the Thirty Years War (1618–48), when many parts of central Europe suffered over 30% population losses. Generally such periods of warfare and social disruption between phases of civilization within a region are termed 'dark ages', and Europe in the first half of the 17th century was a place of doom and despair for most of its inhabitants.

But the resolution of the Thirty Years War was not like earlier culminations of 'dark ages'; untypically no new world empire emerged. The candidate in Europe at this time was the Hapsburg dynasty with their vast holdings in Iberia, Central Europe, northern Italy and the Low Countries. Linked to the Counter-Reformation against the Protestant princes, we can discern an imperium project by the Hapsburg family to reconstitute a true catholic Christendom in Europe. But the Hapsburgs were the great losers in the Thirty Years War. There are many reasons for this failure, and one crucial factor was the resistance of the Netherlands within the Hapsburg realms. The Dutch rebellion was an 80-year war of which the wider Thirty Year War was merely the final phase. By creating an independent United Provinces in the city-rich Low Countries, the Dutch constructed a new type of state ruled by economic elites. Merchants had ruled city-states many times before, but this was a completely new territorial state comprising numerous cities represented in government. In this way economic and political policies were effectively merged at a new scale of organization. The result was remarkably successful. While other states had perennial fiscal crises to pay for their war activities, the United Provinces budgeted with relative ease for the necessary military expenditure to protect their territory and capital. The greatest military power of the era, the Hapsburgs, was comfortably kept at bay with no destruction of the major Dutch cities: while the rest of Europe suffered the 'crisis of the 17th century', the Dutch enjoyed their 'golden age'.

The new kind of state was a hegemonic state. It was hegemonic in two crucial ways. First, it was instrumental in preventing the construction of a new imperium, and second, it provided an alternative organization to an imperium – new political-economy criteria to rival the traditional world of political–military imperatives. It is this change that made Europe so peculiar and set it on a unique path to global dominance. In short, the customary imperium project was replaced by a new hegemony project. Hence the success of the Dutch did not mean that they simply replaced the Hapsburgs as the main threat to all other states. Quite the opposite: they had no policy of conquest in Europe; rather they wished to use the multiplicity of states in order to continue to accumulate capital.

Unlike a world empire run by a single political elite, an inter-state system of many independent political elites provided the opportunity for Dutch merchants to buy cheap and sell dear across Europe and beyond without any overarching political interference. This manoeuvrability for capital provided the conditions that enabled economic elites to emerge from the suffocating dominance by political elites. But for this to work, the states had to modify their political imperatives of conquer or perish. In other words, a new *raison d'état* was necessary in which economic considerations took their place alongside political ones. This is what the Dutch invented for their new territorial state; and they were so successful that rival states had no choice but to emulate them. The result was the age of mercantilism, state-building through mixing economic and political means – if 'little Holland' could defeat the mighty Hapsburgs, who could ignore such state policy? Instead of Europe becoming a political region of a 'perennial Thirty Years War' until a winner finally emerged, it became a political-economy region of competitive mercantilism where capital accumulation could proceed as never before. This is what made Europe such a special place that it could and did remake the world in its own image as the modern world-system.

Europe is different, therefore, because the nature of its cyclical development was revolutionized in the 17th century. Three hegemonic cycles have replaced the traditional imperium cycle of warring states alternating with empire. Political leadership has been turned on its head: instead of the leading power eliminating rivals by conquest, rivals are expected to copy the leading power and such emulation automatically leads to rivals 'catching up'. This levelling effect of hegemonic leadership among the leading powers means that 'high hegemony', when the hegemon is at its peak, is a relatively short period, but it has been no less crucial for that. Creating three distinct stages of political economy is the first dimension of the 'something extra' about hegemons. Each case of hegemony is consolidated during a period of widespread warfare when one state emerges from the military destruction as an oasis of intensified capital accumulation. In short, as well as being on the winning side, the hegemon has a 'good war' economically. This is the case for the Dutch during the Thirty Years War, and it also fits the British during the Napoleonic War and the Americans during World Wars I and II. Both Napoleonic France and Nazi Germany can be interpreted as imperium projects that successfully incorporated most of Europe before being defeated in a process that devastated all economic rivals, both enemies and allies, of Britain by 1815 and of the USA by 1945.

The opportunities opened up by having a good war were exploited in each case to create a new political economy structure. The Dutch introduced a commercially based world, the British led the way to a new industrial world and the Americans combined production with consumption in an equally unprecedented 'affluent society'. In each case failure to copy the success of the hegemon condemned rivals to oblivion. For instance, after the British industrial revolution, any state that did not follow suit would not only become relatively poorer but it would not be able to equip its armed forces adequately for war. The Ottoman Empire is a case in point: as late as the 17th century it was a real military threat to Europe, but in the 19th century it became transformed into the 'sick man of Europe' due to a failure to industrialize. Similarly the American case is interesting in this respect because whereas Western Europe and Japan adopted forms of American consumerism and were able to 'catch up' economically, this path was rejected by the main political rival, the USSR. The latter's focus on industrialization reproduced the political economy structure pioneered by Britain, but this was inadequate in terms of the new American political economy. Hence instead of catching up, the USSR fell behind economically culminating in its political collapse.

The process whereby Europeans made a new world in their image has been called 'Europeanization' or, more generally, 'Westernization'. However the term 'modernization' is much more common, with its temporal specificity replacing the geographical specificity. The word 'modern' was coined in the 17th century to describe the new Europe and came to be applied to other regions as they were transformed through incorporation into Europe's spheres of activity. 'Modern' is the word we use to describe the nature of such a transformed society; it encompasses the cultural changes that necessarily accompany the constitution of political-economy structures. Hence the capitalist world-economy is the modern world-system. Typically, 'modern' is contrasted with 'traditional' implying, in most analyses, a single duality: societies or institutions are viewed as being either traditional or modern. However, given that the modern world-system has experienced three hegemonic cycles, it follows that there should be three specific cultural structures or, if you will, three modernities. Hegemons not only create new political economies, they are directly implicated in the production of the distinctive cultures which we think of as modern. In short the hegemon is the 'most modern of the modern' in its era. This is the second dimension where we can identify that there is 'something extra' about our hegemons.

Traditionally, societies looked backwards to 'golden ages' for their legitimation. The present has been a prisoner of the past: emperors and kings, for instance, tried to emulate their successful ancestors in quests for glory. Europe in the 16th century was no different in this respect: after all the 'Renaissance' represented the discovery of the classical Mediterranean civilization as a golden age of learning. In the Hapsburg imperium project Emperor Charles V was often portrayed as the 'new Charlemagne'. It was not until the late 17th century that the 'debate between the ancients and moderns' was won by the latter with unique and profound social implications. In 'modern' Europe the temporal perspective of society was turned around with the discovery of 'progress'. The present became a prisoner of the future: the general belief in progress interpreted the present as a stepping stone from an inferior past to a superior future. This idea is one of the hallmarks of modernity and the hegemonic states are directly implicated in its creation. Because of their outstanding economic performances, the Netherlands, Britain and the USA as hegemons came to be widely accepted as representing the future for other states. Visitors came from afar 'to see the future' in these most 'advanced' locales. Obviously this provided an immense cultural power whereby hegemons defined what the future would be for others.

Three 'images of the future' that contemporaries marvelled at are: the harbour full of ships at Amsterdam, the industrial landscape of northern England centred on Manchester and leafy suburbia symbolically represented by Los Angeles in innumerable Hollywood films. These landscapes were recreated in other lands which 'modernized' through mercantilism, industrialization and 'Americanization' in turn. The Dutch made making money respectably modern and in the process condemned aristocratic mores as traditional, to die later as the 'ancien regime'. The British redefined modern as industrial by merging technology with production and relegating traditional rural life to a backward status. The Americans created a third modern by combining mass consumption with mass production to produce the 'affluent society', which defined the poverty of Third World countries as the 'underdevelopment' of traditional societies.

Each of these three conceptions of modern has been contested both from within and without by powerful traditional forces, but modernity has been on a winning role for four centuries now. It swept all before it: what was merely 'greater Europe' became truly global in the 20th century under American leadership. American 'high hegemony' lasted from 1945 to about 1970 and we are now in a period of US relative economic decline when rivals, Western Europe (especially Germany) and Japan, have 'caught up'. What comes next? Those who look for the rise of a fourth hegemon usually pick on Japan as having most of the successful economic attributes upon which to build another new political economy. But there are many problems with Japan as hegemon-in-waiting which we need not rehearse here. This is because in this tale there is no time for a fourth hegemon. Instead 'world impasse' is on the horizon.

The world we live in is based upon capital accumulation as we have seen. This has been the underlying stimulus to the overall expansion of the system. The modern world-system cannot stand still; accumulation is ceaseless. Those that do not innovate and expand disappear: they are either taken over or they go bankrupt. This driving force has stood the modern world-system in good stead in its relations with other social systems which have all succumbed to its power on the battlefield and in the market-place. With the elimination of all other societies – 'global closure' occurred about 1900 – expansion proceeded 'internally', that is by intensification of production and its necessary adjunct, consumption. The creation of mass production and mass consumption has been America's historic role in our story. But can such capital expansion be forever?

European elites have generally looked down upon Americanization as populist and vulgar. Their distaste is based upon two things. First there is the natural dislike of the new modern by the purveyors of the old as they are made more and more 'out of date'. Second, and more important, one of the distinctive features of Americanization has been its cultural popularism transcending economic classes. The 'American dream' as 'world dream' promised the good life for all. The people enjoying life in suburbia are not the super-rich, they are ordinary people doing an ordinary job in a modern world. In this political economy the job is defined as a contribution to mass production and its organization, the good life is defined as consuming the products of mass production. The political economy supporting this 'ordinary modernity' has proven to be voracious of the Earth's resources. The rise of consumption across the world has sparked an avalanche of warnings about the future sustainability of our world which has generated a global environmental movement. The radical green position is that the world is not big enough for capitalism. Ceaseless accumulation of capital based upon ever-increasing production and consumption in more shopping malls in more suburbias across the world spells doom for the system: a world impasse. The argument against this doomsday scenario is based upon faith in human inventiveness to find a way out of the impending crisis. A world of plenty was always the goal of progress based upon the exploits of science and technology; why give up now just as science and technology are on the threshold of greater and greater advances? But, of course, science as technology is implicated in the production that feeds the consumption. The fundamental role of science in the modern world-system is to be an enabling factor for producing new and better products to sell on the world market. Hence rather than saviour, science as practised in the modern world-system brings the hour of doom ever closer.

Identifying a world impasse is not defeatist. Being pessimistic for the future of capitalism is not the same as doubting that humanity has a future. Equating humanity with capitalism is a much more fundamental devaluing of human ingenuity than a scepticism that technological magic tricks can save capitalism. Ceaseless capital accumulation is not the only social logic for ordering human life. It was organized differently in the past and it would be arrogant of us 'moderns' to suppose that future generations will not respond to the social tensions that will arise with the demise of the modern world-system and devise many social experiments leading to alternative sustainable postmodern worlds. World impasse will collectively concentrate the minds of people as they cope with a situation that no longer automatically rewards capital accumulation. We cannot predict the outcome, but we can explore the range of possibilities. And having disposed of the metaphysics of progress, we should be able to accept that although some outcomes can be better than capitalism, there will be just as many worse than capitalism. With world impasse impending, the future becomes especially open. Hence our tale is not a tragedy; in the future people can still live happily ever after.

This audacious romp through modern history verges upon a crude historical functionalism. Humanity, living in whatever social system, consists of individuals and they have been largely conspicuous by their absence in the tale above. The purpose of the book that follows is to put some flesh on the skeleton of the argument just presented to make it at least a little more plausible. Broadly, the method I employ to attain this goal is to make humanity especially visible in my analysis through a particular emphasis upon the cultural components of hegemony. Although I adhere to a world-systems' analysis because of its holistic qualities, it is a fact that this form of social analysis has tended to neglect the cultural. This is most clearly seen in its treatment of the modern and modernity. Although the terms 'modern world-system' and 'capitalist world-economy' describe the same entity, there has been much more concern to investigate its capitalist properties than to explore the meaning of its modernity. In this book I reverse this bias. Hence, if it is necessary to pigeon-hole the writing before you into a single category — always notoriously difficult for a world-systems' study — I would be happy for the book to be viewed as a simple cultural corrective to less human world-system analyses.

In more conventional world-systems' terms, the book also has a historiographic point to make. Many, possibly most, general histories of the last half-millenium have plenty to say about the activities of the British and the Americans but rather less about the Dutch. This is partly due to the common focus upon power politics, and hence neglecting economic changes, so that first Hapsburg Spain and then the France of Louis XIV eclipse the Dutch in the story of the 17th century. It is also due to the historiographical circumstances of British historians (and later American historians) largely writing the Netherlands out of their Whiggish script of early modern European history. This script emphasizes the English political upheavals in the 17th century that culminated in the 'Glorious Revolution' and a liberal constitutionalism that both the UK and the USA are heir to. In this tale the Dutch only have a walk-on part in the person of William of Orange becoming William III of England. Needless to say in the story that unfolds below the Dutch are given equal due with their fellow hegemons. If the readers of this book are like students I have tried these ideas out on (in both British and American universities), then they will be certain to learn something with respect to the Dutch golden age because of the low knowledge level they start with.

But whatever previous historical knowledge readers have of the three countries I focus upon, the contribution I am trying to make here is to interpret existing histories within the framework of a particular model of social change. Since I believe all history is ultimately about the present in order to influence the future (ie we use the past), it is very important whether we interpret contemporary US relative decline as similar to royal Spain or republican Netherlands. Comparison with the former, which has become popular as a model of military overreach, does not lead to a world impasse, employing the historical analogy of hegemony does. Hence the reader may surmise that the crucial concern that has inspired this book is the prospect of the end of the world as we know it.

But there is still plenty of time to read this book. There are six chapters which can be grouped together as three pairs: the first two delineate the basic historical model, the middle two describe the normal operation of hegemony and the final two provide materials for contemplating the future. Chapter 1 elaborates upon much of the first half of the tale told above. We add further material to the Europe-is-peculiar argument and then define the concept of world hegemony we used. This is employed to show how hegemony can be related to the overall development of the modern world-system and thus to forms of modernity. Chapter 2 looks specifically at hegemonic creation of modern politics. This is intended to help balance the literature which tends to emphasize the economic practices of hegemons. Chapter 3 deals with the fundamental hegemonic process of presenting the hegemonic state's self-interest as the general interest. This is to invent new universalisms which we relate to liberalism as the political ideology of hegemony. Chapter 4 concentrates upon the receptive audience that is out there ready to accept the hegemonic message. This is about the hegemonic state defining the rest of the world's future. Chapter 5 looks at the downside of the hegemonic cycle as post-hegemonic trauma. Past Dutch and British impasses are compared to the contemporary American conundrum and a new phase of ultra-hegemony is projected. Chapter 6 finally brings us to world impasse, which, we argue, results from an ordinary modernity built upon consumption. Alternative eco-Fascist and deep green world-systems are briefly described as outcomes of contemporary thinking on a world in crisis.

1   World hegemony

The exotic is no more. We live in a world where there are no longer 'unknown lands' about which fabulous stories can be told. In the late 19th century the public would flock to the meetings of geographical societies to hear the tales of the great explorers of the times. Today we have a global media that can bring events across the world into our living rooms instantaneously. Our world is pre-eminently global in scope. This 'communications revolution' is just one aspect of contemporary 'globalization': economic organization, political competition, social mores, cultural clashes and ecological crises are all, today, fundamentally global in nature. Put another way, depletion of the ozone layer, religious conflicts, ubiquitous blue jeans, new world (dis)order, 'cocacolarization' and McWorld — we are all in this together. This scale of social organization is novel: by eradicating the exotic and creating 'one world', we, as a society, are geographically different from all that has gone before.

How did we reach this global outcome? There was certainly no smooth evolutionary path. Historians interested in long-term patterns are apt to find continuities in the social record that suggest the 20th century as 'global times' is an inevitable culmination of humankind's progress. But there was no incremental increase in the geographical scale of social organization prior to our modern world. Earlier social organizations were 'regional' in scope, with no likelihood of ever becoming global. The largest empires were either quite ephemeral – lasting just a few generations – like the Eurasian Mongol conquests, or more stable but with seemingly definite limits to their geographical expansion like the Chinese and Roman empires. These latter impressive political systems were undoubtedly very substantial, but they reached logistic obstacles in their programmes of conquest and incorporation. In general the historical record shows that empires waxed and waned rather than exhibiting any nascent drive to globalization. Hence we define an historical disjuncture between our world and what went before. In the 'long 16th century' (c. 1450–1650) a society emerged in Europe that was to throw off the traditional shackles and embark on an expansion that led to its economic and political domination of the world by 1900.

Postmedieval Europe waxed but did not wane. Europeans became the 'great destroyers' of all other societies. Beginning in the Americas and then moving to other continents, non-Europeans have had their social organizations destroyed as they have been incorporated into the world of the Europeans. Crucially Europeans evolved a double attack on the societies they encountered. As well as traditional political incorporation through military might, Europeans brought with them the economic imperatives of the market. With or without a political take-over, the production capacities of non-European societies were reorientated to a world market dominated by Europeans. By 1900 the whole world consisted of one great economic functional region centred on Western Europe.

How and why was this able to happen? Understanding this historical disjuncture has been termed the 'central intellectual problem' tackled by historical and social thinkers over many generations.[1] Starting from different theoretical positions, writers have viewed the disrupture in a variety of ways: 'European miracle', 'rise of the West', 'transition from feudalism to capitalism' and 'origins of modernity' are the four main formulations of the problem. These scholars all agree that something extraordinary occurred in Europe about half a millennium ago but disagree on how to conceptualize it. They all suffer from the same basic conundrum. In trying to find the secret of Europe's success, they have searched through medieval and early modern European history to find what made this place and its people so special they could conquer the world. But whatever arguments they have come up with for European exceptionalism, critics have always found it relatively easy to point to non-European societies that experienced similar situations but without the same effect.[2] For instance in the classic Marxist formulation, the free (wage) labour that lies at the heart of the transition from feudalism to capitalism argument is by no means unique to Europe and can be found in other places at other times but without leading to an expansive capitalism.

If no special ingredient, what? Behind every supposed miracle a mundane explanation can usually be found and Immanuel Wallerstein provides just such for this European case.[3] In his 'conjunctional explanation', Europe is interpreted as an 'aberrant case' to the normal pattern of historical change. Wallerstein argues that the concomitant collapse of four crucial elements in the development of Europe in the 15th century created a unique situation. A failure of production led to the collapse of economic elites, a breakdown of order led to a collapse of political elites and the social glue provided by the church was eroding in a collapse of cultural elites. These three internal collapses were related and not necessarily unique to 15th-century Europe but in addition there was a collapse of the external threat to Europe with the demise of Mongol power. The internal crises made Europe a society ripe for military conquest but there was no external power strong enough to take advantage. Hence, with elites in disarray, European society could be reinvented in a new form. An opening was provided in which the rewards for different social activities were turned upside down. Strategies of capital accumulation were found to be better able to cope with the internal collapses than more traditional forms of behaviour. In other words economic elites were able to rival the traditionally dominant political elites in the influence they wielded during these trying times. The result was that during the long 16th century, a new type of society emerged which Wallerstein calls the 'modern world-system' or 'capitalist world-economy'. It is this social entity, born of contingencies in Europe, that has expanded to take over the whole globe.

Geographically it consists of an entrenched hierarchical division of labour with core and periphery plus a semi-periphery in between.[4] The core is where most of the capital accumulation ends up, the periphery is the zone of cheap labour and the semi-periphery mixes these two characteristics. This geographical structure — first created in Europe in the long 16th century as western European core, southern European semi-periphery and eastern European periphery — is now writ large across the world with western Europe still core but sharing this status with the USA and Japan, and with the 'south' and 'east' comprising mixes of semi-periphery and periphery.

This modern world-system is just one of many world-systems that have existed. Their prefix 'world' has no global connotation: they are so-named because they define the 'worlds', both material and imagined, in which their inhabitants live out their lives. Physically they consist of integrated areas of economic production that are relatively autonomous in their internal development. Historically they have taken the basic form of 'world-empires' under the political control of a military–bureaucratic class. Economic surplus is redistributed upwards from agricultural producers via political mechanisms. It is just such a system, feudalism, that collapsed in 15th-century Europe. Its replacement was a different type of world-system, a world-economy where a world market is crucially implicated in the distribution of economic surplus. There had been many incipient world-economies in world history before 1450, but none found a political mechanism to prevent coersion resulting in subordination to a world-empire. This is why Europe forms an aberrant case – the only time a nascent world-economy was able to develop fully into a world-system.

Framing the rise of Europe in this manner leads us to consider its success in a different light. Instead of focusing on its origins, we are drawn to consider its survival. There is no doubt that the capitalist world-economy has been vulnerable to what we may term a traditional political take-over and conversion into a form of world-empire. The question is: why didn't the political elites capitalize on their formal monopoly of violence to bring the 'upstart' economic elites back into line as in other world-systems? The answer seems to be that 'ruling the world' has been the goal of very few modern military and political leaders; survival of the system has relied upon this grand aim being kept off the political agenda. Rather than a politics versus economics contest arising, a particular political economy has been created where a mutuality between political and economic elites was developed. In this way, what were potentially rival elites found themselves partially dependent upon one another: politicians needed the wealth created by business to enhance their power, the business community needed the politicians to provide the conditions for creating wealth. It is this almost symbiotic relationship that lies behind the survival of the modern world-system. This was reflected directly in the 'double attack' — political and economic — experienced by non-Europeans, but its full development was to be found in Europe itself. The result was that a fragile modern world-system was able to develop from strength to strength.

For four centuries economic growth was facilitated, in part, by geographical expansion. Destroyed societies were reconstructed and their production reorientated to the world market. In the highly competitive search for economic advantage, the physical logistic problems that had always limited the growth of world-empires were overcome leaving no obstacles in the way of geographical expansion. Hence the basic logic of capital accumulation resulted in region after region being 'opened up', the term used to denote integration into the world market. The unique situation was thus created in which there were no longer any limits to prevent this world-system from expanding over the whole world to create our contemporary global society.

The political economy based upon a 'symbiotic' relationship between political and economic elites in the modern world-system has always had a crucial geographical

Plate 1   *The Battle of the Strong Boxes and the Money Bags* (*c*. 1565) by the Flemish painter Pieter Bruegel the Elder engraved by Jan Galle (Kress Library, Harvard University). This is a vivid early expression of the new capitalist world-economy showing its different form of competitive chaos but depicted in traditional military mode

dimension. Two distinctive spatial structures have been created. On the one hand an economic space of nodes and flows facilitates the movement of labour and capital for production and commodities for consumption. On the other hand the political space of the system consists of a mosaic of sovereign territories, separate units of law and order. The two spaces interact every time an economic flow crosses a political border. These contrasting spaces provide a necessary manoeuvrability for economic elites in relation to political elites. In other words politicians are unable, ultimately, to control business. Through the whole history of the world-economy economic elites have been able to profit from this circumstance. Even in wartime when borders are especially controlled, any number of businessmen have been able to have very profitable wars. In the construction of the political economy that enabled the modern world-system to prosper, therefore, a divided political system was crucial. It is this feature that has, as it were, liberated an economics to stimulate the whole process that has led to globalization. In this chapter we focus on the states as necessary, though not sufficient, facilitators of capitalist expansion.

The chapter is divided into three key arguments. We begin by elaborating on the crucial role of states in the capitalist world-economy. However we find that the literature on this topic is peculiar. Whereas we are concerned for both the political and economic dimensions of a states system, this is not the focus of mainstream studies. Either the importance of the economic dimension is recognized but at the level of a single state, for instance by the many Marxist theories of the state, or a system of states is recognized but with a neglect of economic processes as is typical of international relations' studies. In the first part of this chapter we focus upon political processes as we describe how Europe turned the concept of sovereignty upside down – from a single universal property to a multiple territorial property. However, when we move beyond construction to the survival of the system, we find the international relations focus on political–military processes wanting. This justifies our recognition of a political-economy basis for the survival and, in our second key argument, we consider how the mutuality between economics and politics was achieved.

Economic elites as a group cannot combat the violent potential of political elites and their states; what is required is a new type of state activity that promotes political economy over traditional political–military state imperatives. Enter the hegemons. We argue that there have been three hegemonic states – the Dutch Republic in the 17th century, Britain in the 19th century and the USA in the 20th century – who have led the world-system towards political-economy imperatives. In the second section we deal with three hegemonic cycles – the rise and fall of the hegemons – as a historical analogy through which we gain the necessary insights for understanding the survival of the inter-state system. Hegemons are unique to the modern world-system, and in the final key argument we consider their contribution to the overall development of this world. Hegemons define the basic stages and trajectory of the system and therefore are implicated in delineating the very nature of the system. What is it that makes the modern world-system 'modern'? In the third section we take the argument beyond political economy to the social–cultural realm by implicating the hegemons in the creation of three critical forms of modernity. Hence this chapter follows a path from political–military through political economy to social–cultural to set out the basic arguments upon which the rest of the book builds.

The political organization of world-systems

On 14 September 1793 Qianlong, the Chinese emperor, attended his 57th birthday celebrations since becoming 'Son of Heaven'.[5] As part of this annual fête, delegations from vassal states took the opportunity to pledge their allegiance to the emperor. For the celebrations that year three such delegations were present: from Burma, Mongolia and Great Britain. Britain was placed on the official list of 'kingdoms of the western ocean' accepting Chinese suzerainty. The only indication that the British may have been different was the fact that the leader of the delegation, George Lord Macartney, did not kowtow on presentation to the emperor. Ever since the British had arrived in China the previous year there had been a crisis of ritual which was resolved by agreement that Macartney would only kneel before the emperor. But the British remained just a small part of the celebrations and were quickly returned to the ranks of the vassal foreigners.

Plate 2 *A Meeting of Two Worlds:* 'The Reception of the Diplomatique and his Suite, at the Court of Pekin' (1792) engraved by James Gillray. This shows Lord George Macartney, representing George III of Great Britain, kneeling but not kowtowing before the Chinese Emperor Qianlong. The dispute over ritual reflected two opposing conceptions of world politics, traditional universal sovereignty and modern multiple sovereignty. The Macartney mission to China is so fascinating because it brought together, face to face, the greatest of all world-empires and the leading state of the only world-economy to fully develop

The British delegation was 700 strong and they interpreted their role somewhat differently. At this time British merchants were confined to the southern Chinese port of Canton far from the centre of power at Beijing and it was Macartney's job to change this situation. But the omens were not good: 15 previous European missions to the emperor had failed. Britain, and Europe in general, suffered a severe trade deficit with China due to the popularity of Chinese fashions – tea, porcelain, lacquer, plants, vases – in 18th-century European society. To resolve this economic problem Macartney wanted to establish a permanent embassy in Beijing to negotiate the opening up of the Chinese market to British products. This involved persuading the emperor on two key matters, one political and one economic. First the emperor would have to accept some formal political equality between China as the great land power of the East and Britain as the great sea power of the West. Second, Macartney had to convince the emperor that Britain could furnish China with the most advanced commodities available on the world market. To prove the latter the British

Table 1 Populations of cities of half a million or more in 1800

Beijing (China)	1 100 000
London (Britain)	861 000
Canton (China)	800 000
Constantinople (Ottoman Empire)	570 000
Paris (France)	547 000
Hangchow (China)	500 000

Source: Estimates from Chandler and Fox (1974)

bore gifts for the emperor that illustrated the progress in science and arts that their country had undergone. A planetarium, a ship's model, a telescope, lenses and two globes of earth and heavens respectively were among the gifts.[6] But, with the exception of music boxes, they did not impress the emperor. They were not even accepted as presents. This was made clear, but not to the British, on the banners announcing the river flotilla transporting the delegation to Beijing. The Chinese word 'li' meaning present had been changed to 'gong' indicating tribute. Similarly the Chinese rejected Macartney's title of 'legate' and referred to him as simply 'conveyer of tribute'.[7] It is obvious that the economic argument could not progress without acceptance of Britain's political assertion of equal status. The problem was that the latter made no sense whatsoever; George III, whom Macartney represented, could not possibly be the equivalent of the current Son of Heaven!

Needless to say the Chinese rejected the British overtures because, as their reply put it, they had not 'the slightest need for your manufactures'.[8] The gifts were accepted as protocol required by the 'Department of Foreign Tribute' and the British were expected to swear 'perpetual obedience' to the emperor. Notice that the Chinese could have no 'Department of Foreign *Affairs*', hence no embassies or foreign trade, since that implies relations between equals. However the Chinese position was not as fanciful as it may, at first, seem. It is easy today to dismiss the Chinese Empire as traditional and backward. Peyrefitte refers to it as 'the immobile empire', reflecting its resistance to change and progress as represented by Europe.[9] But at the time this empire was an immensely successful social entity. In fact we can argue that it was unrivalled in the degree of its success. For instance Beijing, the imperial capital, was the only millionaire city (one with over a million inhabitants) in 1800: there were only six cities with over half a million people at this time and three were in China (Table 1).

Such comparisons are instructive because before the great rise of urbanized industrial production in the 19th century, the size of cities is a direct index of the power and success of a social system based upon agriculture. Inhabitants of cities have to be fed by rural production and the larger the city the greater the necessary surplus extraction from the countryside. On this count China, with a further four cities over 200 000 far exceeded Britain – Glasgow was Britain's second city in 1800 with a population of only 85 000. Hence there is a very strong material basis for Chinese cultural arrogance in allocating the British a bit part as music-box makers in their annual celebration of the emperor's birthday.

From our position of historical hindsight we know that all this was to change in the next century. Another British mission was rebuffed in 1816, but in the First Opium War of 1841 the British defeated the imperial army and took Hong Kong as its prize. With a series of unequal treaties through the 19th century involving all the major European powers, China was humiliated and the empire finally disintegrated in the revolution of 1911. It is easy to read European superiority into this process but, of course, this was not the first Chinese empire to collapse. All empires have their broad pattern of rise and fall, and the European successful encounter with the Chinese coincided with the latest phase of imperial demise. Europeans were by no means the first foreigners to take advantage of such circumstances, but there was a crucial difference this time. In the past the foreigners, such as the Mongols, were absorbed into the Chinese orbit and became the genesis of a new empire. In the 19th century it was the Chinese who were incorporated into the world of the foreigners. This was the ultimate defeat; the Chinese world-system was no more and China became a state, large but weak, in the inter-state system of the capitalist world-economy.

What makes this clash of worlds so fascinating is not so much the outcome but the initial lack of comprehension between representatives of the two systems. Their mutual misunderstandings were based upon the fact that they represented two very different types of political organization, a centralized empire and an inter-state system. As a traditional empire, China's conception of sovereignty was singular: all the world consisted of either China and her provinces or vassal states. This accounts for the treatment of the British in 1793. In total contrast, the modern world-system that Britain belonged to was a world of multiple sovereignties. It was not 'Europe' that encountered China in 1793 but one sovereign part of it, Great Britain. It is this 'modern' conception of sovereignty that the Chinese could not understand. The request for China to become Britain's trading partner seems self-evidently reasonable to us because of the mutual benefits that could result. But this presupposes exactly what the Chinese could not accept: trading partner implies relations between equals. A world of many sovereignties was simply something the Chinese could not imagine.

This example shows a clear political chasm between European and Chinese politics at the end of the 18th century. Although both sides found the other's politics incomprehensible, from a world historical perspective we would have to say that it is the Chinese who represent the political norm and it is Europe, as we noted earlier, that is aberrant. Since it is Europe that expands and China that is 'opened up', it is a reasonable inference that the nature of European politics is implicated in this process. Indeed this idea has already been introduced above. But before we can accept that Europe's decentralized politics has been in some way instrumental in its phenomenal growth, we must go beyond a single comparison, albeit one pregnant with contrasts. The simple fact is that there have been other cases of decentralized political organization in world-systems, and we have to compare them to the European case before accepting such an inference. In the first part of this section we put the modern inter-state system into just such a context to explore in what ways it was indeed 'unique'. In the second part we concentrate specifically on the construction of the inter-state system in early modern Europe. In a final part we look at the reasons international relations scholars have given for the survival of the system and find them wanting. Returning to a political-economy argument, we introduce the idea that it is hegemony that is crucial in this matter.

Cycles of centralization and decentralization

It is commonplace to talk of the rise and fall of empires. Even the greatest empires in history have eventually stopped expanding and suffered a demise when their unified rule is destroyed. From our perspective this can be viewed as alternation of centralized and decentralized political organization. Many scholars of civilizations have tried to find temporal patterns in the existence of unified empires and multiple states. The general view is that a system of multiple states is an unstable situation that will eventually be transformed into a single empire. However, given the subsequent demise of the latter, an alternating sequence of multiple states with unified empires can be posited. This has been broadly confirmed in a recent study of civilizations by David Wilkinson based upon study of 23 unified empires and 27 states systems.[10]

Comparative civilization studies suffer severe problems of definition. Different scholars use different criteria to identify separate 'systems', so that a region deemed autonomous in one study is combined with other regions in another. This impinges directly on our concerns here because narrow definitions favour the finding of single empires whereas broad definitions invariably produce states systems. This is no place to enter the debate; fortunately we can avoid it for our purposes here by focusing on the Chinese case. This is the great civilization that, according to Adam Watson, 'evolved in virtual isolation'.[11] This simple geographical fact has meant that definitional problems are minimalized and we can proceed with a consensual position on the sequence of centralization and decentralization in the Chinese cultural area.

The sequence of empires and states systems in China is shown in Table 2. This is a classic story of empires rising and falling with multiple state sequences in between. There is some uncertainty about the initial political organization. The Zhou system was given imperial status by later writers to legitimate empire, but there is no doubt their capital city was sacked in 770 BC decisively ending whatever level of rule they claimed. Half a millennium of multiple states then ensued in which mutual recognition

Table 2 Centralization and decentralization in China

Period	Political organization	Name
?–770BC	Uncertain, possible empire	Zhou suzerainty
770–221BC	Multiple states	Era of Warring States (from 403 BC)
221BC–220	Unified empire	Qin (to 206BC), Han dynasty
220–589	Multiple states	6 dynasties, 16 kingdoms, etc
589–907	Unified empire	Sui dynasty to 617 T'ang dynasty from 624
907–979	Multiple states	5 dynasties, 10 kingdoms, etc
979–1126	Unified empire	Sung dynasty
1126–1280	Multiple states	Northern and southern empires
1280–(1911)	Unified empire	Yuan dynasty to 1367 Ming dynasty to 1644 Ch'ing dynasty to 1911

required the ability to defend territory. Culminating in the era of warring states, this initial competitive states period shows how the process of reconstituting empire worked: a situation of multiple states is destroyed by one state defeating all others. In this case the victorious Qin empire was short lived, but its unification of China was maintained by the Han dynasty. The demise of this empire led to another states system and a repeat of the previous era: the military winner, the Sui, formed a short-lived empire but its unification was maintained by the T'ang. With the demise of the latter there are three short phases: first decentralization with various mixes of competitive kingdoms and dynasties, a short unified empire interlude with the Sung dynasty and finally a division of China as the Sung are defeated in the north. The Mongols take over the north as a prelude to creating a new unification of China as the Yuan dynasty. Although the dynasty lasted less than a century, this unification was to be long lasting, being continued by the indigenous Ming dynasty followed by the exogenous Manchus. The latter created the Ch'ing dynasty, to which Qianlong belonged. His dynasty finally fell in the republican revolution of 1911, but the empire had already been absorbed into the modern world-system by the mid-19th century; from that time the Ch'ing emperors were no longer sovereign in their own terms.

What does this tell us about Europe? In previous multiple states systems it seems that the states have two imperatives. The first is survival, success at which enables a state to strive for the second: to eliminate rivals and become the next empire. Given the situation of perennial war, this military activity will appear as one continuous process since, with sufficient success, imperative one will transmute into two. Hence, through all these changes in political organization, universal empire remains the social ideal. Unification brings peace and prosperity so that empires become the 'golden ages' of the imagination in times of turmoil. For instance Confucius, writing in the era of warring states, provided the blueprint for subsequent Chinese centralized bureaucracy and justified his work by looking back to a mythical centralized Zhou empire. It is in this process that we can find clear parallels with pre-modern Europe. There is no doubt that the Roman Empire took on the role of golden age for Europeans despite the fact that, unlike the Chinese, they were never able to recreate such a unified empire themselves. In Europe, before the 16th century, the concept of sovereignty derived from Roman Law in which there could be only one legitimate ruler above all others: the Roman Emperor was *dominus mundi*, lord of the world.[12]

But in western Europe there was no Roman Emperor, no single supreme political authority for a thousand years before the modern era. Instead there was a highly complex and decentralized pattern of political organization. In feudal Europe there was a hierarchical political system with allegiance building up from local manorial land rights though a sequence of territorial ranks from counts (counties) and dukes (duchies) to princes (principalities) and kings (kingdoms). All such territorial rights were hereditary; but, in addition, there were other forms of territory holders ranging from bishops and religious orders to free cities and city leagues. Despite all this complexity the idea of emperor and sovereignty did not disappear. After the fall of the Roman Empire in the West, the Papacy kept alive a notion of unity to which a German emperor was added in 800. Taking the name of Roman Emperor, Charlemagne's military successes formally reconstituted an empire that became the medieval 'Holy Roman Empire' and survived, in name at least, until 1806. Although the political power of this emperor was never great enough militarily to dominate all Europe, his overall status was understood. For instance, we are accustomed to describe the 16th-century Spanish conquests in the Americas as the 'Spanish Empire', but this was not as contemporaries saw it.[13] The conquests could not constitute an 'empire' because there could only be one emperor within the political system and he resided in Germany. For a period in the 16th century the Americas were ruled by an emperor, but this was only because the Spanish king Charles was also Holy Roman Emperor. His imperial title had nothing to do with the size of his American territories and everything to do with the influence of his family, the Hapsburgs, in central Europe.

Hence the decentralized nature of medieval Europe did not define a fragmented sovereignty: there remained an imperial ideal harking back to the stability and prosperity of the Roman Empire, albeit only weakly expressed in the actual politics. After the demise of the Roman Empire in the West there was a period of multiple states (235 – 800) before the constitution of feudal Europe. In a pale shadow of the Chinese pattern, the Carolingian dynasty was able to re-establish the imperial title in 800 but did not have the capacity to go on and construct a centralized empire. Nevertheless medieval Europe did emerge as a unified 'Christendom' with a single political pyramid at the top of which were the Bishop of Rome and the Holy Roman Emperor. This produced an unusual 'joint sovereignty' based on the theory that the emperor embodied temporal supremacy and the pope spiritual supremacy. Such a concept of sovereignty was inherently problematic in practice. The overall effect was that the papacy prevented a strong empire reappearing in Europe. Political competition at the top of the hierarchy was largely settled in the 12th century by the victory of the papacy over the emperor.[14] But the pope never commanded the secular power to replace the temporal role of the emperor; a power vacuum resulted. This provided the context in which new political practices could emerge, leading to modern multiple sovereignties.

Turning sovereignty on its head: inter-stateness

The weakness of the empire enabled city-states to form in Italy in a highly competitive political system: 300 city-states in 1250 were reduced to just 40 by 1500.[15] At the same time there developed in Western Europe what Joseph Strayer has termed 'law states'.[16] These were medium-sized polities – that is between city-states and empire – which became relatively centralized states through the king curbing local feudal powers within his realm. During the crisis of feudalism of the 14th and 15th centuries some of these states disappeared, notably Burgundy in 1477, but some survived the incessant warfare to emerge as recognizable modern states in the 16th century. Portugal, England and France are the classic cases; and Spain also emerged after the union of the crowns of Castile and Aragon in 1479. However, feudal Europe's dynastic organization of territory did not necessarily generate compact and contiguous realms since family claims to territory depended upon inheritance and marriage which provided no locational logic to land accumulation. For instance, the Hapsburg unification of Castile and Aragon created a compact modern Spain but at the same time this constituted less than half the Hapsburg territory, which was spread discontinuously across Europe with major land holdings in Italy, Burgundy and Austria. In the 16th century, however, we begin to see the consolidation of territories. This is symbolized, according to Edward Luard, by the peace settlements of 1559 between Spain, France and England where

Spain gave up claims to parts of Burgundy, France to northern Italy and England to Calais so that 'the shadowy outline of national states, with more clearly defined territorial boundaries, started to be discernible'.[17]

This geographical reorganization went hand in hand with new political concepts of political authority as sovereignty came to be linked to territory through the state. Before the 16th century the term 'state' merely referred to the 'status' of a prince's realm with no sense of a public power separate from ruler and ruled as supreme authority in a territory.[18] This modern abstract notion of state begins to develop among the city-states of northern Italy and, according to Quentin Skinner, Machiavelli's treatment of politics in *The Prince* in 1513 can be considered transitional to the modern conception of the state.[19] The process is fully accomplished in France, the classic early modern centralized state, in Jean Bodin's *Six Livres* in 1576 in which he analyses the state as an omnipotent yet impersonal power within a bounded territory. Hence Skinner concludes that by the beginning of the 17th century 'the concept of the State – its nature, its powers, its right to command obedience – had come to be regarded as the most important object of analysis in European political thought'.[20] In particular, he argues that with Bodin's study 'we may be said to enter the modern world' of politics.[21] But this is only partly true. The modern state claims omnipotence within its territory to be sure, but this is only part of its necessary condition. As well as this 'internal sovereignty', there is the question of recognition by other states in the system or 'external sovereignty'.

Quite simply sovereignty cannot be unilaterally proclaimed however firm the political control of a piece of territory is. We can illustrate this with recent failures of political units to become recognized as sovereign. For instance, after the Turkish invasion of Cyprus in 1974 the 'Turkish Republic of Northern Cyprus' was declared, but this has never received international recognition. Similarly the South African attempt to create new black states as part of its apartheid programme was never recognized as legitimate outside that country. Hence neither Northern Cyprus nor the 'Bantustans' were allowed to join the international club of sovereign states with, for instance, seats in the United Nations. In short, sovereignty requires an international capacity as well as control of territory.[22] We will term this external sovereignty condition 'inter-stateness'.[23] By this we mean the fundamental presumption of a multiplicity of states who mutually recognize one another's sovereignty. Hence states as territories constitute a mosaic of sovereign parcels of land that are mutually dependent on each other; in Rosenberg's neat simile: 'A modern state out of the state system is like a fish out of water.'[24] Inter-stateness is vital to our argument here since it expresses the division of sovereignty that distinguishes modern political authority from the traditional imperial assumption of a singular omnipotent locus of power.

The condition of inter-stateness emerges with the development of internal sovereignty and can be traced through the idea of foreign policy. Obviously the Holy Roman Empire and papacy, like all other traditional imperial entities, could not formally have a foreign policy since they were above all other polities in the system; no country was outside, that is 'foreign' to, their authority. However, the law states that emerged from the 12th century were also bereft of any notion of foreign policy. They developed internal administrations to centralize law and tax collection through the creation of 'high courts' and exchequers, but no organs of government dealing with foreign affairs were devised.

Strayer provides a simple explanation: 'The concept of "foreign affairs" could hardly exist in a Europe that . . . was not quite sure what states were sovereign': relations between political units remained entwined in warfare and complicated dynastic relations.[25] In the city-states of northern Italy, some features of modern international politics emerged, notably ambassadors representing one state to another, but this did not constitute recognition of foreign affairs. Quite simply city-states did not consider each other to be 'foreign' so that there was no conception of separate politics relating to internal and external matters.[26]

This distinction between domestic and foreign affairs – the hallmark of the modern politics – had to be created. It is usually traced back to the Peace of Augsburg in 1555 when the principle of non-interference in the internal religious affairs of a prince's realm was recognized for the first time.[27] Non-interference presumes the existence of separate domestic and foreign spheres of politics.

This notion was repeated at the Treaty of Westphalia in 1648 which has come to be viewed as the foundation treaty for the establishment of the inter-state system.[28] Although it can be reasonably argued that Westphalia only confirmed political practices that were well established by the mid-17th century, its importance should not be underestimated. It formally provided the roll-call of who was and who was not sovereign. Coming at the end of the Thirty Years War in which the emperor failed to impose his sovereignty on the northern German Protestant princes, the Holy Roman Empire no longer existed as a meaningful political unit although the title was to continue for another century and a half. Three hundred effectively sovereign units were recognized within the 'empire', each with the international capacity to make treaties with other states. In addition, the independence of Switzerland and the Netherlands were both finally confirmed outside the empire. Thus, the sovereign apex of the medieval political arrangement was finally removed. Coupled with the earlier disciplining of local power bases – barons, cities and so on – by the 'law states', modern states became defined as a single level focus of authority at an intermediate scale: sovereignties above localities but below the system.

Although a legal contradiction to his very being, the Holy Roman Emperor accepted inter-stateness and concentrated on making his Austrian lands a major power in the inter-state system. He was a signatory of the Westphalia Treaty and to him it represented the harsh reality of practical politics: he had to salvage what he could from a most unpromising military situation. For the Papacy, as custodian of the true Catholic church, it could not be viewed as a political question: universal sovereignty remained a matter of highest principle that could never be given away. No wonder Pope Innocent X was to condemn the Peace of Westphalia famously as 'null, void, invalid, unjust, damnable, reprobate, inane, empty of meaning and effect for all time'.[29] But the Papacy no longer had the power to make any difference; inter-stateness with its mosaic of sovereignties had arrived.

Beyond sovereign equality

Inter-stateness is premised upon sovereign equality between states. In international law states are interpreted as 'corporate persons' with equal rights and obligations. A unanimity rule follows from this legal equality: no state can be bound to decisions to which it has not given consent. But international politics has never been limited to international law. In fact quite the opposite has been the norm. In Orwellian terms, all states are created equal but some are more equal than others. Viewed in this manner, the modern inter-state system is not very different from earlier state systems. Codes of inter-state behaviour were devised before the Europeans invented 'international law', but these never prevented military successes leading to elimination of states and a reconstitution of empire.[30] Why should the formal equality of European states agreed at Westphalia have fared any better?

Probably the most ambitious and sustained attempt to answer this question through rigorous comparative studies of states systems has come from the 'British Committee on the Theory of International Politics'. This 'study group' operated under the auspices chairmanships of Herbert Butterfield, Martin Wight, Adam Watson and Hedley Bull for a period of twenty five years (1959–84). Their basic interpretation of the inter-state system is outlined in Martin Wight's *Power Politics*.[31] Since sovereign states recognize no rule above themselves, Wight interprets the inter-state system as international anarchy. This is the traditional 'realist' international relations viewpoint of competition between states with no holds barred where 'vital interests' are concerned. Within this context states are designated 'powers' whose nature it is to expand. Hence war in general is 'inevitable but particular wars can be avoided'.[32] The latter follows from Wight's argument that anarchy does not mean total disorder, rather there is organization without rule — what he terms 'international society'.[33] Adam Watson conceptualizes this as a *raison de système*, 'the belief that it pays to make the system work', in addition to *raison d'état*.[34] This 'society' is constituted through diplomatic ties and alliances between states and by the practices of statecraft such as balance-of-power strategies. Therefore survival of the inter-state system is due to international society countering the destructive tendencies of international anarchy.

Wight treats the inequality of states by defining several categories of powers.[35] 'Great powers' are the leading states of an era as recognized in contemporary diplomacy. 'Dominant powers', however, are defined by their actions and aspire to be more than one Great Power among many. These are states that have attempted to gain mastery over the system: disregarding the sovereignty of all other states, their expansion has constituted an aggrandizement whose goal is universal empire. Wight identifies Hapsburg Spain, Louis XIV's France, Napoleonic France and Hitler's Germany as classic dominant powers. In each case their plans were only thwarted by the construction of an unusually broad alliance of other great powers. Hence we can say that dominant powers try to take advantage of international anarchy while their opponents have survived by bolstering international society.

For David Wilkinson this success against incipient empires results from a learning process.[36] Over many centuries political elites have developed strategies that make imperial projects harder and harder to complete. He portrays earlier imperial successes as a 'duck shoot' where the strongest state has been able to pick off rivals one at a time in increasingly unequal contests. He argues that by pursuing counterintervention tactics and devising balance-of-power strategies, a statecraft has been invented which has prevented conversion of the current states' system into a universal empire. This process behind the growth of international society is not really borne out historically. The problem is that Adam Watson, in his impressive historical analysis of state behaviour, *The Evolution of International Society*, has comprehensively shown that the management of relations among states is as old as states themselves and it is unclear how the Westphalia Treaty, for example, represents any new survival tricks of statecraft.[37]

Let us try another tack derived from Wight's original analysis.[38] As well as classifying states quantitatively, he recognizes different projections of power: sea power and land power. The classic dominant powers were all land powers. The Netherlands, Britain and the USA are classic cases of sea powers. Although leading members of the alliances that defeat the land-based dominant powers, the relative neglect of sea powers in his subsequent discussion of power is suggestive of the poverty of this international relations theory. Of course the simplistic notion of sea power does no justice at all to the complex political entities that have come to power on both sides of the North Atlantic. If we did not know the historical outcomes, on reading realist international relations books we might well conclude that dominant land powers routinely lead the inter-state system. The narrow theoretical focus on politico–military activities has directed international relations scholars away from a full understanding of where power ultimately lies in the modern inter-state system. The bottom line is that each time there has been a major world war, it is the sea powers that have come out on the winning side. The reason is because the sea powers in question have been so much more than mere war machines.

The Dutch, the British and the Americans may have been the 'great learners' – they certainly contributed to new strategies of statecraft – who countered the imperium threats, but that does not explain why they, in turn, did not seek to create a world empire. Surely their emphatic victories over their major rivals could have become a springboard for an alternative world empire. After all this was the route France took after the defeat of Spain in the 17th century and Germany took after the defeat of France in the late 19th century. But it was not a route pursued by the Dutch, British and American states. At the peak of their powers these three states did not threaten the sovereignty of other states in the system. They were a different sort of state to that portrayed in the traditional international relations literature. Theirs was a sophisticated economic expansion rather than a crude war strategy to gain territory. Instead of the political–military imperatives that are expected to dominate international relations, these states had very definite economic agendas in which political elimination of rivals was simply not relevant. They pursued political-economy imperatives.

It will not have escaped the attention of the reader that the three 'sea powers' with unusual attitudes to territorial aggrandizement are the hegemons we have previously identified. Therefore we conclude that the creation of a world ordered through political-economy imperatives is the mark of a hegemon. Here we follow Christopher Case-Dunn's argument that the modern inter-state system survived because of the emergence of hegemony in the system.[39] After millennia when empires rose to eliminate state systems, in the capitalist world-economy a new type of leading state emerged which used its power to maintain state competition rather than eliminate it. This enabled the modern world-system to follow a unique trajectory among world-systems. This is the fundamental difference that hegemony makes.

The difference hegemony makes

Hegemony is a highly contested concept so let us begin at the beginning. Hegemony can be traced back to the classical Greek term *hegemonia*. This was used in two distinctive ways.[40] First, it could mean the dominance and supremacy of one political group over others and so was little different from the idea of empire.[41] A second, more subtle, usage identified the *hegemon* as leader in the sense of guide, the political group 'who does things first and therefore shows the way for others'.[42] The latter implies much more than coercive political power and has led to the widespread modern use of the term.

This is associated with name of Antonio Gramsci, who famously defined hegemony as 'intellectual and moral leadership'. He argued that the attainment of hegemony within a country by a social class made them appear to be the 'natural' leaders of the country so that their rule could be based as much on consensus as coercion.[43] This is made possible through the interests of the 'hegemonic class' appearing as universal interests.[44] Gramsci developed his ideas while a political prisoner in Fascist Italy in the late 1920s and 1930s. As a leader of the Italian Communist Party he wanted to understand why the politics of his country diverged from the more liberal regimes in north-western Europe. Traditional Marxist ideas did not seem to account for the rise of populist Fascism, but Gramsci devised a quite sophisticated answer to this conundrum. He argued that the Italian bourgeoisie had never achieved an hegemony within Italian society as they had long enjoyed in, say, Britain. Hence there was a political vacuum in the Italian state which Mussolini's Fascists were able to take advantage of through coercion to produce a non-hegemonic rule of the country.

For Gramsci, the concept of hegemony enabled him to develop a Marxist theory that broke decisively from the mechanistic and deterministic ideas that have dominated so much of Marxism.[45] By providing a more humanistic reading of Marx, he has been attributed with bringing cultural factors back into critical social analysis.[46] Hence, while 'official' Marxism continued its long march down the political cul-de-sac it created for itself, Gramsci's ideas have taken on a new lease of life. As one commentator quips: Gramsci is 'the Marxist you can take home to mother'.[47] Thus 'cultural hegemony' is an important concept in many contemporary social analyses, and I will draw on it freely below, but my use of hegemony will relate to a wider sphere of social activities.

Gramsci was concerned with the nature of power within states and he borrowed the concept of hegemony from its classical usage referring to relations between political entities.[48] Most contemporary users of 'hegemony' have returned to using the term to describe such relations, specifically at the inter-state scale of analysis. Within the field of international relations, the concept of hegemony has been used to try to make sense of the relative economic decline of the USA and its consequences since about 1970. One school of thought has developed a hegemonic-stability theory to explain why the world has become more unstable, especially economically, after the breakdown of the Bretton Woods system of fixed exchange rates and the return of volatile currency markets.[49] In this theory the earlier post-war period of relative stability was explained as an artifact of US hegemony.

Like Britain a century earlier, the USA was economically powerful enough to provide and maintain a general infrastructure through which much of the rest of the world would benefit. For instance the fixed-rate dollar facilitated secure and certain exchange payments for trade in a similar manner to the pound sterling and the gold standard in an earlier era. The international instability that was experienced after 1970, therefore, was interpreted as being due to the ending of American hegemony in the same way that the relative decline of Britain had created so many problems in the first half of the 20th century. Although not originally couched in Gramscian terms, this analogy between Britain and the USA has been reinterpreted as examples of 'intellectual and moral leadership' based upon their respective economic, political and cultural pre-eminence. The translation from the original Gramsci analysis is quite straightforward. For Gramsci the subjects competing for hegemony are social classes and the object is the state as the locus of power. In this analysis the subjects are states and the object is power within the wider world. To avoid confusion this will be referred to as 'world hegemony' on account of its object.[50]

In this book we develop the concept of world hegemony through a world-systems' interpretation of the modern world. This has two specific implications that are not found elsewhere. First, we go beyond British–American comparisons: in a system that is half a millennium old, the Dutch Republic is treated as a third case of hegemony centred on the 17th century. The addition of the Dutch is highly controversial for the simple reason that as a state they never appeared to be anything like as powerful as either Britain or the USA at their peaks.[51] But much of the criticism misses the point on two counts. First, the power that accrues to the hegemon is much more subtle than many of the critics seem to appreciate; they have been looking for the wrong clues. Second, and more important, we shall see that the Dutch as 'foundation hegemons' are arguably the most important of the three rather than a poor and doubtful relation. The key point is, however, that in what follows the quite commonplace Britain–USA comparisons are complemented by discussion of the Dutch case in a world hegemonic tryst.

The second implication of our approach follows from our promotion of the Dutch as hegemonic. World hegemony is seen as a property of the whole system and not just of the hegemon itself. Hegemonic states are particular core states that appear at specific conjunctures in the development of the world-system and are implicated in the overall development of the system. In short the capitalist world-economy has evolved through rather long cycles we term hegemonic cycles. These are the eras that encompass the rise, achievement and subsequent decline of an hegemonic state and which define the changing nature of the whole system. We explore this property of hegemony in the final section; here we concentrate on our hegemonic trio as they make the difference between continuing world-economy and conversion to world-empire.

In essence we use the concept of world hegemony as a very powerful historical analogy. Throughout the book we will be drawing on comparisons between the three cases to develop our arguments. Hence the Dutch, the British and the Americans appear in every chapter. In this first chapter we provide the basic framework for understanding how world hegemony operates. In this section we present the historical analogy in its simplest form: we highlight the four realms of activity in which the comparisons are clearest.[52] First, we deal with the role of the hegemons in

Plate 3 *World War*, 'The Plumb-pudding in danger' (1805) by James Gillray and published by H. Humphrey. This cartoon features British Prime Minister Pitt slicing off the maritime world west of the British Isles and Napoleon taking the juiciest piece, most of Europe, for France (Hulton Deutsch)

resisting imperial threats in world wars. Second, we argue that the hegemon is more than just a victor, it is the only state that has a 'good war' economically. This leads to the heart of the hegemony analogy: our third concern is the economic prowess of the hegemons. Finally we show how the hegemons have behaved as 'liberal champions', a role which leads the discussion towards consideration of the wider implications of hegemony in the next section.

World wars

World hegemony has triumphed over attempts to create world empires. In this argument three critical threats to the inter-state system are identified: the Hapsburg dynasty in the 16th and early 17th centuries, Napoleonic France in the early 19th century and the German Third Reich in the second quarter of the 20th century. On each occasion the effort was repulsed after a long '30 years' world war in which the imperial threat was utterly defeated: the 'original' Thirty Years War (1618–48), the Revolutionary and Napoleonic Wars (1792–1815) and the 20th-century World Wars I and II, which are interpreted as a single contest begun in 1914 but not finally resolved until 1945.

There have been many more wars involving the great powers, but these three wars are exceptional. We can make this case first on quantitative grounds: the great powers suffered far more deaths in these three wars than others (Table 3). Although the 20th-century wars stand out because of their means for unprecedented levels of violence, the two earlier '30-year wars' are also outstanding for great power commitment of lives. More important, qualitatively the outcome of these three wars fundamentally determined the nature of the system: they were 'world wars' in the sense of deciding what sort of world was to follow. Their great disruptions of the status quo were the enabling factor in the construction of hegemonies. But before we come to that we need to consider the threats to the inter-state system that required a 'grand alliance' of most other great powers first to curb then defeat them.

The Hapsburg inheritance of Charles V was immense. As well as succeeding to the unified Spanish throne he became Holy Roman Emperor in 1519 (Figure 1). Until his abdication in 1556 he was undisputably the most powerful man in Europe. His son Phillip II of Spain did not become the German emperor, but the title stayed in the family to continue its dynastic domination of European politics. With the launch of the Counter-Reformation, the idea of a universal monarchy was given a fresh goal and impetus in the late 16th and 17th centuries. But it also stimulated the revolt of the Protestant Dutch. Despite military setbacks, Spain was able to use its diplomatic leverage to establish a 'pax Hispania' in Europe; in the decade after 1610 Phillip III seemed, according to Hugh Trevor-Roper, to be 'monarch of the world'.[53] With the onset of the Thirty Years War in 1618, the Hapsburgs went on the offensive. J. P. Cooper argues that there was still the possibility of a Catholic Hapsburg domination of Europe as late as 1635: in that year the Hall of the Realms was finished in Madrid providing the classic iconography of universal monarchy.[54] But in the same year the Netherlands and France entered into an alliance, joining with the northern German Protestant princes and Sweden in the grand alliance that was eventually to force an end to the Thirty Years War and Hapsburg European ambitions at Westphalia.

In 1804 Napoleon took the title Emperor of France. This meant there were briefly two emperors in Europe, but war with Hapsburg Austria soon led to the final elimination of the title Holy Roman Emperor. Napoleon could have become the new king of France but he chose, instead, to evoke the memory of Charlemagne who had

Table 3   World Wars among major wars with more than half a million Great Power deaths

War:	Numbers of Great Powers	Great Power deaths (thousands)
World Wars I & II (1914–45)	8	20 703
Revolutionary & Napoleonic wars (1792–1815)	6	2532
Thirty Years War (1618–48)	6	2171
War of the Spanish Succession (1701–13)	5	1261
Seven Years War (1756–63)	6	992
Korean War (1950–3)	4	955
War of the League of Augsburg (1688–97)	5	680

Source: Estimates from Small and Singer (1982)

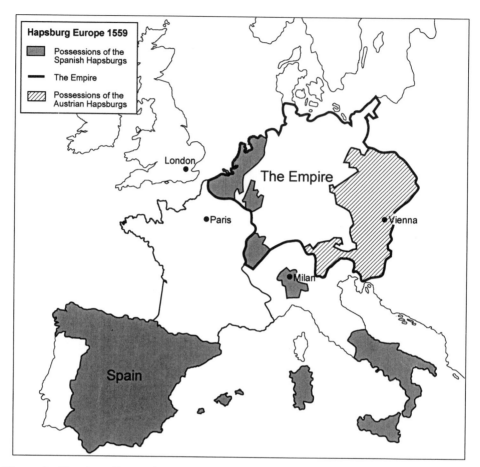

Figure 1   Hapsburg Europe in 1559

been ruler of France as well as the traditional Holy Roman Empire lands of Germany and Italy. Napoleon's European pretensions were thus laid bare. The Westphalia arrangement of nominally equal sovereign states was to be overturned in favour of a federated system of states with France at the centre. Since the emperor's dictat was the ultimate rule of law, this system of very unequal states was in reality a European empire (Figure 2). Stuart Woolf writes of 'echoes of Charles V's realm extending across Europe' and with the continental blockade against British trade he sees 'the progressive transformation of the universal system into the mirage of an universal empire'.[55] This project reached its greatest extent in 1812 before succumbing to a British-led grand alliance including Russia, Austria and Prussia.

Adolf Hilter expected there to be a German state of 250 million people within a hundred years.[56] Contemporary boundaries defined a territory far too small for such an eventuality. Germany was, therefore, in Hitler's eyes, a space-deprived state: the space-owning powers would have to relinquish their possessions in a new and just share-out of the world's lands. This need for *lebensraum* (literally 'living space') was the basic geopolitical theory behind the military aggression of the Third Reich. But Hitler's goals went beyond *lebensraum* to world domination. This was planned in three

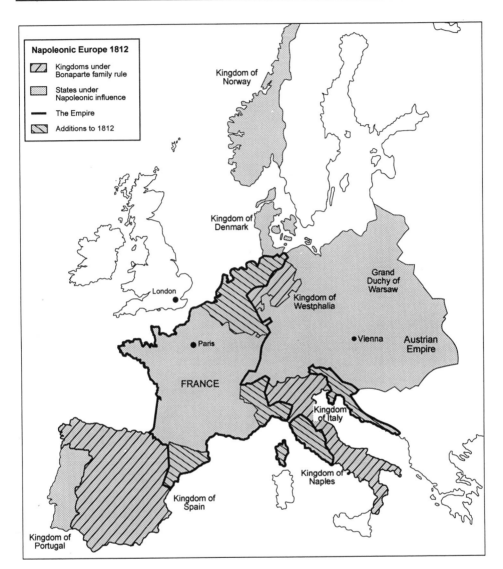

Figure 2   Napoleonic Europe in 1812

stages.[57] First, France was to be defeated to give mastery of Europe. Second, Russia was to be defeated to provide mastery of Eurasia. Third, as master of the great 'world island', Germany would be able to dominate the rest of the world converting them into satellite states. Only one and a half stages were completed by late 1942 (Figure 3) when Hitler's armies began to suffer the same fate as Napoleon's on the great Russian steppes. Final defeat was organized under the auspices of American leadership in a grand alliance including the USSR, the British Empire, France and China.

Comparing the three cases above defines quite a neat historical analogy. This first cut at the analogy can be portrayed as a trajectory of the modern world-system through time in which imperium and hegemony are opposite tendencies away from a balanced distribution of power. The trajectory of the modern world-system defines

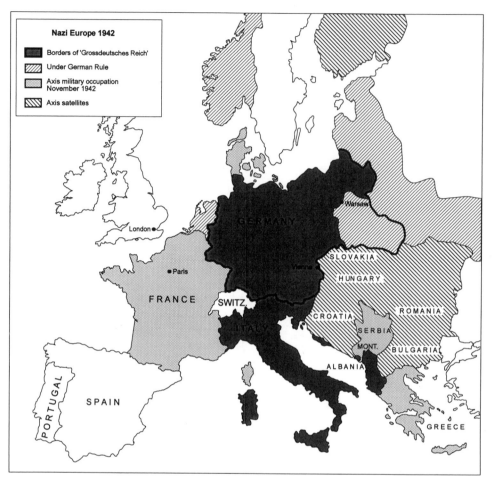

Figure 3   Nazi Europe in 1942

a spiral: competitive tendencies move the system towards imperium but the three world wars, instead of consolidating a new world empire, reverse the direction to create the very different power concentration we call hegemony.

Having a 'good war'

At the end of each of the 30-year world wars the state we have identified as hegemon was just one military victor among the several great powers that made up the grand alliance. What, therefore, makes the hegemons special? Remarkably, in each case, while all around them were being devastated, they were prospering economically. Wars, especially ones that last 30 years, are incredibly destructive of capital, but they also create a continual demand to replace what is destroyed. World war, therefore, is a major economic opportunity. The Dutch, British and Americans grabbed the opportunity with both hands. As well as being military victors, they had a 'good war' economically.[58]

How were they able to achieve this most auspicious outcome?[59] There are two reasons for this. First, their specific role as sea powers in the world war is important. Conflict at sea is much less destructive of capital than land war, and the initial role of the hegemon-to-be is to use its navy to maintain economic networks. But a land power can only be finally defeated in the field. In this process the hegemon-to-be subsidizes allies to do most of the fighting throughout the long conflict. In the defeat of France and Germany, it is only towards the end of the conflict that the hegemon-to-be enters the land war as a major player and, through its crucial final contribution to the decisive defeat, has a leading role in making the peace. Great Britain defeated France at sea early on, but the victorious supreme commander, Wellington, is a relatively late arrival on the scene just like Eisenhower 13 decades later. The Dutch case is different, but similar principles are at work. The Dutch certainly kept the seas open in the Thirty Years War and subsidized allies. But they were never leaders in the land war and kept carefully to their sector of the war, although in the process their neutralizing the Spanish forces in the Low Countries was probably decisive in sapping Hapsburg military might. The key point in all three cases is that the hegemon's land war is carefully controlled so as not to become dehabilitating.

Second, and the key to subsequent leadership, the hegemon-to-be is the economic powerhouse behind the victory. Although in hindsight we can see that the Dutch, British and Americans had the most potential for economic growth before each war, by the time we come to the end of the war this is plain for all to see. The Dutch 'golden age' and the British 'industrial revolution' both coincide with world war: each country emerges from the war with its economy immensely boosted. The case of the USA is even more remarkable: American GNP more than doubled in the years from 1939 to 1945.[60] Economic success is always relative, of course, and this enhances the hegemon-to-be's position. All other countries, enemies and allies alike, suffer different degrees of devastation and effective economic bankruptcy. This is why world wars are the launching pads of hegemony. As well as defeating the threat of empire, the world war economically exhausts all great powers except one: the hegemon is the only power to come out of the war economically stronger than when the war began. With all economic rivals temporarily eliminated, the hegemon is in a position to use its unique economic clout to ensure that the post-war reconstruction of the world-economy is compatible with its interests.

Economic edge

Usually the historical analogy underlying the world-systems' interpretation of hegemony begins with economic comparisons. Hegemonic economic prowess not only acts as the enabling factor in world wars but is also used to define hegemony and the nature of its rise and demise. Hence Immanuel Wallerstein's approach to hegemonic cycles has at its core a material base.[61] The hegemons have an economic edge over their rivals which is built in three stages. First, in the realm of production the hegemon becomes the most advanced and efficient to such a degree that it can even compete in other core states' home markets. Second, this leads to commercial supremacy with merchants from the hegemon dominating the world market. Third, the wealth that accrues from these activities stimulates the financial sector with the hegemon housing the world's bankers. Full hegemony only occurs when this triple economic dominance is in place. Sometimes referred to as 'high hegemony', this is a relatively short phase – Wallerstein dates the three periods 1620–72, 1815–73 and 1945–67.[62] On the other side of the cycle economic leadership is lost in the same order, first in production, then commerce, leaving financial pre-eminence as the last economic vestige of hegemony. Let us flesh out the economic analogy.

Hegemony specifies uneven development among the core states of the world-economy. It is based upon technological and managerial innovations within the hegemonic state which give it an unusual economic lead over its rivals. In short each of the hegemons experiences an 'industrial revolution'. The least well-known is the Dutch case, but it is well documented.[63] Focused upon shipbuilding and sea trans-port from about 1580 to 1620, the Netherlands experienced a concentration of techni-cal and managerial innovations that set it off from the rest of Europe. From this leading edge, innovations spread through other sectors of production such as brew-ing and sugar refining. In contrast, the case of Britain is universally known as 'the' industrial revolution with technological and managerial innovations initially centred on textiles and steam power before diffusing across the economy. For the USA the managerial revolution of mass production and the technical advances in electronics define a third industrial revolution that has yet to be completed. But already the US is losing its production edge to Japan and Germany just as Britain began to fall behind the USA and Germany in the late 19th century and the Dutch increasingly succumbed to English competition towards the end of the 17th century.

In the case of commerce, the crucial Dutch contribution was the invention of modern charter companies. Given the uncertainties of foreign trade in the 17th century, these companies spread the risk and created regional trade monopolies. The most successful was also the first, the Dutch East India Company established in 1602.[64] Commerce in the Netherlands was organized around the arrival of the great fleets from East Indies, West Indies, the Mediterranean and the Levant, and the Baltic.[65] Other countries, notably England and France, copied the Dutch example and established their own charter companies which out-traded the Dutch in much of the world in the 18th century. By the 19th century charter companies were con-sidered unwieldy economic agents and under British tutelage we enter the classic age of international trade with family businesses and limited companies producing in one country and trading – buying raw materials or selling their finished products – with companies set up in other countries. Import–export is the name of the game, and the British created the largest-ever merchant marine to facilitate this inter-state commerce under the protection of the Royal Navy. There were, of course, common ventures between companies across boundaries, but the great transition to very large companies occurred in the USA at the very end of the 19th century. This led to a very different kind of commerce. In the 20th century America has pioneered multinational corporations that produce and sell in many countries. Commerce un-der American hegemony has become more a matter of intra-firm transactions than trade between countries. Nevertheless one of the symptoms of US decline has been the loss of the 'trade war' with Japan.

Financial dominance has been at the very centre of hegemony. As the final piece in the economic jig-saw, as it were, financial pre-eminence is closely associated with the world wars that confirm hegemony. In 1607 the Bank of Amsterdam was formed to facilitate the great expansion that was occurring in international trade. By offering bills of exchange the bank provided the financial basis for transactions across the whole world-economy. It is this banking role above all others that is stimulated by the Thirty Years War: the Spanish even used the Bank of Amsterdam to pay their troops fighting the Netherlands! Amsterdam was, in Fernand Braudel's terms, the world-city at the centre of the world-economy.[66] It kept this role through the 18th century and although rivalled by London — the Bank of England was formed in 1696 — it continued to finance Britain's debt until the Napoleonic Wars. French conquest of the Netherlands spelt the death knell for Amsterdam's international role, and London finally took over as the world financial centre during the Napoleonic Wars. Based upon the gold standard and the pound sterling as the world's exchange currency, plus the City of London as the major provider of finance capital throughout the world, London was indisputably the world-city of the 19th century. This lasted into the 20th century, but British financial pre-eminence was fundamentally undermined by the costs of the World Wars I and II. The major task of financing the wars and the subsequent economic reconstructions fell on the Americans, and New York became the new world-city. The global repercussions of the Wall Street Crash in 1929 confirmed the overwhelming importance of New York. However, it was only after 1945 that the dollar became the cornerstone of the Bretton Woods fixed-currency exchange-rate system that ended in 1971 with the floating of the dollar on the currency market. Recently, American financial prowess has been challenged by Japanese banks, and Tokyo has become a rival to New York, although the dollar remains the leading currency of exchange in the world-economy.

It seems that the idea of each hegemon experiencing similar rise and decline patterns from initial production edge to final financial fall is reasonably consistent with the historical record. There is much detail to be added which will inevitably lead to some caveats, but the basic analogy would seem to be a sound one. Here we are at the heart of what it is to be a hegemon. Although not military weaklings, the power of hegemonic states is fundamentally economic in nature. As such they have most to lose from conversion of the system to a universal empire. They rely on a political economy based upon a multiplicity of states to provide the manoeuvrability that is not possible in imperial structures under the control of political elites. Their role is to lead the modern world-system in an altogether different direction.

Liberal champion

Economic pre-eminence has had many repercussions for the three countries involved. Perhaps the most basic has been the hegemon's promotion of a more open or liberal world-economy. Obviously it is in the interests of the country with the most efficient economy to free the world market from political restrictions that would nullify its market advantages. The mid-19th century and the period after 1945 are rare periods in the history of the modern world-system when restrictions on trade were lowered producing a relatively liberal world-economy. This is central to the hegemonic stability theory described earlier. The Dutch case is far less clear-cut, but they do pioneer opening the seas to free passage for all, the basic prerequisite for a liberal world order.

Although the reasons for promoting an open world-economy reflect the hegemon's self-interest, they have portrayed their preferred economic arrangements as of universal utility against the particular interests of others. The key concept they have used is freedom: in Nicole Bousquet's words 'the freedom to sail of the Dutch, the freedom to trade of the British, and the freedom to invest of the Americans'.[67] By wrapping up their economic interests in a philosophical garb, hegemons have projected their needs on to a universal plane in true Gramscian mode: this is a classic example of intellectual and moral leadership. The intellectual investment in this process, both for and against, has been immense (Table 4). The three 'universal' claims have been promoted by great theorists: Grotius in the 17th century, David Ricardo following Adam Smith in the 19th century and the whole weight of the very orthodox discipline of economics in this century. Although relatively successful in getting others to accept their ideas during 'high hegemony', their chief rivals have developed alternative theories and politics to lessen the hegemon's economic advantages. A notable feature of this process is the prominence of hegemons-to-be as economic dissenters in the period before their promotion of economic freedoms. The English are the great mercantilists against the Dutch and the Americans the great protectionists against the British which implies their subsequent conversion to the universal is a mite hypocritical. On past records the Japanese will undoubtedly be the leading proponents of economic freedoms in the future!

In converting their economic needs into universal pleas for freedom, this philosophical concept has been transmitted into the political sphere of activities. In all three hegemonic cycles the hegemons have developed states in which power is unusually diffused. In the Dutch case there was no single power focus; there was a continually changing balance of power between the pseudo-royal Orange family and the representatives of the cities. In Britain a similar balance emerged between the constitutional monarchy and Parliament, while the USA is the archetypal state with a division of powers and restrictions on the executive. Dutch merchant republicanism, British parliamentary politics and American democratic federalism

Table 4 Trade Policies of Hegemons and Major Rivals

Hegemonic Cycle	'Universal' Theory	Rival 'Particularism'
DUTCH	Grotius's *mare liberum*	England: Mun's mercantilism. France: Colbertism
BRITISH	Smith's *laissez faire.* Ricardo's comparative advantage	Germany: List's protectionism. USA: Republican tariff policy
AMERICAN	Modern economic orthodoxy's free enterprise	USSR: Stalin's 'socialism in one country'. Japan: 'hidden protectionism'

constituted the most open governments among the major powers in their eras of high hegemony.

We can conclude, therefore, that the hegemons have been the modern world's liberal champions both economically and politically. As well as their negative role in preventing the rise of a world empire, hegemonic states have a crucial positive role in defining the nature of the modern world-system. Of course these two roles are not separate. Liberalism – either the idea of a liberal economics based upon open markets or a political liberalism based upon diffused power – makes little or no sense in a universal empire. By preventing the latter, the hegemon creates space for the former. In short, hegemonic cycles represent much more than the rise and fall of particular hegemonic states.

Hegemonies, world development and modernities

Historical analogies vary greatly in their credibility, but I think we have shown above that the hegemonic analogy can be reasonably well drawn. However neat and compelling the analogies may appear, they cannot be judged solely in terms of similarities between cases. There is, of course, no such thing as the perfect analogy – if the cases are so close as to be the same it is no longer an analogy. Ultimately the value of historical analogies is not measured by 'goodness of fit' but by their utility. A good analogy is pregnant with suggestions for how to take the analysis further. It points to new ideas that are not obvious from the original cases but emerge in the process of bringing them together. Historical analogy is a tool for understanding social change, no more, no less. The purpose of the discussion below is to illustrate just how suggestive the idea of hegemony can be for understanding our modern world.

Before we embark on this task we must recognize that historical analogies have their limitations. They can be very blunt instruments for understanding both the present and the past. The worst analogies abstract the cases being compared out of their historical context. The historical analogy we have developed avoids this pitfall because we have not presented comparisons based upon unchanging processes but have set them within an overarching historical context, the modern world-system. This is not a static system and therefore the context within which hegemony occurs has changed greatly among the three cases. But a world-systems' analysis implies much more than appreciation of changing contexts. Wallerstein describes hegemony as a 'processual concept'; it goes beyond a taxonomical ordering of events to describe a process through which the modern world-system operates.[68] This is the basis of the analogy's special utility. The emergence, maintenance and decline of world hegemonies define a basic set of transformations that distinguish the modern world-system from all earlier world-systems. We argue below that hegemonic cycles define the stages of development of the modern world-system, are implicated in the overall trajectory of the system and specify what it is about the system that makes it modern. In short, the utility of the hegemony analogy is to be found in the reach of its significance.

Stages of world development

Giovanni Arrighi emphasizes that the hegemony we are dealing with is world hegemony.[69] As such each case defines a world development, the stages through which the modern world-system has progressed: hegemony is a process of supersession in which each hegemon creates a new order in the world-system that is more complex than its predecessor.

In his model, Arrighi brings together many of the ideas we have previously presented. The anarchy of the inter-state system and the world wars are at the centre of his analysis. He treats anarchy in the orthodox manner as indicating no rule but with working arrangements between states creating an order of sorts. World wars on the other hand represent a breakdown of that order which he calls 'systemic chaos'.[70] However this chaos denotes a broader concept than world war. As well as inter-state conflict organized by the political rulers, there is an equally serious rebelliousness among the ruled. The Thirty Years War is a culmination of the religious rebellions we call the Reformation, the Revolutionary and Napoleonic Wars are the centre-piece of the 'age of revolutions' (1776–1848) and World Wars I and II coincide with the rise of socialist threats to the system from the Russian Revolution (1917) through to the Chinese Revolution (1949). In these dangerous circumstances with wars feeding off revolutions and vice versa, there is a general demand among the political and economic elites for order. This is not just a matter of war being followed by peace, a pacification must be imposed to stabilize the system. The hegemon is the only state able to provide the necessary order and in doing so creates a particular stage of world-system development.

The Dutch are instrumental in creating the simplest pattern of order which Arrighi terms the 'Westphalia system' after the treaty that confirms the inter-state system.[71] The chaos of the Thirty Years War derived directly from a lack of respect for political boundaries: great armies marauded across Central Europe leaving swaths of destruction in their wake. It is just such behaviour that is outlawed at Westphalia. The new Europe of boundaries around sovereign territorial states produced separated spaces of peace, a mosaic that kept religions apart while simultaneously providing new units of economic competition. This first pacification, therefore, was at the scale of individual sovereign territories.[72] This most certainly did not bring an end to war – the sovereign states remained war machines – but general war is replaced by border wars. This is an anarchic system *par excellence*, but it is no longer chaotic.

Systemic chaos reappears with the French Revolution and Napoleon. Once again armies march across Europe with little or no concern for political boundaries. The order that is imposed at Vienna under British tutelage is a more complex one than at Westphalia. Arrighi calls this 'Free Trade Imperialism', a new stage of order that is less anarchic than the Westphalia system.[73] Britain was able to maintain a balance of power within Europe through the formal existence of the Concert of Europe while having a free hand to dominate the rest of the world-system. The Concert was a very weak organization but none the less represented organization above the states that impinged on the sovereignty of smaller states. Hence the new scale of pacification is Europe as a whole.[74] In addition, through free-trade policies, the world-economy is centred upon the hegemon's economy at a new level of integration.

In the systemic chaos of the first half of the 20th century, the demand for order is satisfied by the USA in a further stage of system complexity Arrighi calls the 'Free Enterprise System'.[75] The international organizations centred upon the United Nations are a quantum step above the 19th-century Concert of Europe. First, they are global in scope; second, they cover a far wider range of issues beyond the strategic balance of power; and third, they are part of a general tendency for political and economic state associations that severely curtail simple territorial sovereignty. The zone of pacification becomes larger again, this time encompassing the whole of the 'North' as the Cold War 'freezes' alliances from the North Atlantic to Siberia.[76] In addition the world-economy has been further integrated through global corporations, financial markets and telecommunications to continue eroding the anarchic sovereignty of states.

This is a clear example of world hegemony as a system-wide property. Hegemony is more than the attributes or behaviours of a particularly favoured state; it is part of the nature of the world-system itself. Hegemony defines the basic steps in the evolution of the system in terms of stages of economic development and the associated political order. But hegemonies can define even more.

The rise and demise of the system

All world-systems are historical systems in the sense that they are created, they develop and they come to their end. This 'system cycle' defines the rise and fall of world empires we treated earlier. But how do the hegemonic cycles within a world-economy fit into this historical pattern? Following Chase-Dunn we have argued that hegemons have replaced imperiums as the dominant engine of social change, but unlike new empires each hegemon does not define a new world-system.[77] On reaching their zenith hegemons soon decline, but the renewed system they have been instrumental in creating continues to thrive. The capitalist world-economy, therefore, has discovered the trick of renewing itself as stages of development in its evolution. This does not mean that renewals can continue forever: the modern world-system is a historical system and therefore might be expected to have a system cycle just like other world-systems before it. Hence, although Arrighi's model describes the evolution of the system to the present, he does not suggest the mechanisms he describes are eternal: quite the reverse in fact; he interprets the American Free Enterprise System as the final stage in the process of supersession.[78] In short, the modern world-system has its rise and fall just like any other historical system. Hence in this model the three hegemonic cycles constitute the 'life-span' of our system, they define the overarching system cycle.

Terence Hopkins has provided the argument that relates the hegemonic cycles to the system cycle.[79] Each case of hegemony signifies a critical 'moment' in the existence of the modern world-system. Dutch hegemony represents the moment of 'rise'; it demonstrated that a capitalist world-economy was a realistic historical alternative to world-empire. Without Dutch hegemony the modern world-system might never have succeeded in avoiding the fate of all previous incipient world-economies – incorporation or conversion into a world-empire. The corollary of this is that although on all quantitative criteria the Dutch are, in Wallerstein's term, 'the least plausible' hegemon, in the perspective of the world-system cycle they become the crucial actors that make all subsequent stages possible.

British hegemony represents the moment of 'dominium' when the modern world-system eliminated all rival systems to become truly global. This is the period when the world-economy proved itself to be an exceptional system like no other in history. Its expansion proved irresistible. Through a combination of war and market processes the capitalist world-economy became innately more powerful than all other systems with which it came into contact. Even the greatest world-empire of them all, China, was forced to succumb in the 19th century as we noted earlier. Every part of the world was integrated into a single division of labour as pre-capitalist economic systems were either destroyed or transformed by reorientation to the world market. In terms of the system cycle, British hegemony occurs as the high point of the system trajectory.

Although on all quantitative indicators the USA has been the most powerful of the hegemons, in this argument it represents the moment of 'demise'. This may seem strange to readers used to seeing their history as ever onward progress, but in terms of system cycles the turning of the tide comes at the very limits of the social system – a success too far. In the case of the modern world-system, the American Free Enterprise System has been so successful it has created the basis of a trans-state world that supersedes inter-stateness. Both increasing political interconnectedness and the massive globalization of economic processes have become what Hopkins calls 'state-subversive'.[80] The inter-state system is being undermined not through another attempt at world-empire but through its own development.

Hopkins's thesis is controversial.[81] We cannot know the future; so that describing American hegemony as the demise moment is conjecture. Nevertheless it is a thesis that we explore and develop in later chapters. Hence, this is a question we will return to in some detail later in the book; at this stage we can leave it as a provocative idea of the sort we expect from the better type of historical analogy.

Modernities

The fact that we have called our current world-system 'modern' has elicited no discussion thus far. Although the word is often used simply to mean contemporary, we use modern here as more than a temporal reference. The idea that something is modern implies a social or cultural content. Hence the concept of a modern world-system implies more than a capitalist world-economy narrowly conceived in political-economy terms. The socio-cultural sphere of activities has been relatively neglected thus far, but it will be remembered that we began with Gramsci's cultural definition of hegemony as intellectual and moral leadership. The cultural has been lurking in the background; the time has come to bring it back to the fore as we contemplate what is modern about our system. We will argue that it is in their role as definers of modernity that the hegemons most display their world-leadership qualities.

The cultural dimension of all world-systems is represented by its civilization. The major world-empires have been the great civilizations. Since the appellation 'modern' is used to denote the world-system we are dealing with, we can designate its culture as modern civilization. Just as with other world-systems, outsiders have been viewed as barbarians in contrast to the civilized who inhabit the system. Since about 1900 there have been no outsiders left, and the civilized–barbarian antithesis has been replaced in our civilization by the internal conflict of modern versus traditional. Modern people living in modern society consider themselves superior to those unfortunate enough to be 'still' living in traditional societies. But just as barbarians can be civilized, so too can traditional societies be modernized. Thus incorporation into the modern world-system sets in train the process of modernization: traditional customs and mores, sometimes termed 'moral economy', are converted into a new culture compatible with producing for the world market.

Modernization theory was very popular in the 1950s and 1960s as a way of conceptualizing social change after decolonization in the Third World. Political independence was seen as only a first stepping-stone to a new existence as a modern state. In order for the state to develop, its people and institutions were expected to modernize. That is to say, the society had to be functionally organized into classes rather than tribes, and people had to be more economically rational rather than behave in customary fashion. In this approach, modern is treated as a self-evidently good condition, barely disguised from the contemporary society of the theorists (the USA or Western Europe).[82] The key point here, however, is that this stereotypical modern society became the universal goal of development. The result was a singular concept of the modern that stifled all creative thinking about possible futures for poor Third World countries. But historically there have been many modernity projects, and those recently devised for the Third World should not be seen in isolation.

Once we ask historical questions about modernity, we come to the vexed matter of the origins of the modern.[83] Probably the most common approach has been to interpret the industrial revolution in late 18th-century Britain as the great watershed between traditional and modern. This created the conditions for the massive increases in productivity that led to mass urban society with all the breaking of links with the rural past that that implies. But for many writers who equate modern with systematic rational thinking, it is the 17th century's European scientific revolution that marks the breakthrough to modernity. However, we do not have to choose between these different conceptions of the beginning of modernity if we allow modernity to be a multiple concept. Given the existence of several modernities, the task becomes to describe the general historical context in which alternative modernities have arisen. World hegemonies have provided just such contexts.

What is this experience we call modernity? The modern world-system is one of perpetual change as capitalist entrepreneurs are forever shifting their focus to gain advantages in the market-place. The need for ceaseless accumulation of capital is the basic driving force. Such a world is a very paradoxical place. Men and women experience rapid change as both opportunity for a better world and as destroyer of their existing world. According to Marshall Berman to live in the modern world is to live in 'a maelstrom of perpetual disintegration and renewal, of struggle and contradiction, of ambiguity and anguish'.[84] The modernism movement which burst on to the arts scene in the closing years of the last century explicitly provided the visions and images to try to capture, or make sense of, the maelstrom of modern life. Of course coping with modernity extends far beyond artistic movements, ordinary people have to deal with it in their daily lives.[85] In this discussion we are concerned

Plate 4 *Apocalyptic Landscape* (1913) by Ludwig Meidner (Los Angeles County Museum of Art). This is a typical modernist painting that attempts to capture movement and change. Although resembling the chaos of a town after an earthquake, it is the painter's image of his home city of Berlin representing modernity

with culture in its general meaning as the way of life in a society rather than as the 'high culture' of a society's elites.

There are several political regimes that have portrayed themselves as agents of modernity. Emphasizing the rationality core of modernity, they have often attempted to control change through bureaucratic planning. Revolutionary and Napoleonic France were explicit modernizers as they rationalized the government of their own country and then attempted to export their modern bureaucracy to the rest of Europe.[86] In our times the USSR thought it could capture modernity in its planning mechanism and so steer change in its preferred direction. Both of these projects were spectacular failures. Their bureaucracies proved to be far too crude as social engineers to cope with the modern maelstrom – these, and other similar projects, quite rapidly slid from the renewal to the disintegration side of modernity. However, although modernity cannot be captured by a particular state apparatus, that does not mean that particular states are never implicated in the renewal aspect of the modern. By taking advantage of opportunities that arise, states can certainly nurture modernity; in certain circumstances they may generate new forms of modernity.

Berman identifies three main phases of modernity: the first extending from the 16th to the 18th centuries, the second in the 19th century and a contemporary modernity in this century.[87] At the cultural–ideological level these phases can be defined as intellectual attempts to come to terms with a rapidly changing world by ordering knowledge so that people are subjects as well as objects of change. Three periods of major ordering are usually identified: in the 17th century a Cartesian world was devised with 'man' at the centre, the 19th century was the high mark of change interpreted as human progress, and in our century the idea of change has been globalized and repackaged as 'development' in modernization theory. Each of these is a theoretical taming of the perpetually new by application of a rationality privileging science and technology.

The reader will note immediately the temporal correlation with the three hegemonic cycles. The argument of this book is that the crucial aspects of the social–cultural dimension we call 'modernity' have evolved with and through the hegemons. This follows from our definition of hegemony. Although rapid change is the norm in the modern world-system, the rate of change that has to be coped with is not a constant. In fact the rate of change will accelerate precisely when hegemons are creating a new world through their restructuring of the world-economy. This stimulates a basic need for intellectual reassesssments and the creation of a new rationalization of the newness. New forms of modernity are the socio-cultural reaction to this hegemonic creation of uncertainties. Hence each hegemon has been responsible for creating its particular version of what is modern about the modern world-system. The first modern world is that of the merchants, the everyday life of commerce and the massive coterie of activities that is generated. There had been many influential networks of merchants in the past but in the 17th century a new rationality came to dominate the world-system in which the calculating behaviour of the merchant was the archetypal practical form: navigation became the great enabling applied science. The Dutch more than anyone else created this modernity: they made making money respectable. In the 19th century great commercial ports gave way to massive industrial towns as the archetypal modern. In this industrial world, modern society became mass society — for Marx the modern became an alienated way of life. As the merchant gave way to the industrialist, mechanical engineering became the great enabling applied science. There is no doubt that Britain is the country most implicated in bringing this second modern condition about.[88] In the 20th century the alienation has been countered in selected countries by a spread of affluence to ordinary people. The suburban mall has become the focal modern place in the new consumer society where people are encouraged to buy commodities endlessly. Here it is management science with its communications and computer technologies that has been the major enabling applied science of our era. There can be no doubt that Americans have been the major purveyors of contemporary modernity. Hence the hegemons have been directly instrumental in creating new ways of life that have dominated the modern world-system; they have been the leading architects of modernities.

We should expect nothing less from world hegemons, of course. As the prime actors in the history of the modern world-system, it is they who should define what is modern about the system in their respective eras. Because each hegemon is indisputably a great success story in its path to high hegemony, their rivals try to emulate if they can. After the success of the Dutch, other states commercialized their activities in a process known as mercantilism. After the success of the British, other states industrialized to prevent 'falling behind'. After the success of the Americans, other states that could created their own 'affluent societies' based upon mass consumption. This is what is meant by hegemonic 'intellectual and moral leadership' at the world-system scale. Emulation implies no coercion, merely a general consensus about what it is to be modern in a given era.

The limits of hegemony

This chapter has covered an enormous amount of material within its relatively short length. We have introduced large claims – some would say they are heroic – which we elaborate upon in subsequent chapters. But before we go any further we need to be clear and specific about the scope of our analysis. Like all historical analogies, the idea of world hegemony has its limits. As will be well appreciated by now, this is a very wide-ranging book but there is obviously much that is missing. Hence it is incumbent on the author to spell out the limits of hegemony before developing its multifarious insights.

The first point to make about limits is that I am not unduly concerned about questions of degree of hegemony. As we have seen, the Dutch are usually viewed as the 'least hegemonic', or indeed not hegemonic at all, but there are differences of opinion on whether Britain or the USA has been the 'most hegemonic'. Such questions are not unimportant, but we can spend too long on them; ultimately they come down to definitions and interpretations whose resolution can only be to agree to differ. My position is that the idea of hegemony must be analytically distinguished from the actual historical situations. This is the old hoary chestnut of the difference between theoretical model and concrete cases. All three hegemons are partial examples of hegemony as an ideal case. How could it be otherwise? But they are not so partial as to make my argument redundant.

There is a second more important limit to hegemony that is integral to the analysis. The relative importance of consent in the relationship between hegemon and other states means that the former's interests only prevail, in Gramsci's words, 'up to a certain point'.[89] Whereas world-empires can impose their interests by coercion, the fact of not relying on this option is what makes a hegemon a hegemon. In this form of rule, the interests of the other states over which hegemony is being exercised have to be taken into account. In constructing a moral leadership, again in Gramsci's words, 'a certain compromise equilibrium' has to be formed which will inevitably mean short-term sacrifices by the hegemon to achieve its longer-term goals.[90]

Although very different in kind, both of these limits point to the same corollary: there will be much for which the hegemon is not directly responsible. Since this is a book about hegemony, we are selecting episodes from the historical record that show the difference hegemony makes. Certainly there is another book to be written about the role of the 'Number Twos' (France, Germany . . .) in the modern world-system.[91] And, of course, the hegemons as defenders of the system have not been the major players in the development of anti-systemic movements – socialism, national-ism and their various combinations. This is not to say that Number Twos and anti-systemic movements are missing from our analysis but rather that they are mar-ginalized in our particular focus. Like all histories, this one is highly selective.

But we do argue that world hegemony has had an exorbitant influence on our modern ways of living. Hegemons have provided the economic and political struc-tures through which we live our lives and the dominant world-views and moralities by which we live our lives: they have defined what makes us modern. This chapter has had the task of providing the foundation for this assertion, which the remainder of the book attempts to confirm. In the next chapter we focus upon modern politics and define it in terms of the nature of the modern state. In the following two chapters the key processes of universalizing and emulating are explored further. All of this is a prelude to the concern for where we have reached today and where we may be going. The penultimate chapter identifies contemporary American dilemmas as a case of 'post-hegemonic trauma' and uses our historical analogy to see what we can learn from the British and the Dutch when they faced their great 'impasses'. In the final chapter we return to the question of system cycle and discuss what happens next as America's impasse transmutes into a world impasse. That completes our intellectual journey from world hegemony to world impasse.

2 Creating modern politics

We are right to feel somewhat ambivalent when we think of modern politics. As a 'modern' activity it incorporates all the ambiguities we have come to associate with this adjective. On the one hand modern politics has had its great successes notably in increasing popular participation in the political process. The spread of democracy across more and more countries is to be celebrated. But there is another side to popular participation; mass politics has led to genocides both in the hearth of modern politics, Europe, and in regions where it has tried to diffuse such as Africa. In fact soldiers have continued to be at least as prominent as voters in modern politics. This is despite the fact that the pursuit of peace has been and continues to be a major activity in modern politics. We can easily become cynical about it all. In a political world of popular elections and popular genocides, of perennial bloody wars and perennial peace conferences, the contradictions can seem like a great conspiracy: surely no 'cock-up theory' of history could create such tragedies alongside the triumphs. But it is neither conspiracy nor cock-up. In order to cope with a modern world of perpetual change, political elites are forever adapting old institutions and creating new ones. The endless difficulty is that as soon as an institution answers the questions asked of it, fresh challenges arise for which it is found to be wanting. Whether we think that on the whole modern politicians have done a good or bad job overall, we can admire their inventiveness in recreating politics time and again over the past five hundred years.

It is this political practice that is our main subject matter here. We will be concerned with how politicians have dealt with the matrix of opportunities and risks that is the modern world-system. Their creativity is bounded, however. In fact it is by observing what is constant in the changing politics that we can discern the critical features of modern politics. First and foremost, all modern politics is premised upon the existence of the state within an inter-state system. Although we may generically define politics as the wielding of power irrespective of context, in the modern world politics is crucially about states. Political elites are state officials and members of governments, voters and soldiers are state citizens, and to escape a genocide is to escape across a state's borders.

States are, in Anthony Giddens's famous phrase, power containers.[1] They are so powerful that they have become 'naturalized' – state boundaries on the world map appear to be as natural as rivers, shore lines and mountain ranges.[2] As part of our taken-for-granted world, states define and confine politics. The corollary of this is that modern politics is essentially territorial in organization. It is divided into two spheres of activities, a politics within states and a politics between states. Hence every state has a dual character; it is 'Janus-faced' in the sense of looking two ways at once – inwards to its own society and outwards to the rest of the inter-state system.[3] Since the nature of relations with society and with other states are of two different kinds, it follows that a defining feature of modern politics is its division into two separated realms of politics.

Domestic politics is about state–society relations. The term commonly used to describe the state's partner in this duo is 'civil society'. Unfortunately this concept has developed two related but distinctive meanings that can cause confusion. On the one hand civil society is that realm of activities that exists between the private world of the family and the public world of the state. Neither household nor state can function properly without the existence of civil society; households are never self-sufficient but need the co-operation of other households in civil society, while the state needs civil society as a source of order and organization within its territory. On the other hand, economic activities can be separated out to create the trio: state, civil society and economy. This leaves civil society with just cultural and social institutions, and the market and production relations as a separate sphere. In our discussion here we will use the former definition although future reference will be made to a separate sphere for the economic. Basically civil society equates with the idea of 'society' as generally used to describe the people living within a state territory – for instance, American society, French society, and so on. The adjective 'civil' reminds us of the state relation since it is citizens that make up such societies.

Two examples of contemporary failures of civil society illustrate this meaning. In the European communist states in the period before 1989, the state through the party dominated all organization within its territory leaving little space for a civil society to exist. In fact the Communist Party, instead of carrying out the usual party-political role of linking civil society with the state, effectively became part of the state, a parallel state apparatus. In 1989, therefore, any civil society that existed in these countries was weak. Consequently, the transition to a new state–society relation for both economic development and political democracy has proven to be much more difficult than originally expected. As well as lifting the burden of the state, new civil society relations have had to be built. The second example is the post-colonial states of inter-tropical Africa. Spatially defined by their former colonial boundaries, the initial modernizing elites attempted to build economic and political development with a civil society that only scratched the surface of the multiethnic peoples in the new states. The small civil society comprising an educated elite and urban workers proved insufficient to prevent these largely rural states from becoming military fiefdoms based upon ethnic allegiances.[4] The consequent deterioration of the colonial economic infrastructure of roads and railways, which was the only physical basis for integration of the territory, has often been dramatic: the Belgians, arguably the colonists with the worst record, left Zaïre with 88 000 miles of roads in 1960 but within 25 years this had reduced to just 12 000 miles.[5] It makes no sense to talk of 'Zairean society' or 'Liberian society' or 'Somalian society'; in Africa there are many states without a civil society. The lesson is that without civil societies, states implode into a type of anarchy.

Anarchy is traditionally seen as the condition of international politics. This follows from its definition as the opposite of domestic politics: a politics without 'society'. As we related in Chapter 1, international relations scholars do identify the existence of an 'international society', but it has none of the integrating power of civil society. Hence, it is argued that this realm of modern politics is much closer to a pure power politics as evidenced by the assertion that war is natural and cannot be abolished. As our previous discussion has shown, this realist international relations argument worked best in the period between the Treaties of Westphalia (1648) and Vienna (1815) but subsequently international politics has become much more complex. This is aptly illustrated by the cases of the imploded states referred to above. In the 18th century, signs of serious weakness in a state could lead to its elimination. Predatory states waited in the wings to take advantage; Holsti lists eight planned partitions of which three were executed.[6] Contrast this to the case of Africa today. There are plenty of inherently weak states but none have, or look like being, removed from the political map. Even without a government, a state such as Somalia is under no threat of outside partition such as befell Poland between 1772 and 1795. Whatever the mechanisms of modern international politics, they are certainly more complex than the unchanging realism by which it is often portrayed. States are not self-sufficient and need the co-operation of other states, but the key point is that this has been met by organization at far less than the level of functioning civil societies. Internationalism and cosmopolitanism take second place to nationalism and patriotism in the politics of the modern world-system.

As a social construction to cope with an uncertain world, there is nothing natural about this duality of modern politics, but this does not make it any less real as political practice. Despite some notable exceptions, bipartisanship has become the norm for US foreign policy, for example. Any politician who violates the convention that party political disputes end at the water's edge risks the ultimate condemnation of being disloyal. Such conventions are common in the politics of many other countries: you can attack your government at home but not abroad. Dual politics is imbued in political practice and will be used, therefore, as part of the framework of this chapter. But we must be careful not to fall into the 'realist trap' of really believing there to be two autonomous spheres of politics.[7] The duality of modern political practices is integral to how states organize their affairs, but that does not mean the domestic and international are unrelated. As was demonstrated at length in the last chapter, world hegemony is not about the international at the expense of the domestic. What happens within the borders of the hegemonic state is crucially enabling for extra-mural activities and vice versa. Therefore this chapter is organized chronologically, taking each hegemon in turn, rather than treating the two sides of modern politics separately.

We argued in Chapter 1 that through ensuring the defeat of prospective universal empires, the hegemons are directly instrumental in the survival of the inter-state system and thus in the development of the basis for a Janus-faced modern politics. But they have also contributed much to the content of modern politics both within and between states. In their quite different ways the Dutch, the British and the Americans have developed three exceptional political practices that are central to the nature of modern politics. First, hegemons have domesticated the state. Unlike the states of other systems, the modern state is socially enabling: the purpose of the state is to satisfy the needs of its society. In order to do this the state as war machine has had to be relegated from *raison d'état* to but one function of the modern state. This defines the second hegemonic practice of promoting peace within the inter-state system; for all earlier states systems war was 'natural': under hegemonic leadership it has come to be no longer accepted as such. Third, the hegemons have been the chief purveyors of the idea of freedom in their political practices. So much so that their self images have been closely bound up with concepts of freedom. These three political practices provide the framework for investigating each hegemon's contribution to modern politics; we will briefly elaborate on the meaning of each before treating them historically for each hegemon in turn.

In modern politics we are used to thinking of states as instruments for attaining some social goal. All free elections, for example, are premised on the idea that the winners can form a government to use the state apparatus for their policy ends. This is what I mean by a state being socially enabling. In premodern systems such relationships only pertained in relatively small political communities. Traditionally it is states that use 'society'; land and people were seen as resources to be deployed by state rulers to attain their own political and military goals. Hegemons have turned this relation on its head: it is society that uses the modern state to further its economic and social goals. Hence to contemporaries living in rival states, hegemonic states have often seemed superficially 'weak' because they do not pursue traditional military imperatives; the reality has been otherwise. The three hegemonic states have each created their own distinctive state–society relation with the latter in command.

The idea of converting the inter-state system into a peaceful community of states can be traced back to the Dutch in the 17th century, and such idealism has certainly been well represented in pacifism and peace movements in Britain and the USA at their peaks.[8] But this is not primarily what I mean by the hegemonic contribution to creating a more peaceful system. Hegemons have been created in world wars, as we have seen, and they certainly do not turn pacifist after this success. Rather we can think of hegemons as pacifiers in the sense of being crucially instrumental in creating more order in the inter-state system. The new political organization set up at the end of each world war has involved increasing sophistication in curtailing the states as war machines. The consequent 'peaces' have been top-down pacifications, first at the state level after Westphalia, then Europe-wide after Vienna and finally encompassing the 'North' with the Cold War after 1945.[9]

The final contribution of the hegemonic state combines looking inwards to its society and outwards to the rest of the inter-state system through a common development of a politics of freedom in both spheres. The hegemons operate in the name of freedom. Although the 'pursuit of liberty' is never monopolized by the hegemon, they do come to encapsulate it in both their domestic and foreign relations. This is a quintessentially modern concept: politics in the modern world can be said to revolve around freedom and its multifarious interpretations. Each hegemon has constructed a politics of freedom in opposition to a particular negation of freedom. Defining Self as free, an Other is defined as the archetypal unfree. For the Dutch their republicanism opposed royal absolutism, British parliamentarianism contrasted with Asiatic despotism and American democracy has been the foe of communist totalitarianism. As well as defining an external opposition, each of these contests was equally important in the process of defining a social self-identity as tolerant republican, liberal parliamentary and free democratic societies respectively.

It is in our discussions of hegemons as champions of freedom that we definitively escape from the realist trap and treat modern politics as one.

Having identified these three hegemonic contributions to the creation of modern politics, I must now add a crucial caveat that will cover all our subsequent discussion. In their practical politics all three hegemons have been pragmatic in the application of their ideals. Their power politics may not be as crudely militaristic as some of their rivals, but no hegemon ever got to dominate the inter-state system by pursuing idealist goals. In order to win, hegemons have been as pragmatic in their policies as any other state. This is especially obvious in the world war triumphs. The Dutch may have been fighting a Catholic monarchy, Spain, but their chief ally was another powerful Catholic monarchy, France. Similarly the British combated Napoleon's France in alliance with the Czar of Russia, and the USA combated Hitler's Germany in alliance with the USSR – hardly appropriate bedfellows for champions of freedom. These can be dismissed as necessary in the exigencies of world war but pragmatism did not end with the war. The Dutch as the leading Protestant republican state fought wars with the new Protestant republican England after 1648, the British extended their repressive rule in India after 1815 and the Americans continued to support many repressive regimes after 1945 as long as they were not communist. In all three cases these practices were adopted because they made political sense despite being contrary to the political principles represented by the hegemons. Hegemons have been, above all else, pragmatists.

The Dutch as pragmatic republicans

There is a crucial component of modern politics missing from Dutch hegemony. Popular nationalism is a product of the revolutions of the late 18th century, came to the fore in the 19th century and only dominated world politics in this century. This new political movement greatly strengthened the link between state and civil society. With the people within a country deemed to be a nation with a common origin, the state could become 'nation-state', so that the terms 'state' and 'nation' are used interchangeably in modern political language.[10] But Dutch political elites in the 17th century could not claim to be acting 'on behalf of the nation': Dutch hegemony occurs before the age of nationalism in a world-system without the popular concept of nation. Although some historians have interpreted the Dutch rebellion in the late 16th century as the first national revolt, this is only an exercise in creating a national myth. As Simon Schama points out, it tells us more about 19th century historiography than 16th-century politics.[11] The United Provinces remained a collection of localisms throughout its hegemonic period and, like all other states of the early modern period, it was a state without a nation.

The leaders of the Dutch rebellion did create a patriotism, however. Patriotism, meaning love of one's country, is much older than nationalism and does not include the latter's populist core. Patriots do not appeal to the people; patriots form a privileged elite within a state and love their country accordingly. Patriotism grew with the rise of the new territorial states in the 16th century, notably in France and England. In the case of the Dutch the initial 'patria' were the towns and provinces, but during the rebellion William the Silent and his supporters cultivated a larger patria as *'bons patriots'* of the Netherlands.[12] This was a move to shift the focus of loyalty among the political elite: the concept of treason was changed from acts against 'majesty' (ie Philip II of Spain) to acts against patria.[13] The outcome was a state with a political elite, the 'regents', of about 2000 persons at the head of a larger oligarchy of perhaps 10 000 economic and political leaders.

Can the Dutch be said to have had a civil society within their state, therefore? Although not as powerful as nationalism, patriotism at the head of society and economic integration further down did create what is commonly viewed as the first 'bourgeois society'. This term implies a functioning social collectivity based upon economic linkages, even if a cultural commonality is relatively weak. The connectedness of social activities within the United Provinces can be easily shown in the transport system.[14] In the 17th century the Dutch created a 'unique' transport system as a true precursor of later 'infrastructures' underpinning 'national economies'. Canals transported goods, information and people between 30 cities throughout the country to produce a single, large integrated economic space. Both the prior investment indicating the need for integration and the subsequent enabling of economic transactions point to the existence of a civil society above the localisms at the level of the state. It is difficult to supplement this physical evidence with actual collective behaviours operating below the activities of the oligarchy, but one example stands out.

In the 1630s the Dutch were seized by 'tulipomania'. Tulips had been introduced into the Low Countries in the 16th century from the Ottoman Empire and they soon became flowers of great prestige. More and more exotic varieties were created leading to speculation as their prices rose. Single bulbs changed hands at incredible rates – as high as $50 000 at today's prices.[15] This was the first of many examples of what Kenneth Galbraith terms 'financial euphoria', and like all the others it soon led to a crash leaving most investors with large losses. The key point here, however, is that 'people of all grades converted their property into cash, and invested it in flowers'.[16] Charles Mackay lists the following investors: 'Nobles, citizens, farmers, mechanics, seamen, footmen, maid-servants, even chimney-sweeps and old clotheswomen.'[17] Markets for the sale of tulips were established in all the major cities; even in the smaller towns taverns became 'show places' for trading in the bulbs. Whatever lessons may be drawn from tulipomania, I think we can interpret it reasonably as Dutch civil society in action.

It is, of course, important for us to establish the existence of this pre-nationalist civil society for our subsequent arguments. In fact we will show that this was not just any society because, unlike populations in other countries, the Dutch created a society that was more than a match for its state. The Dutch state pursued wars as necessary in the very dangerous early modern period but it did not make this its *raison d'état*. The 'man on horseback' was kept in check as a new enabling state was created, one that facilitated the operation of this new society at home and abroad.

Looking inwards: a domesticated state

The Netherlands were part of the Burgundian inheritance of the Spanish Hapsburgs which included today's Netherlands, Belgium, Luxembourg and a part of northern

France. In 1548 this original Netherlands was redefined within the Burgundian Circle of the Holy Roman Empire as part of a reorganization of Hapsburg territory. But the Netherlands remained a hotchpotch of territories. When Phillip II succeeded to the Spanish throne in 1555–6, he inherited '17 Netherlands'. Among his titles he was duke of four places, count of another six and simply lord of a further five.[18] It was into this heterogeneous political region that the Spanish introduced the Inquisition in the 1560s. As a land of many cities the Reformation had made some ground in the Netherlands, thus creating conditions for resistance to imposition of Catholic orthodoxy. In 1565 four hundred 'lesser nobles' signed the Compromise of the Nobility which repudiated the Inquisition.[19] A religious rebellion across all the Netherlands ensued but was soon defeated with the leaders forfeiting their lands.

One of those stripped of his territory was William of Orange, sometimes known as William the Silent. Although he held his land and position in the Netherlands from Phillip II, he was a sovereign in his own right as Prince of Orange, a territory in today's southern France. With this independent status he became leader of the rebellion. Despite the King of Spain's instructions, the province of Holland retained William as their Stadtholder, or military governor, which definitively located the centre of the rebellion to the northern part of the Netherlands.[20] The fortunes of the rebel and royal armies fluctuated in the 1570s with neither side being able to defeat the other. The final north–south split occurred in 1579 with the Union of Utrecht and the Treaty of Arras. The former led to a defensive alliance of seven northern provinces – Holland, Zealand, Utrecht, Gelderland, Freisland, Overijssel and the Ommelanden – leaving the remainder of the Netherlands affirming their loyalty to the king at Arras. In 1581 the Act of Abjuration by the northern provinces finally deposed Phillip II.

Although for many years William and his successors aimed at uniting the whole of the Netherlands in a new independent state, the division of the country soon solidified into two separate political entities. The north was independent and Calvinist, although with a substantial Catholic minority, whereas the south remained under the Spanish crown and with the church of Rome. Since the whole area was known as the Netherlands, there was no clear name for the new independent country; the name 'United Provinces' was coined by an Englishman to overcome this potential confusion.[21] The boundaries between these two countries fluctuated with the war but, from about 1590, neither side was in danger of being overrun by the other. The war continued until the Truce of 1609 when the United Provinces was effectively recognized by other states: ambassadors were exchanged, for example. The war resumed in 1621 and petered out in the 1640s when the United Provinces was finally recognized as sovereign at the Treaty of Westphalia in 1648.

The circumstances of the United Provinces' origins are vital to the subsequent success of the country. Religious differences provided both the general context for the rebellion and specific organizational bases, but its political essence was resistance to centralization.[22] The major trend in state development in the 16th century was centralization of power, and Hapsburg activities in the Netherlands were part of this tendency. The northern provinces, according to Anthony Duke, were the least well integrated of Hapsburg possessions: 'By reason of their remoteness, their peculiar social structure and independent political traditions, these [provinces] could more easily detach themselves from the king'.[23] But the rebels were not republicans. In the 1580s a royal replacement for Phillip II was sought and offers made to German, French and English candidates but to no avail. The main problem was the conditions attached to the position: it made no sense for the United Provinces to get rid of one king and seat another with similar centralizing plans. The preservation of traditional local political rights was at the heart of the rebellion and the corollary, which took a decade to be realized, was that a form of republic was the only organization compatible with these needs. The search for a monarch was abandoned at the end of the 1580s and the United Provinces as Dutch Republic emerged on to the world scene.

There was no blueprint to create a new state; what emerged was a unique mixture of old institutions and new arrangements of power.[24] With the defence arrangement of the Treaty of Utrecht as the basic law of the new state, a complicated federal government structure emerged. Each of the seven provinces had its own policy-making forum known as 'Estates' in which cities and nobles were represented. For instance, in the largest province 18 cities were represented in the Estates of Holland. Delegates from these bodies then formed the States-General that made the policies which affected the United Provinces as a whole. In addition there was a parallel pattern of power relating to the office of Stadtholder. Originally royal military governors, each province had its own local Stadtholder but the positions were monopolized by the Orange family. Certainly not kings, nor even 'half kings', there was, none the less, a hereditary tendency that developed for these positions which made the Orange family and their court effectively the coercive arm of the state. On the whole this dual arrangement worked well although the balance of power between the States-General and Stadtholder varied over time: in periods of military threat the power of the Stadtholder as military governor was of course enhanced.

The particularly distinctive periods of the United Provinces were when the power of the States-General comes to the fore. In such times the Dutch Republic was run by a civilian leader, a situation unprecedented for the great powers of the time. During most of the 12-year truce (1609–21) Johan van Oldenbarnevelt as 'advocate of Holland' was the effective chief executive of the republic. In the 'Stadtholderless period' (1652–72), John de Witt as 'councillor pensionary' took on the same role. Note that there is no common title for the civilian executive position, reflecting the improvisation by which Dutch government evolved.

There is no doubt that the Dutch produced a very unusual political structure. It certainly did not look like any other state in the early modern period. This has led to two serious misinterpretations of the nature of the Dutch Republic. First, it is sometimes alleged that the United Provinces was not actually a state at all but merely a collection of local jurisdictions pragmatically coming together for defence needs.[25] Second, even if it is conceded that this was a state, it is interpreted as merely a city-state, as Amsterdam and its hinterland.[26] Both of these positions show a failure to understand the decentralized nature of the Dutch Republic. The Dutch were bucking the European-wide political trend towards centralization, but that does not mean they did not create a state — their's was simply different. And its difference was not reflected as a throwback to late medieval Italian city-states. Our position is diametrically opposed to both these arguments: after 1590 a great new state power emerged on the European scene, almost from nowhere as it were. This position is so far apart from the other two that we need to refute the counter arguments in detail.

The concern as to whether the United Provinces was in fact a state is based upon a quite narrow interpretation of power. France is usually interpreted as the 'model' state of the era since it led in centralizing power in the king's government. As part of the centralization, the state apparatus was functionally organized in recognizably modern departments. This is a standard the Dutch Republic cannot match. Lacking centralization, the republic was slow to differentiate functions: John de Witt, for example, has been described as prime minister, foreign secretary, minister of finance and even navy minister – he found time to accompany the fleet during war.[27] But the reason why the Dutch did not meet French standards is quite simple: their state was formed precisely to avoid such politics. It was a different political animal. One of Louis XIV's diplomats commented in 1660 that the Dutch had a 'government of 2,000 people' in which de Witt was 'a servant who guided his masters'.[28] In other words he skilfully played off the States-General against the other concentrations of power, the Estates of Holland, the largest province, and the City of Amsterdam. Decision making might be cumbersome in such a situation, but the outcome was a very strong infrastructural power. That is to say, there is power inherent in the nature of the state–society relation itself, a power which is less overt than crude military displays but which is invariably more effective. The strength of the Dutch in the 17th century was largely hidden behind its decentralized shell, but it was real enough to all its enemies. A key test of infrastructural power is the ability to mobilize sufficient resources as and when necessary. The Dutch had a clear dictum for this: the state should be 'as lavish in wartime as it is miserly in peace time'.[29] In effect there was specialization in the Dutch state apparatus but in only one function: war. This specialized activity was 'subcontracted out' to the House of Orange who recruited a mercenary army to do the business.[30] This proved very efficient and effective: for rival states war was a burden creating perennial fiscal crises; for the United Provinces it was an unfortunate but necessary part of the Budget.[31]

The spatial organization of the United Provinces lay at the heart of its infrastructural power. In the initial revolt, the rebels soon learnt to use 'geography as an ally' in this region of four great rivers and numerous dikes.[32] 'The military and geographical strength of their position', as Geoffrey Parker calls it, was written into the defence provisions of the Union of Utrecht.[33] The territory of the state was treated as two zones, the maritime core of great trading cities and centres of production, and a surrounding land buffer to act as a bulwark against invasion.[34] In the Union treaty, the fortifications and defence of frontier towns were to be paid for jointly by all seven provinces.[35] It was William the Silent's successor as Stadtholder, Maurice of Nassau, who operationalized this policy in the crucial 1580s. He saw his key task to 'close the fence' through control of waterways and strategic fortified cities in the general frontier zone.[36] The result was that the war with Spain was contained in an outer zone of siege warfare leaving the major cities to carry on their business as normal.[37] This frontier policy operated through the 17th century: John de Witt's strategic view of the Dutch Republic in mid-century was as a citadel with a broad ring moat around it.[38] The policy saw its severest test in the French assault of 1672, when the French army reached as far as Utrecht. But Amsterdam and Holland did not fall. The dikes were opened and the core of the United Provinces was converted into 'a fortified island' that the French could not reach.[39] This strategic crisis is usually taken to define the close of Dutch hegemony – de Witt was assassinated and

William of Orange (later William III of England) took the Stadtholder vacancy and managed successfully to hold off the French. But the fact remains that the core defence strategy did work right to the end of hegemony.

The model of central core and defensive hinterland has been a common strategy of city-states. So was the United Provinces a city-state? The case for answering 'yes' has been made by V. Barbour who refers to the Dutch golden age as 'the reign of a city . . . unsustained by the forces of a modern unified state'.[40] In this argument Amsterdam follows the examples of Antwerp and Venice as world-cities, to use Fernand Braudel's terminology. Braudel agrees with Barbour and argues that Amsterdam is more like earlier Venice as a city-state than later London within a territorial state.[41] Subsequently he changes his position by suggesting the Dutch Republic 'lies between' city-state and territorial state organization.[42]

There is no doubt that Amsterdam was by far the largest and wealthiest of all Dutch cities. As such it paid the greatest contribution to the running of the United Provinces in both war and peace. This gave it a special leverage in Dutch politics, but it did not make it omnipotent. It certainly did not govern in the way Venice administered its territory. The United Provinces was a state comprising 58 cities with voting rights in the provincial Estates.[43] In this decentralized structure decision making operated through political patterns of shifting coalitions in which Amsterdam can be said to be 'first among peers' but no more.[44] For instance, Amsterdam was not the seat of government. This honour was given to a minor city with no voting rights, The Hague, in order 'to avoid all rivalry'.[45] Amsterdam could dominate in this political process but always had to co-operate with other major cities and could be checked by a coalition of rivals.[46] For instance, in the negotiations with Spain after 1629, the Dutch split evenly into a war party and peace party each made up of coalitions of provinces and cities. Divisions reflected Europe trade versus Indies trade and commerce versus manufacturing. Hence the peace coalition was led by Amsterdam and Rotterdam, whereas Haarlem and Leiden were at the head of the war party opposition. The latter were able to bring the truce moves to a halt and the war continued for nearly another two decades.[47] Peter Burke summarizes the situation as Amsterdam usually getting its own way but not always, hardly the politics of a city-state.[48] Hence we can conclude that the argument for the United Provinces as Amsterdam's city-state cannot be sustained.

If the United Provinces was not created on the basis of the template of either sovereign-centred France or city-centred Venice, we can return to the idea that this decentralized political structure was a new type of territorial state. It operated like a league of cities but was enclosed in a contiguous defensible territory.[49] It was this combination that was unique and was crucial for the initial success of the United Provinces. The capture and sack of Antwerp by Spanish troops in 1585 was central to this process. As the leading world-city of the time, the destruction of Antwerp led to the diaspora of its commercial classes and most went north to Amsterdam.[50] It was this process that converted Amsterdam into the new world-city. As one immigrant wrote in 1594: 'Here is Antwerp itself changed into Amsterdam.'[51] But why Amsterdam? There were many other important trading cities that the merchants could have moved to, especially in Germany. Hamburg was perhaps the favourite.[52] However, Amsterdam possessed one key advantage: a territorial state, which is precisely what was missing in politically fragmented Germany. In these troubled times, refugees from a sacked city were looking especially for the 'protection and active support of a powerful state'.[53] It was not only Amsterdam that profited from the chaos in the southern Netherlands; Leiden benefited from the flight of the textile industry. Hence the new defence proficiency is crucially implicated in the early building of the Dutch economy.

Initial establishment is one thing, but why did this decentralized state continue to prosper in a world of increasing political centralization? The key point is that the decentralization was a symptom of something much more fundamental. In this new territorial state the traditional relationship between state and society was reversed. According to J. C. Boogman, 'in the United Provinces the State was already at an early stage regarded as a function of society'.[54] World hegemony requires just such a state so that it can be a tool for harnessing economic pre-eminence and forging a wider dominance. The Dutch were the first to develop this type of state-society relationship, in Immanuel Wallerstein's words:

> the state was an essential instrument used by the Dutch bourgeoisie to consolidate an economic hegemony that they had won originally in the sphere of production and then extended to commerce and finance.[55]

In short they invented a new *raison d'état*.

The concept of *raison d'état* is itself a modern concept derived in the first instance to separate the political interests of sovereigns from strictly religious motives.[56] This secularization of the state created a *raison d'état* that focused on the glory of the monarch and thus justified the state as a war machine. This is exactly the trap the Dutch avoided. Without the luxury of a king to waste their resources on war for territorial expansion, the Dutch could concentrate on enhancing the wealth within their territory. The result was an integrated territorial economy for the purposes of begetting more wealth. The new function of the state was to maintain, sustain and aid in this process,[57] a crucial element in the Dutch success and therefore of their hegemony.

By the time we reach the zenith of Dutch power in the Stadtholderless period (1652–72), contemporaries were well aware of the special nature of the Dutch state and its advantages. We can find a wonderful metaphor for the nature of the Dutch state in a famous tract written in 1661. Treating the international realm as a jungle full of wild animals, the destructive habits of 'great monarchs' as various 'beasts' are rehearsed and contrasted with Holland which follows 'the commendable example of the Cat':

> For she never converses with strange beasts, but either keeps at home, or accompanyes those of her own species, meddling with none, but in order to defend her own; very vigilant to provide food, and preserve her young ones: she neither barks nor snarls at those who provoke or abuse her; so shy and fearful, that being pursued, she immediately takes her flight into some whole or place of natural strength, where she remains quiet till the noise be over. But if it happens that she can by no means avoid the combat, she is more fierce than a Lion, defends herself with tooth and nail, and better than any other beast, making use of all her well-husbanded strength, without the least neglect or fainting in her extremity. . . . A Cat indeed is outwardly like a Lion, yet she is, and will remain but a Cat still: and so we who are naturally merchants, cannot be turned into soldiers.[58]

In short, the United Provinces is a state that, like the cat, has been domesticated.

Looking outwards: a pacific state

Once we turn towards the external relations of the Dutch state we soon lose any remaining doubts about its great power in the 17th century. As one commentator would have it, the strength of the United Provinces was 'demonstrated by their foreign policy'.[59] By 1598 the Netherlands had become the focus of European conflict; the war with Spain had even overspilled into the first global conflict in history as the Dutch began to attack Spanish colonies.[60] The many bilateral wars of the 16th century were gradually converted into a single 'inter-bloc' war in the first half of the 17th century with two international diplomatic networks centred on Brussels (the royal capital) and The Hague.[61] According to Gustavus Adolphus (the Swedish king) in 1625, 'The Hague was the stage on which all negotiations and actions of Europe took place'.[62] Geoffrey Parker thinks that it was the Dutch who created the new polarization for their own ends. He quotes a contemporary Dutch writer in 1617 as likening the Dutch–Spanish conflict to 'a mouse against an elephant' with the implication of the need for a balance-of-power policy to even the score.[63] Certainly diplomatic histories often credit the Dutch Republic as having invented the modern system-wide balance-of-power strategy.[64] First devised for survival needs, balance of power has come to be a major modern political strategy for maintaining order in the inter-state system. But the United Provinces' contribution to modern international relations extends far beyond inventing this one strategy.

According to one standard history of peace: 'The seventeenth century brought to the world the first unfolding of the idea of international peace in a large and comprehensive way.'[65] The Dutch Republic deserve the credit for this: they were self-consciously pacifist. In an anonymous work of 1666, a list is constructed of 21 countries in Europe with claims and counter-claims on each other's territory.[66] The United Provinces is number ten on the list and is the only state with no claims. As a state with no plans for territorial aggrandizement it was unique in Europe. New territory required defending and would likely not meet a Dutch cost–benefit analysis. In fact contraction as an option was always more likely than extension within the republic's overall core/frontier strategic plan. This was a state that threatened no other.[67]

There is, of course, a paradox that a state conceived in war, and a war that lasted 80 years, should have become a pacific state. Pacifism could not be seriously contemplated before full sovereignty was attained in 1648, but even in the war with Spain there were unusual features in the Dutch manner of war. As we have seen, from the very beginning the state was formed as a defensive alliance which precluded attack. In a critique of the Union of Utrecht in 1580, William the Silent argued that this would cause problems in waging war because the other side would always have the initiative.[68] But the Stadtholder view representing the coercive side of the state did not prevail. The result can be seen in the nature of the war with Spain. Unlike all other wars in the early 17th century, the conflict in the Netherlands was devoid of gross savagery and wilful destruction found elsewhere. Concentrated siege warfare enabled large areas to escape unscathed and, in addition, by agreement between the armies, the usual heavy war damage of towns and villages was avoided.[69] The result was that during the Thirty Years War there were two very different conflicts going on in the Netherlands and Germany.[70] Hence when the United Provinces made the treaty with France in 1635 they 'took care lest their war with Spain should be absorbed into the [general] Thirty Years War'.[71] This was, according to Kossmann, 'a characteristic proof of their refusal to pursue power-politics in the grand style'.[72]

Dutch pacifism was never idealistic. It was a pragmatic policy that was in its own interests: as one contemporary argued in 1661, 'there is more to be gotten by us in a time of peace and good trading, than by war and the ruin of trade'.[73] But what peace policy? In the middle of the 17th century the Dutch debated policies which we have come to expect of hegemons. Two opposing positions were advanced. First there was peace as isolationism. In 1668 Lydius defined the purpose of Dutch power to be peace and derived as a corollary a 'pure' policy of non-interference.[74] But how realistic was this? The United Provinces more than any country was dependent on affairs beyond its borders; its trade was its lifeblood and it could not allow it to dry up because of someone else's war.[75] For instance, in the Concert of the Hague of 1659, the Dutch, with England and France, imposed a peace on Sweden and Denmark who were threatening the Baltic trade. But such 'trouble-shooting' only created a piecemeal peace. The Dutch at this time began to think about the possibility of 'perpetual peace'.[76] This took the form of the United Provinces having an international responsibility to promote peace and spread the message of their domestic liberty. In 1650, Schele defined this as the Dutch Republic's 'great task' in a manner that both the British and the Americans were to take up in their periods of hegemony.[77]

Peace as an idea is fine, but what were the practical political achievements of the Dutch during their hegemony? At first sight the results do not seem impressive. Certainly there is no era of 'long peace' that characterized both British and US hegemony: it was closer to perpetual war than perpetual peace during Dutch hegemony. Although world war ended in 1648 at Westphalia, 'an unavoidable tension' was created between the rights of the new states and the demand for inter-state order.[78] The result was a mixture of opposing tendencies promoting both war and peace. First, the legitimation of a system of sovereign states created what Gross terms the 'liberty of states', which provided the context for endemic warfare.[79] In short, territorial states became platforms for war. Second, the nature of the war represented a genuine advance towards a more peaceful world. By creating sovereign territories, order was promoted internally so that the quantity of war activity lessened.

In effect the less-destructive Dutch–Spanish war before 1648 was writ large across Europe after 1648. Alexander Hamilton, looking at Europe from the outside a century and a half later, described the changed situation thus:

> The history of war, in that portion of the globe, is no longer a history of nations subdued and empires overturned, but towns taken and retaken; of battles that decide nothing; of retreats more beneficial than victories, of much effort and little acquisition.[80]

He could well be describing the conflict in the Low Countries between 1621 and 1648. Europe was transformed into a spatial mosaic of oases of relative peace with war commonly occurring around them along the borderlands. That may not seem much in comparison with later peaces, but it was a giant step forward for the 17th century. It is the Dutch contribution to creating modern international politics.

Self and other: 'True Freedom' republicans versus royal tyrants (absolutism)

The United Provinces was a state created by improvisation as we have seen. By adapting old institutions to new needs the Dutch resisted the Europe-wide trend towards state centralization. In the process they became a republic at a time when a strong king as sovereign was widely believed necessary for social stability. Elsewhere in Europe a tradition of political theory was developed that legitimated monarchical forms of government; in contrast, the Dutch never became a source of political treatises advocating republicanism to the same degree.[81] Dutch political writers did draw upon the precedents of Venice and Switzerland as successful republics. Their work, however, remained primarily practical in orientation and purpose. For instance the most influential statement justifying the Dutch lack of a sovereign prince comes in 1654 in 'The Deduction' written by John de Witt to justify Holland's Act of Exclusion to the other provinces.[82] This act terminated the role of the House of Orange as Stadtholder and therefore legitimated the 'Stadtholderless period' to 1672. It is in the Deduction that we find the first elaboration of the theory of government known as 'True Freedom'.

The basic argument against monarchs was quite straightforward. Since all individuals are selfish, in the case of a sovereign prince this will inevitably lead to a conflict of royal private interests and public state interests.[83] There will be times when the prince acts to bolster his own position at the expense of the country. It is ironic that a classic example of this occurred near the end of the Stadtholderless period and which was to end True Freedom. At the Treaty of Dover in 1670, Charles II of England, for personal and family reasons, joined with France in an anti-Dutch alliance that was to lead to the French invasion of the United Provinces. This was clearly against England's long-term interests: a French-dominated continent including the Netherlands would pose a severe threat to English independence. When the invasion came in 1672 it failed, as we have seen, but the resulting emergency did bring back the latest William of Orange as Stadtholder. In the meantime the theory of government espoused by Dutch republicans was to reach its apogee in Peter de la Court's *The True Interest of Holland* written in 1662.[84] This was a highly controversial book written anonymously and with some material provided by John de Witt. It boldly set out to show that Dutch successes were due to Holland's 'free-state' or 'free Commonwealth Government'.

De la Court's basic theory was a formulation of the relationship between public and private interests. Having dismissed monarchies as deficient, he argued that although individuals are selfish, the sum of their selfish actions defines the public good. Hence the best government is one that enhances private economic interests for the benefit of all. Corollaries included minimalizing the general tax burden and removing the restrictive labour practices of the guilds. No wonder Caton has remarked that 'This was Adam Smith a century before *The Wealth of Nations*'.[85] It was, in fact, an explicit definition of the new *raison d'état* of government promoting

THE TRUE

INTEREST
AND

Political Maxims,
OF THE

Republic *of* HOLLAND·

VIZ.

I. Of the Nature, Product, and Advantages of *Holland*.	*land* in Relation to foreign Princes and States·
II. Of the Fishing-Trade, &c. of *Holland*.	IX. That a free Navigation ought to be kept.
III. Why heavy Taxes have not drove the Fishing-Trade, &c. out of *Holland*.	X. Of Alliances, particularly with *England*.
IV. Of the antient State of Manufactures, Fisheries, and Navigation in *Europe*.	XI. That *Holland*, under a *Stadholder*, was in continual Broils and Tumults.
V. That *Holland* is a richer merchandizing Country than ever was in the World.	XII. That *Holland*, during its free Government, is very well able to resist all foreign Power.
VI. That all Monopolies are prejudicial to *Holland*.	XIII. That *Holland*, united with *Utrecht* only, is able to defend herself against all the Potentates of the World, &c. &c. &c.
VII. The great Advantages of Colonies to *Holland*.	
VIII. Of the Interest of *Hol*-	

Written by that great Statesman and Patriot,

JOHN De WITT,

GRAND-PENSIONER of *HOLLAND.*

Translated from the Original *Dutch.*

To which is prefixed, (*never before printed*)

HISTORICAL MEMOIRS of the Illustrious Brothers *CORNELIUS* and *JOHN de WITT.*

By JOHN CAMPBELL, *Esq;*

LONDON:

Printed for J. NOURSE, at the *Lamb*, opposite *Katherine-Street*, in the *Strand*. 1746.

Plate 5 *The True Interest of Holland*, written by Peter de la Court and first published in 1662 with additions by John de Witt. Both French and English translations, the latter's frontispiece is reproduced here, attributed the work to de Witt. Highly controversial among contemporaries, this book can claim to be the first modern manuscript that sets out liberal prescriptions for a political economy preceeding Adam Smith's *Wealth of Nations* by over a century. Note chapter VI 'That all monopolies are prejudicial to Holland'; chapter IX 'That a free navigation ought to be kept' and chapter XII 'That Holland, during its free government, is very well able to resist all foreign power'

economic well-being. Productivity was identified as the basis of wealth within the 'four pillars of prosperity': manufacturing, shipping, fishing and trade.[86] All public policy should be aimed at supporting these private pillars; for instance by having low duties on raw materials. The end result is the 'perfect free state' where there is a unity of interests between the governing class and the people in the republic.

This is a modern theory of freedom and liberty in which the Dutch develop a self-identity as 'free' in contrast to an unfree Other – the absolutist monarchies in the rest of Europe. Absolutism is the name given to the early modern political practices of the centralizing states.[87] It is usually interpreted as a sort of proto-modern state between feudalism and the nation–state. Although traditionally using religion to justify the centralization – the divine right of kings – the absolutist state was an original creation of the period. Although the Spanish Hapsburgs can be viewed as the initial absolutists, this form of state really prospered in the aftermath of the Westphalia agreement.

By providing a 'liberty of states' in which sovereigns were given unchallenged authority over their territories, royal governments were able to escape from legal constraints and constitutional controls. The classic example is the France of Louis XIV (1643–1715) in which a bureaucracy was built to rationalize fiscal policy and reform the legal system. In the 18th century such reforms when enacted by Frederick the Great of Prussia and Catherine the Great of Russia were widely praised as 'enlightened absolutism'. The stimulus for such state reorganization remained a very traditional one: how to find the resources to fight more and more expensive wars. Hence whether Louis, Frederick or Catherine, the *raison d'état* remains very much a military one. From the Dutch perspective, far from being enlightened, such absolutism bred tyrants who enslaved their people and wasted public wealth for private adventures. The Dutch provided the alternative in this 'age of absolutism'; they showed that a more representative government did not mean chaos but, on the contrary, could provide major advantages. Peter de la Court understood this well: 'Where there is Liberty, there will be riches.'[88] The idea of freedom as necessary for success was unleashed upon an unsuspecting early modern world.

The British as pragmatic parliamentarians

The period between Dutch and British hegemony is much longer than that between Britain and the USA. The 'inter-hegemonic' phase of intense state competition that precedes the systemic chaos of world war lasted about three times longer in the first transition period (1672–1792) than the second (1873–1914). This greatly diminishes the role of the Dutch in the building of the new hegemony. Although we can draw a historical analogy in terms of 'special relationships' between old and new hegemons which makes sense for both Dutch–British and British–American relations, in the case of the former this had no relevance by the time the crucial world war erupts. Although the English supported the French in their 1672 assault on the Dutch, in a very short time the alliance pattern reverted to England and the United Provinces versus France. This was cemented by the English 'Glorious Revolution' of 1688 when William of Orange, as husband of Mary Stuart, became King of England. By the time of the Treaty of Utrecht (1713) when peace was made with France, England, or rather now Great Britain after the Act of Union between England and Scotland in 1707, was clearly the senior partner and partly sidelined the Dutch in the negotiations. But we are still more than a century from British hegemony. The British–Dutch alliance becomes like other international agreements in the 18th century, highly brittle; and when world war comes the Dutch Republic is soon defeated by the French and plays no major role in the war. Hence although the financial arm of Dutch hegemony lingers into the early 19th century, in terms of politics the key relation preceding British hegemony is that between France and Britain.

State competition in the 18th century operated in two distinctive arenas. First there was the mercantilist competition for the increasingly important colonial production and market. With the Dutch declining and the Spanish largely eclipsed, this had become a straight battle between the British and the French by mid-century. In the Seven Years War (1756–63) Britain defeated France and forced her out of both North America and India. From this time forth Britain is the leading world power. Second, however, there was the competition among the great continental states: France, Austria, Prussia and Russia. Notice that France appears in both contests; it is often suggested that France's failures in the 18th century were due the political tensions between maritime and continental strategies.[89] Whatever the truth in this, France failed to recover its world position despite supporting the American rebellion, but she remained the strongest power in Europe up to the French Revolution. This situation suited British mercantilism, but in 1789 the nature of the French challenge changed fundamentally. From being failed mercantilists, the French were transformed into the purveyors of a profound ideological challenge to the British state.

In introducing the concept of world hegemony in the last chapter, we were extremely careful not to claim that hegemons account for everything of importance in the development of modernity. Here we have arrived at a classic example of this. The French Revolution defines an ideological watershed in the history of the modern world-system.[90] In terms of politics, it is commonplace to trace the origins of key modern political ideas and movements back to the social and political upheavals in France in the 1790s. One example is of particular relevance here: the French Revolution is the crucible of nationalism as a popular movement. Since nationalism lies at the very heart of contemporary modern politics we can reasonably designate the French as central contributors to the making of modern politics. But where does this leave France's great rival, Britain, as a creator of modern politics? In becoming the leading opponent of the French and their revolution, the rising hegemon found itself in the camp of the enemies of political change.

But hegemons should be managers of change not its enemy: we consider this conundrum in detail in this section. The Dutch managed to create a new politics before nationalism as 'patriots' and we shall see that Britain initially took a similar route to counter nationalism. From a hegemonic perspective, the most dangerous political effect of nationalism was to strengthen the state by making it popular, as the French demonstrated only too well. Instead the British developed a patriotism which avoided populist nationalism and to this day the English consider nationalism to be a particularly vulgar politics, something only foreigners do. The end-result was a very peculiar British 'nation-state'.

Looking inwards: 'aberrant' England

In his historical discussion of the western European state, Kenneth Dyson identifies England as an 'aberrant case' of political development.[91] According to Dyson, English politics became exceptional in the second half of the 17th century: in the initial development of modern European states in the 16th century, Tudor England shared in the common centralizing practices of the times and the English civil war

(1642–9) can be interpreted as part of the general crisis of the 'renaissance state'. Thereafter England diverges from the general pattern of European state development. Dyson's key point is that the political and legal concept of the state, so central in France and Germany for example, was not constructed for English politics.[92] The idea of a state only appeared as an external sign to mark England's role in the inter-state system. Hence the use of the Royal prerogative in foreign policy became known as an Act of State; otherwise there was no reference to the state as a part of the politics. Certainly the notion of the state as a distinct corporate authority above society was never developed with respect to domestic policy. Why no state? Dyson's answer is very apposite to our concerns here: the state that was created 'lacked the idea of emancipation from civil society' because 'it was composed of members of civil society'.[93] In other words, like the Dutch before them, the English reversed the relation between state and society: society used state and not vice versa.

According to Tom Nairn 'a spontanously emergent bourgeois "civil society" created the [English] state' in the 17th century.[94] The outcome of the conflicts from the civil war to the Glorious Revolution was the rise to political power of a commercial landed elite allied with the urban merchant class to produce their own 'patrician state'.[95] With the accession of William and Mary to the throne by invitation of the 'patricians', a new state was created whereby sovereignty lay with the Crown in Parliament. This combination of a private court and public arena proved to be a very flexible formula for rule; through its many reincarnations in the next three centuries, civil society has been able to continue domination of the state. Hence just at the same time when the latter's abstract mystique was being promoted elsewhere, in England any vestiges of a 'state spirit' were being eliminated by a more personal and informal rule. The result was 'non-bureaucratic and relatively decentralized control' of the country.[96] This decentralization was premised on a division between 'high politics' and 'low politics'. The centre jealously guarded control of the former – largely fiscal and foreign policy – allowing all other matters to be dealt with through negotiation with the communities and interest groups outside the centre.[97]

The transition from such a 'low-profile state' of patrician origins to the liberal ideal of a 'nightwatchman state' during British hegemony in the 19th century was relatively smooth.[98] While other countries experienced revolutionary political change Britain continued its famed political evolution. By investing sovereignty with the Crown in Parliament a flexible political system of checks and balances was created in which the politics could change from Tory royalism or Whig aristocratic control to constitutional liberalism without any need to change the state apparatus. Only two options were precluded by this political formula: a royal absolutism and a radical popularism.[99] At the time of the Great Reform Act of 1832, the rising middle-class political interests required just such a political formula. In their agitation for change they confronted traditional aristocratic power, but the middle classes were simultaneously watchful of new working-class political aspirations. The reforms widened representation in parliament and changed the balance of power in favour of the elected House of Commons but stopped far short of creating a democracy. It was under the leadership of the new House of Commons that the task of creating the minimal state fit for a hegemon could begin.

The reformed parliament was an opportunity to eliminate the traditional mercantilist state and bring British political practices into line with contemporary political-economy needs. Half a century earlier Adam Smith had argued that economic success depended on the free operation of markets and therefore that state interference in these processes was against the public good. This left the state with little to concern itself with 'but peace, easy taxes, and a tolerable administration of justice; all the rest being brought about by the natural course of things'.[100] This ideal 'nightwatchman state' could never be created in reality, but the term captures the spirit of the reformers. In fact the mid-19th-century British liberal state can be viewed as a transition between two alternative interventionist states: mercantile state and welfare state. Hence while political economists were having their great success with the abolition of the Corn Laws, there was also increasing recognition for the need to regulate rapid industrialization and its consequence, massive urbanization. Factory Acts with state inspectors, local Boards of Health and Housing Acts for slum clearance all make their appearance at this time: the nightwatchman had a wider role than merely protecting life and property. Nevertheless, by any historical standards, this was a minimal state and marked Britain out as different from her European rivals.

Writing in 1867 in his classic justification of this liberal state, *The British Constitution*, Walter Bagehot described Britain as being a 'disguised republic'.[101] This was because executive power was vested with the prime minister and his cabinet based upon an elected majority in the House of Commons leaving the monarchy and House of Lords with primarily ceremonial functions. He famously presented these as the 'efficient' and 'dignified' parts of the constitution respectively. The division of labour was clear-cut: the 'dignified parts' legitimated the state in the eyes of the people while the 'efficient parts' carried out the business of government.[102] Bagehot's use of the word 'republic' to describe this arrangement may seem to be a little odd at first, implying as it does the irrelevance of the monarchy, but a more careful reading reveals the vital importance of the Crown in this scheme of things.[103] In any modern state a balance has to be achieved between providing the conditions for capital accumulation while simultaneously maintaining legitimacy for this exercise. Hence the state has to cultivate the allegiance of its population, and in the British case this has been represented by loyalty to the Crown. Thus the monarchy is not a sideshow, it was an integral element in the creation of the British 19th-century liberal state.

The survival of the monarchy is often interpreted as evidence for the antiquity of the British state. For instance, Bagehot identified only the efficient part of the constitution as 'modern', leaving the Crown as a residue from a previous age. Nairn takes the argument even further: he does not concede that any part of the British state is modern. For him Britain missed having a bourgeois revolution and therefore has remained stuck in a transitional time warp between late feudalism and modern times.[104] We must be careful at dismissing one of the most successful states in the modern world-system in this way. Certainly England and then Britain was different, that is after all a hallmark of being a rising hegemon, but it is disingenuous to describe this as not modern. Such an interpretation relies on a narrow definition of what is politically modern and thereby misses the special modern cases. Britain, like the Dutch before her, adapted old institutions to new requirements and invented some new political practices in a unique combination. This was what Walter Bagehot described for 19th-century Britain: the invention a new form of rule, the constitutional monarchy. In the 18th century the king was used as the head of an aristocratic government, which was Britain's version of the ancien régime. It was this order that was put at risk by the example of the French Revolution. England had experienced the early stirrings of popular nationalism in the years before 1789, and therefore the surge of radical nationalism in France was a threat to the British status quo.[105] Nairn has called the solution to this problem the 'modernization of George III'.[106] Whereas the more authoritarian monarchies had to confront revolutionary popularism head on, the British with their relatively weak monarchy could take a completely different route: the monarchy itself was popularized to act as a focus for popular politics. Nationalism was designated 'foreign' and English 'royal patriotism' developed to take its place. New ceremonies were invented to show the 'authentic antiquity' of the monarchy; and George III, despite his mental illness, became a safe symbol of popular devotion. This was crucial in these dangerous times since the world war led to a politicalization of populations throughout Europe. But in England, the people were never called upon in their own name, sovereignty remained with the Crown in Parliament. The result was that the state ruled in the 'public interest' rather than on behalf of the people, with the term 'public' denoting a restricted civil society.[107]

The invention of a popular constitutional monarchy created a peculiar conservative nationalism. This had little relevance for domestic policy mobilizations in the 19th century but was periodically useful for supporting the government in foreign affairs. As J. H. Grainger has so aptly put it: 'It seemed as if Britain pre-eminent had inoculated herself against an eighteenth century epidemic.'[108] Hence as well as inheriting an aberrant state, the British created an aberrant nationalism on the eve of their hegemony.[109] This allowed Britain's relatively narrow civil society to go about its hegemonic business in full knowledge that it operated a political machine where neither absolute state nor popular nation were a threat to its interests.

Looking outwards: the long peace

The international contrast between the 18th and 19th centuries is one of the big historical questions of the modern world-system. Whereas the 18th century was a period of almost continual war among European powers, in the 19th century they enjoyed what is commonly referred to as 'the long peace'. Quantitatively battlefield deaths declined by a factor of eight between the two centuries and this despite the increasing destructiveness of the weaponry.[110] Why should this be so? One obvious approach to answering this question is to study the various actors in the two centuries and to work out why those that came later were far more successful in securing peace. It would seem at first sight that 19th-century diplomats and statesmen were far better at their job than their predecessors in the much bloodier of the two centuries. However, it is hard to see why the quality of political elites should have suddenly improved to such a degree to create such a remarkable transformation in the balance between war and peace. In fact this was not the case. As Paul Schroeder points out, there were many skilful practitioners of international affairs in the 18th century who were just as competent as those in the next century.[111] Hence, he concludes, the differences between the two centuries cannot be explained by the behaviour of political elites, but must reflect, instead, a structural change in the nature of inter-state politics. This is the position we take here: the Congress of

Vienna marks a watershed in the inter-state system at exactly the time Britain becomes hegemonic.[112] This is not mere coincidence.

Structural change in the inter-state system means that the fundamental way the system works, and is perceived to work, has altered in terms of what sort of behaviours are penalized and which are rewarded. This abrupt change incorporated two basic features which both curtailed the 'liberty of states' set up at Westphalia. First, there was the recognition that states could not keep their right to declare war on other states. This was justified in 1820 by the Austrian Count Metternich, one of the architects of the new order, as follows: 'since no state is any longer isolated . . . we must never lose sight of the *society* of states which is the essential condition of the modern world'.[113] Second, the distinction between war and peace was more sharply differentiated. In the 18th century over much of Europe war was a 'natural activity' carried out seasonally in a multitude of forms ranging from banditry and rebellion to civil war and inter-state war. In contrast in the 19th century peace broke out in Europe and war became clearly demarcated precisely because it had become 'unnatural'.[114] In considering Britain's role in these changes we will take each in turn.

Hinsley calls the framework agreed at Vienna in 1815 the 'modern international system'.[115] Although it did not set up permanent international institutions – these were to come later – it did provide for the management of inter-state relations for the very first time. Management took two forms that were strictly separated geographically. In Europe the Great Powers agreed the territorial arrangement for ending the Napoleonic war and guaranteed the new boundaries. This pacification of Europe is known as the Concert of Europe, which consisted of irregular meetings of the Great Powers to whom boundary changes had to go for approval. In this arrangement Britain was one of the Great Powers. But what of the world beyond Europe? The Napoleonic war had led to conflict across the world resulting in many changes of colonies. Britain insisted that these issues were not discussed at Vienna. Instead a *Pax Britannica* was created across the oceans of the world.[116] The overall result for Britain as hegemon was ideal: Vienna ensured a peaceful 'back yard' in Europe leaving her free to pursue her global agenda.

Britain's role at Vienna was similar to the Dutch at Westphalia: she was the only participant with no territorial ambitions in Europe. Kenneth Bourne describes this neatly as 'politically satiated' but with her 'commercial appetite unsatiated'.[117] Hence her motives were very different from her conservative allies in the world war. The main concern of Austria, Prussia and Russia was to prevent revolution reappearing within their realms. This genuine reactionary political position fitted Britain's needs only to the degree that the ensuing political stability would be good for trade: Britain was looking to capture new markets in Europe denied to it by Napoleon's Continental Blockade. When the three reactionary powers agreed the Troppau Protocol in 1820, claiming the right to intervene in states to prevent a revolution, Britain declined to sign. France had been readmitted to the status of a Great Power in 1818, and by the 1830s she formed a sort of informal 'liberal alliance' with Britain to counter the influence of the Holy Alliance of Russia, Prussia and Austria. However, this ideological division among the Great Powers never threatened to become the basis for another great war. It was not in the interests of any of the Great Powers to disturb the controlled balance of power provided through the Concert of Europe. The 1848 revolutions put pressure on the system, but it survived

Plate 6 *Balancing Power*, caricature engraving of the Congress of Vienna (1815) by L. Lutz (Historisches Museum der Stadt Wien, Vienna). The three persons behind the table discussing the map are (from left to right) Francis I of Austria, Czar Alexander I and Frederick William III of Prussia. Britain is represented by the supreme allied commander, the Duke of Wellington, symbolically seated next to the globe and showing no interest in the details of the boundary drawing since his country's territorial interests were all extra-European

with no major war. The closest it came to breakdown was the Crimean War (1854–6) when Britain and France fought Russia; this proved to be a war that 'wouldn't boil', as A. J. P. Taylor has so aptly described it.[118] Other states refused to get involved and the war ended with Russia humiliated but without doing too much damage to the balance of power in Europe. It is in the 1860s that the system gets out of control, especially with the conversion of Prussia into Germany through the defeats of Austria and France. Again the system soon settled down into its new balance with no threat to Britain for the remainder of the century. Hence for Britain the long peace built upon the agreements made at Vienna in 1815 worked very well.

The term *'Pax Britannica'* was coined in the 1880s to describe the world domination of Britain in the 19th century.[119] It is dated from 1815 when at the close of hostilities the British kept control of islands and ports across all oceans. These 'keys' to the world, as the Foreign Secretary Castlereagh called them, provided strategic, communication and commercial advantages to the British throughout the 19th century.[120] This meant Britain and her navy were the only power with a global reach. With this capacity Britain could conduct 'gunboat diplomacy' throughout all continents beyond Europe and protect its citizens around the world, as well as promoting legitimate trade through its anti-piracy and anti-slavery campaigns. Hence it provided the basic infrastructure for both Britain's continued imperial ventures, especially in India, and the new 'economic imperialism' conducted in the Americas and China. It was the dominance of the Royal Navy in the Atlantic that ensured no European intervention when the Latin American provinces rebelled against their Iberian imperial masters in the 1820s. This enabled Britain to gain a new market in the new independent states; the British foreign secretary Lord Canning is reported as remarking at the time: 'Latin America is free and she is ours.'[121] No wonder Latin America came to be known as Britain's 'informal empire'!

The *Pax Britannica* was a pacification, not a peace by agreement; nevertheless it did figure in the development of ideas for a 'perpetual peace'. This phrase is the name given to a pamphlet written by Immanuel Kant in 1795 in which he provided the philosophical case for peace as being in the interests of both individuals and states.[122] As countries came to depend more and more on external linkages and internal cohesion, then, according to Kant, war would become increasingly 'artificial'. This was the basis of the 19th-century liberal assumption that an international economy would generate a universal peace. The heyday of this dream occurred in Britain in the mid-19th century. *Pax Britannica* was seen as promoting modern industrial society across the world which would eventually destroy all motives for making war.[123] For the British liberal Richard Cobden there were just two contending parties in the world: 'commercial interests' as the party of peace and 'territorial interests' as the party of war and it was the latter that was declining.[124] Hence, like the Dutch before them, Britain as hegemon claimed to be a pacific state: in the mid-1850s H. T. Buckle reported that in Britain the love of war is 'utterly extinct'.[125]

Hence the long peace, as well as being a pacification, also reflected the aspirations of a liberal pacificism promoted by the hegemon of the day. The result is that whereas the Dutch generated a scale of peace at the level of states, the British contributed to a peace at the level of Europe and the oceans. Competition among states did not disappear, but it took a new form in the 19th century that reflected a new *raison d'état* to create a modern international system in the image of the hegemon. In Schroeder's words:

> It was essentially [state] competition for advantage, like the competition for shares of the market . . . The main advantage sought was the ability to profit from the international system at little cost, to enjoy freedom and choices others did not, and to escape burdens and payments that others had to bear.[126]

This was the key structural change that created the long peace of the 19th century.

Self and other: liberal parliamentarians versus Eastern despots (Orientalism)

Although they did not use the term, the British understood themselves to be the purveyors of 'True Freedom' in much the same way as the Dutch. By the 19th century the circumstances surrounding the relations between free and unfree had radically changed: the idea of liberty was no longer a minor irritant in a largely absolutist Europe as it had been during Dutch hegemony. Although Britain had allied with the traditional monarchies of Austria, Prussia and Russia in order to defeat Napoleon, this political convenience did not reflect the cultural dimension of British hegemony. This is most obviously shown in the fact that in the 19th century London became the haven for intellectual exiles to the chagrin of continental rulers just as Amsterdam had been earlier – for Descartes read Marx. However the British did not condemn the great monarchs of Europe as tyrants in the manner of the Dutch since they had to work with them in the Concert of Europe. British concern for free and unfree took on a much broader perspective in both cultural and geographical terms. Absolutist tyrants are replaced by oriental despots as the measure of un-freedom.

With the incorporation of more and more of the earth's surface into the world-economy, the British faced the particular problem of defining the limits of liberty. There needed to be a way of justifying what seems to be one of the great paradoxes of British hegemony: the coincidence of 'liberty and empire'. How could Britain's treatment of India be reconciled with all the talk of freedom and constitutional monarchy? This was not necessarily seen as a paradox to contemporaries imbued with 'orientalist' notions of ranking Asian people below Europeans.[127] The greatest British political theorist of the 19th century, John Stuart Mill, made clear that the arguments in his liberal classic *On Liberty and Representative Government* did not apply to India.[128] Mill worked for the India Office and had no doubts that the inferiority of people from Asia made them incapable of responsibly governing themselves. Left to themselves, Asian civilizations created despotic emperors whose cruel arbitrary rule reduced their subjects to the status of slaves. Hence British rule in India could be justified as a much preferable form of law and order, even if it could not replicate the representative government enjoyed in Britain itself.

Such reasoning is known as 'Orientalism'. According to Edward Said, Orientalism is an imaginary world geography based upon an East–West dichotomy that emerged in the late 18th century to dominate European relations with Asia in the 19th century.[129] It developed into a discipline of scholars who provided a particular description of Asia from a distinctively Eurocentric perspective.[130] Although the idea of 'Asiatic despots' can be traced back to Aristotle, the Orientalists gave this theme a new twist: Europe was now 'modern', which relegated Asia to the realm of the 'unmodern'. Whereas European civilization was progressive, the civilizations of Asia had stagnated and remained trapped in a state of backward traditionalism. Karl Marx explicitly incorporated this argument in his social analysis by designating an 'Asiatic mode of production' outside the progressive European sequence from feudalism through capitalism to communism.[131] Marx, like Mill, was not himself an Orientalist, but both were trapped by its imaginary world geography into supporting British imperialism in India as the agent of progress. Because Asiatic civilizations were interpreted as lacking in progress, Orientatists studied them as an unchanging pattern of social relationships; scholars typically focused on the ancient texts to understand their contemporary subjects. They concluded that 'orientals' were everything that Europeans were not: above all they were irrational and did not have a European capacity for logic. In short, the Orientalists provided the ideal world theory for Britain's pragmatic parliamentarians: the British in India were providing the intellectual service of introducing rationality into a subcontinent where parliamentary politics was impossible.

Beyond its obvious geopolitical utility, Orientalism incorporated a much broader facility for Britain and Europe. As Europe's Other, it defined Europe's Self.[132] Rana

Kabbani identifies two striking themes in the East's otherness: 'lascivious sensuality' and 'inherent violence':[133] 'The Orient of Western imagination provided respite from Victorian sexual repressiveness. It was used to express the exotic longings that would have otherwise remained suppressed.'[134] Kabbani is referring here to popular travel writing introducing the reader to the exotic. The message is clear: whereas Victorian values can be exported westward from Europe to America there can be no equivalent export eastwards to Asia. Orientalism defined the limits of British-led bourgeois culture and therefore of freedom. The latter was a responsibility not everybody was capable of shouldering.

The Americans as pragmatic democrats

By definition hegemonic states are not just special polities, they are unique political artifacts of their eras. This was true for the USA in its period of high hegemony as it was for the United Provinces and Britain. But in each case their exceptional natures did not just appear as hegemony was achieved; antecedents of their unusual characters can be easily found in their pre-hegemonic existence. In these circumstances we have to be careful not to produce a 'whig' historical account that leads inevitably to their condition of hegemonic triumph. Alongside the antecedents of hegemony there are counter political tendencies that point in other directions – the Dutch did search for a replacement monarch and the British aristocratic state of the 18th century, known as the 'Old Corruption', hardly promoted freedom. In the case of the USA, exceptionalism is integral to the national consciousness so we have to be particularly on our guard not to mix up popular notions that America was destined for greatness with our search for hegemonic antecedents.

There is no doubt that the USA was exceptional from its origins as the first case of decolonization. The successful War of Independence produced a completely new state that was distinctive from its European origins in numerous ways. Having conceded this point – and we will return to it again below – it does not follow that there was a continuous history of exceptionalism through to hegemony. From a world-system perspective American history can be divided into four periods. The initial exceptionalism gradually gave way in the late 19th century to produce a quite 'normal' Great Power by 1898 which in turn gives way to a new exceptionalism in the first half of the 20th century, culminating in hegemony from 1945. Normality begins to return in the aftermath of hegemony in the final third of the 20th century. The middle period of behaving just like other major states of the period provides the key break that gives the lie to the popular notion of continuous American exceptionalism. At the turn of the last century the USA was far from unique as it joined the ranks of the Great Powers with some relish.

In 1900 the USA was organizing the spoils from its victory in the Spanish-American War of two years earlier. By defeating one of Europe's weakest imperial powers, the USA found itself in possession of colonies in the Caribbean and Pacific. US policies in Puerto Rico, Cuba and the Philippines were hardly what we might expect from the first decolonized state: the USA acted in the spirit of the age and became imperialists themselves. In the process they put down a Philippines revolt as ruthlessly as any more practised European imperialist state. In general they pursued a typical imperial policy of using colonies for metropolitan ends, in this case project-ing American power south to Panama and west to east Asia. At the turn of the century such aggressive foreign policies were popular in all imperial states. This is evidenced by what we may term 'imperial elections', when right-wing governments consolidated their positions on the back of nationalism stoked by imperialism. In 1900 President McKinley easily saw off the challenge of the 'Great Commoner' William Jennings Bryan in a campaign that has parallels with the Conservative government's defeat of a divided Liberal Party in Britain's 'khaki' election in the same year and during the Boer War. This was not America joining Britain as special, the latter had long since lost her hegemonic status and was, by this time, one imperial state among many in a highly competitive world. America had become just another imperial state.

Domestically the main prop of the argument for continuous American excep-tionalism has been the failure of socialist parties to become a major force in electoral politics as became the norm in Europe. But even here there was no exceptionalism in 1900. The USA had a tradition of radical trade unionism in the late 19th century and first half of the 20th century that matches anything in Europe. In addition socialist politics, from the Knights of Labor in the 1880s to the Socialist Party of America in the first two decades of the 20th century, was as strong in the USA as most other industrial states. Certainly until 1920 the American Socialist Party was doing at least as well as the British Labour Party.[135] The exceptionalism came later when, from a similar base, American socialists were unable to become a major party. But there was nothing distinctively exceptional about the rise of this class conflict within American politics during its pre-hegemonic era.

If the USA was a 'normal' state at the beginning of the century, it most certainly was not so by mid-century. It created a new modern politics that promised the benefits of progress much wider than ever before. The previous two hegemons had been careful to define the limits of their political incorporations, the Americans had no such inhibitions. In terms of the state–civil society, America's inclusive tradition culminated in the first society in history where most people considered themselves to be 'middle class' and behaved accordingly. The 'American Dream' became a reality for millions of ordinary families in what John Galbraith famously dubbed the 'affluent society'.[136] In addition the American dream was deemed exportable. In terms of relations with other states, a 'free world' was designated that in principle covered every country, although the Cold War was to limit its scope in practice to about two-thirds of the world until 1989. Whether looking inwards or outwards, the USA as hegemonic state created a new pragmatic politics of democracy.

Looking inwards: politics for an 'affluent society'

In the late 1950s the chairman of President Eisenhower's Council of Economic Ad-visers was very clear on the relationship between the US state and civil society. He declared that the 'prime purpose' of the US economy is, at least as far as his govern-ment was concerned, 'to produce more consumer goods. This is the goal. That is the objective of everything we are working at; to produce things for consumers.'[137] This represents a massive cultural shift from an earlier 'work ethic' associated with thriftiness to a 'consumer ethic' based upon leisure and shopping. Most writers agree that the origins of the consumer society can be traced to the changing behaviour of urban elites in the last two decades of the 19th century. With 'the emergence of a new stratum of professionals and managers, rooted in a web of new organizations', such as giant corporations, universities, new government departments and the mass media, there arose a national advertising industry to persuade the new salariat to spend rather than save.[138] At the beginning of the 20th century, this was still a small minority activity.

But, according to John Lukacs, something happened in America around 1920 that was totally without precedent: American society had taken on a new economic 'shape'.[139] All previous large societies have had pyramid social structures with few very rich tapering down to many poor. Although the angle of taper may have varied, the basic pattern was constant — until, that is, American society developed its unique 'onion' shape. Somehow the middle had expanded at the expense of the bottom to create a completely new form of society and a very different politics. In the 1920s the advertising industry became a major national industry and as consumption spread, questions began to be asked whether America was beginning 'a new historical epoch'. Viewing these changes from Europe, Antonio Gramsci coined the word 'Americanism' to describe 'a new beacon that has been lit over there'.[140] He interpreted this as an intensification of European society which had 'acquired a new coating in the American climate'.[141] The new coating was a new culture being built in the USA for the next hegemonic stage of the modern world-system.

With great prescience, Gramsci focused upon the high wages paid to workers, notably by Ford in the motor industry, and the reorganization of production through 'Taylorism', or scientific management, which made the high wages possible. Although interrupted in the 1930s by the economic crisis, in the post-1945 period this is what became known as the Fordist regime of accumulation when mass production generated a high paid workforce for mass consumption. This neatly bypassed the economic blockage of under-consumption which was widely blamed for the economic catastrophe of the 1930s. The agreement between General Motors and the United Auto Workers' Union in 1947 is usually taken as the symbolic capital–labour deal when high wages were given for guaranteed high productivity. Auto workers won the 'good life', the ability to buy their own house in a spacious suburb and fill it with all manner of new domestic gadgets coming onto the market. The good life came also to the workers producing the gadgets for Hoover, Whirlpool and others. 'Buying itself became a way of life' or more precisely the 'American way of life'.[142] When Vice-President Richard Nixon confronted the USSR's Nikita Khrushchev on the relative merits of their different societies in 1959 he argued that the American system worked because '44 million families in America own 56 million cars, 50 million television sets, 143 million radio sets, and . . . 31 million of those families own their own homes'.[143] American civil society had become overwhelmingly a consumer society. Even voters became converted into consumers of carefully packaged politicians whose expensive advertising campaigns dominated elections: presidential candidates came to be 'sold' just like washing powder.[144]

Where is the state in all of this? According to Dyson, the US state continues its English legacy as a state denied.[145] That is to say, it has an external persona to face the rest of the world but is inconspicuous in American debates on domestic policy. In the US government the Foreign Ministry and its chief minister are called the State Department and the Secretary of State respectively, but when Americans 'beyond the beltway' criticize what comes out of Washington, DC they have traditionally moaned about poor government in the form of an incompetent president or an unresponsive Congress but far less about an oppressive state. In fact the American state is a relatively weak state apparatus compared with other industrial countries. Of course this is no accident. There are two quite distinctive historical bases for this situation. First the USA was designed to be a weak state by its founding fathers in the late 18th century. Like the Dutch before them, they were not about to be rid of one oppressive state in order to create another. But unlike the Dutch their federation was not an improvisation. After the initial loose confederation was found to be wanting, the framers of the federal constitution produced a stronger central government but under a system of checks and balances between executive, legislature and judiciary as well as between the centre and the states making up the federation. The product has been called 'fragmented government', a unique mixture of hostile bodies in a disorderly federation where the president is more 'bargainer-in-chief' than the state's chief executive.[146] Hence despite all the debate about the 'rise of an imperial presidency' or the perennial call for 'states rights', the American Constitution ensures that the American state remains unique in its limited power *vis-à-vis* its civil society.

If this was not enough, in the 19th century a second national tradition arose that made the USA's state–society relation even more exceptional. The essence of American identity was deemed to derive not reactively from its original resistance to European imperialism but proactively from the subsequent authentic American winning a continent. The frontier thesis was devised by Frederick Jackson Turner to provide the USA with a new historical basis from which Europe was banished.[147] The gradual western expansion of America throughout the 19th century acted as a safety valve for social conflict, according to Turner, allowing for the emergence of an ideal harmonious society in contrast to Europe. The frontier became mythologized as a font of liberty and freedom where the individual could prosper without political interference. The result was a new politics:

> The frontier had enabled American ideology to develop differently from its European counterpart. It permitted a novel model of the state to evolve with a different concept of its roles and tasks . . . According to the tenets of American liberalism society took precedence over the state.[148]

There is an irony to this American exceptionalism in that Turner was writing to warn of the end of the frontier which would thus curtail America's distinctiveness. The political solution for his supporters was to continue territorial and commercial expansion beyond the USA which was, in fact, what turned America into a fairly typical imperial state abroad. The frontier ideal remained to buttress civil society against the state in the 20th century and produce the quite distinctive suspicion of public policy – what Andrew Shonfield terms 'the uncertain role of public power' – in America to this day.[149]

We can see this process in operation in the period just before American high hegemony. As we have seen, the 1920s appear as an initial age of affluence cut short by the 1929 financial crash and consequent depression. The 1920s were a period of minimal state involvement in society and economy, but the catastrophic economic outcome led to the political rethink in the 1930s which we know as the New Deal. Under Franklin Roosevelt the USA conformed to the general international trend for more state intervention in attempts to compensate for the disastrous failings of the market. The degree of intervention varied between countries; in much of Europe there was a turn to the state dominating civil society as in Fascist regimes but even elsewhere, such as Britain, national planning, however rudimentary, made its first peacetime appearance. The USA's New Deal policies were initially somewhere between these two positions. Shonfield argues that there were two New Deal doctrines.[150] At first (1933–4) the new Roosevelt government took a corporatist turn by trying to get state and business to collaborate in agreed economic objectives. This major national planning exercise was the responsibility of the National Recovery Administration (NRA). However New Deal opponents challenged the constitutionality of the NRA and the Supreme Court ruled in their favour in 1935. Hence the separation of powers in the US Constitution allowed the executive to be blocked and the new corporatism to be effectively defeated. The government was forced to fall back on a much weaker supervisory approach to the New Deal which was little different from earlier progressive politics. A regulatory state was created as the immediate antecedent to hegemony. However, this proved to be particularly suitable for the new regime of accumulation after 1945 where state intervention was unnecessary since production and consumption were handled within civil society by negotiation. And, of course, the subsequent rise of the 'affluent society' led to less demand for further state intervention. This contrasted with European states that developed corporatist states after 1945 with large welfare provisions and economic planning.

The USA remains the industrial state with the poorest public provision for welfare throughout the period since 1945. It is sometimes argued that with the onset of the Cold War, the USA created a warfare state in contrast to the welfare states constructed elsewhere. Even President Eisenhower warned against the rise of a military–industrial complex dominating the state–society relationship. Certainly the USA consistently spent more than its economic rivals on war preparation. Although very frightening at the time, we can see in hindsight that in many ways this operated in lieu of the industrial development policies America's anti-public power doctrine would not allow but which were pursued with vigour by its rivals. This was the strong external face of the American state impinging directly upon the domestic sphere. We are only beginning to appreciate the economic importance of this after the Cold War and the consequent depression in the 'defence industries'.[151]

Looking outwards: Cold War as 'long peace'

Like British hegemony, the international regime presided over by the USA has been termed a 'long peace', this one lasting since 1945.[152] But it is, of course, a very different peace to the one that existed through most of the 19th century. This is a long peace that has been called a war: the Cold War. The effective zone of peace has far outgrown Europe to encompass a 'North' spanning the globe from Vancouver to Vladivostok, but it has been a highly militarized peace, a peace of great tension. Hence although US hegemony has been associated with a further extension in the scale of pacified stability, it has been a very distinctive form of peace that America has been implicated in constructing.

The industrialization of war leading to ever greater destructiveness of weapons has been a major stimulus to international peace moves from the 19th century onwards. World War I led directly to international attempts to ensure its battlefield horrors would never be repeated; in the sentiment of the time it would be 'the war to end all wars'. This was very much associated with the entry of the USA into the war and the attempt by President Wilson to convert it from a traditional war of spoils to a new kind of war to create a new kind of peace. American exceptionalism was evoked as the 'new world' teaching the 'old world' how to conduct international relations appropriate for the 20th century.[153] American idealism may have legitimized the dismantling of Central and Eastern Europe's land empires but it did not create a new international politics at Versailles in 1919. Despite Wilson's proposal in his 'fourteen points' to treat winners and losers equally, in Western Europe the final treaty confirmed the status quo as produced by the outcome of the war.[154] This left France as the major power on the continent, a role she was ill-equipped to sustain once the particular circumstances of war's end were over. With the electoral defeat of Wilson and the USA's failure to join the League of Nations as a vehicle to maintain the peace, the next two decades were marked by a power vacuum in international politics that Germany and Japan were eventually to take advantage of. Although her empire was to reach its territorial zenith at this time (after the award of League of Nations mandates), Britain was long past her hegemony and had neither the will nor capacity to guarantee peace and stability. In 1932 she even abandoned free trade in favour of 'imperial preference' as a protectionist measure aimed particularly at the USA. It is the matching of economic and political instability with the lack of any state leadership in these inter-war years, when contrasted with the reversal of this situation after 1945, that spawned the hegemonic stability theory we mentioned in Chapter 1.

The reaction to World War I did lead to institutions being built for a peaceful world that presaged the 1945 boom in new international institutional creation. In terms of organization, the League of Nations was a massive advance on the old Concert of Europe both in geographical scope and as a permanent body in Geneva. Of particular importance is the fact that both through the League's Charter and in the later Kellogg Pact (1928), states renounced the right to go to war. Although of limited practical significance, this principle was a historic declaration in terms of the changing nature of the inter-state system. The principle was adopted by the United Nations in 1945 so that members have been constrained to fight only wars of defence: overnight around the world War Departments, Offices and Ministries had to drop 'War' from their titles and substitute the word 'Defence'.[155]

Given that this change has coincided with a long peace, scholars of international law have interpreted these new arrangements as being very significant. For instance the international lawyer W. D. Coplin argues that in terms of the traditional assumption about a state's natural inclination to maximise power, the contemporary legal commitment to a just war doctrine represents a profound and historic shift.[156]

Agreeing that there has been a 'fundamental' change, Fred Hinsley believes 1945 marks the end of the 'modern international system' and its replacement by another system 'even more different from the modern system than that was from all its precursors'.[157] Hinsley reserves the phrase modern international system for that created at Vienna in 1815 which we have interpreted as a world politics made to facilitate British hegemony. In our account there have been three modern international systems of which the one identified by Hinsley is the second, following the Westphalia creation as the first modern system. This means that the United Nations-based system constitutes the third modern international system in a sequence that successively curtailed the original 'liberty of states'.

The victorious American war leader in World War II, Franklin Roosevelt, was much more of a realist in international affairs than their war leader of World War I, Woodrow Wilson. Roosevelt has been attributed with having 'a remarkable combination of realism and idealism' but the former is certainly the more evident:[158] national interests of the USA were the first concern of Roosevelt and his administration.[159] Idealism was to be found in an 'emphasis on grand objectives' wherein American interests would prosper.[160] In particular Roosevelt promoted a 'one world' ideal in World War II whereby the allies would continue to collaborate after victory to secure a sound peace.[161] Like 19th-century British liberals, Roosevelt and his administration viewed peace as much more than a question of security alone. The experience of the 1930s convinced the administration that aggressive economic policies, the formation of discriminatory trading blocs and consequent economic breakdown with mass unemployment were the root causes of war. Security arrangements had to be accompanied by new trade arrangements: 'if soldiers were not to cross international borders, then goods must do so'.[162] Hence, unlike the League of Nations, as much effort went into devising new economic institutions as political ones: while the UN General Assembly and Security Council were being mapped out in San Francisco, the World Bank and IMF were being created at Bretton Woods.

Given that the 1930s' depression was seen to result from a lack of demand, it followed that to prevent the scourge of under-consumption reappearing after war demobilization, markets had to be found for US goods across the world. This was urgent in 1945 since US production had more than doubled in the war years.[163] Hence American peace plans were clear: 'to restructure the world so that American business could trade, operate and profit without restrictions everywhere'.[164] Initially multilateral agreements were favoured but these proved impossible in the highly unequal world of the early post-war period. With all other economies disrupted or destroyed, normal trade relations could not be resumed before reconstruction, and the latter could not begin because of a world-wide dollar shortage. The result was that loan agreements became the key American tool for opening up the world-economy.[165]

The first and most important target was Britain with trade preferences in its Empire and currency control in its Sterling Area.[166] Half of all US trade was with the latter region. After fighting an all-out war for six years Britain was effectively bankrupt in 1945 and required a loan to sustain its domestic social programme as well as to rebuild its economy. The US was able to use this short-term British emergency for its medium-term ends, the creation of a liberal economic order. To receive the loan Britain had to agree to conditions that both opened up imperial markets and made sterling convertible into dollars.[167] In fact the hard-nosed US negotiators never fully realized the true scale of the economic differentials created by World War II. The loan failed to stimulate a British economic recovery and dollar convertibility proved to be unsustainable. It took two years for the US to realize that European reconstruction would require a massive aid programme to provide the markets for American goods. This was the Marshall Plan, implemented in 1948; but in order to understand the context of this shift in US policy we have to return to questions of security.

The fact that the USA originally expected to construct 'one world' but had to settle for just two-thirds of the world as its 'free world', shows the limits of hegemony. Although economic pressure is a formidable weapon, it operates through negotiation in an uncertain world.[168] The USA did not possess an imperium power, it could not instruct and expect to be obeyed and the result was that a sizeable portion of the world 'got away', creating a bi-polar world. There are many ideas on how amity between the USA and USSR in 1945 was converted to emnity by 1947; most reduce to either blaming the USSR for political imperialism by stubbornly refusing to relinquish Eastern Europe or blaming the USA for economic imperialism by insisting on opening up markets.[169] The actual process was very complex and has an important ideological dimension, of course, which we deal with in the next section. The key point here is that sometime in the year following the end of the war, the one-world model gave way to a two-world model and with the USSR replacing Britain as the main obstacle to US aims. From being a remote ally with little prior contact and with no reason not to expect friendly future relations, the Soviet Union was converted into a state with a ravenous appetite for expansion. As George Kennan explained at the time, the USSR was not an ordinary state and therefore could not be treated through normal international relations. It had to be confronted and contained.[170] When Britain suffered another budgetary crisis in 1947, she announced a withdrawal of troops from Greece. This sent alarm bells ringing in Washington since it was assumed the USSR would attempt to step into the power vacuum left by the British and hence advance to the Mediterranean, the cherished hope of Russian empires for centuries. This was the spark that meant *Pax Americana* would have to replace the rapidly disappearing *Pax Britannica*.[171]

The American response to Britain's withdrawal from Greece was the Truman Doctrine which publicly defined US foreign policy in terms of two worlds.[172] In his famous speech to both Houses of Congress on 11 March 1947, President Truman promised to defend any country that resisted Soviet aggression. Congressional leaders had been briefed at the White House, when a form of domino theory was used to explain that the fall of Greece would precipitate Russian control of Iran, Turkey and Egypt, then Italy and France, before the demise of the British Empire leaving the USA at the mercy of this new and seemingly all-powerful foe.[173] Although a deliberate overstatement, 'clearer than the truth' as Dean Acheson (who did the briefing) was subsequently to put it, the speech and briefing did their job in preparing Congress, and then the American public, for a new world of Cold War.[174] In the following year the Marshall Plan of aid to rebuild Western Europe could pass through Congress on the grounds that economic impoverishment in Europe only played into the USSR's hands – they would be only too happy politically to pick up the pieces after any economic collapse.[175] When the focus of international conflict switched to Asia in 1949 and 1950, rearmament for the Korean War, just five years after World War II demobilization, attracted little opposition and the Cold War became firmly established as the new international order.

In terms of power politics, one feature made the Cold War unique as an international system. In 1945 the USA detonated the first atomic bomb, and in 1949 the USSR fuelled Cold War paranoia by testing its own atomic bomb. And so began the nuclear arms race. Although other states developed such bombs, the USA and the USSR totally dominated production and their particular status as superpowers came to based upon these oversized arsenals. For John Herz the creation of the 'atomic age' produced a great historical divide at least as important as Westphalia.[176] The traditional role of territorial states was fatally undermined, according to Herz, since there could be no reliable defence against such weapons of mass destruction. Hence although war between major powers continued to be thinkable, it was no longer rationally practical. Past world wars had lasted about 30 years as we have seen; would the next one last 30 days, or was that being optimistic given the cumulative increase in the quantity and quality of weapons? Is 30 hours a better estimate or is it to be just 30 minutes to Armageddon? Instead of the balance of power of British hegemony, US hegemony was premised upon a balance of terror.[177] Furthermore, in the British case the hegemon was careful to manoeuvre from outside the balance, the famous 'free hand' position, whereas the USA was at the centre of the alliance system that dominated its hegemony. Hence the peculiar role of this latest world stabilizer: warfare state in a militarized peace.

This is not necessarily the converse of what we expect to accompany hegemonic status, however. The competition between the USA and the USSR was not only an unequal one simply in terms of a material comparison between the two world zones, the nature of their opposing alliances was qualitatively different. The Red Army stayed on in Eastern Europe after 1945 and became an army of occupation propping up unpopular governments. Remove army support and the governments fall; *ergo* the popular revolutions of 1989. After 1945 the USA did withdraw from Europe and returned only after the Cold War began. NATO was formed in 1949 and was as much a British initiative as American. Hence rather than an army of occupation, US forces in Europe were welcomed as a military insurance policy. America and things American were popular in Western Europe; that is what made the contest with a repressive USSR so unequal from the start.

Self and other: free democrats versus communist dictators (totalitarianism)

America's self-image has always been rooted in its perceived exceptionalism. Traditionally this has taken the form of treating Europe and its ills as the 'Old World' to contrast with a better 'New World' as represented by the USA. This model of America's Other was very much in evidence in Woodrow Wilson's tendency to lecture at his European allies in World War I. With the entry of the USA into World War II and the defeat of isolationism, the vision of America in the world transmuted into becoming a model for the rest of the world. This was the basis of the idea of one world, American ideals would be writ large across the globe – initially as a 'global New Deal'.[178] President Roosevelt used the language of liberty to encapsulate these ideals as 'four freedoms': freedom of religion and speech, freedom from want and fear. Practical implementation began with the Atlantic Charter agreed between Roosevelt and Churchill in 1941. As well as agreeing to free trade, the right to national self-determination was reiterated and, unlike the earlier Wilsonian version that only applied to Europe, this was intended to include the whole world. Its implementation would mean the end of the British Empire. Stalin followed Churchill in appeasing Roosevelt and in 1945 agreed the Declaration on Liberated Europe which effectively precluded Soviet control of Eastern Europe. As consummate power politicians, neither Churchill nor Stalin saw these agreements as anything more than necessary tools to placate the USA during the war. Hence once hostilities came to an end, the inherent contradictions between these agreements and national interests came to the fore. As we have seen, Britain as initial obstacle to the one-world vision was effectively bought off by the loan agreement, leaving the USSR to become the obstacle that was not overcome. In the creation of a bi-polar world, the USSR came to be defined as America's new Other, representing totalitarianism against its own democracy. In one of the most remarkable historical political turn-arounds of the modern era, the USSR was converted from heroic ally to an intrinsically evil enemy in less than two years.[179] It set the ideological and cultural basis for American hegemony.

It would seem that America's assumption of leadership in the inter-state system needed more than the development of new policies. George Washington had warned America never to become embroiled in Old World conflicts. Although both World Wars I and II had been seen as necessary, in 1945 the idea of withdrawal, as had happened in 1919, remained strong. In early 1946 the passage of the Bill authorizing the loan to Britain was having trouble in its passage through Congress. Practical business arguments for a liberal world-economy were not succeeding; the Bill only passed when reinterpreted as a measure to combat communism.[180] This success with Congress and public opinion was duly noted by the executive, and foreign policy was soon to be converted from the usual mundane international relations transactions to an ideological crusade. We can see this in President Truman's words in the Truman Declaration as a struggle to the death between two ways of life:

> One way of life is based upon the will of the majority, and is distinguished by free elections, guarantees of individual liberty, freedom of speech and religion, and freedom from political oppression. The second way of life is based upon the will of a minority forcibly imposed upon the majority. It relies upon terror and oppression, a controlled press and radio, fixed elections, and the suppression of personal freedoms.[181]

This uncompromising language depicting two opposing worlds may have only been devised for short-term Congressional needs, but the reality was that such a fundamental shift in the nature of the American state required a popular political crusade. Unlike 1919, the American people were now given a reason for assuming a world leadership role. Once unleashed, anti-communism was not something that could be turned on or off at a politician's whim.[182] America had changed, she had become a country ready to assume world hegemony.

The basic theory devised to legitimate American peacetime political involvement in the rest of the world was that of the totalitarian state. This argued that in the 20th century the irrational legacy of the French Revolution had come to fruition in the guise of totalitarian regimes. These were not traditional repressive states but were based upon a new politics that required total state control of civil society. Three examples of this ultimate negation of freedom were identified: Fascist Italy, Nazi Germany and Soviet Russia. With the end of World War II, the first two cases were despatched to history, so that the conflict with the USSR represented a continuity, the second stage, of the great contest between the free and the unfree. This was very convenient because it explained how so recent an ally should be properly viewed as an arch enemy. In this way the Soviet Union took on the role of 'red Fascists'.[183] In addition, the theory helped make the USSR less unpredictable in its behaviour: lessons could be learnt from relations with Italy and Germany in the 1930s and policies devised accordingly.[184] The message was an easy one to understand: it is useless to negotiate or compromise with a totalitarian state, diplomacy can never work since conflict is inevitable. The USSR was, according to this view of the world, an innately expansionary state bent on imposing its politics on the rest of the world. Hence even if an agreement were reached, it would only be used as a breathing space for the Soviets in their preparation for the final showdown.

But anti-communism was always about more than inter-state relations. Nine days after his Declaration, President Truman issued an executive order that set up the Loyalty-Security Program. Anti-communists had to be vigilant at home as well as abroad: communists were to be rooted out of public service. A similar programme was instituted in Britain where the governing Labour Party also expelled some of its more radical MPs. In France and Italy popular-front governments including communists were replaced by anti-communist administrations. It was in the USA, however, that the repression of alleged communists went far beyond the state apparatus and created a more intolerant civil society.[185] McCarthyism, as a virulent form of political repression using lies and innuendoes to break individual lives and careers, penetrated deep into civil society so that anti-communism became entrenched in American culture. The result was that with communism definitively portrayed as anti-American, the state had a free hand in its anti-communist foreign policies with little or no opposition until the Vietnam débâcle.

The main area of communist activity in the USA in the 1930s had been in labour organizations. This was resisted by the trade-union leadership with their close ties to New Deal policies. When communism officially became anti-American, US unions, the AFL–CIO, were ready to support the government both domestically and internationally. American unions had long been political lobbyists for labour interests rather than purveyors of a distinctive labour politics and by 1947 their aims had become clear: the workers whom they represented were not to be raised as a class, they were to be given the individual opportunity to join the middle class. To be American came to mean to be middle class; as Barbara Ehrenreich sees it, 'this class plays an overwhelming role in defining "America": its modes, its political direction, and its moral tone'.[186] As the American 'universal class', the middle class set the social norms and centred them upon consumption. Hence to be middle class, that is

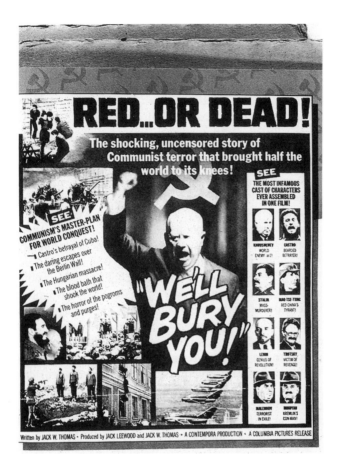

Plate 7 *We'll Bury You* (1962), a documentary film released by Columbia Pictures. USSR leader Nikita Khrushchev had used the phrase 'We'll bury you' with reference to the Soviet economy overhauling American capitalism as part of his boisterous debates with Richard Nixon in 1959. But in the atmosphere of the Cold War, a more sinister meaning was soon given to his comment leading to this remarkable anti-communist propaganda film

to be American, you no longer required a white-collar occupation; rather, a mortgaged home full of the latest appliances became the entry requirement. It is of little surprise, therefore, that social surveys consistently show most Americans think of themselves as middle class. In his study of a New Jersey working-class community, David Halle has shown how this worked for blue-collar workers.[187] Their rationalization of their status depended entirely on the division between work and home. In the former, typical working-class attitudes are held – 'we do the real work, bosses get paid for sitting down all day'. However, rather than leading to a class identification, this workplace identity was individualized to being a 'working man'.[188] Class identity was then freed to be linked to home and consumption – all Halle's workers thought they were middle class. Clearly for these workers communism could never be attractive, it could only be a threat to their middle-class homes. Mobilizing the American working class behind anti-communism was therefore never a major political problem during US hegemony.

But what of the rest of the 'Free World'? The theory of totalitarianism had two very different implications for relations with friendly governments in different parts of the world. In core countries, including recently defeated enemies, the theory justified US financial support to rebuild economies to keep the spectre of communism at bay. In the case of Western Europe this meant working with socialist or labour governments as long as they were anti-communist. American liberalism could live with European 'democratic socialism' because both opposed totalitarianism. But in Western Europe anti-communism was different from the USA version since it blended into long existing conflicts within the labour movements. The Cold War provided the opportunity for 'moderates' to rid themselves of 'radicals' and define for themselves a new respectability. Certainly the British Labour government was a leading proponent of isolating the USSR to precipitate the Cold War.[189] Initially the consumption levels enjoyed by American workers were unattainable by their counterparts in Western Europe. But they knew all about them through images of the good life purveyed by Hollywood. America as hegemon was showing, literally, what was possible. Hence while European political parties were protecting ordinary people from poverty through welfare policies in their new corporate states, these same people were striving for an 'American standard of living'. With high levels of economic growth in the 1950s and 1960s, the relative importance of public provision and private consumption was reversed in a process often referred to as Americanization. Eventually it was not Roosevelt's 'four freedoms' that united the USA and Western Europe but the Hoover Vacuum Cleaner Company's 'Fifth Freedom' announced in a 1944 advertising campaign: 'freedom of choice' meaning, in more recent parlance, 'shop 'til you drop'.[190]

The result was that when the USA came to dominate the world it was not through a 'global New Deal', as radical members of Roosevelt's administration had assumed in the 1940s, but rather by an internationalized version of Say's Law.[191] This controversial 'economic law' stated that supply would always find a demand; the 1930s disproved its applicability at the state level with massive under-consumption, but by the 1950s it seemed to be working at the international level. As T. J. McCormick has pointed out, it became generally assumed that 'maximising global production would maximise global consumption and per capita standards of living'.[192] In this way America could present a plausible hegemonic face to its allies that the American system was not self-serving but good for all who voluntarily embraced it.[193] This argument worked for Western Europe, but it did not for most of the rest of the world. For millions of people in Latin America, Africa and Asia, the promise of the good life was found to have strict geographical limits.

The second implication of the theory of totalitarianism is the reason why the term 'free world' has always had commas around it in this discussion. American ideals of freedom were not extended to non-core countries. In the so-called Third World, the allies of America were a very mixed bunch and included a large number of dictators whose power depended on their American-supplied army. Although nominally on the side of freedom in the great world contest, these dictators were often more repressive, and usually more bloody, than the 'real' opponents of freedom, the communist regimes. Having such 'not-wholly savory allies', as two apologists for the policy described them, was admittedly an embarrassment: 'All things being equal, Americans want to spread their values and domestic moral standards around the globe, and helping tyrants hardly advances the cause.'[194] However, by drawing a distinction between totalitarian and authoritarian regimes, 'friendly tyrants' were legitimated within a 'free world'. Unlike the totalitarian states, non-communist authoritarian government was deemed reformable: with proper policies directed towards them they would eventually see the error of their ways and become democracies.[195] Hence American foreign policy was based upon a stick-and-carrot theory of action for freedom: it was the stick for communist dictators and the carrot for dictators opposing communism. This is obviously as convenient a theory for US geopolitics as Orientalism was for British geopolitics a century earlier. In this case it was a simple codification of that old power political maxim that 'the enemy of my enemy is my friend'. Here, more than anywhere else, the Americans revealed themselves as very pragmatic democrats. This was so very hegemonic; hegemons have never been prisoners of their own ideologies of freedom.

Whither modern politics?

The downside of the American hegemonic cycle has begun and therefore the time is ripe to consider where modern politics is proceeding. This can be approached at two different levels. At a structural level, the political organization of the modern world-system seems to fit uneasily with the rampant globalization of the late 20th century. There is a large literature debating the demise of the state and we consider this matter in later chapters. All I will say here is that the existence of such a serious debate at this time is indicative of the real threat that state sovereignty is under. At a behavioural level, the political practices pioneered by the hegemons define a political development in the modern world-system that may also be under threat. Obviously the structural and behavioural are closely related but in what follows I will continue the discussion of this chapter by focusing on the contemporary prospects of the three key hegemonic contributions to modern politics.

The first point to make about the political practices is that there is little contemporary evidence that past hegemonic contributions are being eroded. There are many short-term political changes as we would expect in the first decades of a hegemonic decline but there is nothing more fundamental to report. For instance the relationship between state and civil society appears not to be at risk. Society uses the state, albeit in a variety of ways, in all contemporary states in the core of the world-economy. There appears to be no imminent state threat to civil society. This is very different to the 1920s and 1930s when states were eclipsing society in a majority of European countries. There continue to be threats to civil society in semi-peripheral countries, of course, but this is to be expected. This zone of the world-economy represents the area of greatest political conflict and will typically alternate between state domination, such as military regimes, and civil administrations. The recent history of Latin American politics bears this out, and we may expect some post-communist Eastern European countries to follow a similar sequence in the future. The important point is that there is no authoritarianism spreading from semi-periphery to the core as happened in the second quarter of this century. In fact quite the opposite is happening as democracy in the form of competitive elections has diffused across the world. Hence the hegemonic placing of civil society above the state is safe, for the time being at least.

At first sight, on looking outwards to the inter-state system, the contributions of the hegemons seems less firm, but this is not the case. The post-Cold War world seems to be a place of perennial crises. It is obviously true that the certainties of the Cold War are no more, but we have not moved into anything approaching systemic chaos as happened earlier in the century. Part of the problem today is that expectations were raised by a post-hegemonic USA and its promise of a New World Order in 1990. But the Americans can no longer deliver a world order. In the inevitable political turmoil following the demise of communism, the USA and its allies have acted more like fire-fighters and policemen rather than respected statesmen. This does not mean that past hegemonic constructions of a more pacified world are being diminished. The key point is that armed conflicts are being contained within international boundaries as recognized by the United Nations. Not only is violence localized, the political order represented by the boundaries is being respected. There has been one exception to the latter: the 1991 invasion of Kuwait by Iraq. Acting in traditional state style as a crude war machine, the Iraqi government attempted to solve their domestic problems by territorial aggrandizement. The ease with which the USA was able to get a large majority of states to support a United Nations' counter-invasion to reconstitute the status quo really proves the point. The rigidities of the Cold War may be gone, but the hegemonic contributions to a pacified world where states as simple war machines are 'outlawed' remains firmly in place.

The demise of communism has had an obvious effect upon the hegemonic practice of focusing on a free/unfree dichotomy. With no totalitarian foe, the 'free' – pragmatic democracy – has been able to claim victory in the battle of ideas but this leaves a lacuna in world politics. To be confident about our self-identity there is a need to define an Other that encapsulates what we are not. However this 'situation vacant' position has attracted candidates and two in particular stand out. First, 'Islamic fundamentalism', with in Western eyes its overt intolerance and disrespect for pluralism, is a ready-made replacement for communism as the archetypal unfree. Some commentators expect a future geopolitics to split along 'civilizational fractures' in what looks very much like a new Orientalism. Second, and much closer to 'home', there is a quite different challenge from those who would impose an ecological imperative on world politics that transcends state boundaries. Saving the planet as a living world marginalizes all other political concerns including democracy. We discuss the implications of both these potential 'others' in later chapters but to the degree that these challenges gain ground, it will be business as usual for the free as they continue the battle for their particular universal goals.

On the horizon, however, not all is rosy for the politics championed by the hegemons. As we have mentioned previously, we will argue that the USA is the last hegemonic state. This means there will be no state agent to renew modern politics after the current round of political competitions. If the hegemons define the main thread of political development in the modern world-system, it follows that this process is coming to an end. After the hegemons, all that may remain of the hegemonic legacy to world politics is the pragmatism without the ideals. Probably less hypocritical, definitely more dangerous, modern politics is sure of future fundamental change despite contemporary continuities.

Universality: what's good for the hegemon is good 3 for the world

Taking a long view of history there are two basic models of social change. In the modern world our thinking about change has been dominated by the idea of progress. But this is not how people in the other world-systems have viewed their history. Typically the past is interpreted as distinct epochs to which are attributed extreme characterizations: golden ages and dark ages. The crucial difference between the two seems to have been social stability. For any social system to work it needs the glue of shared values to hold it together. Without some commonly held beliefs about how to behave in the system and for what purpose, social turmoil is an inevitable result. But such 'social glue' has to be constructed and this has been the prime cultural role of 'universal empires'. Hence golden ages generally coincide with politically centralized world-systems when a single polity was able to impose a dominant culture which provided the norms of what we identify as 'civilization'. By providing peace and order, these eras of 'high' culture are marked out as golden ages to subsequent generations living in the less stable conditions of dark ages. Since the latter are typically periods of political fragmentation, it follows that this model of good and bad times correlates with cycles of decentralization and centralization. Extrapolating to the modern world-system, this argument implies that the coming of the inter-state system heralds a new dark age in which there is no place for civilization and its cultural universalism. But this is precisely where we should not extrapolate, since the modern world-system is a different type of social entity, a world-economy. As such it has generated a new 'social trick' for creating cohesion, a universality for a decentralized political era.

It is the thesis of this chapter that the emergence on to the world stage of a new social actor, the hegemonic state, has made possible the generation of 'golden ages' in a competitive states system. Although the political opposite of an imperium, as we argued in Chapter 1, in cultural terms the hegemon shares some crucial universalizing attributes with erstwhile world-empires. As the most successful capitalist state, the hegemon is able to promote its economic interests and in this way further capitalist values throughout the system. Of course, the state that is doing best out of capitalism will promote ideas that support its success. But in this multiple world of polities, why should other states necessarily take that much notice of this economically powerful neighbour? This is where the notion of hegemony is crucial: the hegemon is not merely the first among equals in the inter-state system, it is qualitatively different from its rivals. It is not just successful, it has cornered the market in success. As such it is in a unique position to define what works and what fails in social behaviour in the modern world-system. Hence its values can be projected not just as representing the interests of one state but of being universal in nature in true Gramscian mode. This is the ultimate mark of a hegemon. When a large enough proportion of the rest of the world accepts its ideas as universal ideas to define the very nature of the times, then we know we are in the high hegemony phase of a hegemonic cycle. Or in Gramscian terms: the ideas of the hegemonic state are the ruling ideas of the modern world-system.

The successful transmission of ideas involves two sets of actors, those propagating their message and those willing to receive it. Hegemons lead, above all, by example. All other states want to be as successful as the hegemon and so seek to emulate its behaviour to varying degrees. Hence there is a receptive audience out there trying to ape success. This process of emulation is the subject matter of the next chapter. Here I will concentrate upon the ways in which the hegemon projects its own interests as the world-economy's interests. The sub-title of this chapter is my 'globalization' of a famous American saying with unabashed hegemonic overtones: 'What's good for General Motors is good for America.' The ruling ideas of our century, America's hegemonic cycle, have been good to General Motors and their ilk just as similar universalisms suited both British and Dutch capitalist interests in their times.

There is a basic arrogance behind this conversion of one country's special interests into general world interests. It is only credible because of the nature of the hegemonic state. Its period of high hegemony is a time of supreme collective self-confidence. It seems the hegemon can succeed at whatever it turns its mind to. What is created is what we may term a 'can-do' society. This is the basic platform from which universalism is projected on to the rest of the world and is the subject matter of the first part of this chapter.

Universal ideas are awe inspiring. By definition hegemonic ways are what have worked, their very success has 'proven' their innate correctness. As holder of this 'truth' the hegemon has a duty to the rest of the world to disseminate the right ideas to those not yet enlightened. Hence agents of the hegemonic state have felt they have a mission to transmit the good news of their success for the benefit of the rest of the world. Such missions are the subject matter of the second part of this chapter. But we should not view the activities of the hegemon in simple idealistic terms. The hegemon achieved its exalted position through a series of very pragmatic policies and such concerns continue throughout its whole cycle. There is a fundamental contradiction at the heart of this hegemonic practice: looking after, literally, number one is never lost sight of in all the universalizing. The mission to the world is very much of this world and its materialist message creates a curious form of politics. Following our discussion of the hegemonic role in the creation of modern political practices in the last chapter, in the third section we focus upon political ideas and identify liberalism as the basic political ideology of the modern world-system. It is shown that liberalisms have been implicated in the projection of hegemonic power and thus can be directly related to the stages of development of the system described in Chapter 1. In a concluding section we introduce the process of embedding liberalism in which liberalism broadly conceived becomes integral to the idea of what it is to be a modern society.

The can-do society in a no-can-do world

In the late 1950s, contemporary observers of American society discovered a peculiar dilemma: 'the problem of problemness'. Ehrenreich quotes one newspaper editor as complaining: 'What are we to write about? All the problems are solved. All that is left are problems of technical adjustment.'[1] We can term this the ultimate problem of hegemony. In a similar vein, the two-time US Democratic presidential candidate (1952 and 1956), Adlai Stevenson, expressed his extravagant faith in the times:

> Science and technology are making the problems of today irrelevant in the long run . . . This is the basic miracle of technology . . . It is in a real sense a magic wand that gives us what we desire.[2]

Other periods of high hegemony brought similar expressions of faith in technology: 'We are capable of doing anything,' the young Queen Victoria is quoted as saying during her preview tour of the Great Exhibition at the Crystal Palace in 1851.[3] Even today we can recognize that she sounds just like a mid-20th-century American politician. According to Hyam, the decades 1838 to 1858 were 'great ones to be alive and British'.[4] A similar euphoric attitude has been identified in the United Provinces. Again using American-style language, one writer on 17th-century Amsterdam, for example, has described it as having 'a boom town atmosphere'.[5] Continuing with this rather appropriate language style, such situations can be termed 'can-do societies' defined by their immense self-confidence where anything seems possible once they set their mind (and resources) to it. Where does this leave the rest of the world? Lacking in the 'know-how' of the hegemon, other countries are incapable of reaching the hegemon's achievements, at least without the hegemon's expert assistance. This crude dichotomy of a can-do society in a no-can-do world is the starting point for considering hegemonic promotion of universal values.

A third 'world technology cluster'?

Before the modern world-system, universalizing projects generally followed the sword. The creators of empire took their cultural ideals with them into the field and as success built upon success their gods legitimated their expanding rule. The link between success and universalizing is maintained in our system, but the definition of success has changed. Although by no means unrelated, military prowess gives way to technological prowess as the basis for diffusing a general culture. The hegemon is the 'high-tech' champion of its age and this advantage is projected beyond politics and economics to define the leading world ideas.

No one country has ever had a monopoly of important inventions, but it has often been pointed out that innovations, the practical application of inventions, do cluster in both time and place. Hence, according to Joel Mokyr in his wide-ranging survey of 'technological creativity and economic progress', *The Lever of Riches*, 'The historical record of technological change is uneven and spasmodic'.[6] He cites the classic cases of the British industrial revolution and 20th-century American prowess in technology — sometimes known as the 'second industrial revolution' — in making this point. In choosing these examples of technological clusters Mokyr is being quite conventional in his relative neglect of earlier Dutch technological achievements.[7] In fact the very idea of a British industrial revolution presupposes no such technological change had occurred before: the Dutch have been largely written out of the script. It is important to our story here to understand that, as Israel describes it, in the 17th century Holland became 'the technical research laboratory of the western world'.[8] That is to say, the Dutch in their time were technology world leaders just like the other two hegemons. However, since 'so much ink has been spilled to explain why Holland did not industrialize that we tend to overlook the fact that it did do so', we need to elaborate briefly upon this claim.[9]

Returning to Mokyr's work, we find that although he has no place for the Netherlands in the organization of his text — they appear in a chapter on technology from 1500 to 1750 entitled 'The Renaissance and beyond' — their technological prowess nevertheless stands out as pivotal in his survey.[10] Describing the 17th-century Dutch as 'the *wunderkind* of Europe', he lists an impressive catalogue of innovations matched only by the later British and Americans.[11] In order of appearance these are: the Dutch plough, the new windmill, the *Hollander* paper-maker, ship top masts, peat-based manufacture (bricks, madder dye, salt, bread, bleach, and tiles), new ships (the flute and buss), the telescope, trigonometric triangulation for mapmaking, the Dutch loom for making ribbons and Delft tile enamel wares imitating Chinese porcelain.[12] Here indeed was the 'first' industrial revolution and its identification as such requires a renumbering of the British and American revolutions as the second and third examples of such rapid spurts of technological change.

Part of the recognition problem for the Dutch industrial revolution is the image of industry and technology derived from the later British achievements. The Dutch excelled in a different form of engineering: 'Holland became the centre of the wood mechanical era'.[13] This is clearly illustrated by the large industrial district of Zaanstreek to the north of Amsterdam. This was a wholly new centre of economic growth that used a radically improved windmill to provide the motive power creating a new scale of manufacture.[14] As well as the traditional milling of grains into flour, the new technology expanded into very many types of mill to make, among other things, papers, dyes from both wood and minerals, hemp, snuff, pepper, mustard and paper. All of these uses involved crushing material, but the most important innovation was the creation of sawmills. Powerful saws produced cheap and regularly shaped planks which in turn were the basis for Europe's largest and state-of-the-art shipbuilding industry. By mid-century the Dutch shipyards were producing over 2000 sea-going ships annually plus of course the barges for the canal transport system.[15] In the case of the latter, Mokyr notes that, 'The Dutch shipbuilding industry led the movement towards specialization, building at least 39 different types of canal and river boats alone.'[16] But the most important shipbuilding innovation was the flute, which in these most modern yards was cheap to build and, crucially, was also very cheap to operate. Combining small crews with large cargoes, the Dutch could undercut their rivals by between 30% and 50% in the carrying trade. Clearly, we should not underestimate the technological prowess and production successes of the Dutch in their period of hegemony.

Having confirmed the Netherlands as a world technology cluster, we have provided the basis of their can-do society alongside those of Britain and the USA. In the remaining parts of this section, we present three cameo sketches of audacious achievements that epitomize the immense self-confidence of these very special societies. For the Dutch we continue our consideration of the windmill, but on this occasion we highlight the unprecedented scale of their land reclamation. For the British we turn to the Great Exhibition of 1851 which, as an international exhibition, was itself a new invention but whose main attribute was showcasing the hegemon's technological leadership. Finally, for the Americans, we choose the Apollo Project, that most spectacular of all technological feats — putting a man on the moon. The crucial point about all three cases is that no other country at the time could have replicated their success: only the Dutch could produce so much from the sea; only the British could have brought all the other countries of the world together to show their inferiority; only the Americans could set a timetable for space travel and keep it. Here we get a real sense of the basic hegemonic mood that 'anything is possible'.

'God made the world but the Dutch made Holland'

Simon Schama has shown that during the 80-year struggle for independence the Dutch thought of themselves fighting two wars simultaneously against the 'tyrant' Hapsburgs and the 'tyrant' sea.[17] The parallelism of these battles on two fronts against ocean and absolutism focused on the winning of strategic territory to extend and consolidate the land that was the new state. The final defeat of the most powerful empire in Europe was impressive but no less so than the great reclamation projects of the time converting sea into farmland.

The building of dikes and reclamation was not new to Western Europe, of course, but the medieval practice largely terminated about 1350 only to begin slowly again after 1500.[18] Technology kept all such schemes small scale until the late 16th century. Originally the draining was by gravity and although windmills had been introduced in the 13th century by crusaders returning from the middle east, their application to drainage was very inefficient and hence limited. However a key Netherlands innovation in the late 16th century completely changed the potential of wind-driven water pumps. The invention of the moveable cap meant that sails could be larger and the mill built taller.[19] The 'can-do' society of the United Provinces converted this new potential into a successful investment explosion in creating new land, some 200 000 acres in the period from 1590 to 1640.[20] Whereas before 1590 the instigators of reclamation had been the landed nobility and the Crown, now it was the burghers who were investing in the making of farmland: land reclamation schemes became 'thoroughly capitalist undertakings'.[21]

The great reclamation schemes of the early 17th century were a classic example of the successful combination of capital with technology. The process was personified by the partnership of the Amsterdam director of the East India Company Dirk van Oss and the great civil engineer Jan Adrianszoon Leeghwater.[22] Their largest project was at Beemster begun in 1607 and resulting in over 30 000 acres of new land pumped dry by 42 windmills in 1612.[23] To accomplish this end, van Oss had to attract capital and, with the help of the Republic's chief minister Johan van Olden-barnevelt, persuaded 123 investors to come up with the huge sum of almost one and a half million guilders. They were well rewarded. In the first year after draining, the polder was divided into 207 new farms which paid a total rent of a quarter of a million guilders for a first dividend of 17%.[24] But the project was more than a quick return on capital. By 1640 it constituted a large rural community with three schools, two wharfs, corn mill, church and village hall. In addition wealthy Amsterdammers, including van Oss, were building luxurious villas as new family country seats. With the rapidly growing urban population such polders were necessary for feeding the city dwellers. Hence the new nearby lands supplemented the grain trade from the Baltic with local market-garden and dairy products. Demand was, of course, greatest in Amsterdam, and in the region to the north of the city farm land was increased by 40%.[25] The growing city was matched by a growing rural production, the source of the investors' return on their capital.

The mark of a can-do society is the self-confidence it has in its capacity to go beyond what had previously been thought possible. In fact the project does not necessarily have to be a success; enterprise can sometimes be even better illustrated by outlandish plans that never come to fruition. This is the case with the Dutch reclaimers. After Beemster, Leeghwater proposed the draining of Harlemmermeer, a huge project involving hundreds of windmills to drain over 75 000 acres.[26] Although a consortium was set up, it was unable to attract the huge three and a half million guilders of risk capital that was required. The drainage had to wait two centuries and for a different technology, the coming of steam pumps, but it does show the audacity of Dutch engineers with only windmills to work with.

At Beemster and other successful reclamation schemes the Dutch were quite literally creating their own country. While winning land militarily from Spain in the south and east, they were simultaneously enlarging their land area by reclamation in the north and west. It was the latter that was very special. Armed conquest was nothing new but actually creating your own state territory was. In medieval times land drained had not had the same feudal restrictions placed on it, and Dutch independent republicanism is sometimes traced back to this circumstance.[27] In the 17th century the surge in reclamation made the whole state unique. As the Dutch saying goes: 'God made the world, but the Dutch made Holland.' In other words other states may have received their land directly from God, but the Dutch used their God-given skills to create their land.[28] This was the ultimate expression of the can-do society in a no-can-do world.

The geopolitics of the Great Exhibition

The idea of an exhibition of wares and wonders was not a British invention. That honour must go to the France of Napoleon who used such exhibitions to promote French commodities on the world market. In fact the original proposal for an exhibition in London in 1851 was to be a 'British Exhibition of National Design and Manufacture', as a direct copy of what had become a French series of such events. The organizers even visited the Paris *Exposition* in 1849 as part of their planning.[29] But the British product was to become a very different sort of national showcase. Rather than keeping the rest of the world out of their exhibition, the British invited them in and used them to highlight the technological leadership of Britain. R. F. Jordan describes it thus:

> The international character of the Great Exhibition was not due to any enlightened interest in foreigners; on the contrary it was a patronizing and Philistine gesture from a Herren Volk, fearless of competition.[30]

Hence it is the British who invented the *international* exhibition. This is the mark of a hegemon and its can-do spirit – to take an existing idea, even that of a rival country, and transform it to such an extent that it comes to symbolize what is unique about the hegemon.

The Great Exhibition of 1851 symbolized many things, but at the very centre of its meaning was the portrayal of Britain as a very special place in the world. Officially called 'The Great Exhibition of Industry of all Nations', the exhibits were arranged to make 'British eminence perfectly clear' to all visitors:

> 'the exhibition layout essentially balkanized the rest of the world, projecting a kind of geopolitical map of the world half occupied by England, half occupied by a collection of principalities vying for leftover space.[31]

The contents of the exhibits justified to visitors this extreme spatial inequity.[32] The western half of the building was reserved for British exhibits where the full fruits of its industrial revolution were on display. At its centre was the great hydraulic press in the Machinery Court that left visitors in awe of the technology that Britain had developed.[33] In contrast the east end of the building which was allocated to the rest of the world was a disappointing menagerie.[34] Visitors could gasp at the beauty of French porcelain, inspect elegant Spanish firearms and quaint Austrian toys or they could wonder at the Tunisian bazaar and the carved ivory furniture and fabled Koh-i-noor diamond from India, but it was only too clear that they were all qualitatively different from what Britain had to offer. In the contest between the exotic and enterprise, those leaving the show would have no doubts who had won. Britain through the enterprise of its people was truly the incomparable centre of the world.[35]

The Great Exhibition was more than a collection of exhibits, the building that housed it was very much part of the mystique of British technology being projected. The great iron and glass building covered almost 19 acres enclosing some 33 million cubic feet; it has even been suggested that 'the sheer size of the Great Exhibition of 1851 was its most impressive feature'.[36] It was dubbed the 'Crystal Palace' by *The Times* and the name stuck to symbolize the uniqueness of this place that was the 'crystal focus of the world'.[37] Other countries had long had their great palaces but there had never been a building such as this one. And the manner in which it came about only enhanced the can-do image of mid-Victorian Britain.

Although the exhibition was to open on 1 May 1851, the Royal Commission to oversee the operation was only formed in early 1850. The architect of the revolutionary building, Joseph Paxton, only met the Commission's Building Committee in June with less than a year to go to opening day.[38] Paxton was a builder in iron and glass for greenhouses in stately house gardens and he determined on the same model at a far greater scale, a glass palace no less. Given nine days to design the building, he completed detailed specifications on time, including 3300 iron columns, 2150 girders and 293 655 panes of glass. Builders took possession of the site on 30 July 1850 and the main structure of the building covering nineteen acres was completed by the end of the year. Panes of glass were being fixed at the rate of 18 000 panes a week.

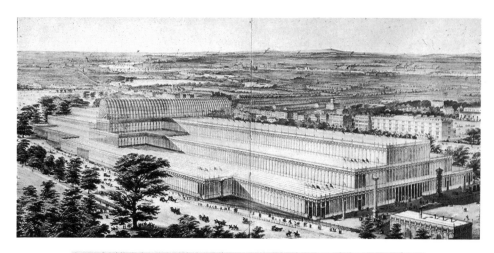

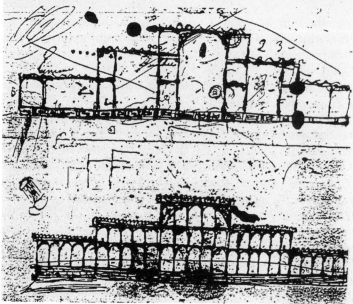

Plate 8 *The Crystal Palace*. A unique construction of its age, it was designed and built in less than a year. The main picture, from the exhibition's illustrated catalogue, shows the huge scale of the building which was ready for the opening of the Great Exhibition on 1 May 1851. The rough sketch is Joseph Paxton's famous 'doodle' on blotting paper at an unrelated business meeting on 15 June 1850 which he transformed into plans for the building and delivered to London on 22 June. Notice that the right end of the building closely corresponds to the 'doodle', which is in the South Kensington Museum

Glaziers were followed by painters and then came the joiners who in the first months of 1851 built eleven miles of stalls ready to display 100 000 exhibits. These exhibits arrived from all over the world over a period of three months and each was channelled to its correct place in the stalls. On 1 May 30 000 people assembled for the opening ceremony with Queen Victoria, Prince Albert and the Archbishop of Canterbury in a unique building 1848 feet long, 408 feet wide and varying from 64 to 108 feet high.[39] From levelling the site to completing a building organized into a geopolitical map of the world took just nine months. This was a can-do society at work: the construction was as much a wonder as the marvelled building itself.

Shooting for the Moon

We could say that, figuratively speaking, the hegemon as can-do society develops technology and 'shoots for the moon'; the US did this literally. From windmills to steam engines to space rockets the technology gaps may seem tremendous, but we find the same basic attitude of mind with programmes devised to take technology to its limit. Perhaps the most outstanding example of all was the Apollo programme. Like the British and their Great Exhibition, the Americans were following in the footsteps of their great rival. In the early 1960s the USSR had a definite lead in the space race with a number of crucial firsts including first orbital satellite and first man in space. But like a good hegemon, as soon as it committed its mind and resources to the project, the USA was able to take the lead and win the big prize – landing a man on the moon. This was what space travel was all about – going to other worlds – and just as the Crystal Palace eclipsed all previous French *Expositions* so Neil Armstrong's first step on the moon relegated Russian achievements in space to the second division.

The decision to set up the Apollo Project combines some of the audacity of Dutch drainage engineers with the ad hocery of the British creation of a Crystal Palace. Before John Kennedy's presidency there really was no space race with the Soviet Union. The USA maintained a clear military lead in missile strength and its leaders were uncertain about how to interpret Soviet achievements in space. Kennedy realized that the issue was more than a practical question; it impinged directly on America's position as world leader. It was what Theodore Sorensen called 'the world-wide political and psychological impact of the space race' that particularly interested Kennedy.[40] Quite simply, the USA could not afford to neglect this most visible area of advanced technology: it was not possible to be first on Earth and second in space.[41]

Kennedy had used the 'space gap' in his criticism of the Eisenhower administration during the presidential campaign of 1960, and he made good his promise to do something about it when he entered the Oval Office in 1961. The space budget for 1962 exceeded all pre-1961 budgets combined.[42] But it was more than resources that was needed; what was to be the purpose? The USA was starting late in the race and was clearly and substantially behind. America had shot its first astronaut into space in 1961 but Commander Alan Shepherd had merely gone up and come down; Yuri Gagarin had earlier orbited the Earth. Soviet leader Khrushchev had teased America with an evolutionary analogy: whereas the USSR had reached the stage of flying

Plate 9 *Conquering other worlds*. The USA 'won' the space race by planting the Stars and Stripes on the Moon. Although an American achievement, the rhetoric was consummately universal in nature: on climbing down to the Moon's surface, Neil Armstrong caught the mood of his world-wide television audience by announcing 'one small step for man' (Hulton Deutsch)

insects, the USA was still only jumping.[43] The hegemon was being mocked by its greatest rival but not for long. Kennedy asked for a report on different levels of space achievement to judge where the USA might safely be able to overtake the USSR. The answer was that in near space the Russians would be hard to compete with, but moon shots were another item altogether. This led to the audacious commitment by the president at a special second State of the Union Address in May 1961 to land a man on the moon and return him to Earth 'before this decade is out'.[44] The fact that a Moon programme could not be justified on scientific grounds was beside the point; this was hegemonic bombast. In the president's own words: 'No single space project will be more impressive for mankind.'[45]

With this clear focus, the personal support of the president and with Vice-President Lyndon Johnson in charge of a revitalized National Space Council, the Apollo project was a huge technological success. The first time in history human beings physically left Earth was on Apollo 8 which reached lunar orbit on Christmas Eve 1968. But the big prize was still to be claimed.[46] When Apollo 11 took off for the first Moon landing six months later success seemed inevitable – America could do anything. Of course that was the point: the Apollo Project was always more than a technological exercise. To be sure it confirmed American scientific pre-eminence but the goal was always much broader: to strengthen American world leadership.[47] This it achieved in two ways. First as an event, the landing on the moon televised across the world was the great adventure of the century, and it was an American taking 'one giant step for man'.[48] Second, this American achievement had captured the world's imagination in the one area where there had been doubts about US pre-eminence. After the defeat of the Soviets in the race to the Moon, there could be no doubt which country was the true can-do society of the 20th century.

The medium of universality

World hegemony implies more than simply a special technological ability. If the can-do society is to reach out to the rest of the world, its achievements must be suitably packaged not just for the here and now but in epochal terms that relate to all humanity. In their tongue-in-cheek assertion that God made the world but they were responsible for Holland, the Dutch were interpreting their achievements as going beyond the Creation. Such blasphemy points towards a later secular modernity, but even in our times it strikes us as an audacious claim to parade before the world. The British claim is slightly more modest: their 'industrial revolution' was offered as the second great transformation in social organization equivalent to the 'agricultural revolution' of several millennia earlier. The Americans 'go over the top' in their definition of extra-specialness. Walter McDougall argues that landing on the Moon defines a 'Space Age' that goes beyond both industrial and agricultural revolutions to something unique for humanity.[49] He draws a geological analogy: travelling in space is 'another cleavage in natural history' equivalent to the Devonian 'amphibian revolution' when sea creatures first colonized the land.[50] What wonderful hyperbole; drawing such parallels with the past enables the hegemons to set their contemporary pretensions in a suitable epochal context. There was nothing mundane about can-do technology; it provides the foundations for new universalisms.

Hegemons have been enthusiastic purveyors of the good news of their superiority to the rest of the world. They have often used the religious language of 'missions' and 'crusades', but the spiritual has not been a central plank in hegemonic messages for the world. Rather a secular universalism has been invented wherein the particular interests of the hegemon are cloaked in the language of general principles. The self-confidence of a can-do society is translated into a certainty in prescriptions for the no-can-do remainder of humanity. Hence the creation of a universal body of ideas for all.

Although the leaders of all three hegemons were no doubt sincere Christians in their personal beliefs, they did not develop their political projects within the intellectual confines of Christendom. This is most important in the case of the Dutch since their hegemony marked the transition from a world image of a Christendom surrounded by unbelievers to be converted to one of Europe surrounded by a world of economic opportunities. This was well understood by contemporaries. In 1651 Benjamin Worsley, in discussing English trading problems, complained that 'just as Spain aimed at "the universal monarchy of Christendom", so the Dutch had "aimed to lay a foundation to themselves for ingrossing the universal trade, not only of Christendom, but indeed of the greater part of the known world" '.[51] Ten years later another English critic of the Netherlands, Sir William Temple, referred to the Dutch as 'citizens of the world' which really sums up the Netherlands at its most pretentious.[52] In many ways this title, and its associated arrogance, was effectively claimed later by both the British and the Americans at their respective peaks. To be thus recognized presupposes not just economic leadership but a cultural pervasiveness, including an important moral dimension, that only a hegemon can fully generate in the modern world-system.

In the very different contexts of the three hegemonies, the medium of universality varied but the same basic format prevailed. We illustrate this below by focusing upon the intellectual universalisms that the hegemons created to understand the new social worlds they were in the process of making. All three produced very powerful theoretical frameworks that codified hegemonic practice as universal laws. Although by no means original to the hegemon – they adopted and adapted many earlier ideas of their rivals – it is only when the intellectuals of the hegemon create their theoretical structures that the ideas come to dominate social thought and epitomize their hegemony.

In the case of the Dutch, the medium in which they made their intellectual mark was jurisprudence. Deriving from medieval and Renaissance scholarship, the Dutch were responsible for bringing it up to date as it were. In other words they made jurisprudence relevant to the modern world. For the Dutch the main intellectual task was to counter an existing universality, Roman Christian thought, with an alternative general scheme of principles in keeping with needs of the new world-economy. The result was a philosophical legitimation of Dutch activities in the world as a universalism based on past authorities but relating to a completely new ideal world.[53] In our discussion below we introduce the ideas of the classic Dutch jurist Hugo Grotius (1583–1643). A member of the first generation to be born in an independent Netherlands, Grotius was a child prodigy chosen to accompany a Dutch diplomatic mission to the French court at the age of just 15 and famously introduced to the King as 'the miracle of Holland'.[54] Working for the young Dutch state in the first half of his career, he seemed to be destined for political leadership until caught up in religious conflict which led to his arrest and eventual exile in Paris. It was here he composed the work for which he is most well known. A true cosmopolitan, in the latter part of his life he acted as a diplomat for Sweden.

For the British, their medium of universalism was political economy. Although the French *économistes* were the leading formulators of early economic thought, it was in Britain that the school of political economy emerged that was definitively to replace mercantilist ideas, representing particular vested interests, by the 'hidden hand' of the market. This universal institution gave favours to none but the efficient, who in the 19th century just happened to be the British. In our discussion below we will consider the efforts of Richard Cobden to propagate the gospel of free trade beyond Britain's borders. Cobden was a Manchester manufacturer and leader of the Anti-Corn Law movement, the crucial political lobby whose success set in train the free-trade era of the mid-19th century. We will follow Cobden from the heart of can-do England on his mission to Europe to sell his political-economy universalism.

For the Americans, the medium of universality for understanding their social world was social science. By the 20th century the holistic approach of political economy had become unfashionable, and its core concerns had been reduced to the discipline of economics. Although there were many differences between old political economy and new economics, they shared a belief in universal economic laws. Universalism lived on, extended beyond economic relations. Economics was one of a set of social sciences, the two other main members being sociology and political science. The self-proclaimed purpose of all three was to produce general laws of social behaviour in the same way that natural sciences produced laws covering their physical subject matter. This was the universalism in social thinking that the USA as hegemon promoted. It described a world of social, economic and political systems with models purporting to predict how societies, all societies, and their component parts worked. In our discussion below we describe the attempted production of one such general model that would predict dissent in poor countries. This 'Project Camelot', with its hegemonic self-confidence in its ability to encompass all societies in the world through a family of general models, for a brief moment represented the apex of social science.

Secularized jurisprudence, political economy and social science, although very different in content, are remarkably similar in their intellectual roles as projections of hegemony.

The jurist's universalism of Hugo Grotius

In his Cambridge lectures nearly a century ago, John Figgis argued that the Netherlands in their heyday became 'the University of Europe'. Excepting the achievements of Francis Bacon, Figgis argued that if Dutch intellectuals are removed from the history of ideas in the first half of the 17th century 'the European record is barren instead of fertile'.[55] The legal scholar and diplomat Hugo de Groot was a major figure in this 'great source of intellectual and moral enlightenment'.[56] Following the custom of his time, he Latinized his name to Grotius. This should not divert us from recognizing his importance as a fundamentally modern intellectual, the person normally credited with being the 'father' of international law.[57] His writings on jurisprudence dominated political theory in Europe for over a century by providing the intellectual framework for engaging with issues of war and diplomacy.[58] Given that most of Grotius's ideas are recycled from existing treatises, his domination of this crucial field of social understanding has often been viewed as surprising. There are two reasons why this should not be so. First, previous writers had been closely tied to the theological schisms of the period, whereas Grotius incorporated Dutch tolerance with a new rationalism to appeal beyond religious disputes, especially in northern Europe.[59] Second, his focus on war and peace meant that he provided guidelines for the most important issue of his times.[60]

Grotius was born in the late 16th century and therefore lived through a period of astounding political upheaval not just in his homeland but throughout Europe. With the demise of feudalism leading to the emergence of new centralized states and with the rise of Protestantism, the traditional universal authority in Europe based upon Papacy and Holy Roman Empire was shattered. In this confused legal world Grotius's 'great accomplishment was to reaffirm the persistent notion of universalism'.[61] The destruction of Roman Catholic universalism provided a licence for warfare within Christendom that was unprecedented. In earlier times of Christian unity there were common rights and duties recognized in opposition to Turk and Moor, but now Christianity was turned against itself. The believer versus infidel contest was internalized as neither Catholics nor Protestants respected each other's Christian credentials. A new non-religious definition of rights and duties was required that was relevant to the emerging inter-state system. Grotius created a new modern universalism by basing it upon international society rather than Christendom.

We can begin to appreciate the scale of Grotius's intellectual achievement by comparing his contribution to other 'founding fathers' of modern politics. What we find is that only in Grotius can we see the full development of the modern state in terms of both internal and external relations. The two classic 16th-century interpretations of the new political world that was replacing the feudal order were those of Niccolo Machiavelli and Jean Bodin. Neither could conceive of an international order above the state. Machiavelli in fact presumed anarchic relations between rulers. In his *The Prince* of 1513, he proposed the ruler be a law unto himself, resulting in unrestrained competition between rulers. With no rules except self-interest governing relations, there could be no concept of universal values.[62] Jean Bodin, in his *Six Books of the State* of 1576, was concerned to justify centralization of the new state structures that were being created and argued that sovereignty was embodied in the ruler. Unlike Machiavelli, he did subject the ruler to a higher authority in that he was accountable to divine law and custom and tradition. But as the agent of divine will, the ruler was only accountable for his actions within the state. Hence there was still no system of rules for accountability among sovereigns.[63] Enter Grotius. As Machiavelli reflected the incessant warring between the city-states of his Italy and Boden codified the centralization of his France, Grotius was equally influenced by the political context in which he wrote. He had to make sense of political authority in the new United Provinces where all relations in the highly decentralized state structure seemed like international relations.

Drawing by convention on classical and Christian sources as well as more recent Renaissance writings, Grotius argued for different tiers of authority in the political turmoil of the first half of the 17th century. In his *magnum opus* of 1625, *On The Law of War and Peace*, he argued that individual states did not constitute separate 'universal societies' but were practical political divisions of humanity.[64] Therefore there were two levels of law, civil law and law of nations or *ius gentium*. In Roman Law the latter originally applied to private law as opposed to public law, with particular reference to the regulation of the customs of people in the empire who were not Roman citizens. It had evolved to mean law common *within* many nations, but with Grotius it became the law governing relations *between* nations and therefore the basis for international law.[65] Hence we arrive at the idea of rights and duties for rulers, universal obligations that constitute a higher law under which sovereign power existed. For this to be effective there had to be a clear definition of which 'divisions of humanity' could be juridical persons within this area of law. In other words territorial sovereignty was reaffirmed. It is with Grotius that 'territorialism . . . becomes an integral part of the system of International Law'.[66] This accounts for his very strict rulings on the conditions when resistance to a sovereign is legitimate which, perhaps, are surprising for a Dutch theorist. Figgis memorably commented that Grotius's 'definition of the cases in which resistance is justified is so narrow that it may be doubted whether any case but that of the Netherlands ever fell within it'.[67] Inviolate territorial states may not be universal societies in their own right, but they were the basic building blocks of the new international law as envisaged by Grotius.[68]

In the preface of *On The Law of War and Peace* the author expressed his abhorrence at the terrible atrocities in the religious wars of his times.[69] Obviously the pen is unable to quell the sword at a stroke, and the Thirty Years War was to continue in all its savagery for two more decades. But his work was widely recognized as pointing towards a way of bringing some order to international anarchy. We know that the Swedish king Gustav Adolphus carried a copy of the book with him everywhere and is even reported to have slept with it under his pillow during his great military campaigns.[70] (Given the social anarchy generated in Germany by these campaigns, this is perhaps not the best recommendation for the new ideas!) Grotius died before peace came to Europe, but his ideas were influential with the peace makers. Although the details of the Peace of Westphalia were not exactly consistent with his writings, nevertheless we can agree with Hedley Bull in his assessment that 'in the broad impact on the course of international history the theory of Grotius and the practice of the Peace of Westphalia marched together'.[71] This makes him, according to Hedley Bull, the 'intellectual father' of 'international society'.[72]

In Chapter 1 we mentioned that the Dutch pioneered the right to sail through the concept of freedom of the seas. This derived from earlier writings of Grotius, and we will use this here to illustrate his secular derivation of universalism. In his 1609 pamphlet *Mare Liberum*, Grotius provided the principles for what we today call the Law of the Sea.[73] This work was written to justify Dutch trading in the East Indies against Portuguese monopolistic claims. He based his whole argument on the existence of a universal human society.[74] From this he derived two conclusions: first, the sea cannot be occupied and therefore cannot be property; and second, the sea (like the air) is limitless and cannot be possessed and therefore is common to all.[75] Using these general arguments, Grotius justified Dutch navigation and commerce in Asia and later Dutch fishing off the English coast. It is hard for us today to understand how revolutionary these universal pronouncements were, but at the time he was writing 'closed waters' were the norm: Venice lay claim to the Adriatic, Denmark and Sweden disputed the Baltic, England claimed the seas around her shores and Spain and Portugal had huge claims, the Pacific Ocean plus Gulf of Mexico and Indian Ocean plus South Atlantic respectively.[76] These particular claims based on criteria such as proximity, strategic necessity, conquest, discovery and even Papal award were all swept away by Grotius's universal law. This remains a classic case of the interests of one country being equated with the general interest. We shall leave the last word to Grotius. In a quintessentially hegemonic statement in *Mare Liberum* he urges his fellow Dutch: 'Arise, O nation unconquered on the sea, and fight boldly, not only for your own liberty, but for that of the human race.'[77]

Richard Cobden and political economy universalism

It has often been pointed out that there was a 70-year delay from the publication of Adam Smith's *Wealth of Nations* to the repeal of the Corn Laws in 1846 which is taken to symbolize Britain embracing free trade. Why the time lag? We can scotch two possible causes straightaway: Smith was never an isolated scholar with little influence, nor was his work an 'ivory tower pursuit' with little practical application. Smith soon found a major disciple in France, Jean Baptiste Say, and his ideas were widely taught in German universities by 1800.[78] But it was in Britain that, as we might expect, he had greatest impact. A school of political economy developed, including such leading figures as Thomas Malthus and David Ricardo, which set out to perfect the science that Smith had founded. Although the new economists made important theoretical contributions, they were always concerned to go beyond their academic discipline and inform the practical economic problems of the day.[79] Ricardo, for instance, dealt with monetary theory and policy in response to the inflationary pressures consequent on the war against Napoleonic France.[80] Political economists certainly achieved political respect for their work, but implementation was not immediately forthcoming. We can see why in another policy area where Ricardo made important contributions, trade policy. As the first major theorist to separate international from intra-national econ- omic transactions, Ricardo developed a theory of the distribution of the national product among rents, profits and wages that argued the 'artificial' (ie tariff protected) high price of corn raised wages and therefore depressed profits to the detriment of capital accumulation.[81] His policy prescription of free trade would lead, he subse- quently argued, to efficient specialization across the whole international trading sys- tem. Although presented as 'scientific', it was, of course, highly political. All changes in economic policy produce winners and losers: in this case the major losers would be the immensely powerful landowning class.[82] Clearly, providing prescriptions for pol- icy would not be enough; there was a major political battle to be won. This was the task taken up so enthusiastically by the Anti-Corn Law League under the leadership of Richard Cobden. They never doubted the truth of political economy; their job was to persuade government to implement this natural system of economic behaviour.

The political task was daunting because of the conservative role of Britain in its victorious world war. Prior to the war the influence of Adam Smith seemed to be spreading in the world of policy making. The prime minister, Pitt the Younger, considered himself to be a disciple of Smith's, and in 1786 the Eden Treaty was signed which lowered tariffs with Britain's major trading partner, France.[83] This treaty was to become an early victim of the great war with France. The world war was fought economically as well as military so that by 1815 tariffs were higher than those criticized by Smith in the 18th century. In addition a new Corn Law in that year effectively prevented imports of grain. This reflected the domestic ascendency of the Tories during the war and their power base within the landowning classes. Hence although British hegemony is dated from world war victory in 1815, this conservative domestic political situation delayed the pursuit of hegemonic economic policies. Trade was liberalized in the 1820s through tariff reductions and bilateral reciprocity treaties, but it was not until Robert Peel's government in 1841 that major policy changes occurred: further reductions in tariffs culminated in the 1846 repeal of the Corn Laws.[84]

The triumph for the Anti-Corn Law League in 1846 vindicated the great political agitation for change. The tactics of the League had been to emphasize the national interest in repealing the Corn Laws, eschewing any broader appeals for foreign support. In this way Tory opponents were deprived of sole use of the nationalist card in the debates.[85] Once the Corn Laws were repealed the situation was completely changed and the international implications of the reform were embraced, especially by Richard Cobden.

As a result of his successful activities in the Anti-Corn Law League, Cobden had developed a huge reputation across Europe. He had, as one biographer has put it, 'captured the European imagination'.[86] And so he embarked on his triumphant European tour of 1846–7 proclaiming grandly that 'I will be an ambassador from the free-traders of England to the governments of the great nations of the continent'.[87] This was perhaps one of the most remarkable journeys in history. The economist J. A. Hobson has quite aptly called it a 'triumphant progress' like a conquering hero returning home.[88] The tour took Cobden through France, Spain, Italy, Austria, Prussia, Russia and back to England via Hamburg. Everywhere he was fêted with parades and banquets and he had audiences with the kings of France, Naples, Sardinia and Prussia as well as with the leading statesmen Metternich and von Humboldt – and all for a private individual who wanted to talk about economics![89] This was, of course, no abstract theorist. Here was a crusader for a new world, an industrial order modelled on Britain where free trade was but the first step to an internationalism where peace would be the norm. In this ideal liberal world of free-trading states there would no longer be any need for war. This was the same universalism propagated just four years later by the Great Exhibition which was promoted as a festival of peace as a consequence of technological success and industrial progress.[90]

Cobden's crusade was not an immediate political success, however, and he returned to Britain disappointed. This only betrayed his overblown expectations:

> Cobden's initial confidence that Europe would adopt free trade . . . sprang from a strong, widely shared conviction that the teachings of contemporary, orthodox British economists, including free trade, were scientifically exact, universally applicable and demanded assent.[91]

He did, however, make one very crucial contact. During his European tour in 1846 at the Paris banquet in his honour he met Michel Chevalier. Chevalier was an ardent free trader and after 1852 became an adviser to Emperor Napoleon III. When tensions between Britain and France increased in 1859 Cobden put this contact to good use.

Although officially on a private visit to Paris, Cobden travelled with the British government's authority to explore the possibility of a commercial treaty with France. The French had prohibitively high tariffs on imports at this time, but Cobden's motives were as much to do with peace as with trade. He wrote to Chevalier that the increasing belligerence in Europe was 'not in harmony with the spirit of the age'.[92] In his audience with the emperor he argued that a commercial treaty was the only reliable basis for an *entente cordiale* between their two countries.[93] Although he argued typically that 'Free Trade is God's diplomacy', his concern for peace overcame his free-trader's distrust for commercial treaties with their usual exclusionary character.[94] However, he assured his chief supporter in the Cabinet, William Gladstone the Chancellor of the Exchequer, that his negotiations were based upon 'sound principles of political economy' and proceeded finally to produce the first bilateral treaty concerned with more than simple bilateral effects.[95] After giving the French minister of state 'the first lessons of political economy', he concluded a deal that applied the most-favoured nation clause whereby any future negotiated reduction of tariffs to either one of the countries was automatically extended to the other country.[96] In this way liberalization of trade was made a cumulative process.

Cobden realized the importance of the treaty he had negotiated. He wrote triumphantly to his political ally Henry Richard that it had 'virtually knocked on the head the whole European protective system'.[97] He was to be proved correct in his assessment. Within the next decade France was to sign similar treaties with Belgium, Austria, the German *Zollverein*, Switzerland, Italy, Denmark and Sweden. In addition these countries signed further treaties with each other. Liberalizing trade had certainly come to be part of the spirit of the age. Even Russia and Spain moved towards some liberalization. Something approaching free trade had finally arrived in the 1860s under British tutelage, albeit some decades late for the hegemon to gain full benefit.

We will leave the last word on political economy universalism to an opponent of Britain's hegemonic project. As an architect of the German customs union, the *Zollverein* set up in 1834, the economist Friedrich List supported tariffs to protect 'infant' German industry and considered contemporary political economy 'the English trick': 'It is a very common clever device that anyone who has attained the summit of greatness, he kicks away the ladder.' His contemporary understanding of British hegemony and its political-economy legitimation is unimpeachable. This is his interpretation in 1840:

> How vain do the efforts of those appear to us who have striven to found their universal dominion on military power compared with the attempt of England to raise her entire territory into one immense manufacturing, commercial and maritime city and to become among the countries and kingdoms of the earth that which a great city is in relation to its surrounding territory . . . A world's metropolis which supplies all nations with manufactured goods and supplies herself in exchange from every nation with those raw materials and agricultural products . . . The world has not been hindered in its progress but immeasurably aided in it by England . . . But ought we on that account to wish that she may erect a universal dominion on the ruins of other nations?[98]

DAME COBDEN'S NEW PUPIL.

Plate 10 *Dame Cobden's New Pupil*. This famous *Punch* cartoon of 28 January 1860 illustrates hegemonic arrogance by showing Richard Cobden as teacher and the French Emperor Napoleon III as schoolboy. It celebrates Cobden's trip to Paris which led to the crucial Franco–British trade agreement of 1860

The *Zollverein* states were leaders in the reduction of tariffs in the 1860s, so we may say that Cobden finally triumphed over List; but who can deny the German's greater understanding in cutting through the universal pretensions of British political economy?

Project Camelot and social-science universalism

Writing in 1941 as the war was exposing Britain's economic fragility, Henry Luce in his influential *The American Century* vigorously promoted the USA finally taking over world leadership.[99] He saw it as America's 'duty' to use its influence to mould a new and better world.[100] As heir to the great principles of Western civilization, America was viewed as the combination of can-do and missionary society. There were four elements in this vision of America's role in the world: (i) America as the dynamic centre of enterprise; (ii) America as a centre of leadership in skills to act as 'servants of mankind'; (iii) America as Good Samaritan; and (iv) America as 'powerhouse of the ideals of Freedom and Justice'.[101] The result was another explicit linking of the national interest to the universal: 'we can make a truly *American* internationalism something as natural to us in our own time as the airplane or the radio' (the italics are Luce's own emphasis).[102] Here was that 'moral fever and national interest in an indissoluble amalgam' once again.[103] Critics were quick to draw the obvious parallel: 'He has achieved what some of the great British statesmen of the last century achieved, complete identification of his own country's interests with the interests of humanity and of moral law.'[104] In other words, the USA was beginning to come of age as hegemon.

With a new hegemon we get the same message but through a new medium of transmission. The 'proof' of universality had moved from juristic philosophy through political economy to social science. The rise of the social sciences in the 20th century has been America's great contribution to knowledge of the human condition. Although drawing heavily on 19th-century European antecedents, largely German and sometimes French, a distinctive American product was created and disseminated to Europe and the rest of the world in the mid-20th century. This 'Americanization of European thought', as Touraine terms it, divided social knowledge into three 'disciplines': economics, political science and sociology.[105] In each case the prime units of investigation were the domestic societies within state boundaries so that relations at the scale of the world-system as a whole were severely neglected. The partial exception to this was political science in which a subdiscipline of 'international relations' developed into an almost separate body of knowledge.

The realist study of international relations we introduced in Chapter 1 focused upon British contributions towards understanding long-term 'international' political changes. Although their identification of inter-state anarchy was fairly typical of the subdiscipline, their historical focus was much less common. International relations studies have been mostly concerned with contemporary affairs and have been mostly carried out by Americans. This is a good illustration of US dominance of social thought after 1945. Although the modern 'founding father' of realist international relations is the English historian, E. H. Carr, it was an American political scientist, Hans Morgenthau, who formulated these studies into a science of international politics in his best-selling text of 1948.[106] His approach to international

relations rapidly diffused through US universities and beyond in the next two decades to 'flood this field of study in the noncommunist world' to such a degree that
'non-American writing on international affairs accepted the agenda and perceptions
of Americans'.[107] Hence instead of the development of a 'neutral' science, what
David Wightman calls an 'intellectual imperium' was created, geared to the intellectual needs of US foreign policy making.[108] Yet despite its 'self-serving provincial-
ism', its ideas were widely accepted as definitively encompassing the discipline.[109]
In our terms, US political scientists were world disciplinary leaders and US studies
of international relations were hegemonic.

The classic case of this hegemonic process is sociology, the modern social-science
discipline that more than any other is an American creation. Sociology as the scientific study of society was developed into a comprehensive theory of social action
under the American leadership of Talcott Parsons. His functionalist sociology
viewed modern society as a differentiated set of social relations which together
formed a social system. Again although quite culture-bound and parochial in content, this new sociology became globally dominant.[110] For instance, according to
Alvin Gouldner: 'Its techniques are everywhere *emulated* and its theories shape the
terms in which world discussion of sociology is cast.'[111] In a neat illustration, R. W.
Connell has pointed out that in terms of citations, Polish sociologists quote Polish
and American work, Italian sociologists quote Italian and American work, British
sociologists quote . . . there is no need to go on; the only sociologists who stick to
work from their own country are the Americans, of course.[112] D. A. Chekki explicitly
refers to this as America's 'hegemonic influence' in world sociology.[113] This is not of
mere academic significance. Touraine argues that 'American sociology is one of the
intellectual creations that has most deeply influenced our century.'[114] In what ways?
Connell provides a succinct answer:

> The hegemonic . . . stance in US sociology might be characterized, by an analogy
> with the phrase 'corporate liberalism', as 'professional liberalism' . . . American
> power shapes American sociology . . . It is itself an aspect of American power.[115]

In sociology, and in the social sciences in general, American interests have been
made universal by being designated 'scientific'. In the intellectual pecking order of
the modern world-system, the natural sciences have achieved most prestige for their
advancement of the enabling knowledge behind technological achievements.
Science is popularly viewed as objective truth with which there can be no disagree-
ment. By calling the study of social relations a 'science', social scientists are trying to
make some of the prestige of physics rub off on to their highly contestable knowledge.[116] In the two or three decades after 1945, social science was remarkably successful in this aim. As a 'science' it emulated the physical sciences in its methods
with the ultimate purpose of producing universal laws. This meant that rigorous
study of social relations in any one part of the world could produce findings applicable everywhere else. In practice this meant that a functionalist conception of American society was writ large as universal social theory.

The universal nature of social-science knowledge meant that it could be applied to
countries very different from the USA, even to the poor countries of the world. In
1949 when President Truman introduced his 'Point IV progam' to provide aid to the

'underdeveloped areas' of the world, the new social scientists considered themselves to be 'pressed into action' to produce the necessary knowledge about this 'no-man's land of the social sciences'.[117] Within a decade there were development models aplenty; the 'undeveloped' countries became first 'underdeveloped' then 'less developed' or simply 'developing' as an optimistic social-science profession of development was created.[118] The job of the development profession was to eliminate material poverty throughout the world using the objective models of social science, a task that was 'so worthy of the best brains', as one of its early proponents argued.[119] But the idea that social science was producing knowledge for a better world was always politically naïve. We can argue, for instance, that if it is the purpose of natural science to provide the knowledge to control the natural world, then a corollary is that it is the purpose of social science to provide the knowledge to control the social world. This was soon understood in political circles: in the words of a Report of the House Subcommittee on International Organizations, social science is 'one of the vital tools in the arsenals of free societies'.[120]

The zenith of American social-science influence came in the early 1960s and is symbolized by Project Camelot. Irving Horowitz has described the project succinctly as 'big-range social science', combining 'the enlightenment syndrome' of belief in rationality with 'Americanism as an ideology accepted as a basic positive value'.[121] Its scientific purpose was to predict rapid social changes in Third World countries. However, from a political perspective, it is easy to see how useful it would be if threats to order and stability across the world could be predicted ahead of time. There was a need for analyses that would tell US policy makers where and when revolts, riots, strikes or unfavourable election results were likely so that the US could pre-empt their occurrence and social scientists, suitably remunerated, were willing to meet this need. This was the true agenda of Project Camelot as its origins make clear. In 1964 the Army's Special Operations Research Office, in conjunction with the Defense Department, announced the largest ever research grant to social science: $6 million over four years.[122] According to the original press release, its goal was

> to determine the feasibility of developing a general social systems model which would make it possible to predict and influence politically significant aspects of social change in the developing nations of the world.[123]

After this feasibility study there was talk of funding at the astronomical level of $50 million a year: social science was entering the big league.[124] Not surprisingly social scientists came flocking to the bird tray and preliminary plans were made for this global study to find the necessary universal laws. Over 20 countries were recommended for comparative historical study, survey research and intensive field work.[125] The criteria for country selection mixed general social-science requirements with US national interest. But, as the documents show, the latter came first: 'Most significant is the relevance of selected countries to US foreign policy interests.'[126] Here we are at the zenith of social-science influence, of American interests wrapped up in the myth of scientific objectivity to justify its maintenance of the global status quo. Radical social change is anathema to functionalist systems models just as it is to hegemonic political interests. This commonality generated a programme of 'stress management' of foreigners that is perhaps the most audacious hegemonic project of all.[127] But it never transpired in its full glory. Foreign governments, especially Chile, objected to being laboratories for American social scientists, and the State Department was shocked at the Department of Defense interfering in foreign-affairs matters.[128] After a chorus of protests leading to a House investigation, the project was aborted leaving us with a most interesting episode in hegemonic behaviour.

The ultimate failure of this very ambitious social-science project should not blind us to the fact of the domination of social science in the study of humanity in the middle of the 20th century. As is so often the case, the meaning of the project transcends its particular failure. In fact the latter might be due merely to inept politics in failing properly to involve the target countries: if the State Department had sponsored the research it might have got much further. The key irony is that the uproar in Chile and elsewhere shows that its intended victims did in fact believe that Camelot could provide what it promised. It was accepted that countries in the rest of the world could be successfully modelled as if they were imperfect models of American society. Hence the controversy itself represents a victory of this particular universalizing project.

Liberalism as the politics of universalism

In the last chapter we emphasized the pragmatic nature of the modern politics created by the three hegemonic states. But their political practice was never cast solely in terms of self-interest; in the projection of hegemonic political influence, ideas are as important as actions. A general world-view or ideology is required that is broadly supportive of capital accumulation and which can act as a political rallying call against the enemies of capitalism. Hence, in addition to the cultural universalism developed by intellectual elites described in last section, other intellectual elites have been busy creating a political universalism. Liberalism has been the result. Several generations of political philosophers have produced a political theory that articulates a relationship between government and individual which defines a free and stable environment that facilitates capital expansion. This basic interpretation follows Harold Laski in his 1936 classic *The Rise of European Liberalism* where he argues that liberalism first emerged as 'a new ideology to fit the needs of a new world' four hundred years ago and has been 'the outstanding doctrine of Western Civilization' ever since.[129]

Of course, political theories of liberalism despite their universal pretensions, were devised in particular social contexts which inevitably influenced their content. There have been several important contexts highly conducive to spawning liberal ideas but none more so than the societies of the three hegemons. This is because, as we showed in Chapter 2, all three have actively developed politics which define themselves in opposition to 'unfree others'. It is this hegemonic self-identity as free societies that is projected on to the rest of the world as an image of multiple free societies to generate liberal ideologies. This has been accomplished by translating the particular merits of hegemonic societies into general principles of political behaviour. Liberal ideologies are, therefore, ideal hegemonic practices writ large; but this simple formula hides as much as it reveals. In this section we view some of the political complexities that have accompanied the making and maintaining of liberalism as the prime political theory within the modern world-system.

What exactly is this political theory of liberalism? As we would expect, such an important set of ideas is highly contested and who was or is, and who was not or is not, a liberal is a focus of much dispute. We can come up with simple definitions such as 'a belief that progress, leading to final perfection, could be achieved by means of free institutions'[130] but even this is problematic since there has never been agreement on what is meant by 'free institutions'. The truth is that there has been a great variety of political ideas that have been designated 'liberal'. In different times and places, what it is to be a liberal politician has been a product, in part, of different political situations. This has generated a major debate among those that write on liberalism. On the one side there are writers who emphasize the unity of liberalism and find a strong continuity of key concerns over several centuries.[131] Liberals writing about themselves represent the main proponents of this view. On the other hand, many critics identify more than one liberalism, often resting on fundamentally different philosophical foundations. For them changes in the politics of liberalism represent much more than adaption to new political circumstances, the very nature of the ideology has altered.[132] In our discussions below we use elements of both unity and disunity positions. Following Laski, we accept a certain unity of liberalism over the history of the modern world-system. But in addition we introduce hegemonic cycles to define different liberalisms for different political contexts within the overall development of the modern world-system.

The diversity within liberalism derives from many sources. At any one point in time, the main influence is probably the national tradition within various state politics — German liberalism in the 19th century is normally viewed as being more state-orientated than British liberalism, for example.[133] But taking the long view over the entire history of the world-economy, it is differences between the hegemonic cycles that are the most revealing.

Following on our discussion in Chapter 1 on stages of modern world-system development, if liberalism is the 'outstanding doctrine' of the system it follows that the ideology should reflect the rise, dominium and decline phases previously identified. This clarifies the source of much of the variety of liberalism. In the Dutch hegemonic cycle liberalism was emerging in a largely defensive role, focusing upon tolerance as a way to resist the tyranny of absolutism. In the British hegemonic cycle this threat from above was marginalized and the threat from below not fully developed, so that 19th-century Britain is commonly viewed as the heyday of liberalism. In the American cycle the threat from below produces a socialist rival, socialism, which forces liberals to accommodate to a new social democracy. This is the source of many critics doubting a philosophical continuity between 19th- and 20th-century liberalisms. Hence we identify the rise of liberalism in the battle against threats from above, dominium when liberalism holds sway over both threats from above and below, and demise as liberalism struggles to come to terms with threats from below.

Liberalism as hegemonic centrism

The model of liberalism within hegemonic cycles defines a changing location for liberalism in the right–left spectrum of modern politics. Put simply, over time liberals have moved to the right. First, in its 'rise phase', liberalism was a radical ideology to combat an illiberal status quo. Second, in the 'dominium phase', it was the dominant political ideology and took the position of a moderate world-view between extremes of right and left. Third, in its 'demise phase', liberalism appears on the right of the world political spectrum in its opposition to new radical movements. These relocations of liberalism have been a major reason for doubting the unity of liberalism as a political ideology. Closer scrutiny, however, shows this not to be the case. The classic position of liberalism, its situation during British hegemony, is at the political centre and this position is confirmed in part throughout its history. The positions described for rise and demise relate to defence against the main threat to liberal politics, but liberals have resisted responding by simple conversion to either radical or reactionary positions. Liberalism appeals to bourgeois interests, to the middle classes of the modern world-system, in opposition to both upper-class aristo- cratic politics and lower-class proletarian politics.[134] This middle position is epitomized in the founding document of our very first hegemon. In the Union of Utrecht of 1579 not only was the process of moving power from the monarch to a new ruling oligarchy begun, it also reduced the rights of guilds in the towns.[135] In this way the change that came about was twofold, with the losers located above and below the regent class that was leading the rebellion. This remains a classic example of the process of hegemonic politics, in this case hegemon-to-be taking the political middle way.

We can refer to this as 'hegemonic centrism', which defines the main way liberals have exercised power over four centuries. On the international stage this is illus- trated in the manner through which the hegemon's pragmatic power politics has combined with its political ideology to steer a path between the political extremes of each era. On all three occasions, the hegemon's rise through world war was accom- panied by a radical revolution in a rival state – the English, French and Russian revolutions respectively. In each case the hegemon showed itself to be no friend of revolution. In some ways the most surprising case is that of the United Provinces and the English Revolution. The latter was fought against the absolute pretensions of a sovereign monarch exactly as the Dutch had done in their rebellion. In addition it added a republican Protestant state to the European scene as a likely international ally of the Netherlands. But this was not to be.[136] The English revolution revealed a very radical side in the Levellers and Diggers – still revered by English socialists today – and although ruthlessly suppressed by Cromwell, the Dutch did not ap- prove of the latter's regicide. Hence despite some initial ambiguity in relations between these two Protestant republics, they soon went to war becoming each other's 'natural enemy'. The exiled king, Charles II, even took up residence in the Dutch Republic and returned in triumph to England from The Hague in 1660. This does not mean the Netherlands was the friend of reaction. England was the sea enemy, France the enemy on land. The Dutch might have temporary alliances with the French and other monarchies such as Denmark and Sweden but these were all highly pragmatic. The politics of the Dutch represented a middle way between the extremes of the radicals, briefly glimpsed in England, and the reaction of the conser- vative regimes elsewhere; they would ally with either side depending on who rep- resented the most serious threat to international order.

This ideological pragmatism is well represented by the British in their reaction to the French Revolution and the subsequent Napoleonic wars. Although Britain was the leader of the coalition resisting change and hence allied with the arch-conservative regimes in Russia, Austria and Prussia; Britain itself was a very different type of state. After the war was over and order imposed through the Concert of Europe, Britain very soon distanced itself from the reactionary policies of the Holy Alliance (of Russia, Austria and Prussia) and by the 1820s was closer to the new more liberal France than its war-time allies. The lesson seems to be that while world war forces the hegemon to take sides, once the battle is won it can revert to its middle way, supporting neither revolution nor reaction, as the British did for the remainder of the 19th century.

The same is true for the USA in this century but with a different sequence of political positions. In 1917 both American liberalism and Russian communism entered the world stage as major forces. In fact the period to 1989 can be interpreted as a great contest between two ideologies, Wilsonianism and Leninism. The USA intervened in the Russian Civil War and clearly opposed the new Soviet regime in the period to 1941. When, however, World War II came, the threat of reaction – Nazi Germany – was considered the greater menace to world order. Pragmatism demanded alliance with the USSR which duly enabled European Fascism to be destroyed. Only with the coming of the Cold War did the USA dispense with its erstwhile ally, and the revolutionary regime in Moscow became the enemy. As we noted in the last chapter, the Cold War resulted in some of the most reactionary regimes becoming US allies as long as they opposed communism: the theory of totalitarianism meant that such regimes were not irretrievably lost to liberalism.[137] Nevertheless, the political tension in this liberal position is obvious and has been caught perfectly in the opening lines of FitzSimmons's *The Kennedy Doctrine*:

> In his Inaugural Address, President John F. Kennedy invoked America's revolutionary heritage as the inspiration of his foreign policy, yet under his administration this nation became the leading defender of the international status quo. Because we were so strong – militarily, economically, technologically – we became the world's most effective counter-revolutionary power[138]

Hence American liberalism has wound its way between radical and conservative alliances in what we can now identify as a typical hegemonic manner.

In all three cases the hegemon has negotiated the political tension of periods of great change with a pragmatic dexterity offering a middle way between the illiberal extremes of opponents. But this continuity encompassed quite different forms of liberalism associated with each hegemon.

Rise: Holland as the 'first secure foothold'

Although liberalism as a self-conscious political ideology is a product of the 19th century, it is generally agreed that its ideas and practice go back to earlier periods.[139] How far back do we need to search to find antecedents? Some liberal writers claim paternity for their ideas in classical Greece – Socrates as first liberal martyr – but this is to pick and isolate ideas, considering them outside their social context. If liberalism is an ideology of the modern world-system we must look much closer to home for its origins. The most common argument has been to draw parallels with the Protestant concern for individual religious conscience and the individualism at the heart of liberal ideals. Hence liberalism emerges naturally out of the Reformation, or so the story goes.[140] The problem with this, however, is that the new Protestant churches were every bit as illiberal in their practices as the Roman church had ever been. By this I mean that they were intolerant, not just of Rome, but initially of each other. Protestantism did not so much spawn liberalism but a whole new swath of accusations of heresy.

Nevertheless, Anthony Arblaster does suggest that the Reformation was directly implicated in the emergence of liberalism, not because of Protestant teachings but rather through a politics of necessity.[141] With the rapid spread of different Protestant creeds in the 16th century, there arose numerous potential areas of conflict in central and northern Europe, producing several political responses to try to maintain order. In the Holy Roman Empire the fact of religious variety was accepted in Germany by the Peace of Augsburg of 1555; each prince was given the right to determine the religion of his realm.[142] This did not resolve the problem in countries with very large religious minorities. In particular, the Huguenots in France were perhaps the first to begin to devise constitutional arguments about religious toleration between sovereign and subjects of a different creed. But accommodation to religious pluralism was always fragile in France, and the gradually increasing repression of Protestantism there made other religious minorities in Europe fear for their future. There was another country where constitutional issues concerning the role of the sovereign were equally debated and where a mixed religious community had all the makings of a serious conflict: the new state of the United Provinces. It was here that repression was stemmed and religious tolerance emerged as a fundamental condition for later liberalism. For, as Arblaster sees it, although:

> it would be anachronistic to describe the Dutch Republic as 'liberal'. Nevertheless, in the difficult, piecemeal, haphazard process of the establishment of liberal principles in Europe, this middle class republic represents their first secure foothold in modern history.[143]

Our first hegemon is the first state to begin to look like a modern liberal country.

Religious toleration in the Dutch Republic was by no means uncontested. Since the original Dutch rebellion had a religious base and the early successes were the result of Calvinist resistance to Rome, the new state was established with an official Reform Church. This was in keeping with the emerging international tradition of every state being identified with one religion: the United Provinces was formally a Calvinist state. But in the case of the Dutch, the situation was far more complicated owing to large minorities of Catholics, other Protestants and Jews. Hence the state existed in perpetual tension between degrees of intolerance from the official church and the claims for tolerance both within and beyond the official church. However the seeds of toleration can be discerned from the very beginning. For example, in 1575 a new university was established at Leiden, the first in the Low Countries north of the rivers, with the expressed purpose of bolstering 'the political and religious separation of Holland and Zealand'.[144] Its contribution to serving the needs of the church was always deemed secondary and it was not placed under the authority of the

South Holland synod. The result was that the new university was 'freer from ecclesiastical sway than any other in Europe'.[145] By the second quarter of the 17th century, Leiden was one of the great universities of Europe, an international institution with over half the students coming from outside the United Provinces.[146] But the path to success was not smooth; the aura of toleration in which the university prospered fluctuated with the politics of the United Provinces.

The great crisis for toleration came with the deep divisions within the official church, culminating in the overthrow of Oldenbarnevelt's government and the old man's execution in 1619. This involved the purges of 1618–20 in which Oldenbarnevelt's supporters were sacked from public offices which included the dismissal of many professors.[147] However, with the new Stadtholder Frederik Hendrik in 1625, the 'Calvinist revolution' gradually subsided so that, according to Jonathan Israel, 'The Dutch Republic became a freer, more flexible society after 1630.'[148] By the end of the 'Golden Age', the United Provinces was famously proclaimed to be, in J. B. Stouppe's *Religion des Hollandais* of 1673, the most tolerant society in Europe.[149]

Tolerance does not mean the eradication of discrimination, of course, since all public offices were only open to members of the official church. But gradually, at different rates in different places, others were allowed to worship without harassment. That the large Catholic minority was allowed freedom of worship symbolized the unique nature of this early European society. In his writings, Peter de la Court places 'liberty of serving God' before 'liberty of gaining a livelihood'.[150] Walzer has even suggested that it is this tradition of tolerance, rather than the usual explanation of the Westphalia treaty keeping religions apart, that accounts for the rather abrupt termination of the cycle of religious wars in Europe in the 17th century.[151] But, perhaps most important, religious tolerance provided the intellectual space in which secular ideas could be mooted in a foreshadowing of the 18th century Enlightenment.

The tolerant United Provinces attracted intellectual dissidents from the great French natural philosopher René Descartes to the great English political philosopher John Locke. Descartes is particularly important for the Dutch because his new philosophy showed how the materialism of making money could be made compatible with Christianity. Descartes centred his philosophy on human reason and is generally regarded as the father of modern rationality. In his *Discourse on Method*, published in 1637, he constructed a dualism that separated experience from what cannot be experienced: Descartes provided the metaphysics that enabled Isaac Newton to produce his modern physics. Of much more immediate importance was the fact that Cartesianism allowed Europe 'to keep its God while it unmade and remade its material world at will'.[152] In other words it provided the basic philosophy of the modern world that would promote a separation of capitalism and its products from religion and its restrictions in thought and practice. Although proscribed as blasphemy by Catholics and Protestants alike, by the end of the 17th century Cartesianism had 'spread over Europe like a tidal wave'.[153] Science was released from religious restrictions to become the great manipulator of the natural world in the search for new commodities. Clearly, toleration as the first foothold of liberalism flourished to a large degree because it served Dutch interests and the needs of capital in general.

Dominium: England as the 'home of authentic liberalism'

The rise to pre-eminence of both liberal ideas and British power seem to be indelibly entwined in the 19th century:

> what was extraordinary was the manner in which the liberal solutions of the political economists and philosophical radicals [Benthamites] seemed to fit so perfectly both the self-interest and moral principles of [the] new industrial class . . . If there was an opportune time and place for liberalism, it was nineteenth century England.[154]

For Anthony Arblaster, it was nothing less than the 'home of authentic liberalism'.[155] This was certainly the view of the British political elite in the period of high hegemony. Alongside the mission to spread the benefits of free trade there were parallel movements to project the blessings of Britain's political liberalism on to the world.

The rise of 19th-century humanitarian movements provides exemplary examples of hegemonic behaviour. Oliver Furley has argued that:

> [Britain] felt she had the power to be the moral guardian of civilization every-where. Not only British Christianity, culture, industrial and commercial life, but also democracy and law were considered to have reached a perfection hitherto unknown: to export them to less fortunate peoples was a moral duty.[156]

The clearest case of this moral duty came in the anti-slavery movement. Britain abolished slavery in her territories in 1807 and insisted on an anti-slave-trade clause in the peace treaty signed in 1815. Thereafter she actively prosecuted an anti-slavery policy through the Royal Navy with its 'right to search' obtained from foreign governments. Throughout the 19th century the logic was a simple one. In the words of Donald Horne, 'Britain's self-interests were humanity's' and therefore 'Britain served the world', so that 'to fail to serve British interests was a dereliction of duty to mankind'.[157] This is hegemony rampant.

But there was a much more subtle projection of hegemonic political influence that was of more general importance than humanitarian movements. Britain's liberal reputation was based firmly upon the country's constitutional form of government. Alone among the European states before the French Revolution, the British were governed by a system of checks and balances in which the authority of the sovereign was constrained and parliament had genuine power. But there was no attempt to diffuse this system to countries of the *ancien régime* in 18th century Europe. Quite the opposite in fact: constitutionalism was only established elsewhere at this time in the USA and France as the result of revolutions the British opposed. All this changed after the defeat of Napoleon in 1815.

The British parliamentary form of government offered a middle way between the democratic 'Jacobin' constitution briefly offered by the French Revolution and the continuation of the *ancien régime* as practised by the victorious allies of central and eastern Europe – Russia, Austria and Prussia. It had the advantages of both keeping a semblance of the old order in place through the 'constitutional monarchy' while allowing elements of the new middle classes access to government power through parliament. In addition this constitutionality was extremely flexible in that the same basic form could be used to legitimate very different balances of power between Crown and parliament.[158] Given these advantages, this type of government spread throughout Europe between 1815 and 1875.

Beginning with the political reconstruction of France in 1815, it was adopted next in the Low Countries and Scandinavian countries. After the revolutions of 1848 it spread eastwards to Piedmont, Austria and Prussia before being confirmed in the new states of Italy, Austria–Hungary and the German Reich in the 1860s and 1870s. Obviously the political process of adoption of liberal constitutionality varied greatly among countries as did the nature of the outcome in terms of power of parliaments relative to the executive, but the fact remains that there was a liberal upheaval of governing practices in this period. And we should not restrict our attention to Europe. The new independent states of Latin America all experimented with liberal constitutionality and parliaments also appeared throughout that continent in the 19th century.

What was the role of the hegemon in all this? It is inconceivable that the temporal correspondence of British hegemony and liberal constitutional victories was mere coincidence. D. R. Watson, for instance, considers that, with the adoption of a parliamentary monarchical government in Germany after 1871, 'the triumph of the British model of constitutionalism was complete'.[159] But the processes of the relationship are hard to unravel. There was no direct political intervention as for instance when the British wrote the constitutions of their ex-colonies a century or so later. However, although the constitutional changes described above are all the direct outcome of internal politics, they betray the existence of a pervasive British political ambience promoting the same constitutional agenda across different national politics. For instance, in faraway Brazil one legislator even went as far as to declare, in 1866, that 'When I enter parliament it is as if I am under the influence of Gladstone. I am an English liberal in the Brazilian parliament.'[160] In this way the British were able to translate their economic pre-eminence into a political influence which was very different from the Dutch two centuries before. As well as championing economic liberalism, the British were able to project a political liberalism in their own image. Unlike the Dutch, the success story that was Britain was seen, from both inside and outside, as being both economic *and* political. In the 19th century a 'middle way' in politics triumphed through the impact of the British. This is what John Bright, Cobden's colleague in the Anti-Corn Law movement, meant in 1865 when he referred to England as 'the mother of parliaments'.[161] We have not previously come across this maternal metaphor to describe hegemony, but it is a good one: hegemon-as-mother nurtures, coaxes and teaches by example.

Demise: America's 'offensive liberalism'

In his influential book, *The Arrogance of Power*, J. William Fulbright, the leading critic of US foreign policy in the Senate in the 1960s, suggested that Americans had become like the British of a century before with their 'world arrogance' in allocating to themselves the moral duty of looking after the world.[162] The new liberal universalism of our century certainly had some of the characteristics of past missions but it

Plate 11 *Vote for Liberalism*, British Liberal Party poster (1895). In the 19th century the Liberal Party in Britain was the leading political promoter of liberalism in the world. In this image liberalism is the knight that kills the dragon of reaction to ensure progress and reform

was also distinctive in nature. Anthony Arblaster has argued that the Americans produced a very narrow form of the universal ideology – Cold War liberalism.[163] Its particular characteristic is that it was defined more in terms of what it was against than what it stood for: above all it was anti-communist. In pursuit of this aim many of its adherents abandoned what were usually thought of as inherently liberal ideals. Foremost among these were the civil rights of their opponents. In the atmosphere of the 'McCarthyism' in the USA in the 1950s, large numbers of Americans effectively lost their civil rights through actual or assumed support of communism with relatively little public objection to this severe case of intolerance. In American hegemony, liberals found themselves on the same political side as their erstwhile conservative opponents. Arblaster concludes that Cold War liberalism hardly deserves the name liberalism, arguing that its central ideas were indistinguishable from what had in the past been identified as conservatism.[164] These, however, were self-professed liberals and the US claimed to be the epitome of the liberal state. Rather than remove this Cold War variant from the pantheon of liberal theory and practice, we will interpret it in terms of its context, the rise of US hegemony and the threat from below as promoted by the USSR. We find once again the hegemonic penchant for the middle way.

American liberalism in the 20th century has swung from centre-left to centre-right. In its progressive phase at the beginning of the century through to the New Deal in the 1930s, it promoted constructive state intervention to curb the excesses of capitalism against the vehement opposition of conservative forces. On the international scene this enabled the USA to be a liberal world power, foremost under Woodrow Wilson in World War I, and then again under Franklin D. Roosevelt in World War II. In the latter case the war ended with the Democratic administration using New Deal rhetoric in foreign policy, a global New Deal, no less. Although against the Soviet Union from its inception, the main rival to the USA taking over Britain's mantle as world leader was undoubtedly Germany. Both the German Empire to 1918 and the Third Reich after 1933 could be reasonably portrayed as illiberal regimes, allowing US opposition to them to take centre-left positions in international relations. All this changed after 1945 with the coming of the Cold War. The enemy was now the revolutionary left, and the result was Cold War liberalism and the swing to the right.

How the USA built a credible anti-communist 'left' alternative to communism is a fascinating story. It required the building of international institutions among civil groups such as trade unions to fend off communist influence. The Congress for Cultural Freedom was the major vehicle for mobilizing intellectuals to Cold War liberalism and is representative of covert US institution-building during the Cold War. Formed at a conference in West Berlin in 1950, its headquarters were located in Paris and its leading journal, *Encounter*, was published from London.[165] But we should not doubt its pedigree as a US global project. Secretly funded by the CIA, at its height in the 1950s and 1960s the Congress had representatives in 35 countries, employed 280 staff world-wide, had a network of at least 22 political and cultural magazines, sponsored conferences and seminars on all continents and published books across the world.[166] A huge undertaking, originally intended to be 'a sort of cultural counterpart to the Marshall Plan' to aid in the US 'cultural reconstruction of Europe', it grew with the Cold War to become, in Peter Coleman's words, 'the crusade for the world'.[167]

The Congress for Cultural Freedom fell into disarray with the revelations of CIA funding in the 1960s and was dissolved in 1967. During its lifetime it was highly instructive in showing how US liberalism coped with the Cold War. Although the inaugural meeting in West Berlin produced a manifesto introduced by Arthur Koestler with the stirring words 'Friends, Freedom has seized the offensive', it was essentially a negative message, a mission to counter communism.[168] The choice of West Berlin as the site of the conference was by no means without symbolism. In fact one of the oddest things about this 'movement' was that its international structure and large-scale funding came *before* the existence of 'a clear program or sense of direction'.[169] No doubt this was partly due to liberalism adjusting to the requirements of the Cold War, but when a sense of direction was discovered it was quintessentially hegemonic liberal in nature.

The distinctive form of America's political universalism was its expression of a negative value. Following on from the theory of totalitarianism, the Congress came to embrace an anti-ideology position as its fundamental motif. This maintained its central position between right and left despite the fact that in practice it could only be anti-communist. Edward Shils is usually attributed with the expression 'end of ideology' in a 1955 article in *Encounter* where the phrase was presented as a question.[170] In Daniel Bell's book of the same name five years later the question mark is removed.[171] 'End of ideology' refers to both the failure of the Soviet Union to provide a progressive lead to the world after the revelations of Stalinism and to the movement in the West bringing reform socialists and liberals together in a new politics. Old passions were spent because there were no more radical causes to espouse:

> In the Western world . . . there is today [1961] a rough consensus among intellectuals on the political issues: the acceptance of the welfare state, the desirability of decentralized power, a system of mixed economy and of political pluralism . . . the ideological age has ended.[172]

In particular, the welfare package of practical reforms seemed, on the back of the economic post-war boom in the West, to make revolutionary prescriptions for change no longer necessary for ordinary workers. World War II had destroyed the ideology of the right; now the ideology of the left was no longer attractive even for the people for whom it was intended. Hence the end of ideology.

Of course, it was soon pointed out that the very idea of an end to ideology was nonsensical, in E. H. Carr's memorable put down: 'To denounce ideologies in general is to set up an ideology of one's own.'[173] That it could become the hallmark of Cold War liberalism reflects the degree of arrogance we have come to expect of hegemonic powers – the ideas of the hegemon are the only legitimate ideas in the world. Dismissing rival world-views as ideologies beyond the pale of respectability was America's way of defining its cultural universalism. Under President Kennedy this arrogance resulted in an enormous expansion of the US role in the world. Simple military containment of communism gave way to active counter-insurgency employing 'the full range of political, economic, psychological and sociological activities'.[174] It was for this 'non-ideological' mission that 'objective' social science could come into its own, as we described above for the Camelot Project.[175]

Embedding liberalism I

What does this all add up to? Can-do societies, new universalisms and political liberalisms come together in the story of how hegemons promote their interests and project their power. We can summarize this whole process as 'embedding liberalism'. By embedding I mean the way in which liberalism becomes integral to the new society evolving in the hegemon and in those countries that emulate it. By liberalism I have in mind a broader concept than the political liberalism of the last sections: I include all the things, economic and cultural as well as political, that at any one period go together to create a self-consciously free and open society. Through embedding, this broad liberalism comes to be seen as essentially right and proper, the only way for a truly modern society to organize its affairs. Liberal and modern are brought together through hegemony to defeat their twin opponents conservatism and traditional society.

The name we have given to this process is derived from John Ruggie's concept 'embedded liberalism'.[176] He uses this term to describe the state of affairs during American hegemony in which economic liberalism between countries operated in conjunction with social democracy within countries to reduce adverse world market effects. His attempt to relate the domestic to the international is very interesting and is followed up in the next chapter. Here we conclude this chapter by describing our somewhat broader process of embedding as it operated within each hegemonic state to define consensus in foreign policy. This aspect of embedding liberalism is chosen because the subjugation of anti-hegemonic forces is so clear-cut and visible. Embedding liberalism at the international scale involves a deal of emulation and will therefore be left until the conclusion of the following chapter.

There was never anything inevitable about the victory of liberalism within the politics of each hegemonic state. Given its technological leadership, why should the hegemon not sit back and enjoy the fruits of its production successes? For contemporaries, all the evidence pointed towards the hegemonic state as very special; surely here we have a 'chosen people' with all the exclusiveness that this phrase implies. In the British case this was humorously expressed as 'God is an Englishman', and both the Dutch and the Americans made much of their special exceptionalism.[177] An important political corollary of such thinking has been the development of a very strong isolationist streak in each hegemonic state. This has perhaps been described best by Simon Schama in his interpretation of 17th-century Dutch relations with the non-Dutch:

> the Dutch certainly did suffer from a peculiar false consciousness about their use of power. Force in the hands of others was consistently portrayed as an infringement on the laws of nature; force in their own hands was, however, a defense of freedom. . . . in this moral isolationism, they disdained to deal with the rest of the world on its own slightly soiled terms. By adhering instead to the principles that were said to have separated them from the 'Old World', they imagined that they might transcend the grubby bartering of *raison d'état*.[178]

We can immediately see that replacing 'Dutch' by either 'British' or 'American' at the beginning of this quotation produces a statement equally relevant to later times. For instance, for the British we read the 'Old World' as 'the continent' or Europe minus

Britain; for the USA it is Europe including Britain. In each case the reality was that there was only one world; as 'New Worlds' the hegemons were part of this larger whole. In all three hegemonic states the debate about relationships with the 'Old World' was an important one which the isolationists had to lose if the full fruits of hegemony were to be enjoyed.

For each case of hegemony there was one party whose policies were quintessentially hegemonic in nature. These 'hegemonic parties' were the 'states party' in the United Provinces, the Liberal Party in Britain and the Democratic Party in the USA. In the process of embedding liberalism, the policies of these parties had to transcend mere party politics: their opponents, the 'Orange party', the Tories and Republicans respectively, had to abandon counter positions and embrace the new hegemonic politics. It is with the collapse of domestic anti-hegemonic positions that hegemony becomes fully operative.

The clearest case occurred in the USA, where the Republican Party gradually abandoned its isolationist stance through the 1940s. The leader of the isolationists, Senator Arthur Vandenberg, dated the end of isolation precisely: 9 December 1941 with the Japanese attack on Pearl Harbor. Vandenberg and other leading Republicans, such as the 1940 Republican presidential candidate Wendell Willkie and the editor of *Life* magazine Henry Luce, developed a 'one world' foreign policy agenda compatible with that of Roosevelt's Democratic administration and which culminated in the Cold War. We can see how far the Republicans had moved away from their traditional position by noting the fate of the first US attempt to develop hegemonic policies. This had occurred with Woodrow Wilson's Democratic administration in World War I and its universalistic programme for a 'new world order' based upon 'new world prescriptions'. By promoting free trade and the use of the USA's financial power, Wilson hoped to impose an American peace on the world. It was not to be. With the return of the Republicans to power in 1920, the USA reverted to its traditional protectionism and relative isolation. Hence it was the next Democratic administration in the next war that completed Wilson's work. Again using US financial power, first Roosevelt's and then Truman's administration began the construction of a liberal world economy first in opposition to the British Empire and then to the USSR. On this occasion the Republicans were brought into a Cold War foreign policy which made a return to isolationism impossible. Thus during American hegemony a general bipartisanship of foreign policy was created with differences between the parties becoming matters of emphasis rather than substance.

The emergence of British high hegemony coincides with the conversion of the Tories into the modern Conservative Party. Although British hegemonic practices most commonly stemmed from the so-called 'Manchester Party', the radical faction of the Liberals led by Cobden and Bright, the crucial change of government policy occurred under a Conservative administration. Robert Peel is commonly viewed as the founder of the modern Conservative Party, and his repeal of the Corn Laws was carried out through an alliance of a minority of Tories loyal to the government with the opposition Whigs. The split among the Tories in Parliament ensured that Peel's government fell almost immediately, but there was no turning back. Britain entered the period of classic two-party parliamentary politics: of Liberals versus Conservatives. Although the Liberal Party was to become the hegemonic party *par excellence*, especially under William Gladstone a former Peelite Tory, this new party system was founded upon a broad consensus on Britain's commercial policy. From being the great parliamentary issue of the 1840s, free trade became a cornerstone of government policy whichever party was in office. This was the bipartisanship upon which British hegemonic practices were built.

The Dutch case is somewhat different since there was no party political politics through which opposition to government could be mounted. George Modelski refers to the existence of 'proto-parties' — the 'Orange party' and the 'States party' — but we must be careful not to confuse 17th-century political competition within the United Provinces with a modern party system.[179] There were genuine political differences between the Regents and their merchant allies in the cities on the one hand and the supporters of the Orange family with their land-owning base on the other, but the division of interests was always very fluid. Given that the major foreign policy issue of the first half of the 17th century was the war with Spain, the two 'proto-parties' are sometimes identified as war party and peace party. Whatever the label, the hegemonic party in this case is represented by the States and/or peace political interests. The anti-hegemonic tendency in this case was finally overcome with the early death of Stadtholder William II in 1650, leaving only a young child, the future William III, as heir. This was the opportunity for the 'States party' under John de Witt to carry out Dutch hegemonic practices with little or no internal opposition. The result is the first glimpse of what we, in this century, have called a one-world policy. It was argued that the United Provinces should not only maintain good bilateral relations with other states but also sponsor such relations between 'all the Governments of Christendom'.[180] In practice, the Dutch achieved a series of defence pacts which commanded widespread political support through the Stadtholderless period until the disaster of 1672.

In general we can note that the first step towards embedding liberalism requires a broad internal consensus within the hegemonic state to provide the platform from which hegemonic ideas and practices can be promoted to the rest of the world. But embedding liberalism is a world process. Therefore the second step requires the creation of a receptive world audience for such hegemonic promotions, bringing us to the question of emulation.

To see the future: emulation as the sincerest form of flattery

4

Long before the Cold War was over, the Italian Communist Party declared it was not opposed to Italy's membership of NATO. By any stretch of the imagination this was a peculiar change of policy given that the purpose of NATO was to prevent the spread of communism in Western Europe. As the largest communist party in Western Europe, how could the main party of the left in Italy support NATO? At the heart of the mixture of pragmatism and opportunism that guided the Italian communists towards this unlikely policy, there is a general acceptance of NATO, and with it American leadership, as a simple 'fact of life' in all of Western Europe. This is a sign of an embedded liberalism far beyond the hegemon's borders. It illustrates well the difference between traditional domination by coercion and the hegemon's greater reliance on consensus. Acceptance of US leadership as benign was a necessary but not sufficient condition for embedding liberalism at the international scale. Other states had to want to be like the hegemon, to emulate it so as to produce a world in America's image.

Having a receptive world audience for its extramural manifesto is the very core of the power that is hegemonic. This is built on the hegemonic state's role as an exemplar for other countries, of course – the can-do society described in the last chapter. But there is more to it than this. Technological prowess has certainly been important as a route to riches and wealth, but the alternative route, the traditional military one of conquest and plunder, has still been operative and widely resorted to in the modern world. Since military expansion is so much easier to organize than economic growth *in situ*, why should so many states follow the example of the hegemon during its economic peak? The key point is that hegemonic power relies on right as much as might. In a very important way hegemonic power goes beyond political and economic leadership to impinge on the social and cultural spheres of other countries. This is what we have explored before when we have related hegemony to modernity. The hegemon is seen not only as powerful, it is the most *advanced* country. This brings the time dimension to the centre of our analysis. There is widely perceived temporality operating here which provides the hegemonic state with a fundamental cultural power that is unique to the modern world-system.

Let us consider what it means to be the most advanced country in the world. In literal terms this is a very odd notion since we all share simultaneity of time.[1] Hence when we refer to 'advanced' in this context, we are ascribing a social meaning to time which, in the modern world, can only mean the idea of progress. The theory that social change takes the form of cumulative progress is, according to Robert

Nisbet, 'the cornerstone of intellectual modernism'.[2] To be the most advanced country, therefore, is to be a special place where past and present achievements combine to produce the frontier of modernity. The implications of this are quite profound: it has meant that the hegemon today represented where other countries would expect to be tomorrow. Hence to visit the hegemon is to see your own future. It is hard to imagine a more powerful cultural position. The hegemon is able to universalize its interests so successfully because it is perceived as being everybody else's future. No wonder countries emulated the hegemon: they were not just copying success, they were trying to reach their own better future as quickly as possible.

This process of emulation of the hegemon is our subject matter in this chapter. We begin by exploring the notion of hegemonic states as special places by showing that each in their times have been a 'laboratory of modernity'. In the second section we look at the different ways that modernization has been conceptualized in relation to the three hegemons as precocious enlightenment, the universal theory of progress and scientific models of development respectively. Finally we come to emulation by the rest of the world. In the third section we look at the key ways in which rivals have reacted to the hegemon and how they have tried to adapt to hegemonic practices in order to advance themselves. Here we meet the familiar topics of mercantilism, industrialization and corporatism but treated as the outcome of hegemonic leadership and the process of others 'catching up'.

Laboratories of modernity

I take my title for this section from the phrase in Donald Horne's argument that 'for a time Britain was the world's laboratory of modernism'.[3] The Netherlands and the USA were equally such laboratories in their time at the top. I like the term 'laboratory' in this context because it combines the idea of scientific and technological advance, hegemon as can-do society from the last chapter, with a specific locale in which these processes take place. A laboratory is a place and therefore a laboratory of modernity situates the modern by fixing its geography. The idea of modernity is a very abstract notion, a cluster of ideas with variable empirical referents. A laboratory of modernity, on the other hand, is something concrete, somewhere you can visit and see.

We can trace the concrete territorial nature of this analysis back to our definition of world hegemony. In the original Gramscian analysis of hegemony the subjects are social classes which have no grounding in particular places. One important effect of changing the subject to states – hegemonic states – is to create a fundamentally spatial basis to the analysis. As we have seen, the modern state is defined by its territorial sovereignty which means that our hegemons are territorial units. Given that the hegemonic subject is territorially bounded, it follows that as creators of new modernities they have each constituted themselves as quintessentially modern places. However, unlike sovereignty, which is defined across the whole territory of the state, modernity can be more specific and refer to particular places within the state. This 'uneven modernity' is obvious in all three cases, especially with respect to regions that modernity seemed to have passed by. For the Netherlands, we described in Chapter 2 how the territorial structure of the state consisted of a core of cities centred on Holland surrounded by a bulwark of outer provinces, the military shield for the economic powerhouse. In the case of Britain, the territory of the United Kingdom during its hegemony included the whole of Ireland, western and southern parts of which were to suffer their great famine (1846–51) at the very peak of high hegemony. During America's high hegemony the southern states were the site of bloody conflict over basic civil rights which was hardly in keeping with US world leadership. The Netherlands' outer provinces, Britain's Ireland and the American south all appear to be in some sense less than modern in comparison with the rest of the country. In contrast, each hegemon incorporated cities that appear ultra-modern. In Holland, Amsterdam was the wonder of the age, in England it was Manchester that epitomized the new world and in the USA first New York and then Los Angeles seemed to represent the most advanced places on Earth. However we must be careful not to equate very modern and less modern with an urban–rural division. All three hegemons built their productive edge in part on having a most advanced agricultural sector. The Dutch were the most efficient farmers in the 17th century, the British had their agricultural revolution in the 18th century which was closely linked to their industrial revolution in many complex ways and we should remember that, throughout its hegemony, the USA was by far the world's leading producer and exporter of agricultural commodities. It is a fact that the lagging regions in terms of modernity were rural in nature, but they were not typical of the modern agricultural regions of the hegemonic state which were truly world leaders.

The modernity that is Dutch

As in the previous chapter, when beginning with the Dutch we are forced to start with a 'proof' that they do represent a society comparable in status to the later British and Americans. As with the can-do society, this is not really difficult in considering modernity since again the problem is largely historiographic. That is to say, the Dutch have been written out of the story by later writers, largely 19th-century English, for whom modernity could only be represented by themselves. Here we illustrate Dutch modernity in both its rural and urban precociousness.

In what has developed as the 'standard' account, the geographical focus of the rise of modernity diverges depending upon whether political or economic processes are considered. For the former the exemplar is France and its centralization, for the latter England and its industrial revolution. According to Jan deVries, this has left the 'tantalizing precociousness' of the United Provinces cast in the role of a 'puzzle' that historians have been slow to solve.[4] Politically, the Dutch adaptation of institutional frameworks of medieval origin which were being swept away elsewhere suggests the United Provinces was more a relict of the past than the first laboratory of modernity. We dealt with this argument in Chapter 2. There has been a similar argument consequent upon the economic emphasis on the English agricultural re-volution as the necessary precursor of industrial revolution that we need to deal with here. For instance, in his Marxist interpretation of the rise of capitalism, Eric Hobsbawm has argued that the Dutch ran a 'feudal business economy' whose success emanated from taking advantage of economic opportunities in a still largely feudal world.[5] No sign of modernization here! However deVries, in a seminal statement, has directly confronted the question of Dutch agricultural modernity and has exposed the severe limitations of defining the early process of modernization in terms of English economic history.[6] By focusing on the conversion of agricultural land from communal use to private ownership as the crucial step in modernization, orthodox interpretations have identified the enclosure movement in 18th-century England as the classic locus of this process. This makes the fact that such a process did not occur in the Dutch Republic proof of the latter's relative backwardness. But we should be wary of tying major social changes such as the rise of modernity to particular institutional arrangements. Any superficial glance at the Dutch in the 17th century shows their agriculture to be anything but backward despite the lack of an enclosure movement. The explanation is simple: England's 'crucial step' to a modern agriculture was not necessary.

The legacy of the medieval period in the northern Netherlands provided a framework where a market in land could form with no need for enclosure since feudal arrangements had never dominated in the first place. That is to say, the United Provinces inherited a rural setting in which 'free peasants' were the norm.[6] This was the result of the unattractiveness of much of the land in medieval times until the colonization and drainage schemes that produced societies very different from elsewhere. For instance throughout Holland there were self-governing drainage boards made up of peasants who supervised the dikes and ditches. These *waterschappen* had a 'remarkable degree of independence' including the right to tax.[8] They are generally regarded as 'rural communes' to indicate their similarity to urban communes in terms of local autonomy.[9] Hence whereas elsewhere in Europe town councils operated in a rural sea of feudal jurisdictions, this was not so in northern Netherlands where self-government extended to rural areas. It is this medieval arrangement without feudal restrictions that was easily converted into a land market a century before the English enclosure movement. And, of course, this was all part of the decentralization the Dutch defended against Hapsburg attempts at centralization.

One closely related area of activity particularly emphasizes Dutch modernization at this time. In their wide-ranging survey of cadastral maps, Kain and Baigent highlight the Netherlands as exceptional in terms of early mapped surveys of land property.[10] Instead of the medieval practice of defining property by the written word, in the 16th and 17th centuries the Dutch founded a local cartographic tradition to serve their distinctive land system. The 'rural communes' required maps to assess dike taxes for repairs; they were also necessary for individuals in resolving legal disputes of ownership. The result was a very modern process of labour specialization with one surveyor per 5000 population recorded in the province of Friesland for instance.[11] The importance of this occupation is also shown by the fact that the University of Leiden instituted the first formal training in surveying in 1600; the occupation was being professionalized.[12] Again this is all more than a century before surveyors in the English midlands were drawing up their maps of land ownership for Parliamentary Acts of Enclosure.

We can conclude that the Dutch rural economy in the 17th century was thoroughly modern and they took a different and earlier path to modernity than the English, who have been the standard model for modernization. Of course without the dubious benefit of the historiography of later generations, contemporaries of the hegemon recognized the newness and advantages of the Dutch land market. The

English mercantilist writer, Andrew Yarranton, for instance, in a tract of 1677, re-commended the very flexible land market of Holland for adoption in England.[13] In general the mercantilist writers of the 17th century appreciated the special nature of the United Provinces more than many later economic historians.

Dutch modernity, of course, was to be found in many sectors and places beyond its rural precociousness. At the other end of the economic spectrum from the very tangible agricultural goods, there emerged an international information market in Amsterdam in the mid-17th century.[14] This was part of the Amsterdam information exchange that Woodruff Smith argues played a crucial role in the modernization of European capitalism. In the dispersed markets of the early modern period, there was a strong demand for a central clearing house for information as a means of making improved decisions on buying and selling. Amsterdam took on this role and became the centre of a hierarchy of commercial cities through which information was col-lected and disseminated. Although adopting many existing commercial practices, Amsterdam operated at a new scale of operation and the efficiencies so gained set in train a cumulative process of a more and more sophisticated use of information. In short, we find the invention of information strategies upon which all modern organ-izations depend. Regular business post provided the basic source of private informa-tion and regularly updated commodity prices for different cities were publically listed in Amsterdam. Within the city, we find a massive rise in the importance of face-to-face contacts as the commercial community became the international hub of the expanding trading system. Beyond the city, merchants throughout Europe were served by economic newspapers and merchants' handbooks, both printed in many languages, leading on to market surveys and analysis using statistics. In the early 17th century the keeping of records became converted into the collection of statistics with the possibility of analysis. As early as the 1620s attempts were made to define price cycles in order to anticipate rates of recovery; later long-term time-series ana-lyses were invented as part of the commercial planning of the larger companies.[15] This leads Smith to conclude:

> The orientation of marketing and investment planning around the systematic collection and analysis of long-range information is one of the central characteris-tics of modern capitalism. It appeared first on a substantial scale and in a recog-nisably modern form in seventeenth century Amsterdam.[16]

Quite simply, the Dutch Republic was the 'laboratory' where commercial capitalism was modernized.

Although it could not be recognized as modernity by contemporaries, there was something very distinctive about the new Dutch state that was generally under-stood. Success could not be ignored:

> The Dutch were the original rags to riches story. Lacking all natural wealth, lacking even good harbors, they nevertheless made themselves the wealthiest maritime nation of Europe. They had discovered the secret of acquisition. States-men and political economists of other nations studied their methods in hope of imitating them.[17]

In short they were hegemons, creators of modernity.

Manchester as 'the essence of modernity'

Britain, so Peter Stearns tells us, was a 'peculiar nation' in 1800.[18] It was distinctive because of the rapid economic changes going on within its boundaries that today we call 'industrialization'. This was much more than a matter of economics, of course. A new form of society was in the making that was to transform not just Britain but the rest of the world. This was the second key construction of an advanced, modern society for others to emulate or face inevitable decline. Well into the 20th century the terms 'industrial society' and 'modern society' were treated as being synonymous. It was only in the second half of our century, after the idea of a post-industrial society had been developed, that the automatic link between industrial and modern was broken.

If as the 'first industrial nation' Britain was modern, it follows that the rest of the world had become, by default, 'unmodern'. A visit to Britain became mandatory for anybody who wished to understand what the future had in store for them, and what they saw inspired them. This was a new world that they wished copy. After the end of the Napoleonic war the number of foreign visitors to see Britain's industry 'became a flood'.[19] Quite simply, in the first half of the 19th century Britain was the place to visit for anybody with ambition. Among those who felt the necessity to experience the new industrial wonders of Britain at this time were the New England textile manufacturer Francis Cabot Lowell and the German metal manufacturer Alfred Krupp, both of whom were to play key roles in their own countries' industrialization, of course.[20] Literally thousands of would-be entrepreneurs like them made what can only be called 'a pilgrimage' to the hegemon and the new world it was creating. Stearns quotes one French visitor in 1842 thus: 'I am here in the centre of the most advanced industry in Europe and the Universe.'[21] His last word encapsulates the awe of it all.

It was not the whole of Britain that was attracting admiration and visitors. There was no interest in seeing the old cities like Norwich or Oxford or, for the most part, even London. The shrines for worship were far away from 'old England'. It was in the Midlands and the north of England plus central Scotland, collectively known simply as the 'North', where the great economic transformation was taking place. In his search for the meaning of England, Donald Horne refers to this modernity as the 'Northern metaphor' representing technical skills, enterprise and hard work.[22] He contrasts it with the 'Southern metaphor' of rural backwardness, *rentier* leisure and laziness. As Mrs Gaskell makes one of her characters define the situation in her 1851 novel *North and South*, the north is the present and the future, the south merely the past.[23] As most visitors appreciated, the north was becoming a new country across a gaping cleavage dividing Britain. It is no surprise therefore that the 'southerner' Richard Cobden, after first trying to start up in business in London, soon moved north because, 'In the 1820s Manchester was the obvious goal for any young man seeking his fortune.'[24] To borrow a phrase from another time and place, we could say that the best advice to give at this time was simply 'Go north young man'.

The North was not one continuous, homogeneous zone of industry. It consisted of a number of specialized regions each centred on one or two industrial cities. Cities near or on coalfields developed as world leaders in engineering (Newcastle, Sheffield, Birmingham and Glasgow), other cities developed as great ports (Liverpool and Glasgow again) and in textiles Yorkshire specialized in woollens (Bradford and Leeds) and smaller industrial districts produced lace (Nottingham) and linen (Belfast). All these industrial regions were dwarfed by Lancashire and its cotton textiles. This industrial region was at the cutting-edge of new technologies: by the 1840s some three-quarters of power in the cotton mills was steam. It was no accident that the Anti-Corn Law League was centred here – in the years between the Napoleonic war and the repeal of the Corn Laws, cotton textiles accounted for between 45% and 50% of total British exports.[25] And Manchester was the centre for all this activity, both commercial and political.

Asa Briggs has described Manchester as 'the shock city of the industrial revolution'. It symbolized something new, 'a centre of "modern life" which all students of society were required to understand'.[26] In his collection of contemporary views on Manchester in the decades before 1851, Briggs provides four separate references to the city being a 'cradle' with its association to the birth of the new.[27] In fact Manchester developed two distinctive images relating to its extremes of wealth summed up by Alexis de Tocqueville after his visit in 1835:

> humanity attains its most complete development and its most brutish, here civilization works its miracles, and civilized man is turned almost into a savage.[28]

From the disturbances following the Napoleonic war to the Chartists in the 1840s, Manchester was viewed as a centre of riots and possible revolution, but towards the end of this period Manchester's other image as the centre of a bourgeois social order came to the fore. Briggs dates this change from the depression of 1836 when: 'Manchester was a centre of disturbance again, but it was of a cyclical kind within the framework of a new system rather than the structural change of an old system.'[29] The country was entering a new world and it looked to Manchester for the outcome: 'a new order of businessmen, energetic, tough, proud, contemptuous of the old aristocracy'.[30] Hence, by the 1840s, contemporary observers were generally agreed that Manchester represented a bourgeois world rather than a proletarian one. The Anti-Corn Law League had become much more influential in city politics than the Chartist movement. After the repeal of the Corn Laws, the League disbanded itself in 1846, but its leaders remained influential promoting a broader liberal agenda. This was commonly known as the 'Manchester School' or 'Manchester Party', and its supporters were known throughout the world as 'Manchester Liberals'.[31] But cities cannot shock the world forever. After mid-century Manchester was increasingly taken for granted. Briggs dates this symbolically at 1851 with the visit of Queen Victoria to the city. The orderly crowds contrasted with past agitation and marked Manchester as a respectable city. Nevertheless, by then it had become a new type of world city, an industrial metropolis.

'All roads led to Manchester in the 1840s,' according to Briggs.[32] This was because the city was, in Anthony Arblaster's words, nothing less than 'the essence of modernity . . . the place to which people came to see the future'.[33] For instance, it was the ambition of one Italian visitor to build a 'Manchester' in Istria.[34] It was clear to those who 'understood' the industrial metropolis that the future would consist of a world of Manchesters. The Germans even coined a term, *Manchesterthum*, to denote this new way of life and its international implications.[35] Hence we can say that Britain, through 'the image of Manchester', 'showed where the world was going'.[36]

Americanization

In the first half of the 20th century it became commonplace in Britain, and Europe in general, to treat America as the land of the future. The ugly term 'Americanization' was coined to denote this new metaphor. I date its coming of age to 1899 when the Pope explicitly condemned 'Americanism', a sure sign that this was to be the new modern.[37]

What is Americanization? As a new word for modernity it obviously shares many of the characteristics of our two previous examples.[38] In particular the enterprise of the can-do society is relocated for a second time. Horne is explicit on this when he writes of 'British restlessness now known as Americanization'.[39] But it is much more than this. The 20th century has witnessed another transformation of modernity, this time in the image of the USA. The latest stage in the process of modernization has crucial characteristics missing from past manifestations. In this new phase, modernization is based upon more than production. To be sure the rise of the USA to hegemonic status has been accompanied by key innovations in the production process notably in terms of mass production. But therein lies the problem: who is to buy this massive rise in industrial output? In a society modelled on 19th-century Britain, such technological advance would have started a scramble to find new and massive markets abroad. It would probably have been unsuccessful and certainly would not have been able to sustain an adequate demand for long. The USA embarked on a different solution, it found a new and massive market at home. The hallmark of Americanization is produce and consume.

This strategy had been implicit in American development for some time before it became explicit with the General Motors–United Auto Workers deal of 1947.[40] In return for industrial peace and improved working practices the company conceded relatively high wages that allowed the workers to become consumers at a level previously beyond the reach of the mass of ordinary people. As we have seen, America became the first country where its workers felt themselves to be 'middle class'. The image of modernity was transformed from industrial town to suburbia. The dark side of the old modernity, the grime and poverty of industrial regions, was banished in the spacious suburbs with their detached houses full of the latest home gadgets and a two-car garage. Modernity was redefined in democratic terms as the good life attainable by everybody in John Galbraith's new and unique 'affluent society'.[41] This term was soon superseded by the phrase 'consumer society', emphasizing what Americans did with their affluence. Suburbia became the new and unlikely laboratory of modernity. Unlike Britain a century earlier, this laboratory did not have to be visited physically because by the mid-20th century its nature and mores were known the world over first through films and then TV programmes. Suburbs soon became more than pleasant dormitories, they became the home of the shopping mall. Whereas the cotton textile factory was the shrine of the last modernity, the site of worship for the new modernity has been the ubiquitous mall.

The influence of this produce-and-consume modernity and the great US multinational corporations that grew in its wake has been the subject of some dispute. It is easy to emphasize the triviality of the spread of Americanization as merely consumption. Terms such as 'Cocacolarization' and 'McWorld' suggest a fairly innocuous and unimportant process of little note beyond the profits it brings in.

American blue jeans are now ubiquitous on young people across the world, but so what? This is John Lukacs's question.[42] He has conceded the widespread popularity of Americanization as consumption but argues that it is ultimately superficial. He contrasts it with the very real British influence on 19th-century Europe which left a profound cultural mark.[43] But he is thinking of 'high culture', which is precisely what Americanization is not; its essence is the very opposite of Lukacs's elitism. Lukacs has missed the point; he is viewing Americanization through an older modernity.

The key point is, as John Ney so neatly puts it, 'the people are the Americaniza-tion'.[44] It is this 'everyday Americanization' that makes the new modernity so spe-cial.[45] It has been a bottom-up process of modernization, both in class terms and generationally. In England, for instance, it was the lower class, especially the young, that 'began imitating America utterly, completely and finally' in the post-war years.[46] That is the message of Coca Cola, McDonalds and Levis the world over. Writing in 1970, Ney is able to announce the conquest of Europe by America in his book, *The European Surrender*: 'All Europe is Americanized'.[47] Rather than being superficial, Americanization has redefined modern and universalized it as never before. The whole world, it seems, wants to live in a suburban dwelling and shop at the mall just like in American cinema and TV. The American dream has become the world dream.

Defining the future

Consider again the notion, expressed several times above, that non-hegemonic states can see their future in the hegemon's present. John Ney, writing in 1970, was very explicit of this point: because 'the European present can only duplicate the American past', Europe possesses a 'predetermined future'.[48] Are the Europeans, and non-hegemons in general, to have no say in their future? It is testament to the power of the idea of modern, and the hegemon's particular constitution of it, that such simple determinism can be seriously presented. Further it is implicitly accepted by those designated as 'being behind'. From their point of view, the hegemon seems to be literally 'ahead of its time' as the phrase goes. Visitors may think they are 'seeing the future', but this is actually quite absurd, at least in the absence of any known time travel. Of course, I am being disingenuous here, the concept of time being used in these examples is not physical time but rather a relative 'social time' in which one country can be 'ahead' of another. Well, 'yes' and 'no'; the power of the whole exercise relies on using the simple language of physical time.

It seems to me that what is happening here is that the hegemon is able to appropri-ate world time for itself, and hence deprive others of their time, through its role as the laboratory of modernity. But how can time be taken and packaged in such a way that the hegemon defines the future? This is the task of the laboratory workers specializing in the study of time, the philosophers, historians and development scientists. It is their task to devise a social theory of time in which the rest of the world is ordered behind the hegemon. Such a temporal dynamic is presumed in the notion of the modern, but the form it takes is not determined beyond the necessity to show the hegemon as being 'ahead of its time'. Hence the variety in the treatment of time in the three hegemonic periods. Before we come to deal with these separate cases we need to unravel further the relations between theorizing time and being modern.

Faith in the future

Consider the following statement: 'There will be no end to the growth and develop-ment of human wisdom.'[49] Nothing exceptional about such a sentiment you might think; it expresses a faith in the future of humanity that is commonplace enough. But the statement, made in 1688 by the French intellectual Bernard Le Bovier de Fon-tenelle, is indeed remarkable for it is usually regarded as the first declaration of the modern idea of progress. The idea that the present is the result of past progress and will be superseded by further progress in the future is only commonplace to us 'moderns'. Previous societies were unhistorical in the sense that they had no concep-tion of a social continuity linking past with the present in order to contemplate the future. As Edward Carr so clearly expresses it in terms of the ancient civilizations: 'History was not going anywhere: because there was no sense of the past, there was equally no sense of the future.'[50] Time was seen as a natural cycle, and hope for a better future consisted of a return to 'the golden age'. In medieval Europe, a Chris-tian teleological view of history was only partly of this world. Hence the audacity of Fontenelle to respect neither golden age nor second-coming.

Fontenelle's statement was part of an intellectual debate that has come to be known as the 'Quarrel of the Ancients and the Moderns'. In contradiction to the assumption underlying the Renaissance's rediscovery of classical scholarship, Fon-tenelle and others argued that knowledge is cumulative and therefore however great the thinkers of Greece and Rome, contemporary scholarship must be superior to past knowledge. This idea of progress in intellectual pursuits was to be expanded to cover other social changes during the Enlightenment in the 18th century. Progress came to seem 'natural' – how else should society change?

We now have a problem of chronology. Intellectual modernism would seem to have been constructed some two hundred years after the emergence of the modern world-system itself. We can refer to this as a 'culture lag', the period of time it took intellectuals to come to terms with the new phenomenon of incessant social change that challenged the concepts they inherited from the classical world and Christianity. In fact the discovery of progress is not quite as abrupt as an emphasis on Fontenelle and the famous 'Quarrel' suggests. In his survey of progress as 'the modern man's secular religion', Radoslav Tsanoff traces the emergence of the idea to Renaissance humanism and shows it appears implicitly throughout much of the intellectual ferment of ideas that marked the 17th century.[51] Nevertheless it is not until the Enlightenment of the 18th century that we find a full systematic treatment of social progress and the idea becomes imbued in modern thought. Hence there was a cultural lag between the origins of incessant social change we call 'modernity' and the modern interpretation of its meaning as 'progress'.

Initially the intellectual and social disruption that the new system ushered in was represented by an enhanced geographical imagination rather than a new conception of history.[52] This is to be expected given the nature of the emergence of the modern world-system with the incorporation of the Americas into Europe's orbit. The discovery and exploration of America by Europeans is a very early example of unsettling change and 'newness' that we have identified as the hallmark of modernity. In this case a 'New World' was being defined that was outside the classical cosmology that guided Renaissance thinking. This had provided a comfortable image of one land mass divided into three parts, or continents, surrounded by ocean. By interpreting his discovery as part of Asia, Columbus maintained a faith in classical cosmography, but as early as 1493 the idea of his discoveries being a 'new world' was mooted.[53] By 1502 Amerigo Vespucci's new cosmographic ideas about a separate new world 'unknown to the ancients' were published in many editions across Europe.[54] Very soon America was given a cosmographical status equal to the three 'old world' continents, and in his famous world map of 1507, Martin Waldseemuller modestly tells his readers that he has not followed 'Ptolemy in every respect'.[55] But he is being too modest: this was, in Eviatar Zerubavel words, 'a total cosmographic shock for Europe' which, he goes on to say, constituted a 'psychological threat' to early European modern society.[56]

The modern world-system began, therefore, with a new geographical imagination, a first and crucial challenge to the authority of classical texts. The idea of new worlds was so liberating a notion that it could not remain a scientific matter of cosmography. A new genre of literature was spawned that dealt with fictional new worlds in which fresh possibilities for the human condition could be explored. This literary device allowed the author to define an ideal society on a faraway island in a mythical here-and-now. The original of the genre, Thomas More's *Utopia* (1516), set the pattern of using geography as a shield to explore contemporary social questions. Through Francis Bacon's *New Atlantis* (1626) to Jonathan Swift's *Gulliver's Travels* (1726), the special value of this geographical imagination was, as I. F. Clarke tells it, 'to manifest a new sense of human destiny'.[57]

We can argue quite reasonably that this new fictional geography literature was a cornerstone of early intellectual modernism, but there was one crucial leap of imagination missing. Contemporary society could be compared with such ideal worlds and found wanting, but there was no social theory linking the two; the arguments were, as we still say today, 'utopian'. Contemporary society only becomes self-consciously modern when it embodies a historical imagination of progress. To quote Clarke again, 'the unique understanding of the dynamic relationship between present and future separates the modern from the rest'.[58] Contemporary society could still be found wanting but now with respect to possibilities for a better future. This interpretation of the present based on faith in the future gradually replaced territorial utopias as the latter became less credible with the elimination of unexplored regions in which to locate new worlds: by the end of the 18th century the known world of Europeans was effectively global.[59] Hence in the 19th century all ideas on social change are dominated by the Victorian doctrine of progress wherein it becomes natural to think of the future in terms of the present and vice versa.

How does this pattern of early modern geographical imagination preceding a fully modern historical imagination fit with our sequence of hegemons? Obviously it affects our interpretation of Dutch hegemony in particular. We can note first of all that the United Provinces as hegemon was the world centre for geographical

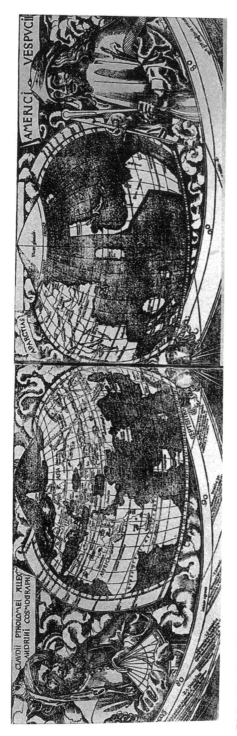

Plate 12 *Detail from Martin Waldseemuller's World Map of 1507* (Schloss Wolfegg, Württemberg, Germany). This was the first map to identify and name America as a separate continent. The author behind this very first modern 'shock of the new' was Amerigo Vespucci and he is explicitly promoted in this detail, alongside Ptolemy with his three continents map, as the discoverer of the fourth continent. Hence the United States of *America* but only the District of *Columbia*

knowledge in the 17th century. This was for both practical and intellectual reasons. On the first count, geographical knowledge was vital for developing trade and commerce in the newly expanding world-economy. But second, there was also Dutch intellectual domination of the development of Europe's geographical imagination. The centre of map publishing moved from Italy to the Low Countries in the second-half of the 16th century and blossomed under Mercator's leadership. Initially centred in Antwerp, the Spanish sacking of the city produced a diaspora of cartographers the most important of whom, Hondius, settled in Amsterdam.[60] From the first Dutch attempt at a world map as early as 1592 using Mercator, through the Mercator–Hondius Atlas of 1606, to *The Great Atlas* of 1662 by Willem Blau (called 'the largest and most beautiful atlas the world has ever seen'), Amsterdam became the world publishing centre of maps, atlases and travel books.[61] This was where the early modern geographical imagination was nurtured and nourished. From academic treatises such as Bernhard Varenius *Geographica Generalis*, for over a hundred years after 1650 the most influential systemic treatment of geography and still viewed by some as a foundation for modern geography in the 20th century, to popular wall maps that adorn Dutch paintings, the United Provinces is the major creator in the 17th century of what Chandra Mukerji calls the 'new world-picture'.[62] The hegemon was most certainly the leader in geography, but without a historical imagination it could not be self-consciously modern. The full systematic development of a theory of progress did not appear until after Dutch high hegemony. This is why any modernity ascribed to the Netherlands will have to be *post hoc*.

Back to the future: the *post hoc* modernity of the Dutch

The Enlightenment was a European-wide intellectual movement of the 18th century centred in France. The goal of the participants was to construct an 'age of reason' to challenge the absurdities and irrationality of the *ancien régime* as they saw it. For instance, the most famous group of Enlightenment thinkers, the French *philosophes*, self-consciously thought their task was to keep alive the truths of reason and liberty in pursuit of human progress despite the absolutist obstacles being laid in their path. Some historians have seen the *philosophes* as 'missionaries of modernity'.[63] But for Dutch intellectuals in the 18th century there was a problem. First, their *'ancien régime'* was a republic where many of the supposed obstacles and absurdities were missing. Second, the Dutch were experiencing a period of relative decline in which ideas of universal social progress hardly seemed appropriate. Many Dutch intellectuals were obsessed by decline, which not surprisingly led to the isolation of the Netherlands within the European Enlightenment.[64] On the other hand and despite the decline, outsiders often praised the Republic precisely for its political distinctiveness. Hence it is important to distinguish between the Enlightenment in the Dutch Republic and the Dutch Republic in the Enlightenment. We will be concerned with the former when we discuss hegemonic decline in the next chapter. Much more spectacular was the symbolic role of the erstwhile hegemonic Dutch for enlightened 18th-century Europeans.

Standing out like 'a spot of light in the black canvas' of the 17th century, the Dutch seemed to be 'the Enlightenment's first ray'.[65] Overworking the light metaphor, we

Plate 13 *Soldier with a Laughing Girl* (*c.* 1658) by Jan Vermeer (The Frick Collection, New York). The Netherlands became the world centre of cartography in the 17th century leading to a market in maps as wall decorations. In this famous Vermeer painting, the wall map takes up fully one-quarter of the picture. In the Netherlands a popular geographical imagination was cultivated

can note that the golden age of the Dutch Republic continued to glow long after it had passed its peak. Due to its tradition of tolerance and the practical business of publishing, the enlightened of the 18th century journeyed to Holland and admired its modernity just as later progressives would visit England and America. According to Simon Schama:

> To say that many of the *philosophes* who sojourned in the Netherlands deferred to its reputation as an arcadia of the wise and the free would be an under-statement.[66]

For the Enlightenment's most famous spokesman, Voltaire, it was nothing less than a *paradis terrestre*.[67]

What is happening here? How can a country rapidly falling down the European hierarchy of states be designated an earthly paradise? The answer is that it is not the declining Republic that is being lauded but an image of it based on achievements of the previous century. The first hegemon became a geographical and historical reference point for the Enlightenment, the most recent staging post in the race for liberty that started in the republican tradition of Socrates' Athens and pre-imperial Rome, had been continued by republican Venice and most recently triumphed in the United Provinces.[68] Hence the *philosophes* visiting the Netherlands were not so much reporting on what they could see as 'gazing through the windows of a Dutch house as into a mirror image of themselves'.[69]

There is a wonderful irony in this acquired status of the Dutch Republic in the 18th century. European contemporaries of the Dutch during their golden age were much less complementary, in fact they were downright derogatory. The Dutch were 'the envy of the present' and that envy was easily turned into malevolence.[70] The great achievement of draining the land was turned on its head – in the animal designations popular at the time, the Dutch were usually portrayed most unheroically as a frog dwelling in the 'great bog of Europe'.[71] The pretensions of the Republic to equal status in the community of states were ridiculed by portrayal as a pig signifying the innate coarseness of this upstart land. Both frog and pig plus their respective associations with emergence from slime and wallowing in the mud were particularly insulting given the Netherlanders' own concern for cleanliness. Even the universality that we described in the previous chapter was not exempt from such attacks: we can find references to both the 'universal quagmire' and 'the buttock of the world' as descriptions of Holland.[72] Hardly the terminology of respect a hegemon might expect!

This was all before the historical imagination of social progress had arrived, and it most certainly does not lessen the importance of the United Provinces for the rise of modernity. Figgis has provided precisely the right interpretation of the 17th-century Dutch:

> Ideas, which might otherwise have been buried for all time, could influence future development because there was now a modern place where they could be seen actually to work.[73]

There was, however, a very special price to pay for developing 'ahead of its time'. Being, in Wijnand Mijnhardt's phrase, 'enlightened before the Enlightenment', the Dutch could only be properly appreciated as a *post hoc* modernity.[74]

The Victorian cult of progress

The Enlightenment concept of progress that developed in the 18th century was 'in the main abstract and speculative'.[75] General schemes of stages of history were devised, but it was the British that gave the idea of progress its decisive subject, the new industrial world. According to Kristan Kumar, in the 19th century, progress 'could only now mean industrialization'[76] The 'logic of industrialism' became generally viewed as the means to raise societies to 'a higher plane'.[77] Hence it was Britain that came to represent progress and it was during her hegemony that faith in the future blossomed:

> The cult of progress reached its climax at the moment when British prosperity, power and self-confidence were at their height; and British writers and historians were among the most ardent votaries of the cult.[78]

For the Victorians it was inconceivable that society did not progress and that they represented the culmination of the process thus far. Quite simply, without progress, so the distinguished historian Lord Acton stated, 'there is no *raison d'être* for the world'.[79]

We have already described the Great Exhibition as a reflection of hegemonic geopolitics but it was also inevitably 'that most splendid revelation in the nineteenth century's belief in the idea of Progress'.[80] The layout of the exhibits not only promoted Britain relative to the rest of the world, it also proclaimed the present to be a spectacular advance on the past. In the British half of the exhibition, for instance, as well as the Great Machinery Hall, visitors could see the Medieval Hall and wonder at 'how far we have come'. Hence, not only was space annihilated by cramming the whole world under one roof, so also was time by locating the past in this present.[81] These were not separate processes. Space and time were combined in the idea that, as one contemporary observer put it, the exhibition contrasted 'one stage of a nation's progress from another'.[82] The world was being scripted as an array of nations all at different stages of advancement. Britain belonged to the highest stage, of course, making it the rest of the world's hope for the future, or in the vivid image drawn by *The Economist*: 'the land will be everywhere adorned with crystal palaces'.[83]

Eight years after the Great Exhibition, Charles Darwin published his *Origin of Species* (1859) in which evolution was firmly located at the centre of understanding the natural world. This was very important because it allowed the 19th-century version of progress to be much more comprehensive than its Enlightenment parent. In the 18th century, although ideas and societies were assumed to progress, this was not how the natural world was interpreted. A static, mechanical model of the non-social meant that the goal of a single knowledge encompassing all experience was impossible. After 1859 this division between the natural and the social was quickly removed as evolution and progress came to be seen as synonymous and therefore able to explain all changes, material and non-material.[84] This way of thinking reached its zenith in the popular school of social Darwinism that flourished in the late 19th century. The leading figure of this school was Herbert Spencer who, in 1872, wrote the seminal essay *Progress: Its Law and Causes* in which he described 'the law of all progress' as follows:

> Whether it be in the development of the earth, in the development of life upon its surface, in the development of society, of government, of manufactures, of commerce, of language, literature, science, art, this same evolution of the simple into the complex, through successive differentiations, holds throughout.'[85]

This has been called the most famous paragraph of the 19th century and it is certainly true that these sweeping ideas diffused far beyond the bounds of academia.

Herbert Spencer was particularly popular in the USA, and he was referred to as 'a power in the world' by *Atlantic Monthly* as early as 1864.[86] In his formative years he supported the Anti-Corn Law movement and his first book, *Social Statics*, attempted to strengthen the argument for *laissez-faire* with imperatives drawn from biology.[87]

Plate 14　*Shooting for the Moon in Fiction.* Although the term 'science fiction' is from the 20th century, this class of modern literature has its origins in the second-half of the 19th century. There were earlier stories of political futures but with the rise of social optimism based upon the new industrialization, the future came to be seen as progress in the form of the onward march of science and technology. The leaders of this field were a Frenchman, Jules Verne, and an Englishman, H.G. Wells, before Americans came to dominate the genre in the 20th century. Space travel is to be found in this literature from the beginning; this illustration is from Jules Verne's *From the Earth to the Moon* published in 1865

However it was after the publication of Darwin's *Origin* that Spencer set about producing the most comprehensive theory of progress through evolution. In 1882 he embarked on a tour of the USA, reminiscent in many ways of Cobden's 1846 tour of Europe except that, instead of being fêted by kings and ministers, it was the great capitalists of the era such as John D. Rockefeller and Andrew Carnegie who hailed him. He was given a hero's welcome on arriving in New York and everywhere he went he was fêted as the prophet of progress.[88] Spencer's crude naturalism precisely legitimated the new barons of capitalism who saw themselves as natural manifestations of 'the survival of the fittest'. For America in general, he told reporters that the USA could 'reasonably look forward to a time when they will have produced a civilization grander than any the world has known'.[89] This was an early example of an English hand passing on the baton of progress to America.

The final blooming of the Victorian cult of progress came with the British Whig School of History as personified by Lord Acton.[90] Widely regarded as the foremost intellectual of his time and a friend of prime ministers and other influential figures, he was asked by the Syndics of the Cambridge University Press to edit their proposed *Cambridge Modern History* series. His task was to select contributors, wherever possible 'from among British historians', to one of whom he described the project thus: 'My plan is to break through the mere juxtaposition of national histories and to take in, as far as may be, what is extra-territorial and universal.'[91] Hence the British would order the rest of the world in their universal history. And universal meant progress – in his 1896 report to the Syndics he defined history as 'a progressive science'.[92] Acton's historical imagination consisted of 'the march of history as an unending progress towards liberty' with Britain at the end of the march.[93] The resulting Whig interpretation of history consisted of a continual battle between the friends and enemies of liberty, favouring the former as 'moderns', and finally glorifying their victory as the present.[94] The great critic of the Whig historians, Herbert Butterfield, described this history as being much more subtle than mere conscious bias: it was 'an unexamined habit of mind'.[95] Examination was not to be long delayed. The optimism of the 19th century succumbed to the horrors of World War I and progress was revised accordingly. John Bury in 1920, in his classic *The Idea of Progress*, relegated progress from a universal law to a mere hypothesis and 11 years later it had become, in Butterfield's words, 'the historian's "pathetic fallacy" '.[96] At the height of the idea's power in the mid-19th century, Czar Nicholas I issued an order banning the word progress throughout his realm; a century later historians find themselves apologizing for using such 'an old-fashioned word'.[97] The time was ripe for the invention by a new hegemon of a new language to describe social change.

Development for all

Under US hegemony the idea of progress did not disappear, but it was recycled in a different lexicon. If progress was the buzzword of the 19th century then 'development' has been all the rage since the middle of our century. Social development, political development and, above all, economic development were the processes Americans promoted as their promise of a better future for the world. Unlike the relatively vague prescriptions of progress, development was seen as a very concrete, measurable property of states, something that could be carefully planned into existence. This had a crucial corollary: development was possible for all states. In this it contrasted with progress which was more a matter of civilization and so might be closed to 'Orientals' and Africans. The idea of development was essentially world-democratic. Americans asked the rhetorical question: 'Why should not others enjoy the good things of life on the same scale as Americans?' This was to translate the American dream into a world dream,[98] and the means were to hand in the form of the universal social science as we described in the last chapter. Here we focus upon how social science treatment of development ordered the world on a time-scale that culminated in the USA.

The basic intellectual concept underlying all models of development was 'modernization'. This was a process devised by sociologists to describe social change in its most general form. It was based on a long recognized dichotomy between modern and 'traditional'. The attributes of modern turn out to be the ideas and values we find promoted in the Enlightenment, above all rational organization and behaviour leading to a functionally differentiated division of labour and the widespread application of science and technology.[99] Of course, this recognized Europe and America – the 'West' – as modern. The traditional became the residual group, all those societies that did not have the attributes of the modern – they were irrational with arbitrary authority unconstrained by democracy; they had a simple division of labour based largely on agriculture; they practised 'pre-Newtonian' science and technology. This turned out to be a very large group comprising by definition all societies before the 17th century (ie 'pre-Newtonian') and most societies since including the majority of contemporary countries. In addition to the Whig interpretation of history devised by the British to distinguish modern from unmodern in the past, American social scientists constructed what we might call 'a Whig interpretation of geography' in which the same categories of modern and unmodern were located in the present. This leap of imagination equating past 'traditional' societies with contemporary 'traditional' societies was very important. It was the basic social science trick that lay behind all the development models devised in this period.

Development models have been based upon two fundamental assumptions.[100] First, all countries can follow the same autonomous path to development. Second, this common path can be discovered by careful study of contemporary countries that are already 'developed'. The contemporary pattern of differences in development among countries reflects variations in how far countries have moved down the common path. The result is an analysis imbued with optimism: however poor a country may be today, given the right policies it is only a matter of time before the country will be just like contemporary rich countries. And the required help was at hand. Social scientists set themselves the task of understanding the common pathway and applied development scientists then devised policies to speed passage along it. As for governments, they are simply left to implement the policies and make the whole process as painless as possible for their populations. Well, that was the ideal.

In order to focus our discussion let us concentrate on just one of these models, probably the most famous, Walter Rostow's *Stages of Economic Growth* of 1960. Using the universalist social science language of the times he begins his book with the remarkable assertion that: 'It is possible to identify all societies as lying within one of five categories.'[101] These are levels of economic development that are functionally linked to produce cumulative stages of growth. The first stage is the traditional society recognized in all modernization theories. The breakdown of this society is termed the 'preconditions for take-off' which leads to the crucial stage of 'take-off' itself. This converts the society into one of self-sustaining growth. This growth is the 'drive to maturity' when the society becomes successively more complex — the modernization process. Finally, there is the stage of 'high mass consumption' – Americanization as we would call it – which is the nature of modern society as Rostow saw it at the time he was writing in the 1950s. In a very useful chart to illustrate the model, countries are lined up in terms of how far they have proceeded along this singular path to development.[102] Britain was the first to take off and reach maturity. Rostow symbolically dates this at 1851 and the Great Exhibition. The USA is the first to reach high mass consumption, but by 1959 she is joined there by eight other countries including Britain. Other countries such as Turkey and China have only just 'taken-off' or are about to. In short, the world is reduced to a single ladder with countries arrayed on one of its five rungs.

Rostow was a student of British and American economic history, and his model reflects this. It consists of a generalization of British economic history to 'maturity', with the USA's 20th-century economic achievements tacked on as a final stage. What he is saying is that every country in the world, at least if they're not ensnared in the communist trap, will repeat British/American history.[103] By now we are familiar with this 'world arrogance' by the hegemon defining its own experience as universal and offering itself as the ultimate goal of social change: in the 19th century becoming more like Britain was called progress; in the 20th century becoming more like America has been called development.

This 'our history is your future' argument has been severely criticized, especially in terms of treating each path to development as an autonomous process. By assuming the developmental autonomy of each state, development theorists avoided awkward questions concerning the influence of the encompassing world-economy on the poorer countries. This means that both the historical pernicious effects of imperialism were transcended and that contemporary international constraints were ignored. The key point is that when the 20th century's high mass consumers were 'taking off' and 'driving to maturity', there was no high mass consumption going on above them at the top of the ladder.[104] Losing sight of this obvious difference in world-historical context between 'us then' and 'them now' was the basic social science trick of development studies.

Although now widely recognized as the 'error of developmentalism', developmentalist thinking continues to include use of the Rostow model, however much it has been discredited. In fact, every time we use the terms 'developed world' and 'developing world' to denote rich and poor countries, we are explicitly using a developmentalist argument. There are two obvious problems with these widely used terms. First, developed world implies an end-point, a process completed with the rich countries reaching the end of the development path. Nothing could be further from the truth: incessant change continues unabated in the so-called 'developed' countries. Second, there is the rather cruel implication that poor countries are truly 'developing' in the sense of catching up with the rich countries, as was generally assumed to be happening in the 1950s and 1960s.[105] Developed and developing simply will not do as descriptions of our modern world which is why we introduced the core–periphery model in Chapter 1, with its terminology that recognizes the whole that is the world-economy.

Rostow's model was devised in a period of great social optimism after World War II.[106] Following the success of US-sponsored economic recovery in Europe, it was assumed that a similar process could stimulate development elsewhere. We can capture this optimism in popular development books of the period. For instance, the 1962 book *World without Want* by Paul Hoffman is full of hopeful headings like: 'The magic ingredient: education and training', 'The magic of science' and 'The promise of tomorrow'.[107] He uses Rostow's model as his framework and identifies Togo as an example of traditional society that with political independence is now 'on the road to a better tomorrow'.[108] 'There is a long way to go,' Hoffman tells us, 'but Togo has begun.'[109] In contrast 'India is nearing the take-off stage' and the only debate is about when it will start 'selfpropelling'.[110] It seems that optimists thought India would start its drive to maturity as early as 1971, the cautious prediction was for 1980 and Prime Minister Nehru compromised at 1972 or 1973. This was all in keeping with the sense of urgency for development: 'Processes that took centuries for us must be compressed into decades for the underdeveloped world.'[111] Hoffman

Plate 15 *Harnessing the power of modernity*. The idea of development for all took some bizarre and deadly turns. Some advertisements marketed baby products using the image of a nurse. This form of marketing of powdered baby milk was common throughout the Third World and the controversy led to world-wide consumer boycotts especially directed at Nestlé (Chetley, 1979). Lack of clean water meant that powdered milk was often linked to infant mortality. Despite the companies admitting breast milk was normally best for babies, many poor people spent large proportions of their meagre incomes on this unnatural substitute. This marketing triumph was based upon pitting a new modern product against the most traditional of products, mother's own milk. It succeeded because consumers thought they were buying into modernity as represented by the smart modern nurse. This cartoon is from *Pan* a newspaper produced during the Rome World Food Conference. Reproduced with permission from War On Want

thought this possible because today we have the 'tremendous new allies' of science and technology. His expectation was that by the end of the Development Decade in 1970, some 20 countries would have graduated to self-sustained growth and would act as an example for the rest of the 'developing countries'. More Development Decades were envisaged and the final sentence of the book contains the prediction that: 'By the year 2000, we can be living in a world that has overcome poverty.'[112] What a wonderful prospect.

Unfortunately, now that we are only a few years away from the date of this vision of the future, we know it to be false: mass poverty and starvation not only remain with us but have increased since Hoffman's prediction. With the decline of US hegemony and the world-economy moving into a stagnation phase, the promise of development for all has taken its place in history alongside British belief in the law of progress and the Enlightenment eulogizing of the Dutch Republic.

Playing catch-up

Let me begin with a sporting metaphor which I believe to be particularly appropriate for understanding the role of hegemons in the world-economy. Given a competitive system of states there are two possible outcomes. As we described in Chapter 1, either one political unit achieves political–military dominance to create a world-empire or else some equilibrium is achieved that results in an inter-state system as part of a world-economy. These two processes can be couched in terms of challenge-cup and league-table types of competition respectively. The historical norm has been for state competition to operate like a knock-out cup in which there can be only one winner.[113] All rivals are, quite literally, eliminated in turn and the final survivor is the cup-holder, the ruler of all. In the modern world-economy, competition can still lead to the elimination of states, but it does not produce a lone winner. However successful the hegemon, it does not rule all. Rather we can think of the modern inter-state system as a league table in which states are ranked in terms of their power. Although the very weak can be relegated from the system, the league itself is never in danger. The hegemon, then, is league champion, the epitome of success for the season of its cycle. As such it is not a threat to competition, rather it takes it to a higher level.

Changing the nature of competition is central to our understanding of the distinctiveness of the modern world-economy. By becoming a positive force rather than a negative force for reproducing the system, competition is enabling rather than threatening. Under hegemonic leadership, rivals are expected to remain in a subordinate position, but they continue to have a role to play in the system. This provides a manoeuvrability for subordinates unavailable, indeed unthinkable, in a world-empire where alternative ruling elites can only succeed by destroying the existing system and instituting a new world-empire. In a world-economy, rival states can work with and use the hegemon by emulating its behaviour in order to catch up.[114] In this case rivals are not out to overturn the system but, by playing to its rules, they actually strengthen it.

This outcome is by no means historically obvious. The basic mechanism of how competition has been positive for our system has to do with the particular relations between politics and economics that have developed. Catching-up is essentially an economic process and its importance is unique to the modern world-system. Other states take notice because one state, the hegemon, seems to have found the elusive recipe for success in the world-economy and its inter-state system. But it has never been purely a matter of economics. Success in wealth-creating always has the potential for conversion into military capability. Try as they might, hegemons have never been able to eliminate war and competition has continued to be expressed militarily. This means that no state can afford not to follow the example of the hegemon, if only to keep up with neighbours in its capacity to arm itself. States had to modernize or risk severe vulnerability in war. Whether an absolutist monarchy in the 17th century, a central European empire in the 19th century or a communist regime in the 20th century, political leaders ignored the example of the hegemon at their ultimate peril. In the 17th century the political theorist Thomas Hobbes saw the relation clearly: 'Wealth is power and power is wealth.'[115] Today we would say that emulating the hegemon is a political-economy imperative.

Emulation can take many different forms and varies greatly in terms of degrees of success. The point is that once the hegemon embarks on a restructuring of the world-economy, all other countries have to respond to the new agenda. Some may try to carve out their own niche avoiding the hegemon, others may closely follow the hegemon's lead, but all have their sights on catching up with the hegemon. They have to be 'modern' first, whatever their ultimate objectives: Lenin's definition of socialism as 'soviets plus electricity' remains the best expression of this political necessity. The result has been that 'modernization' has never required much forced feeding to the world. Whatever envy and suspicion the hegemons might generate, they remain attractive to others for what they have to offer — the means to catch up. In chronological order these means were: mercantilism, industrialization and corporatism. Below we interpret these well-known processes as vehicles of emulation.

Mercantilism: reacting to success in a 'static' world

Nobody in the 17th and 18th centuries called themselves a mercantilist. The 'mercantile system' was a phrase Adam Smith used in his *Wealth of Nations* (1776) to describe the theory and practice of restrictive state economic policies current in his time.[116] It was coined as a pejorative term to contrast with his own proposals for a more *laissez-faire* system. The term 'mercantilism' was used by the German school of economic history a century later when, in contrast with Smith, they looked favourably on the 'nationalist orientation' of these early economic theories. What was relevant to them was the state-building dimension of mercantilism.[117] These two contrary interpretations, negative economics and positive politics, were synthesized to a large degree by Eli Heckscher in his volume, *Mercantilism* (first published in the 1930s and re-published in the 1950s) which have dominated 20th-century discussion on the issue.[118] We will use his work as our starting point.

There are three debates stimulated by Heckscher's work that are directly relevant to our discussion. The first is about the relation between the economics and the politics of mercantilism which Heckscher criticized for overemphasizing the political power motive. In fact, the division inherent in 'plenty versus power' arguments is really false. States used merchants and merchants used states; their relationship was symbiotic and was recognized as such. Wilson describes the relation as a 'partnership':

> Kings' governments and bureaucracy saw in the expansion of mercantile prosperity the chance of larger revenues for themselves, and of a more prosperous and tranquil people to govern. Merchants saw in the 'state' the helping hand necessary to aid and protect them.[119]

Thus wealth-creation and state aggrandizement became 'coexisting ends of national policy which were fundamentally harmonious'.[120]

The second debate has focused upon the question of continuity with economic practices before the 17th century. Most mercantilist practices, such as tariff policies and production licensing, had been common before the rise of mercantilism; Heckscher assumed that the state policies in which he was interested were approximately equivalent. There are two issues here. First, cities had long conducted restrictive economic policies against their rivals incorporating most of the policies we associate with mercantilism. There is, however, a key difference in scale: mercantilism in the 17th century was about promoting large complex economic units that had system-wide implications.[121] Second, as early modern states centralized their functions in the 16th century, they developed new methods and institutions for budget management that were subsequently used for mercantilist ends. Again there is a key difference that is crucial to the development of the world-economy. In the 16th century fiscal policy was seen as extractive: the more the king taxed, the poorer his subjects. There was no notion of using fiscal policy to build the wealth of the country to make the tax-base larger. For instance, this idea is missing from Jean Bodin's classic writings on the state in 1576.[122] In contrast, in the era of mercantilism it was well understood that the richer the subjects, the richer the king. Hence the concern for matters economic and the search for successful policies to boost state economies. This aspect of mercantilism is thoroughly modern; the search is on-going.

The third key debate concerns Heckscher's neglect of the Netherlands. The numbers tell it all: 12 chapters on England, 10 on France but just one on Dutch economic practices in the 17th century.[123] This neglect is because Heckscher, like many other writers, did not consider the Dutch to be mercantilists since they did not fully fit into the concept of mercantilism as a system of economic restriction. This gets right to the heart of our interpretation of the meaning of mercantilism and its relationship to Dutch hegemony. To neglect Dutch economic policy in any treatment of 17th-century economic practices is perverse and can only be justified if their economic exceptionalism is treated solely as a phenomenon relevant to this one state. But this is not the case, of course.

Mercantilism is about multiple state competition in which the Dutch represented the 'problem' for the other states. The latter devised restrictive economic practices, later known as mercantilism, precisely to combat the Dutch. Hence from a system-wide view of mercantilism, the Dutch are not outside the process but at its very centre. The reason why the United Provinces does not appear to behave like a mercantilist state is simply because at its peak it did not have to.[124] H. H. Rowen succinctly sums up this position:

> The heart of Dutch economic policy could not be mercantilism in the specific sense represented by Colbert and defined [and condemned] by Adam Smith, it was in the literal sense a 'mercantile system' *par excellence*; indeed European mercantilism in the seventeenth century was designed specifically to overcome the Dutch 'mercantile system', which had the advantage when trade was most free and its principle channels flowed together in Holland.[125]

Hence mercantilism was created by the Dutch Republic's rivals as a means of coping with this precocious upstart. Not strong enough to emulate the Dutch and join in an economic liberal regime, they responded by making economic policy a crucial prop in their state-making.

The hesitant origins of English mercantilism illustrate this point well. At the beginning of the 17th century, England exported unfinished cloth to Holland where it was finished and re-exported at a profit. In 1614 James I imposed a ban on the export of undyed cloth as a direct challenge to the Dutch textile industry. The stakes were quite straightforward. Most of the final value of the cloth was added in the dyeing and England wanted to stop the Dutch accruing this value from their cloth. This policy was known as Alderman Cockade's project after the London merchant who devised it. But it was an abysmal failure. Dutch mills were the most efficient dye producers in Europe, and England could not compete with her finished cloth on the world market. Over three years cloth exports fell by a third and England had to admit defeat in this early trade war. With the policy abandoned in 1617, the Dutch continued with their highly lucrative finishing of English cloth for the world market.[126]

Partly as a result of this economic débâcle, in the economic crisis of 1622 the English government set up a Commission to investigate the causes of the problems and suggest remedies. One of the members of the Commission was Thomas Mun. As a result of his work for the Commission, he wrote *England's Treasure by Fforraign Trade* which Charles Wilson calls 'the bible of later mercantilism'.[127] The outcome was that the Commission, in what was effectively to define mercantile policy for the next century or more, devised remedies that explicitly targeted the Netherlands. All their main 'principles' can be reduced to economic attacks on the Dutch with the textile industry, merchant marine, Baltic trade and fishing industry particularly targeted.[128] If we agree with Wilson that English mercantilism stems from Mun, then there can be no doubt that it consisted overwhelmingly of economic policy to counter Dutch supremacy.[129]

In the first-half of the 17th century the English could not sustain their mercantilism in the face of Dutch hegemony. After 1650, this situation gradually changed. The symbolic legislation was Oliver Cromwell's Navigation Act of 1651 which, following the advice of the 1622 Commission, required all imports to be carried by English ships or ships of the country of origin. Intermediate carriers, notably the Dutch, were outlawed from English ports. In the second-half of the 17th century, it was not the English but the French who, as leaders in mercantilist practices, targeted the Dutch. Theirs was very much a top-down mercantilism stemming from the perceived state interests rather than merchant interests. It was the mercantilism as state-building so lauded by the German historical school in the late 19th century. The central figure was Jean-Baptiste Colbert, Louis XIV's chief minister for 22 years from 1661. His importance is reflected by the fact that mercantilism is sometimes termed 'Colbertism'. D. C. Coleman states this position neatly when he argues that 'Mercantilism without Colbert has some affinity to Hamlet without the Prince of Denmark.'[130] Like the English before him, Colbert saw the Dutch as an example of what trading could achieve. He reasoned that if Holland's two million people could create so much wealth, France's 19 million could produce so much more.[131] They had to be marshalled for this goal and Colbert devised detailed plans to promote trade and manufacture that have been likened to a planned economy.[132] But it was all a failure; high tariffs hit trade and the new state-planned factories were unsuccessful. Colbert

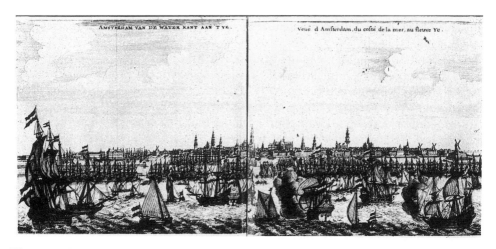

Plate 16 *The Port of Amsterdam seen from the Ij* (1665) from Caspar Commelin et al, *Beschryving der Stad Amsterdam* (Houghton Library, Harvard University). This very popular 'history and gazetteer' included a 'shopper's tour' with prices and values (Schama, 1987, 300–2). The hundreds of ships in this illustration represent the competition facing all other mercantilists as they tried to catch up with the Dutch

missed the essence of the Dutch success because he 'carried the principles of absolutism into the economic field'.[133] His ultimate purpose in all this was to enhance the glory of his king and such 'royal mercantilism' provided an unsatisfactory political-economy balance for success in the world-economy.

Although these rivals emulated the Dutch in the sense of systematically devising policies to promote their economies for the very first time, the main Dutch role was as economic target. This is not typical of high hegemony for either the British or Americans and needs explanation. In fact it relates back to Dutch hegemony occurring before the ideology of progress had made its mark. For mercantilists, economic competition was a zero-sum game: any benefits accruing to one country were therefore at the direct expense of others. For mercantilists, in Eli Heckscher's words: 'That the wealth of the world as a whole could increase was an idea wholly alien to them.'[134] The Dutch economic success was not perceived as leading the way to a more bountiful world but rather as taking from others. Sir William Temple in 1673 thought the Dutch success, the result of 'a great Concurrence of Circumstances', which was 'never before met in the world to such a degree . . . and perhaps never will again'.[135] Catching-up could only be by 'doing down' rivals, thus proscribing any economic inter-state co-operation.

This pessimism based on 'the pervasive conception of a prevailing inelastic demand' was not necessarily an unreasonable interpretation of economic reality in the 17th century[136] which was a general period of downturn in the world-economy with the Dutch as the great exception. In these circumstances devising policies to take away from the 'greedy Dutch' who were cornering more than their share of commerce and industry was to be expected. Hence the first hegemon became an economic target in this early modern world when the productive potential of technological advances of the capitalist world-economy was yet to be recognized.

Industrialization as 'revolution'

We have previously argued that industrialization was an integral part of Dutch economic superiority in the 17th century. That their achievement was largely forgotten with the invention of the term 'industrial revolution' to describe the later British achievements in production should, nevertheless, not be taken as an excuse for underestimating what happened in Britain in the half-century after 1760. The combination of iron and steam created an engineering that developed manufacturing on an altogether new scale of production. The new world thus created seemed to contemporaries a bigger economic transition than anything previously experienced and to later generations was recognizable as the origins of their modern world. Hence the general acceptance of the phrase 'industrial revolution'. For our interpretation, we do not doubt the revolutionary effects of Britain's new production processes; we place them as the middle case of three such 'revolutions'.

There was one important difference between Dutch and British industrialization. By the time British hegemony was emerging, the cultural context in which technology was viewed was changing dramatically. Contemporaries were expecting change and even beginning to worship it. Thus Britain as the locus of modernity could be a diffusion centre in a way that was impossible for the Dutch. There can be no quarrel that Britain's technological advances had more direct impact. In addition, the new mechanization had the potential for diffusion across other lands that Dutch industry never possessed. Despite Dutch innovations, wind power had scale limitations which the new British technology overcame. A key advantage of British production was the sheer size of its undertakings, enabling it to overwhelm markets across Europe and the Americas to a degree that was unprecedented.[137]

According to Peter Stearns, 'after 1800 imitation became a necessity', for all of Britain's rivals.[138] Even before that date French and German governments were sending representatives to Britain to try to find the secrets of the new industrial advances.[139] Obviously the technological developments in metallurgy were of particular interest given their military relevance and hence potential impact on power politics. This was immediately demonstrated in the wars against Napoleon when Britain alone withstood the French. As Prime Minister William Pitt saw it, 'the country had saved herself by her own actions and saved Europe by her example'.[140] But the impact of British industry reached well beyond power politics. The war had provided a vital stimulus to the British textile industry, and once peace came markets opened up across Europe. Napoleon's continental blockage had isolated and protected European industries; with the coming of peace they were subjected to competition from technically superior rivals, leading to economic collapse. Technological imitation became as much an economic necessity as a political one.

The story of the diffusion of industrialization to Europe from Britain in the 19th century has been told many times.[141] As well as the export of commodities for consumption, Britain was soon exporting capital, machinery and labour. For instance major railway lines were built in Belgium, France and Austria 'by British capital, on British design, using British machines, by British contractors using largely British labour'.[142] In addition, every early European example of a modern engineering plant and textile factory was the result of some similar British import. Until 1843, laws forbade the export of machinery but these never had the desired effect, partly

Plate 17 *View from the Window of the Royal Technical College, Salford* (1924) by W. S. Lowry (City Art Gallery, Salford). Lowry is *the* artist of industrial England and the most popular British artist of the 20th century. Known for his paintings of 'matchstick men and women' — ordinary people in an industrial world — he also left a legacy of pencil drawings of industrial landscapes the most famous of which is featured here. This scene captures both the grime and grandeur of industrialization

as the result of successful smuggling across the English Channel. Europe was becoming one large economic region with the major industrial core in Britain plus minor industrial centres scattered across north-central Europe.[143] These were the economic survivors of the expansion of British goods on the European market after 1815. The survival trick was to avoid direct competition while finding a niche in the restructuring the hegemon was sponsoring.[144] Since Britain, for all its technological achievements, could not supply the entire demand that was growing, there were opportunities for others. In textiles, for instance, the French were soon successfully specializing in high-quality clothes while the Germans were taking advantage of their geographical location between the advanced British and the backward areas on their landward interior to sell to the latter. Although Britain maintained its economic lead into the second-half of the 19th century, the process of industrialization was a European story throughout the century.

The revolutionary nature of this industrialization was more than the diffusion of technology. Along with the machines went a whole new way of life centring on risk for the entrepreneur and discipline for labour. For this reason Britain exported people as well as commodities and machines. The Cockerill family are the classic example of British entrepreneurs introducing industrialization to the continent.[145] Due to the economic depression of 1797, William Cockerill left Britain and after a failed venture in Sweden, settled in Belgium where he was tremendously successful. He began by transforming the textile industry, soon moved on to machine-making and by 1812 had a factory in Liège employing 2000 people. His importance was recognized by Napoleon who made him a French citizen. He prospered under the continental blockade with France, Germany and the Low Countries as captive market. His business not only survived after 1815 but went from strength to strength: for instance, the Prussian government invited the Cockerills to set up the first machine-building factory in Berlin. By the 1830s, when John Cockerill had become head of the family, they operated the largest integrated industrial complex in the world near Liège where iron production and machine-making were brought together. It was said of John Cockerill that he 'had a mission to extend manufactures everywhere and to fill the whole world with machinery'.[146] Here we have the image of a new industrial world that was glimpsed by contemporary observers:

> John Cockerill travels on the great highways in his coach. Here he builds furnaces and there chimney stacks. . . . he erects steam engines which have followed in his wake . . . and which breathe life into the great piles of bricks. And the next day the peasants hear a loud rhythmical noise coming from the factory – like the breathing of some enormous monster who, once he has begun to work, will never stop. And John Cockerill climbs back into his coach and government officials unsuspectingly sign his passport as if it referred to a consignment of wine and they do not realize that this silent man who seldom puts pen to paper is far more likely to turn their world upside down than many a revolutionary who has his pockets stuffed with political programmes and manifestoes.[147]

The peasants did not immediately take to industrial life. British labour was imported to the growing industrial regions of Europe not just for their technical skills but also because of their attitude to work. As well as a factory discipline of work much different from agricultural pursuits, new industry prospered when workers were eager to work long hours and learn new skills. This required an ambitious attitude that considered extra work and training worth doing for the extra money and a better future. The peasant 'mentality' was a traditional one of only working as necessary for immediate needs. British workers were as essential for spreading the modern work ethic as they were for the use of their skills. In the 1820s, for instance, there were over 15 000 British workers in France alone.[148] No country industrialized in the 19th century without British labour. The heyday of this labour migration was the first-half of the century, but even later the foremen of factories across Europe were often recruited from Manchester or the other great cities of northern Britain.[149]

Under British tutelage industrialization, and its concomitant urbanization, became defined as modern. The economic superiority of the hegemon produced a sense of inferiority among rivals just as the 17th-century Dutch had stimulated such feelings. Some contemporaries thought the British to be a special type of people, like the Dutch before them, that could not be matched in the new skills of the age.[150] Many more thought the economic gap could be closed and they worked accordingly. In this modernization process the idea of 'catching up' was part of the spirit of the times. Everybody tried it and before the century was out some countries had achieved their goal of becoming modern, that is industrial, societies. They joined Britain at the top of the international league table thus concluding British hegemony.

Corporatism and the political primacy of economic growth

In the 20th century the prime purpose of government has been to stimulate economic growth within its territory. Governments are judged on this criterion throughout the world and are elected out of office or otherwise disposed of when they fail to deliver the goods. It is inevitable that in such circumstances the nature of the political economy of states will be changed. The economic dimension of government policy so stimulated by the Dutch and the British will be greatly reinforced if every government's survival depends directly on its economic success. In these circumstances economic growth is too important to be left to the vagaries of the market and private interests. The result has been that the 19th century's era of economic liberalism was replaced by 'the century of corporatism'.[151] Corporatism is basically a political economy where government and industry are partners in the running of the national economy. It has taken so many different forms at different times and places in the 20th century that further refinement of this definition is not fruitful at this stage. We can note, however, the common theme that the perceived necessity of economic growth requires a partnership of private and public interests: both big business and big government have been hallmarks of American hegemony.

The rise of corporatism in all its many forms is a very complex process whose origins predate American hegemony. The competitive capitalism that Marx described in the mid-19th century had given way to a different form of capitalism by the beginning of the 20th century. The concentration of capital that Marx predicted produced a much less competitive economic situation where just a few large corporations dominated the market in many leading industrial sectors. Hence, the second generation of Marxist theorists such as Lenin recognized a new stage of capitalism which they called 'monopoly capitalism'.[152] With the coming of World War I they were confident that this was indeed the predicted final death throes of capitalism, but they were proved wrong. The world-economy survived and ultimately thrived, with state help, in yet another stage commonly referred to as 'state monopoly capitalism'.[153] In a more original interpretation of the increased state involvement in the economy, instead of defining a further stage out of old theories, J. T. Winkler has suggested corporatism represents a new mode of production distinct from both capitalism and socialism.[154] If this were true it would represent the construction of an alternative to the capitalist world-economy. Since the latter has always been a matter of political economy rather than 'pure' market economics, corporatism is better understood as a new political economy within capitalism rather than its replacement. In any case, whatever the potential of corporatism to supersede capitalism, we can be sure the hegemon would not let it happen. Under US leadership corporatism has been accommodated to a reconstruction of the world-economy in the hegemon's image.

Corporatism in the USA has always been very distinctive. It emerged in the first decades of this century as the way in which political elites came to terms with the rise of great corporations. At the turn of the century popular esteem for the reputation of American business leaders was at an all time low. As 'robber barons', their private interests were not seen as compatible with the public interest.[155] For instance the richest man in America, John D. Rockefeller, was also the most hated – leading Progressive politician Senator Robert LaFollette called him 'the greatest criminal of the age'.[156] The progressive movement encompassed both Republicans and Democrats in schemes to reform unbridled capitalism most notably through President Teddy Roosevelt's Anti-Trust laws which resulted in the break up of Rockefeller's Standard Oil Company. Soon it became clear to both economic and political elites that they needed each other; battle lines gave way to the search for a political economy where the great 'captains of industry' could become partners rather than opponents of government. In the 1920s Commerce Secretary Herbert Hoover promoted policies to aid industry through co-operation which came to be known as the 'associative state'. According to Michael Hogan, this is when the basic lineaments of American corporatism were set.[156] Government would deal with autonomous economic groups through joint institutions where the power of government would be geared towards economic growth. The latter was the key for general acceptance of this middle way between *laissez-faire* and 'statism'. Growth was good for business; it also allowed for the construction of a consensus politics where economic conflicts could be dealt with, without any radical redistribution among classes.[157]

With the economic collapse of the 1930s, such corporatism was widely seen as more necessary than ever and Franklin Roosevelt's New Deal confirmed it as the new American political economy. Although assailed from both the Republican right and the radical left, corporatism became the way America did business. As we described in Chapter 2, defeats for the government in the Supreme Court meant that direct intervention in the economy was curtailed and American corporatism became the weaker regulatory variety. Notwithstanding the debates and conflict, Roosevelt was able to bring representatives from both labour unions and business into the government decision-making process. For instance, 'moderate' Republicans such as leading industrialists Averell Harriman and Paul Hoffman began their public service careers during the New Deal on the National Recovery Administration's Business

Advisory Council, a classic corporatist institution.[158] In the wider world this new corporatism 'fundamentally altered the shape of American diplomacy'.[159] Whereas Woodrow Wilson in World War I had been promoting a liberal world order of free-trading states similar to that found in the mid-19th century, the new corporatism implied a much more interventionist policy to promote trade.

America's opportunity to promote its brand of corporatism to the world came after World War II. As the only major viable national economy in 1945, the US was in an extremely powerful position. However, as we saw in Chapter 2, initial attempts to restructure the world-economy to aid US business failed: the use of conditional loans was insufficient to stimulate European economies. Part of the problem, from America's perspective, was that the general trend towards corporatism had taken a rather different course in Europe.[160] Here it had become associated with various forms of socialism and its priorities had become welfare provision and nationalization of key sectors of industry. The international implications of such policies were a tendency towards autarchy: in this form of corporatism, national planning for economic growth would likely involve tariff policies to protect industry. Although the initial US loans prevented a return to 1930s-style protectionism, without an improvement in European economies, it seemed only a matter of time before the tariffs went up, probably after the coming to power of far-left or even communist governments. In these circumstances, the US devised its Marshall Plan to stimulate European economies and set them on a self-sustaining path of recovery.

In June 1947, the US Secretary of State George Marshall gave a speech at Harvard University in which he invited European governments to come forward with a joint economic recovery plan to be funded by the USA. Led by British Foreign Secretary Ernest Bevin, Western European governments formed the Organization of European Economic Co-operation (OEEC), put together an amalgam of plans for economic growth and the Marshall Plan was born. Paul Hoffman was put in charge of the Economic Co-operation Administration which co-ordinated the US aid, and Averell Harriman ran its Paris office as liaison to the OEEC.[161] Although the Europeans were formally in charge of formulating their economic plans, it was clear that the Americans would not approve European corporatism going any further down the statist line. In this respect the new US policy was very successful. In addition, it was, in George Kennan's words 'a psychological success'.[162] The hegemon created an incomparable image of itself as the land of plenty unselfishly sending over boatloads of goods to help a failed Europe. Pro-American moderates — whether they were social democrats, Christian democrats or liberal conservatives — soon had the upper hand in domestic politics. Tailored to fit each country, the Marshall Plan led to alternative types of corporatism across Western Europe but nowhere did it transgress the needs of American business. Corporatisms emerged that were liberal internationally, and their 'socialism' remained largely welfare-orientated posing no threat to US business.[163] The two decades after the Marshall Plan constitute the period of great expansion of US multinational corporations and Western Europe was the main locus of foreign investment. The Marshall Plan ranks as a classic hegemonic economic strategy.

The example the USA offered the European countries was of a corporatism where the class politics of redistribution could be ameliorated by satisfying all classes through economic growth. With the emphasis on economic management for growth, political problems were converted into technical questions for which experts could be found to provide the answers.[164] Everything reduced to productivity; and the USA was only too willing to lend Europe its experts on how to produce more of everything. Soon, as Theodore White has pointed out, the American expert had 'become in the outer world as much a stock character as was the British traveller of the nineteenth century'.[165] Under Harriman in Paris, for instance, there were 2500 'experts' who with their families became a colony of 7500 Americans directly illustrating the connection between living the good life and American can-do attitudes.[166] The Europeans showed themselves to be very good at playing catch-up and the land of plenty was soon to expand to Europe. The post-war success of corporatism ensured the Americanization of Europe.

Americanization represents the most explicit emulation in our story of hegemons.[167] We have previously emphasized the very conspicuous consumption half of this process; the production side was of equal importance. This was *The American Challenge* that so concerned Jean-Jacques Servan-Schreiber in his seminal book written in the mid-1960s.[168] In some ways this was a book of despair for Europe not having imitated America sufficiently. He showed that it was American corporations that had taken most advantage of the European Economic Community; from an American perspective the Treaty of Rome was 'the sweetest deal'.[169] The prescription was clear: we must learn our lessons from the Americans to do better in the future.[170] First, copy American business organization to create major European companies to compete on the world market. Second, activate closer co-operation between government and industry; he uses the example of the US electronics industry and castigates the European Economic Community for its emphasis on agricultural policy. Third, promote investment in high tech; he deplores Europe's failure to enter the space race and its divisions in the computer industry. Fourth, invest in social justice to open up society; he eulogizes American universities and sees a place for his own moderate socialism in building a more equal society on the back of continuous economic growth.

The fact that this popular text appeared near the end of American high hegemony is testimony to the depth of American world leadership. Corporatism and its associated 'mixed economy' had proven to be a highly flexible political economy. Whether 'labourism' in Britain, social democracy in Scandinavia, Gaullist statism in France or Christian democracy in much of the rest of Western Europe, various forms of corporatist institutions searched for the right economic balance to catch up with the USA. But American optimism underlay it all. Let us allow Servan-Schreiber the last word: 'For societies, as for men, there can be no growth without challenge. Progress is a battle, just as life is a struggle.'[171] This is yet another metaphor for hegemony – to stimulate through challenge.

Embedding liberalism II

This chapter has been about embedding liberalism beyond the boundaries of the hegemonic state. Before proceeding, we need to distinguish further between our process of embedding liberalism and John Ruggie's concept of the condition of 'embedded liberalism'.[172] He has coined that phrase to describe the international political economy under US hegemony as specifically different to the one Britain dominated a century earlier. In particular he refers to embedded liberalism after 1945 as a compromise linking economic liberalism between states with safeguarding stability through welfare within states: 'protection' within states but not between them. This is what we have just described as corporatism and is obviously missing from British hegemony. For Ruggie, 'embedded' means a specific integration of international practices with domestic state practices; my use of 'embedding' relates not to states but to the system as a whole with various liberalisms diffusing between, within and across states. Hence Ruggie's condition of embedded liberalism is just one part of the broader process I identify.

Embedding liberalism at the international scale is explicitly captured by the clever phrase 'empire by invitation'. This was coined by Geir Lundestad to contrast US military involvement in Western Europe with the USSR's control of Eastern Europe during the Cold War.[173] For instance, US bases in, say, Britain were never seen by the population as an army of occupation in the way the Red Army was viewed in Czechoslovakia or any other Warsaw Pact country. If indeed Britain was 'occupied' it was by choice, it was a 'hegemonic occupation'. Quite simply Europeans were very keen to be part of an American sphere of influence in the late 1940s and the British politician Ernest Bevin can even be said to be the major architect of this sector of *pax Americana* – he was pivotal in the formation of both the OEEC and NATO.[174] Hence the paradox that is 'empire by invitation'. It is not an imperium in the traditional meaning of direct political control but represents an alternative way of structuring the world to a leader's needs. It is part of the hegemonic way of domination. If the US had its 'empire by invitation', we should expect something similar to have operated through the other two hegemons.

In the case of British hegemony the term 'informal imperialism' was used to describe its international political economy underlying embedding liberalism. The term 'informal empire' was first coined to describe Britain's relations with Latin American states after their independence in the 1820s. Employing 'free-trade imperialism', Britain in the mid-19th century was able to mould the economies of Latin America to its own requirements just as easily as in its formal empire left over from its earlier mercantilist activities. More generally, informal imperialism came to mean the process of economic domination without the costs of political occupation. This was not quite as anti-militaristic as it first appears – much embedding coincided with extension of *pax Britannica* through the auspices of Royal Navy cannon or 'gunboat diplomacy'. Nevertheless this was undoubtedly a very efficient and cheap way of embedding liberalism.

In a similar manner the Dutch had an 'informal empire' in the Baltic region during the 17th century. With no direct political control, the United Provinces was able to maintain friendly regimes in the region that suited its economy. This was crucial to the Dutch for both material and symbolic reasons. Commodities for the Baltic region were generally known as the 'mother trade', the bulk carrying upon which Dutch wealth had originally been built. As in the case of Britain, the Dutch did occasionally use their naval power to get their own way, but generally this was achieved by forming favourable alliances with the most powerful political elites in the region to provide adequate and very cheap attention to their local economic needs.

As this chapter has illustrated, there is much more to embedding liberalism than 'empire by invitation' and informal imperialism. During high hegemony other states are structurally in a position of economic dependence so that to resist the hegemon would have dire consequences for their economic well-being. The arguments against the Marshall Plan from both the right and left could be relatively marginalized in European politics because economic dependence on the USA was recognized as a 'fact of life'. Opponents had no alternative to offer except the most austere of austerities. In Latin America, Britain took over the dependence links that had once led to the erstwhile imperial power Spain, and pro-British 'liberal' parties were, on the whole, able to win state power on the basis of the necessity of this British connection. And in the Baltic region, Dutch support for landowners produced a ruling class with no means of getting their goods to market except through the good offices of the Dutch and their ships. In both these earlier cases, local oppositions had little chance of victory against the hegemon who controlled their access to the world market.

'Empire by invitation?' Not exactly. In the words of a famous mafia film, it is an offer you can't refuse. Very few states in the history of the world-economy have been able to resist the invitation to become 'modern'. That is the ultimate basis of embedding liberalism.

5 Post-hegemonic trauma

I have not been able to resist beginning this chapter with my personal experiences of comparative international change. While having lived all my life in Great Britain, I have been a regular visitor to the USA since 1970. These visits have ranged from many conference trips lasting just a week or two to a few semester and annual visiting positions at US universities adding up to about four years in all. Hence I have had the opportunity to observe America from the inside while remaining very much an outsider. From the height of the protests against the war in Vietnam to the contemporary travails of President Clinton, I have lived with both American hopes and traumas. And in listening to Americans debating the future of their country, one sense has overwhelmed my thoughts: *déjà vu*. To a person from Britain where questions of decline have dominated politics for the best part of a century, recent American concern for its position in the world seems like a remake of an old movie.

On one short trip to the US in 1988 I bought a copy of Paul Kennedy's *The Rise and Fall of the Great Powers* from an airport bookshop.[1] I knew it was number one in the *New York Times* bestsellers' list and therefore read it on my trip home with a view to finding out why. Initial perusal of the text was not helpful: nearly 700 pages on five hundred years of history, including 1300 footnotes, by a Yale professor hardly seemed a recipe for popular success. Of course, the book did not reflect an increased popular curiosity about the demise of Hapsburg Spain and other former great powers; rather the book sold because of its message about contemporary America. Kennedy used the experience of previous great powers to draw lessons for the USA. His book struck such a chord with the American public because it informed their worries about the relative decline of their country. By putting the serious concerns for America's future into a meaningful historical perspective, Paul Kennedy conjured up a monster publishing hit.

Not surprisingly it was his last chapter entitled 'To the Twenty-first Century', and especially the final section 'The United States: The Problem of Number One in Relative Decline' that elicited most response from the American reading public.[2] The marketing men were well aware of this and included in their cover design a cartoon featuring an Olympic-style world podium from which Britain had stepped down, the USA had one foot off the top while Japan was just about to step up. In this chapter I will be concerned with all three podium actors, but obviously it is the idea of America following Britain into decline which initially interested me in Kennedy's book. It showed me that my *déjà vu* feelings were not just a product of a British upbringing; Americans took seriously the comparison with my own country. In

Kennedy's case his explanation of American decline as 'imperial overstretch' was explicitly drawn in relation to late 19th-century British experience. He portrays US military force deployments for 1987 on a world map and argues that they 'look extraordinarily similar to the chain of fleet bases and garrisons possessed by that former world power, Great Britain, at the height of its strategic overstretch' c.1900.[3] With all this in mind, on my next major sojourn to the USA as a visiting professor at Virginia Tech in 1992–3, I was determined to explore this American–British decline link and this chapter is the result.[4]

To set the context, let us begin by looking briefly at some of the ways in which American concern for the direction their country is going closely parallels what the British were thinking a century ago.[5] Both debates began with a major statement on why the country must change direction, using the example of the previous hegemon as evidence of what happens if nothing is done. In the British case the influential lectures of imperial historian J. R. Seeley, presented in 1881–2 and published in 1884 as *The Expansion of England*, began by using the example of the Dutch whose history he interpreted as being 'wound up'.[6] This was a clear warning to Britain's politicians. Certainly the influential Joseph Chamberlain, who in the 1900s was to become the great crusader for tariff reform, understood the message.[7] He was later to refer to Holland as a former world leader that now 'counts for nothing'.[8] Similarly, in his influential 1966 lectures published as *The Arrogance of Power*, US Senator William Fulbright used the decline of Britain for precisely the same purpose.[9] To Chamberlain Britain had become a 'Weary Titan', for Fulbright the USA was a 'Crippled Giant'.[10] Intellectual concern was soon translated into popular worries with, for instance 'shock books' with similar concepts in titles: in Britain *The American Invaders* appeared in 1901, while more recently Americans have been able to read about *The Coming War with Japan*.[11]

If we look at the actual structure of the debate the parallels just get stronger. The external target for Britain's ills was unfair trading practices by its economic rivals. While Britain was playing the game, others were cheating. The cry was for 'fair trade': if only there was a level playing field the results would be very different. For German and American bashing by the British, read Japanese and European bashing by the Americans. Internal targets were also very similar. At the beginning of the century Britain experienced a 'national efficiency movement' that recognized rivals were winning for reasons other than unfair trading. This movement was particularly concerned for the health of the population – a healthy population is a productive one – and education, especially technical education. In the 1992 US Presidential Election campaign nobody, as far as I am aware, used the phrase 'national efficiency' but that was what it was all about: one of the main reasons Clinton won was because he linked proposals to solve both the health care crisis and the education crisis to stemming economic decline.

The call for efficiency was directly related to concern for erosion of each country's industrial base. Being outsold in the world market was seen in strategic terms and pitted manufacturers against financiers. The latter were accused of neglecting investment in home industry, of being cosmopolitan at the expense of their own country. Joseph Chamberlain argued that in the battles ahead, Britain would not be able to fight a war with foreign financial portfolios and a strong pound sterling; it needed a successful industrial base. In fact when war came in 1914 it soon emerged that British

Plate 18 *Unfair Trading*, an Arthur Moreland cartoon postcard produced by C. W. Faulkner (London) in 1903. At first the relative economic decline of Britain was blamed upon the trading practices of rivals. In this case customers cannot even reach the door of John Bull's British emporium because of unscrupulous foreigners. The parallels with US trade debates today are obvious.

reliance on German machine tools was to be a problem. The current US concern for reliance on Japanese computer technology in missile systems, as evidenced by the Gulf War, is recycling another old story.

From the world-systems' perspective pursued in this book, these cases of state decline are more than 'the fall of great powers'; they represent the down-side of hegemonic cycles. As such, this is a system-wide phenomenon whose repercussions are felt by all. As we related in Chapter 1, it was the changing nature of international politics from about 1970, that is after US high hegemony, that stimulated thinking in terms of hegemonic decline to understand contemporary change. While most of this work has, most properly, focused on the international repercussions, there are extremely interesting effects that occur within the hegemonic states themselves. This chapter is about the reaction of hegemons to their decline and the debates that are thus precipitated. We call the effects of the decline 'post-hegemonic trauma' to indicate its distinctive and severe nature. In general, we can note that because the modern world-system is a very dynamic social entity, rises and falls among social groups and states within the hierarchies of the system are quite normal and not at all exceptional. In the case of a particular rise or fall, there will be the inevitable elation of success or worry about failure so that at any one time the inter-state system consists of multiple citizenries displaying varying degrees of elation or worry and rewarding, rejecting or resisting their state politicians accordingly. All this is standard practice for this world-system. Those rare cases of world hegemony, however, add a unique extra dimension to this incessant dynamism.

The rise and fall of a hegemonic state is very special by definition. The elation of the rise leads to the 'world arrogance' we have discussed previously, but what does decline mean? The phrase that comes to mind is 'the higher you climb, the greater the fall' which seems quite apposite here. Hegemonic decline is the greatest fall of all. The experience is particularly traumatic because from defining the future for others, the hegemon discovers a real future where it is in competition with those who were emulating it only a few decades earlier. Instead of a promise, the future becomes viewed as a threat. The supreme optimism of high hegemony gives way to the uncertainties of a new world that was never contemplated. How can the recent epitome of everything modern resign itself to being just another state, albeit still very powerful, in the inter-state system? Since the situation was never envisaged by either elites or public, there are no ideological resources – frameworks for thinking – to draw upon to accommodate relative decline. I suggest that the worry associated with 'normal' decline is multiplied many times over for a hegemon to produce a qualitatively different condition we can interpret as a 'collective trauma'. Being top of the world hierarchy had come to seem so natural, it is almost impossible for the hegemon and its citizens to understand any other future except a continuation of their immense but now past successes.

I first coined the phrase 'post-hegemonic trauma' as a description of *la crise anglaise* but with the firm expectation it would be applicable to both Dutch and especially American circumstances.[12] This is tested out in this chapter. In the first section I interpret Dutch and British relative decline as historical impasses in the sense of collective *culs-de-sac* from which there was no way back to 'greatness'. Post-hegemonic trauma is centrally located in this process. This provides the framework for the core section of the chapter which deals with the American conundrum. It is a conundrum in two senses. First, there is the real mystery of the mismatch between American economic and political fortunes: how US relative economic decline coincides with Cold War victory and sole superpower status. Second, whatever our model might say about American impasse following Dutch and British impasses, such an eventuality lies in the future: historical impasses are knowable in a way that a future one cannot be. Hence, we can only show that the same symptoms of post-hegemonic trauma exist, implying the conundrum will be resolved finally as an impasse. In the third section we consider the USA's great rivals in its hegemony and aftermath. The USSR and Japan are treated as opposite challenges to the hegemon, first a failed political rival and then a much more successful economic one. Both challenges provide important markers for a future world impasse which is the subject matter of the final chapter: ideological alternatives to capitalism are introduced in the discussion of the Soviet Union and the impossibility of another hegemonic state is argued with respect to Japan. This position is developed in a final section, where the case is put that trans-state processes have become so advanced that hegemony can no longer be organized through a territorial state. We suggest an alternative network organization through world cities which we call 'ultra-hegemony'.

Historical impasses

In the British general election of 1987 a new political grouping, an alliance of the Liberal and Social Democratic Parties, seriously threatened the country's two-party system. Part of their appeal was to offer a new politics, a fresh approach to tackling Britain's problems of decline. But how new were they really? The manifesto they presented to the British electorate began with the words 'Britain yearns for greatness' and proceeded to say how they would satisfy this yearning where many before them had failed. Oh dear! Here we are near the end of the 20th century and British politicians still appeal on the dubious promise of greatness. This is a mind-set that seems impossible to get out of. In the previous election of 1983, Mrs Thatcher's Conservatives recorded a landslide electoral victory a year after a crushing military victory in the Falklands. Who put the Great back into Britain? Maggie did. Oh dear, oh dear. By their very lateness, these symptoms of post-hegemonic trauma illustrate the depth of the affliction within the British collective mentality. What makes it worse is that it is all so hopeless: Britannia will never rule the waves again. It is not that the trauma is accompanied by delusions of future grandeur, rather there is an amnesia towards present predicaments. Hegemonic decline is not something that can be turned around; it is a social impasse.

There are two basic reasons we can classify this particular social change as an impasse: one objective, the other subjective. The first reason for the inevitability of decline from high hegemony derives from the liberal nature of the hegemons.[13] With their 'open door' policies, rivals are able to emulate, as we documented in the last chapter, and there is no good reason to assume rivals will remain mere emulators. Given all the prerequisites of the new political economy created by the hegemon, other states will develop and improve production and even apply innovations of their own. The only way in which this might not happen would be if the hegemon really were occupied by a people with unique attributes that made them innately superior to all others. Although such sentiments can be found during high hegemony, this is self-evidently not the case. Hence the hegemon's own nature ensures its pre-eminence is only transitory.

The second reason for impasse returns us to the question of the collective mentality stimulated by experience of hegemony. Very often this relates more to what is not done than what is. There is no wish to accommodate to relative decline so that serious and popular debate to adapt to reduced circumstances goes by default. Instead of realistic appraisals of decline and sensible use of the accumulated wealth of past successes, the goal of restoration dominates all. Political differences focus upon different means towards this overriding goal. Political elites and their publics, nourished on being 'Number 1', debate how to remain a great power and keep all rivals in their place. The result is that the hegemon sets off down a political *cul-de-sac* of its own making which reinforces the impasse resulting from objective factors. In seeking the glories of the past, chances of a better future are eroded. Continual political failure only adds fuel to the collective trauma as the country moves further and further from what its leaders and people see as their rightful position. Hence there is a very important cultural lag which is our subject matter here: the objective loss of hegemony may be a relatively rapid affair – a decade or so; subjective post-hegemonic trauma is a long drawn out affair – a century or so. Hence the politics of restoration as late as 1980s' Britain; and it has been said that the Dutch 'yearning for greatness' was only laid to rest by the revolution of 1848.

In this section we look at the impasse the Dutch and British reached with the downturn of their respective hegemonic cycles and the process of conversion to 'normality' for both states and peoples. This acts as a prelude to consideration of the USA in the next section. We begin with the two hegemons we can be sure are not about to make a comeback, the historical impasses of the Dutch and the British.

Dutch impasse: from hegemon to minor power

Jacob and Mijnhardt have argued that the case of the Dutch Republic in the 18th century is the most extreme example of state decline in the modern world.[14] It is hard to dissent from their appraisal. We offer three key reasons why it is so. First, and as we noted in the last chapter, the European context of the decline provided a paradoxical cultural framework: as the Enlightenment was pointed towards universal progress, the Dutch were contemplating a very recent golden age. Second, there is the simple matter of size. Always small in population compared with their great rivals, in the 18th century the situation worsened dramatically: as the Dutch remained at about two million the British grew from nine to 16 million and the French from 18 to 28 million.[15] Third, there was the fact that the Dutch Republic had no experience of being a minor power.[16] Created at the cockpit of European politics in the late 16th century, it had been a major player from its inception: we could say that it was 'born great'. This was a formidable mixture of factors facing the Dutch after their golden age and accounts for the particular form that their post-hegemonic trauma took.

The facts of Dutch decline are well known and are remarkable for the coincidence between political and economic changes. Politically, the initial watershed is the French invasion of 1672. According to Schama this marked the end of an era altering 'the Republic's sense of its own place in Europe'.[17] He argues that the shock of 1672, when French captured Utrecht and briefly threatened Amsterdam, forced the Dutch to play a role in Europe's balance-of-power system which was a 'dilution of their singularity' making them 'more acceptably ordinary'.[18] But the longing to be a great power was not thereby removed; hence Kossmann's suggestion that the Dutch only became reconciled to a minor status in the international system in 1848.[19] Between 1672 and 1848 there were many political humiliations as the Republic spiralled down the inter-state hierarchy. At the close of the War of the Spanish Succession, the Dutch were out-manoeuvred by their British allies in negotiations with France at Utrecht in 1713. From this time forth the Republic's international influence had clearly fallen behind that of its two main rivals.[20] In 1747 it was invaded again by France and had to accept a humiliating peace. With the fourth Anglo–Dutch War (1780–4) comes another disastrous defeat, this time culminating in the Patriot Revolution put down by an invading Prussian Army in 1787. The Republic was finally extinguished by the French Revolutionary armies in 1795. Reconstituted as a kingdom in 1815 including the former Hapsburg 'southern' Netherlands, it was divided after the 1830 revolution and suffered its final revolution in 1848.

The loss of international prestige was only part of the story. One of the reasons for the French invasion in 1672 was the decision the previous year by the special committee for economic affairs in Amsterdam to retaliate against aggressive French mercantilism. Israel argues that this 'opened a new era in Dutch economic thought, one characterized by more overtly mercantilist attitudes'.[21] The Dutch were becoming less exceptional economically as well as politically. The War of the Spanish Succession (1701–14) saddled the country with a huge debt that contributed directly to international withdrawal and left no part of the economy unaffected.[22] Despite being on the winning side, this was an even greater 'bad war' for the Dutch than 1672. Israel sees the 1740s as the next key watershed when the Dutch entrepôt failed to respond to changes in trade patterns and was transformed from 'an active controlling force in world trade to a passive staple or storehouse'.[23] Only Rotterdam and Amsterdam survived as major ports. In addition the latter prospered in its 'second life' as a great financial centre in the second-half of the 18th century only succumbing to London's pre-eminence in the last decades.[24] This is in complete contrast with industrial developments at the time. The great textile towns of Haarlem and Leiden lost about half their population and in the other great Dutch industry, shipbuilding, by the 1720s the Dutch were even employing English shipwrights to learn the latest techniques.[25] No wonder a contemporary was to lament in 1775: 'We are no longer innate inventors, and originality is becoming increasingly rare with us here. Nowadays we only make copies, whereas formerly we made only originals.'[26] There can be no clearer statement recognizing lost hegemony.

The political and economic decline is usually linked to cultural changes in Dutch society as the last quotation implies. The golden age is usually contrasted with 'the periwig period' when 'aristocratization' of the top economic strata resulted in the creation of an unenterprising ruling elite of wealthier *rentiers* and merchant bankers.[27] According to Julia Adams:

> That the Dutch elite failed to carry out [necessary] reforms was in part due to the fact that they were no longer merchants, so their perceived economic, political and familial well-being had become progressively uncoupled from the immediacies of trade.[28]

Subsequently, with no 'industrial mentality', the Dutch 'missed' the British-led industrial revolution to become a trading and agricultural country appropriate to its minor status in the 19th century.

No wonder Jacob and Mijnhardt view the 18th century as a 'gloomy picture' and 'deeply troubled time' for the Dutch.[29] To show the existence of post-hegemonic trauma, however, we have to go a stage further and consider their political practices. Kossmann is particularly good on this matter.[30] Although there was overwhelming evidence of a very severe problem in their country, the Dutch did not accept their days as a great power were over. Despite many political setbacks and economic stagnation, the faith remained that all could be righted. Kossmann focuses on the opportunity facing William IV when he came to power in 1747, when the weakness of the Dutch was clear for all to see. Why didn't the new ruler use his power to reorientate the Dutch state by ending great power pretensions, and thus reduce expenses, to use its still formidable remaining wealth for economically constructive ends? It was precisely this action that was impossible: to be Dutch was to be an international player. There could be no such politics of change. Rather, the sole political agenda was centred on actions to restore the country's greatness. The Orangist party thought keeping to tried and trusted methods would eventually work, the Patriots had an extreme nationalist reform programme to 'modernize' the state but for the same end. Dutch politics was in a *cul de sac* from which it could only emerge after defeat in war and revolution. In the 19th century the Dutch transcended their impasse and replaced a debilitating post-hegemonic trauma with a simple nostalgia for a past golden age within a minor state at last congruent with its size.

British impasse: from hegemon to medium power

Britain's descent from hegemony is more complicated. In this case decline is masked to a large degree by imperialism. Hence the question of size, ultimately so important in the Dutch case, is confused: Britain was a medium-sized European state but with an empire that made it simultaneously larger than the 'continental' states of America and Russia. Precisely when the domestic British economy was no longer able to dominate within the world-economy, the British Empire grew to its greatest extent. Clearly, there is some sense in which increasing political power was compensating for a weakening economic power. But that is only part of the story for at key times political and economic trends run parallel in the continuing saga of Britain's famed crisis.

Here is the barest outline of the momentous decline. Britain's hegemonic policy of balance of power in Europe, while dominating the rest of the world, began to unravel as early as the 1860s. State reorganizations in the USA and Germany provided platforms for both countries to challenge British political and economic supremacy. The unification of Germany was especially relevant because the declaration of the German Empire in 1871 after the defeat of France meant an end to political balance in Europe. A concert remained in Europe as Germany consolidated its new position, but the new situation was clearly no longer 'balanced'. Similarly in the rest of the world, Britain's quiet control was rudely upset after 1880 as the European powers carved up Africa, Asia and the Pacific in a famous scramble for colonies and spheres of influence. As the leading world power, Britain received the lion's share of the new colonies, but this was still a sign of weakness rather than strength. When it was hegemon, Britain had had no need to fence off zones for its exclusive control and was able to prevent others doing so. In the late 19th century Britain simply joined in the division of the world as another player, albeit the biggest, in the imperial game. Nevertheless the result was the largest empire the world had ever seen – approximately a quarter of the world's land and people – that faced the German challenge in 1914–18 and 1939–45. Victories were only achieved, however, after US intervention. Hence, in 1945, Britain emerged as the 'first lieutenant' of the new hegemon, in the so-called 'special relationship' with the USA. Yet even with the subsequent loss of empire, world pretensions did not cease. British troops were not withdrawn from 'east of Suez' until 1967 when Britain settled for being a European regional power, finally joining the European Community in 1973.

The first signs that rivals were catching up economically came in 1867 at the Paris International Exhibition where Britain's expected dominance of the medals, so conspicuous at the Crystal Palace in 1851, did not occur.[31] With the onset of the late Victorian depression in the 1870s, Britain was still the leading economy in the world; by 1900 both the USA and Germany had effectively caught up and were ahead in key sectors. Within a year or so of the start of both wars against Germany, Britain was relying on US capital to sustain her fighting. In 1945 Britain emerged as bankrupt and having effectively lost control of her economic destiny. Nevertheless, she managed to reconstitute herself as a leading player in world politics until the sterling crisis of 1967 which precipitated the east of Suez troop withdrawal. Fears of another loss of control of economic destiny resulted in confirmation of British membership of the European Community in the referendum of 1975.

The cultural dimension of this downward spiral is hotly debated. One side of the debate argues that there was a major cultural transformation in Britain after high hegemony that took the unlikely strategy of rejecting the core economic success of industrialization. This posits the existence of a pre-industrial English 'gentlemanly capitalism', briefly eclipsed by industrialization but reasserted towards the end of the 19th century.[32] The key characteristic of this capitalism was its separation from the demeaning world of work. Hence the imperative of making money without getting your hands dirty created an elite culture of anti-industrialism.

Arguing against this thesis, W. D. Rubinstein has strongly defended British capitalists in the late 19th century as acting rationally in not investing in industry and seeking better profits elsewhere.[33] From this perspective, the perceived 'anti-industrialism' is not a cultural artifact at all but simply a matter of good economics. Both of these positions fit our hegemony model. In the latter case, having argued that it is the productive edge that is lost first in hegemonic decline, we expect industry to be the first post-hegemonic casualty. Culturally we have already noted how the decline of the Dutch was accompanied by the rise of uncommercial *rentiers*; the rise of a new anti-industrial British elite seems to be a parallel process. This cultural argument is particularly attractive here since self-rejection behaviour can be interpreted as a prime symptom of post-hegemonic trauma. In the remainder of this section we explore Britain's anti-industrialism as a crucial cultural accompaniment of hegemonic decline. The best documentation of Britain's 'decline of the industrial spirit' is by Martin Wiener and we trace the main lines of his argument below.[34]

Weiner highlights the great irony that the country which gave the world its industrial revolution should so soon become 'traditional' in its mores and hence suspicious of technology and progress. The process began not very long after the Great Exhibition of 1851. Rather than form their own new national elite, the industrial bourgeoisie was incorporated into the traditional landed ruling class through a process of gentrification. As early as 1863, Richard Cobden, lamenting that 'the spirit of feudalism is rife and rampant', observed that:

> Manufacturers and merchants as a rule seem only to desire riches that they may be enabled to prostrate themselves at the feet of feudalism. How is this to end?[35]

It seemed as if the English aristocracy had snatched 'a class victory from the brink of defeat'.[36]

Much of the debate about 19th-century British decline, both contemporary and subsequent interpretation, has focused upon education and the neglect of scientific and technical subjects. Wiener argues that the sons and grandsons of the pioneering industrial generation were educated in traditional 'public schools' to become 'real Englishmen' by stripping them of their industrial heritage.[37] In fact the ethos of these schools went back well before the industrial revolution and overturned the victory of the moderns against the ancients of the late 17th century. More reminiscent of the 16th-century Renaissance with its combination of Christianity and the classics, curriculums differed from the latter through their disdain for science. The same classical ethos permeated the ancient universities of Oxford and Cambridge: in 1904 and 1905, for instance, Greek was confirmed as a compulsory subject at both universities.[38] Although there has been some dispute about how influential these elite institutions were numerically, the key point is that they dominated the thinking behind the whole national education system that was emerging at this time.[39] For instance, attempts by the school boards of some industrial towns to devise a science and technology education were stopped by the 'classics lobby' in Parliament who ensured the 1902 Education Act conformed to the elite style of education.[40] Industry coped by being equally disdainful of science in what is known as the 'cult of the practical man'.[41] The preference for technology to come from practical training in the works required little formal schooling and kept demand for science education low and separate from industrial needs. This completed the vicious circle: even for the few scientists who emerged from the education system, jobs were scarce, wages poor and they were held in low esteem by elites and industrialists alike.[42] It is not so much the resulting lack of a science-trained labour force that is important, but the way elite education imbued the whole social fabric with anti-industrial values.

Beyond the classroom, this counter industrial revolution discovered an 'Old England' that had been set on the 'wrong path' by industrialization.[43] England was a 'garden', 'a green and pleasant land' despoiled by 'dark satanic mills' in the conversion of Britain to workshop of the world. In regional terms, the 'south' reasserted its dominance of the 'north'; in urban terms, London eliminated Manchester as a world city.[44] The latter might have its grand Free Trade Hall and its memorial statues of Richard Cobden, John Bright and Prince Albert as instigator of the Great Exhibition, but by the late 19th century this was to look backwards and not forwards.[45] The future of Britain now belonged to a gentrified elite for whom making money was a means to an end rather than the end itself. The Oxford academic Arnold Toynbee went straight to the heart of the 'wrong thinking' that had done so much harm to his England: political economy was a false philosophy of life, he asserted, being based upon nothing more than 'intellectual superstitions'.[46] For replacement, the 'spiritualism' of a traditional England was invoked as the antidote to the crass materialism that had dominated Britain during its high hegemony.[47]

This late Victorian rejection of recent economic successes was consolidated in two subsequent phases of decline: Edwardian England before World War I and Britain between the wars. As Britain's relative decline became more obvious, so the rejection of industry became more widespread. The crucial period when the British realized the seriousness of the challenges they faced came in the Edwardian period just after the turn of the century. This was a curious time. On the one hand, it is sometimes viewed as an 'Edwardian Garden Party', a golden age of stability and peacefulness preceding the disruption of world war.[48] But what of those outside the garden wall? The second view is of a period of severe crisis. The period begins with the débâcle of the Boer War and ends with domestic crises over the constitution (Lords versus the people), Irish independence, women's suffrage and labour militancy, finally culminating in the international crisis producing World War I.[49] No wonder George Dangerfield looked back on this period as, in the words of the title of his famous book, *The Strange Death of Liberal England*.[50] As with the Dutch, there was a general feeling that something had to be done to stem the tide but no agreement about it. On one side were the imperialists, both Liberal and Tory, who favoured a major reform of Britain's policy to create a unified imperial state behind tariff barriers. These extreme nationalists – this was the time the term 'jingoism' was coined – were politically defeated by those who supported a continuation of the free-trade policies that had served Britain so well during her hegemony. Nobody, of course, proposed a political course that would allow Britain to relinquish her international burdens and become a medium-sized power. On this issue radical socialists agreed with the most reactionary imperialists.[51] This was Britain's political *cul-de-sac*.

In the inter-war years, while Britain remained one of the great industrial powers in the world, the anti-industrialism tendency continued unabated. In 1932 one politician, a government supporter, even went as far as saying 'it might well have been better for England if she had never become a great manufacturing country'.[52] Nineteenth-century policies were dismissed out of hand. After the 1932 trade agreement on imperial preferences, the Conservative Party leader Stanley Baldwin, declaring *laissez-faire* to be as dead as the slave trade with the implication that both were contrary to civilization.[53] If competitive industrialism was un-English, something that had diverted England from its true nature, who was now to blame? The new barbarians were the Americans. As brash materialists they represented all that was wrong with the modern world. At this time there was not a communist spectre haunting Europe but an American one. In 1927, even the successful industrialist Samuel Courtauld admitted viewing the 'Americanization of Europe with the utmost dislike'.[54] The British were conducting 'a gentlemanly economy' and new economic successes across the Atlantic looked likely to upset the complacency.[55] In particular the consumerism of the Americans was viewed as especially vulgar – Britain was now distancing herself from the new modernity as well as her own modernity.[56] A continuing world role was not rejected, but now it became viewed as more spiritual than material; Britain would concentrate on 'higher things' and show the world a genuinely civilized society. As one influential commentator wrote in 1940:

> Intellectually and spiritually we [can] continue to make great contributions to the true wealth of humanity. If we do, we shall receive much more sympathy and admiration from foreign nations than when our rather blatant prosperity made us disliked even more than envied.[57]

This statement can stand as the basic rejection thesis within post-hegemonic trauma – 'no' to industry, 'yes' to a world role.

With the coming of US hegemony, some British elites continued along an anti-materialist route, but Americanization's revolution from below finally undermined anti-materialism as a major force in British culture. Nevertheless, post-hegemonic trauma continued to be evidenced in Britain's international politics. Even after conceding the 'Number One' spot to their 'American cousins', the British still hankered after a world role. Churchill in 1947 saw Britain at the intersection of three power circles, Atlantic, Europe and Empire, and he assumed that from this unique position Britain would not merely continue to be a major power, she would be the fulcrum of world politics. Instead, the real test for Britain soon came with the end of empire. In 1962 Dean Acheson, the former US secretary of state, made his oft-quoted remark that Britain had lost an empire but had not yet found a new role. Surely now was the time for a national reassessment to make the country's power pretension congruent with its medium-size. But no; even when the empire was gone, it had to be reinvented as the Commonwealth.[58] In 1964 the new Labour prime minister, Harold Wilson, answered Acheson: 'Britain is a world power or she is nothing.'[59] The particular context for this statement is especially interesting because Wilson came to power on a promise of radical reform to 'modernize' Britain. Technology and industrialization were back on the agenda. Even now it was more a means to a greater end, the restoration of Britain as a world power; Wilson's statement sums up Britain's post-hegemonic trauma. There is no compromise, no middle way; Britain cannot be just another state. For Donald Horne, writing in 1970, Britain 'is still to get a feeling of its real size'.[60]

Horne understands Britain's impasse better than anyone and he can have the last word on it here. Britain, he argued, has been 'gummed up' because it is unable to deal with decline: after asking rhetorically 'What is wrong with decaying quietly?', he answers simply that 'it cannot be done'.[61] Rather than face up to reality, the British have accepted their perennial crisis:

> la crise anglaise . . . has become institutionalized: it is now part of the British way of life. Come to Britain and see the crisis . . . the crisis can end only with a new definition of British society.[62]

When will Britain finally reach its '1848'?

American conundrum

I am a 'declinist'. In the debate about America's current and future position in the world, declinists are opposed by the 'renewalists' who have recently rediscovered the power of the USA.[63] Their counter-thesis is that prospects for America are much brighter than pessimists realize. Although this debate has obvious political overtones – Reaganites saving America from weak, liberal declinists – there is a serious academic argument here that reflects the fact that we are actually living in this period of hegemonic change. We cannot know the future in the way we can marshal facts to interpret the past. Since the future is still to be made, to define contemporary American travails as part of a longer-term American impasse is perhaps jumping the gun. But this is exactly what we have done in our model of hegemonic cycles. By defining the time-span of the modern world-system as three hegemonic cycles when we have only experienced two and a half such cycles, we are projecting our hegemonic historical analogy into the future. As analogies do not prove anything, America's situation remains a conundrum rather than an impasse.

A conundrum is a mystery for which, unlike an impasse, an answer may be found. The conundrum we are concerned with here is what has happened to the USA since the 1960s. The mystery is that American politicians and their publics have been simultaneously grappling with clear signs of relative decline while the country remains a superpower, even sole superpower since 1991. What can this mean? Certainly with the demise of the USSR, American military power has never been as dominant in purely quantitative terms. It is not surprising, therefore, that part of the difference between declinists and renewalists relates to what spheres of social activity are emphasized: renewalists tend to focus on the political–military, declinists on the economic. We have always advocated their combination in political economy so that both signs of economic decline and superpower status should be accommodated in the same interpretation. Hence despite the salutary reminders about the future being open, we will pursue our hegemonic analogy. Historically, impasses begin as conundrums. For the late Victorian British the conundrum was very clear: they produced the largest empire in the world just as Germany and the USA were overtaking them economically. Similarly the Dutch had more direct involvement in European political events in the decades after 1672 than previously, creating a conundrum for contemporaries aware of their relative economic decline.

The discussion of American conundrum as possible impasse is divided into four parts. We begin by briefly reviewing the counter-thesis and conclude that the argument is itself a reflection of post-hegemonic trauma. This sets up the analogy with the Dutch and British cases, and in the second part we draw parallels across all three hegemons to identify common signals of impasse. Bad wars and ostentatious public parades are highlighted as creating and displaying trauma from which there is no way back. This conclusion allows us, in part three, to develop an argument for American impasse that is based explicitly on the stories of historical impasses related in the previous section. Finally we return to the cultural sphere within hegemony which is relatively neglected by our concentration on political economy; the cultural influence of America does not seem to be waning. In the final part we interpret this in terms of the continuities of social practices that live on even after high hegemony is over.

Still 'Number 1'

America is not going quietly. In the USA, post-hegemonic trauma seems to be expressed popularly by what we might call a fetish for being 'Number 1'. One recent best-selling book entitled *We're Number One* provides no fewer than 116 tables in which America is ranked against its rivals.[64] But we must not let this predictable hype divert us from the serious debate going on. Given that the question of relative decline is an unpalatable one for any country to face, critics of the declinist thesis have taken up one of two distinctive positions. First, there is the argument that the USA has not declined in any meaningful way. Second, even if relative decline is accepted, it is argued that there is no reason why the USA should not rise again.

Has America declined? Not according to some leading international relations experts in the 1980s – Susan Strange makes a case for the 'myth of lost hegemony' and Bruce

Russett investigates the 'mysterious case of vanishing hegemony'.[65] Their carefully considered arguments fit into the general ideological conservative backlash against liberal 'declinists' which came to a head with American triumphalism at the end of the Cold War. However, this latest 'renewalist' counter-thesis focused upon military power, their target was more Paul Kennedy's imperial overstretch thesis, with its military cut-back prescriptions, than the broader hegemonic decline argument. In contrast, Strange and Russett engage directly with our hegemony model. Nevertheless our differences with their positions can still be traced to different interpretations of hegemony. For instance, Strange's case for the 'myth' of America losing its hegemony is based upon showing the USA maintaining its leadership in four crucial pillars of 'structural power': knowledge, finance and production as well as military.[66] There is no doubt concerning American power in these areas, and we can admit the United States remains number one in all four, but that still does not add up to hegemony in our terms. World leadership in a hegemonic sense is more than the possession of power, as we have seen. The hegemon is a special state that defines a new world for which being number one is a necessary but not sufficient condition. Power is not enough to make a hegemon, that power has to be presented on a universal plane to define a new world future. This is exactly what has been missing in US relations with the rest of the world for the last two decades. America remains the most powerful state in the world; it is highly competitive but precisely those facts mean it is no longer hegemonic.

Even when the recent trend of US relative decline is admitted, this can be interpreted as an artifact of selecting time periods for measuring change.[67] The period between 1945 and 1950 was a very unusual time when all rival economies were still devastated by World War II. Hence, it is argued, American economic dominance for these years is quite artificial depending as it does on the absence of any other viable economy. It follows that using 1945–50 as a benchmark for comparison is sure to produce a subsequent relative decline in the US economy as rival countries gradually recover in a peacetime world-economy. If an earlier peacetime world-economy is used as benchmark, say the 1920s, then the US economy has had a relatively level economic trajectory, apart from the early post-war aberration. But this is to treat war and politics as separate from economics. It was not just that the USA won the war, it was the manner of the victory and its economic and cultural repercussions that are important. World War II was not an accident that just came along and caused a blip on the economic landscape. It was part of a major world restructuring process through which the USA consolidated its rise to hegemony. The USA had a 'good war', not through good fortune, but as a result of structural factors operating long before the soldiers fighting the war were even born. Nobody dismisses the effects of the industrial revolution on Britain's dominance after 1815 as an aberration of the Napoleonic wars: as we argued in Chapter 1, having a unique 'good war' amid systemic chaos is precisely how states enter high hegemony.

Even if we concede relative decline to be a true reflection of the current situation, does that mean the USA cannot make a comeback? Surely not? John Lukacs laments that for Britain 'a second Holland is not enough', and we now have a literature that says for the USA a second Britain is not enough.[68] Richard Rosecrance notes that 'no truly hegemonic power has ever come back' but then goes on to argue that the current situation is without historical parallel.[69] What he means by this is that previous declines led to severe inter-state rivalry that emptied the erstwhile hegemon's coffers.

Since 1991 and the end of the USSR, there is only one major military power left in the world. This provides the USA with a unique opportunity to use its impressive remaining power to relaunch itself in a second bid for hegemony. Even defeat in the Vietnam War can now be interpreted positively. George Modelski has argued that just as the British made a comeback after defeat in the American War of Independence to reach their zenith in the next century, this can be repeated by the USA after their defeat in the 'Vietnamese War of Independence'.[70] This is President Bush's 'second American century' proclaimed at the height of post-Cold War euphoria. But Bush interpreted the Gulf War as 'curing' the Vietnam syndrome – the American public's reluctance to support major military action. From Rosecrance's perspective, however, this is the opposite of what is required: combining the Vietnam syndrome with the post-Cold War 'peace dividend' provides the opportunity for serious de-militarization.[71] However, the key question is whether the US government and people are able to take advantage of the situation. The omens are not good. For a start, American hegemony was unique in its level of militarization as a result of the Cold War: Britain ruling the waves through its Royal Navy was a much smaller factor in its hegemony than the US high-tech military–industrial complex. The real problem is post-hegemonic trauma; can the USA retreat from striving to be number one in the present world and recreate another new world? Neither past precedents nor contemporary signs are optimistic on this count. End of hegemony circumstances for the USA certainly are different but, unlike Rosecrance, I see enough similarities with previous ends of hegemony to make me doubt America's ability to avoid an impasse.

Finally, we should note that the renewalist thesis can itself be interpreted as a key symptom of post-hegemonic trauma. Viewing this debate from outside, the words that keep coming to mind are: 'they would say that, wouldn't they?' The arguments are so very predictable; America, despite itself, is becoming so very normal.

Signalling the end of hegemony: 'bad wars' and parading against the future

We are now in a position to continue our hegemonic historical analogy by again focusing on similarities between the three cases. Two comparisons are made. First, we look at the objective factor of having a 'bad war' as a trigger of post-hegemonic trauma. Second, we look at the subjective meaning of great public parades that are out of keeping with the event they purport to celebrate. In both comparisons, the Americans look little different from their Dutch and British hegemonic predecessors.

During high hegemony other countries are playing catch-up as we described in Chapter 4. Since some are successful, as the game proceeds hegemonic pre-eminence is severely eroded creating entirely new circumstances. Certainly, to begin with, there will be a lack of belief that such a social change could possibly occur. The first major jolt to the immanent self-confidence of the hegemon is political. If the rise of the hegemon is marked by 'having a good war' when all rivals are destroyed, it follows that a 'bad war' is a particularly relevant signal of decline. By bad war I do not necessarily mean defeat but rather that the war exposes the weaknesses of the hegemon for all the world to see. Instead of world leadership, the hegemon is isolated even from countries it considered friends or allies.

The first instance of a bad war is crucial not because of its size but because it produces the first dent in the collective self-confidence. The crucial Dutch bad war, as we noted above, occurred in 1672 with the French invasion which led to the capture of much of the country including Utrecht. By the Treaty of Dover, the English allied with the French against the Dutch leaving the latter alone to face French military might. Although the Republic survived by flooding its land to prevent further French advances, it was a close call and the first doubts emerged as to whether the Dutch would be able to sustain a Great Power status.[72]

For Britain the Boer War of 1898–1902 marks the point when British global vulnerability is displayed for all the world to see. A relatively small group of farmers employing guerrilla warfare kept the greatest political power in the world at bay for the best part of four years. Britain was universally condemned by friends and rivals alike, precipitating the end of her 'free hand policy' of no defence treaties in 1901.[73]

Similarly another guerrilla army, this time from the small peripheral country of North Vietnam, was able to prevent a US victory in south-east Asia in the 1960s despite the superpower's massive military superiority. With a large body of world opinion marshalled against the hegemon, the Americans were forced to withdraw in 1973 leading to the final North Vietnamese victory in 1975. The surprising thing was how little support the USA received from its major allies despite Cold War alliances. This is where the 'Vietnam syndrome' – an admission of the limits of the possible in its dealings with the rest of the world – began, of course. After their first bad wars, the Dutch and the British experienced similar 'syndromes', which made them shy of ever facing the world alone again.

A bad war may begin the processes of becoming normal, but there is much social resistance. This is expressed in a rise of a vehement form of nationalism that soon begins to eclipse the cosmopolitanism of high hegemony. In the Dutch Republic this culminated with the elimination of the urbane regents' party and the Republic's final years in the 18th century are marked by the traditional Orangist war party opposed to the new 'Patriots' party of renewal. In Britain the cosmopolitan Liberals were gradually eclipsed by the imperial Tories and by the end of the century both parties were offering an imperial politics to the populace, albeit of rather different varieties. In the USA the 1980s marked the rise of a new nationalism under the Reagan and Bush administrations: one of George Bush's most memorable stops in the 1988 presidential campaign was to a flag-making factory! The home-country nationalism displayed at the 1984 Olympic Games in Los Angeles was distasteful to a non-American like myself until, that is, I realized it was showing America to be post-hegemonic – just another flag-waving nation. For the erstwhile hegemonic society, it seems that a rise in national feelings compensates for the worry of decline. Let us illustrate this process of resistance to decline.

America has recently witnessed the greatest victory celebrations in its history. The successful conclusion to the war against Iraq in 1991 evoked a response by all levels of government throughout the USA seemingly out of all proportion to the event. As John Judis has pointed out, these victory parades 'dwarfed those after World Wars I and II' and 'went on twice as long as the war itself'.[74] Clearly such a nationalistic outpouring is about more than this short war. President Bush was using the victory – a little good war for America – to evoke a recent past when his country was indisputably 'Number 1' in the world. Of course in that time of high hegemony there was no need for such extravagant celebrations. It is only when the exalted position is perceived as being under threat that it has to be so brazenly broadcast to the world. The parades were not really about the Gulf War, their sheer size indicates a far greater celebration. They are reminding everyone, including themselves, that: 'We won the twentieth century'.

About a century earlier another extravagant parade was held, this time through the streets of London. Queen Victoria's diamond jubilee in 1897 brought forth celebrations that dwarfed all that had gone before. It was a great imperial jamboree with the Queen's subjects from all over the world displaying their colourful 'native' costumes. In this case, 50 000 troops from all continents paraded in two columns through London before converging on St Paul's for the thanksgiving service. Contemporaries had no doubt as to its historical significance: it was, said the popular *Daily Mail*, a pageant that had 'never been paralleled in the history of the world', while the establishment's paper, *The Times*, was sure that

> History may be searched, and searched in vain, to discover so wonderful an exhibition of allegiance and brotherhood amongst so many myriads of men.[75]

Undoubtedly this was in part a display of loyalty to the long-serving monarch, but the nationalistic element was far greater than the purely dynastic. It was an excuse for Great Britain to remind herself and proclaim to the world: 'We won the nineteenth century.'[76]

In 1655 a splendid procession made its way across Amsterdam behind the city standard. All the city dignitaries – city officials, burgomasters, council members and their staffs – in their full ceremonial attire attended to mark the opening of their great new Town Hall.[77] Festivities lasted all day and the inauguration was celebrated by the striking of a medal with Mercury, the god of trade, on one side and the Town Hall encircled by the inscription *Fuit haec sapientia quondam* (This was the wisdom of the old days) on the other side.[78] The medal inscription and the magnificence of the building are a clue to the meaning of the inaugural parade's true message. Although contemporaries saw the new building as 'the Wonder of the World', Cotterell considers that 'there was something sad about the Town Hall . . . [it] was magnificent and imposing, but it was not Dutch'.[79] Price sees this as a paradox:

> It is a little paradoxical that this building which should have been the symbol of the greatness of Amsterdam, and by extension of the Republic, in fact shows almost nothing of the strength and individuality of Dutch culture.[80]

It was built in a baroque style with clear French architectural influences. The paradox is resolved if we view the Amsterdammers as trying to demonstrate what they were not.[81] An inscription glorifying the past and imitation of a contemporary rival's architecture are hardly the stuff of hegemony; they are extravagantly proclaiming their greatness but displaying symptoms of being just another state. For Cotterell, the celebration represents the beginning of decadence, only 'a whisper' at this time, but unmistakable as a portent of decline to come.[82] It is symbolic that after the demise of the Republic, it was this building that was chosen in the 19th century to become the royal palace, which remains its name today.

From this 'whisper' to the later British and American 'broadsides', although

Plate 19 *Queen Victoria's Diamond Jubilee Procession* through London in 1897 was the greatest political spectacle of the century. But was the pomp and ceremony merely hiding Britain's relative decline in the world from its mid-century pre-eminence?

intended as confirmations of success, all three parades can be interpreted as signalling countries unsure of themselves as the certainties of hegemony are questioned. They serve the same purpose as those military uniforms, with band upon band of medals, worn by contemporary Third World military dictators. Neither fools us: leadership at all levels has to be earned, it cannot be exhorted by flamboyant display. As mere symbols they are papering over cracks; in the case of our hegemons, we can see a new world through the cracks of their imagery where rival countries are coming to the fore to dispute world leadership.

American impasse: from hegemon to major power?

Since we are just in the first decades of America's post-hegemonic route, judgement on it as another case of full-blown trauma should be suspended at this time. However if there are any lessons to be learned from the first two cases it is that avoiding post-hegemonic trauma is extremely difficult, even in circumstances of the stark reality of catastrophic decline. Hence a political *cul-de-sac* to another impasse is a very likely outcome. Why in this situation should American politicians be more imaginative and American society more enlightened than their Dutch and British forebears?

There are important differences that may bear on the outcome. Objectively the Dutch conversion to becoming normal was the most difficult, entailing as it did a drop from hegemony to minor status. Britain, on the other hand, only fell to a medium-sized power and for much of her descent could believe herself to be a large

Plate 20 *The Citizens' Hall in the Royal Palace, Amsterdam*. Built in the 17th century as the Town Hall, the flamboyant style is thought to be quite 'unDutch', signifying an early chink in the self-confidence of the United Provinces. The floor depicts a world map with the prime meridian running through Amsterdam. However, general agreement on the prime meridian had to wait until British hegemony

power on the basis of her huge empire. By any criteria, the USA is undoubtedly a large powerful country so that any movement to make her international standing congruent with her size will entail maintenance of Great Power status. Objectively this will not be such a great decline. However objectivity is not necessarily a good basis for predicting attitudes in situations of hegemonic decline. It can be argued that the tenacity of Britain's world power dream is due in part to it not becoming a small country like the Netherlands. As a medium-sized state, it could devise credible options to maintain its world status that were just not open to the Dutch. If this was true of Britain, it is obviously much more so the case for the USA. Even after the end of high hegemony, the importance of America is such that it can still credibly use its immense power to resist becoming normal. The language is already in place as we have seen: after the Cold War, by self-consciously dubbing itself the only remaining superpower, the USA is refusing to be just another Great Power.[83]

America's post-hegemonic route begins with the 'bad war' in Vietnam, but the influence of this war was not just a politico–military matter. The USA paid a big economic price for Vietnam as well. Inflationary pressures and the drain on the US gold supply precipitated an economic crisis when 'the United States suddenly became aware that the coffers were not bottomless'.[84] The practical effect was the Nixon administration's decision in 1971 to break the fixed dollar–gold rate. Effectively this was a devaluation and gave the US economy an important short-term boost, but at the expense of overturning the Bretton Woods agreement, the American-designed currency system based upon a fixed-rate dollar. A floating dollar meant that though American currency would still be the most important, trading it on the market turned it into just another currency like that of any other country. Vestiges of high hegemony soon crumbled. Domestically the Watergate scandal and President Nixon's ignoble forced resignation in 1974 crucially eroded American self-confidence. Internationally, in the same year, the OPEC oil price hike represented commodity producers resisting Western domination and hence bucking American leadership. In fact this move affected oil-dependent Europe and Japan more than America; effectively the USA was using OPEC in its economic rivalry with other core states illustrating its new post-hegemonic role as another competitive state.

Two alternative strategies were devised by US governments for coping with the erosion of American leadership: either consolidate the position to maintain leadership or try to regain lost ground. With the Vietnam syndrome at its peak in the seventies, the Nixon, Ford and Carter administrations attempted to adapt American foreign policy to the new circumstances by pursuing the maintenance strategy. The architect of this change was Henry Kissinger, a student and admirer of Britain's hegemonic strategies of balancing power without becoming embroiled in every war. As Nixon's foreign-policy adviser and eventually secretary of state, he devised new policies for both enemies and allies.[85] For the former, crude military containment was abandoned for a more subtle approach, playing China off against the USSR. The result was the new China policy, confirmed by Nixon's visit to Beijing and *détente* with the USSR and Eastern Europe. For the allies, a trilateral arrangement was promoted with Western Europe and Japan joining the USA as the head of the West. This produced Nixon's famous pentagon of power – USA, USSR, China, Western Europe, Japan. This realist programme was about sharing responsibility for world order and reflected changing power potentials, but it was also a way for the USA to maintain Number One status. Although superficially a geometry of equal power, the USA were pulling all the strings – for each of the other four, their most important relationship was with America. The clue is the model being copied – Britain's successful 19th-century diplomatic domination of the inter-state system on a small military budget.

There was a fundamental flaw, however. To a majority of Americans, subtle diplomacy appeared to reflect post-Vietnam weakness rather than a realistic reappraisal of American power. The starkest evidence for this weakness was Iran's capture of the US Embassy in 1978 and their subsequent hostage-keeping for the last year of Jimmy Carter's administration. On Christmas Day, 1979, the USSR invasion of Afghanistan seemed to confirm the failure of US diplomatic strategies. The scene was set for a change of strategy for the eighties and this came with the election of Ronald Reagan to the US presidency. Subtle it was not. Riding on a wave of American nationalism, Reagan developed a macho foreign policy directed at the USSR as 'evil empire'. Instead of co-operation for world order, the 'Reagan doctrine' pursued a policy of confronting communism everywhere by funding guerrillas on all 'southern' continents – for instance Angola, Afghanistan and Nicaragua – and fighting safe little wars as in Grenada. In addition the largest peacetime military build-up in US history, including the Star Wars initiative which militarized inner space for the first time, targeted the USSR for the final showdown.

Superficially this second strategy was successful in that it exposed the USSR as no longer able to keep up the arms race, the first sign of both its political and economic disintegration. But there was a cost to the USA as well. We interpreted the late 19th-century growth of the British empire as a political compensation for relative economic decline and, in hindsight, the 1980s' American strategy looks very similar. In Paul Kennedy's terms, America was drawn into a severe case of imperial over-stretch. That is to say, there was a mismatch between the increase in the military budget and the economic resources at the government's disposal. The inevitable outcome was a huge budget deficit that coincided with the demise of the USSR and America becoming the sole superpower.

For America, this economic sacrifice to buy political success was a short-term phenomenon. The zenith of the USA as lone superpower came in 1991 with the Gulf War. Mobilizing a coalition of 34 countries under the banner of the United Nations, America led the successful military campaign to remove Iraqi troops from Kuwait. With America great again, Bush the war leader was rewarded with the highest approval ratings for any president on record. But within two years he was voted out of office with the lowest proportion of the vote for an incumbent president since 1912. The Gulf War and the sole superpower role was seen for what it was: military opportunism with little or no long-term value. Or in the words of the successful Democratic election campaign team of 1992: 'It's the economy, stupid!' But identifying the trauma does not actually solve it, as President Clinton's record in office has shown only too clearly.

Finally, what about the 'rejection' phase of post-hegemonic trauma found so strongly in the British case? Certainly both main political parties in the 1990s are appealing to middle-class values with associated tax cuts to keep consumption levels up. Little sign of any criticism of consumer society there! However rejection of such consumerism did occur at the very start of US relative decline in the late 1960s. Although much has been made of the conversion of sixties' social revolutionaries into the yuppies of the eighties, the fact remains that a sizeable proportion of the generation coming of age in the 1960s rejected the consumption ethos that had blossomed in 1950s' America. As well as the rebellion centred upon music and drugs, there was a vision of a different society, or even civilization, based upon new relationships among people and with the land. In the optimism of the times, Charles Reich proclaimed 'The coming American revolution'. Although his prophecy for the USA looks odd today, his basic thesis of 'the greening of America' is much less anachronistic.[86] The idea of consumption being opposed to environmental sustainability has certainly not disappeared, and we will focus on such a rejection of Americanization in the next chapter.

American hegemony is dead, long live Americanization!

Finally, before we leave the question of American relative decline, we must clear up a common confusion. One reason why we might be persuaded to doubt the declinist thesis is the extent of popular American 'cultural hegemony'.[87] Nowadays, wherever you travel in the world, America is there overwhelming local cultures. Coca Cola, McDonalds, Hollywood movies and American TV programmes all continue to grow in influence taking the American message to every corner of the globe. What could be more powerful? This certainly does express the continued power of the idea of America in the world: the process of Americanization is not in dispute. But we must not confuse an expression with the real thing; culture on its own does not constitute a hegemony.

Although we have focused in this study on discrete time frames such as periods of high hegemony or indeed whole cycles, world-historical processes such as the ones we have described do not just turn on and turn off. The best way to view the three hegemonies is as layers of modernity. The Dutch laid down the commercial foundation which most certainly did not end with Dutch hegemony. As well as becoming the workshop of the world, Britain, to use Napoleon's famous phrase, was also 'a nation of shopkeepers' and, of course, shopkeepers have never done better than in America's consumer society. Similarly, industrialization has continued apace ever since the British industrial revolution and transcends British hegemony and even Britain's own de-industrialization! The point is that the hegemon starts a bundle of processes in train and even though the hegemonic state itself declines, the processes remain as necessary prerequisites for modernity and so develop a life of their own, independent of their creator. The same applies to American hegemony and the popular consumer revolution it unleashed upon the world. America may not be what it was, but Americanization goes from strength to strength.[88]

One of the reasons this remains part of the contemporary American conundrum, however, is that this hegemonic legacy is so very conspicuous. American hegemony is different from previous hegemonies precisely because of its popular dimension. This ensures its widespread penetration as 'cultural hegemony'. Cultural vestiges can however be found from the other hegemons. For instance, that commercially minded Dutch were always careful with their money is still marked with phrases such as 'Dutch treat' and 'going Dutch'.[89] As someone from Britain I am always intrigued by US TV advertisements that find it necessary to use an English-accented voice to sell expensive goods. It seems England is still associated with 'class' in its high-quality sense. America's legacy is exactly the opposite, everyone can eat the burger. Added to this, the fact that Americanization scored its greatest triumph, the end of communism, about two decades after US high hegemony and we can see why the confusion concerning America's contemporary role is so common. Although the Eastern Europe revolutions in 1989 are usually interpreted as resulting from demands for democracy, the fact that Eastern Europeans could observe their Western neighbours enjoying high levels of consumption on their TV screens also had a lot to do with it. No communist politician ever found the answer to why East Germans should have less than West Germans or why Czechs should have less than Austrians. I suggest that for most people on the wrong side of the European political divide that disappeared in 1989, it was a yearning for Western-level consumption which was at least as important to them as political differences. We can explore this thesis further only by considering the curious nature of the Soviet Union.

The rivals

Some time during the 1980s, America's prime rival changed from being the USSR to Japan. By any standards, this was a huge collective leap of imagination. It is hard to conceive of two states more dissimilar. The USSR was a superpower whose economic prowess was suspect. Although there were no doubts about Japan's economic achievements, with no projection of military power, it seemed she did not qualify for major power status. The two states were polar opposites in terms of their world power strategies. The Soviet Union's political challenge faltered and finally collapsed in the 1980s just as Japan's economic challenge came to a head. Hence recognition of a change in America's main rival was accompanied by a re-evaluation of the nature of rivalry itself. Geopolitics, it has been said, is being replaced by 'geoeconomics'. Such arguments are the result of a severe case of historical amnesia – was there never an age of mercantilism? – but they do represent a real change in perception of the contemporary world-system.

The most distinctive political feature of American hegemony was the Cold War, a world order based upon the existence of a rival universal ideology to liberalism promoted by an anti-capitalist superpower. First and foremost, the Soviet system represented an alternative progressive vision of, and path to, the future — a sort of 'counter-hegemon'. There was nothing remotely comparable to it during either Dutch or British hegemony. For most of the period of American high hegemony, when the question of succession to the USA as Number One arose, the USSR was seen as the only viable candidate. The basic Western premise of the Cold War was precisely to prevent this possibility becoming reality. History has disposed of this future scenario as only history can, but the collapse of the Soviet Union should not blind us to its profound effect on 20th-century politics. Our analysis would not be complete without an interpretation of the socialist challenge to the capitalist world-economy which reached its pinnacle with the USSR as superpower. This is our topic in the first part of this section. But this part has an additional purpose: understanding socialism as an anti-systemic movement is a necessary precursor to our consideration in the next chapter of future opposition to the system during its demise phase.

One of the major, albeit short-term, effects of the end of Soviet power has been to promote American triumphalism. Most Americans had always expected they would win the Cold War; to do so without a missile fired in anger was beyond their collective wildest dream. The Cold War was resolved simply as a battle of ideas. With Russia and the other successor states of the USSR pleading for help to create market economies, America's victory could hardly be more complete. But there are doubts: did the USA win the Cold War? The answer is 'yes' if we only consider the political rivalry between the two superpowers. On a broader interpretation, however, we need not be so certain. For instance, contemporary political jokes and cartoons proclaimed Japan and Germany to be the true winners. Playing on the irony of World War II's defeated states' post-war economic successes, these jokes had a serious side to them. The Cold War converted the hegemon into a military super-power under whose protection other states were able to prosper with low military budgets. The greatest freeriders of all were the Japanese. Given the remarkable economic success of Japan, there is really only one way we can consider it in our argument: will Japan be the next hegemon? In the second part of this section we argue why we think this is not possible.

USSR impasse: from 'counter-hegemon' to disintegration

In 1932 Sidney and Beatrice Webb visited the USSR on a journey Beatrice called 'a pilgrimage to Mecca'.[90] The Webbs, by now both in their 70s, were founding members of the Fabian Society, Britain's famously moderate socialist forum. Now they regretted the Society's initial decision, 40 years earlier, to disavow Marxism. The Webbs were not the only Fabians to feel this way. A year earlier George Bernard Shaw had visited the Soviet Union and declared it to be 'applied Fabianism'.[91] This was a momentous ideological turnaround. As middle-class British socialists, they had chosen to name their group, in 1884, after the little known Roman general Fabius Cunctator. This unlikely choice derived from the fact that in opposing Hannibal, Fabius employed cautious tactics – avoiding battles until Hannibal's stretched supply lines eventually led to the demise of the Carthaginian army. The message was clear: Fabian socialism promoted a gradual evolutionist reform agenda which was about as different from revolutionary Marxist socialism as could be imagined. The Fabians devised a top-down socialism focusing on rational organization of society, a socialist version of the Enlightenment faith in experts. Yet near the end of their lives the Webbs had, in the words of Beatrice again, 'fallen in love with Soviet Communism'.[92] They wrote a 'love letter' of nearly 1200 pages entitled *Soviet Communism: a New Civilization?* which Beatrice announced as 'their last will and testament'.[93] This conversion of Fabians illustrates just how attractive the Soviet Union appeared to even the most unlikely people during capitalism's economic travails in the 1930s.

At this time political choices seemed limited and stark. If it came down to choosing between American individualism and Soviet collectivism many on the left throughout the Western world, like the Webbs, favoured the latter, not least because selfish individualism was viewed as the cause of the economic depression. In addition to their overt political moderation, the Fabians are of particular interest to our argument here, however, because of their national affiliation. At the time when other

Plate 21 *'Third World country with rockets'*. The USSR was the great enigma of the 20th century. An economic success story for the first 50 years of its existence, in the Cold War its most impressive achievements were in armaments paraded every May Day through Red Square in Moscow. As its economic system faltered, investment in its armed forces continued leading inevitably to collapse. In the 1980s the USSR economy was rapidly peripheralizing while maintaining superpower status; hence the derogatory description 'Third World country with rockets'. The picture shows the 1982 parade (Hulton Deutsch)

British politicians and intellectuals were retreating into the national anti-industrialism reported above, these British socialists maintained their faith in social progress and transferred their hopes for a better world to a new country with a new system. Instead of America representing the future, the USSR is given the accolade of being this special place. Americanization was explicitly rejected and the Soviet Union given the role of counter-hegemon. Mindful of the lack of democracy and freedom in the USSR, which in any case they thought was exaggerated, these elderly Fabians pondered the relationship between progress and freedom. They concluded that the Soviet system was a rational expression of modernity, with necessary command structures of experts to steer society and ensure orderly progress.

This was, of course, the way political elites in the Soviet Union themselves portrayed their country. In its period of 'socialism in one country' between World Wars I and II, the USSR pursued a dual policy in relations with the rest of the world.[94] It had a foreign policy to normalize relations with other states culminating in membership of the League of Nations. In addition it had an international socialist policy of relations with other communist parties through the Third International. It is in the latter framework that the Soviet Union was designated the 'fatherland' of all socialists, a special place where socialism's new world was being constructed. The need to defend this fatherland at any price caused the many policy shifts among communist parties during the 1930s which so weakened the left in general throughout the world. However the policy seemed to be vindicated in the next decade by the heroic survival of the USSR in the face of the Nazi German onslaught during World War II. The Soviet Union that emerged victorious in 1945 was at the peak of its power. The Cold War only confirmed its place as counter-hegemon, the credible alternative to Americanization.

The idea of the USSR as counter-hegemon, like the Cold War, was premised upon the notion that there were two separate world-systems led respectively by the USA and the Soviet Union.[95] In hindsight this thesis seems rather far-fetched, but that is not how it appeared to contemporaries. At the height of Cold War hostilities in the years around 1950, the idea of two different worlds with contrasting and incompatible goals seemed credible to most people on both sides, although the degree of autonomy of the two 'systems' was generally over-emphasized. To begin with, the two prospective world-systems existed within a single inter-state system. In the realm of international politics there was no separation; the USSR followed up its membership of the League of Nations by becoming a founder member of the United Nations and joining the USA as a Permanent Member of the Security Council. The consequent political rivalry impinged directly on the economies of both superpowers through distortions to their investment profiles in creating 'warfare states'. Over time the key difference of how their arms production was organized – whether through private or public corporations – seemed to reduce in significance as 'civilian powers', notably Japan and Germany, prospered on the back of low military expenditure.

Beyond this overt military distortion of the economy, the economic relations between the two 'worlds' has been a matter of some debate. Proponents of the 'two-worlds model' from the Soviet side have argued that a distinctive world-economy was being created by the USSR and her allies, based upon a new 'co-operative division of labour' as counter to capitalism's long-established competitive division of labour. This argument was supported by the insulation of the communist states from the world market through their collective policies of economic autarky in the early years of the Cold War. These policies were not sustained for long. After the death of Stalin in 1953, the subsequent political thaw was accompanied by a rise in trade which grew steadily to undermine totally the credibility of there being two world-economies.[96] Charles Levinson has argued convincingly that it was economic links that precipitated the political *détente* of the 1970s and not vice versa as is often claimed.[97] By the time we come to the global debt crisis of the early 1980s, there can be no doubt that the world consists of a single capitalist world-economy: communist states featured high on the list of big debtors, notably Poland and Hungary but including the USSR itself. The Cold War was not yet over but any pretence of two separate worlds, and with it the USSR as counter-hegemon, was long since dead.

Given the short-lived nature of the economic autarky, the question naturally arises as to whether there were ever two separate world-economies. In fact attempts to insulate state economies from the world market have been a relatively common policy that can be shown to transcend the economic policies of the USSR and its allies. Protecting 'infant industry' from the competition of more efficient economies is a standard development strategy for countries trying to 'catch up'. As we noted in Chapter 1, although dressed up in very different political rhetorics, there are parallels between English and French mercantilism in the 17th century, American and German protectionism in the 19th century and, in the 20th century for example, import substitution policies by Brazil and controlled trade by the USSR. In this interpretation, the communist states do not represent the making of a new world, rather they define a particular form that semi-peripheral development strategies have taken in the 20th century. In the words of the Romanian academic Silviu Brucan writing in 1979 and drawing on Lenin's rationale for the Soviet Union's 'New Economic Policy' of 1921: 'Development comes first, socialism only afterwards.'[98] Today we know that the failure of the development strategy meant that socialism never did arrive.

Interpreting the Soviet Union as a great experiment in economic development makes its demise readily explicable in world-system terms. The years around 1970 mark an important watershed in recent history; not only did American high hegemony come to an end but the world-economy as a whole moved into a stagnation phase. In the ensuing inter-state economic competition, the pattern of winners and losers broadly reflected the inter-state hierarchy. Peripheral zones, notably Africa, have been economically devastated and famine has returned to the modern world-system. In contrast, in the core, new political agendas have been adopted creating additional economic polarization but with a majority of the population continuing to enjoy their affluent society. The greatest pressure has been felt in the semi-periphery where expectations raised by previous decades of rapid economic growth have been dashed: for instance, both Brazil's 'economic miracle' and the USSR's bombastic predictions of overtaking the USA have been made to look ridiculous. This is not a good time to govern a semi-peripheral country. Political elites can no longer deliver the economic goods, resulting in their regimes being toppled one after another. The political pattern after 1970 in the non-communist semi-periphery is clear: in India the Congress Party cancels elections and rules through a state of emergency for three years, in Iran the Shah is overthrown, in Latin America military dictatorships fall one by one and in South Africa the strong apartheid state finally disappears in the early 1990s. In the communist-ruled semi-periphery, the states are initially powerful enough to stave off the effects of economic decline so that, ironically given their political oppositions, the timing of change approximates that of South Africa. Experiments in reforms leading to 'market socialism' had postponed more fundamental change, but success was elusive except in the relatively less industrialized China. As communism in Europe came to be seen by all as an economic failure, the communist regimes finally fell in the revolutions of 1989, to be followed by the disintegration of the USSR itself in 1991.

Superficially this is quite an attractive world-systems' explanation for the demise of the Soviet Union and the end of communist rule in Europe, but it leaves some rather big issues uncovered. Two in particular are relevant to our discussion here. First, the fall of the USSR and its satellites were not just examples of regime change as happened elsewhere in the semi-periphery: it was a very big fall, one that brought down a geopolitical world order, the Cold War, in its wake. The overthrow of the military juntas in Latin America may have been of regional importance but that was all. Nobody had ever thought Brazil or Argentina represented the future of the world, neither did they aspire to be anything other than states in the throes of economic development. In contrast the Soviet Union had been special as counter-hegemon and its demise changed the way we all think about the world. If this is the case, how was it possible for the USSR to be transmuted into nothing more than another development state sometime in the 1960s and 1970s? The relationship between socialist fatherland and development strategy is subtle, but we can unravel it by returning to our discussions of modernity.

As a place to see the future, the Soviet Union represented an alternative form of modernity. To understand its theory of progress, we cannot start with the Cold War or even the 1917 revolution. Its premises derive from the 19th century, from the writings of Karl Marx. Working in London during British high hegemony, Marx was very clear about the particular modernity with which he was concerned. In the preface to the original German edition of *Das Kapital*, Marx explained to his readers that he had chosen England 'as the chief illustration in the development of my theoretical ideas' because 'the country that is more developed industrially only shows to the less developed, the image of its own future.'[99] Here British industry defines modern society so that progress is equated with industrialization; it could be no other way given the time and place of the writer. This image of modernity survived in the mid-20th century as East European development strategy. In updating Marxism, later theorists and politicians focused upon European developments in their theories of imperialism, largely neglecting the contemporaneous domestic changes occurring in the USA. Hence, while a new modernity was being created in the latter country, Marxists were constructing an alternative society derived from the earlier British version of modernity. The East European model was therefore a development strategy for industrialization with an emphasis on capital goods.[100] The result was that heavy industry – steel, coal, railways, engineering plus, of course, armaments – was promoted to build up productive and defence capacity while sacrificing consumer goods. In many ways the opposite of American affluent society, the USSR came to be denigrated as a 'Third World country with rockets'.

The point is that the communist countries were pursuing an economic strategy which led towards a modernity already superseded by Americanization. The initial successes of the strategy in terms of economic growth were therefore quite misleading. The building up of a heavy industrial base will obviously stimulate production but alone this can only proceed so far. From the first five-year plan in 1928 to 1978, Soviet industrial production increased 128 times.[101] This spectacular quantitative achievement was insufficient: what was lacking was qualitative change to a new modernity. More and more coal and steel was irrelevant in the context of a technology gap that inevitably resulted from emulating a 19th-century model. By the 1970s, growth rates were declining as the advantage of planning based upon a model of a 'known' industrial past was transformed into the disadvantages of planning for an uncertain future. Previously extra investment had created additional growth, but in the 1970s this relationship broke down leaving Soviet planning stranded in a past world.[102] Quite simply, the severely inflexible accumulation of the East could not compete with the new flexible accumulation strategies evolving in the West.

Socialism as a political practice represented by the USSR as counter-hegemon therefore created its own *cul-de-sac* and impasse in the history of the modern world-system. Although a genuinely anti-systemic movement from the 19th century, in the end it could not cope with the new modernity of the 20th century. As counter-hegemon the USSR was peddling a future that had less and less relevance to its own population and those of its allies as Americanization blossomed. The new consumption-based modernity vanquished all before it and took no prisoners. It is best if we refer to the defeated anti-systemic movement as *industrial* socialism. As such it represents a particular phase of opposition within the modern world-system that relates to Britain's industrial modernity. Its theories and practices focused upon the industrial working class, even in agrarian countries where workers constituted a very small proportion of the population. This included the USSR in 1917 and China in 1949, plus all those post-colonial Marxist regimes where the idea of the proletariat as the vanguard of change was simply ludicrous. Industrial socialism was defeated when enough of the ordinary waged population – traditional working class and lower middle class – were won over by consumer society to undermine socialist models of social change.[103] This does not mean the end of anti-systemic movements. Whereas the great contradiction of British modernity was the rise of the proletariat resulting from new production processes, the great contradiction of American modernity is the depletion of resources resulting from the new consumption processes. We deal with the environmental movement as the challenge to the affluent society in the next chapter.

Japan as hegemon?

All future predictions agree that Japan will play a far greater part in world affairs than she has hitherto. But will Japan become the next hegemonic state? Many observers of world affairs seem to think so; Lester Thurow considers Japan to be 'the betting favorite to win the economic honors of owning the twenty-first century'.[104] The crucial point here is the emphasis on 'economic honors'. Japan has developed as a sort of *contra*-USSR, economic power without political power. We have learned from the USSR's calamitous challenge that without an adequate economic base, world political power is extremely fragile. This has seemed to make the opposite challenge as represented by Japan so much more credible.

Since economic power is the basis of hegemony as we have defined it, Japan certainly looks the most likely successor to the USA. It has developed a clear productive edge which has been translated into a commercial power and especially a financial leadership in the world-economy broadly in the manner suggested by Wallerstein and described in Chapter 1.[105] But we have argued that hegemony requires more than economic success. The hegemon does not just do better what other countries do; it defines a distinctively new political economy and rebuilds the world in its image. The first crucial question, therefore, is whether we can find such a 'newness' in the Japanese 'economic miracle'.

In his description of the Japanese challenge, Thurow uses a very interesting metaphor.[106] From the perspective of orthodox Western economists, Japanese companies operate in a way equivalent to water running uphill. That is to say the theoreticians – believers in gravity – cannot understand why the Japanese practitioners are so successful since many of their economic practices run counter to orthodox economic theory. For instance, employees are not rewarded and promoted by merit but rather wages and salaries are linked to an age-based seniority system. Where is the incentive for workers to better themselves and in doing so help the firm? Yet without such incentives Japanese workers in industry after industry have out-performed their American and European counterparts over recent decades. Thurow argues that the Japanese are not just better producers, they are 'exceptional', they have 'organized a different system' and they are 'playing the game differently'.[107] Using the same metaphor, Karel van Wolferson goes even further: Japan, far from 'beating the West at its own game', is not 'playing the Western game at all'.[108] This is all very suggestive of our hegemony model since such distinctive economic practices imply a new political economy. In their own times the Dutch, the British and the Americans invented new political economies against existing orthodoxies – they each made water run uphill, if you will. But the USSR also created a new political economy and it had impressive economic successes for a while. Nevertheless the world repercussions of Japanese economic achievements certainly suggest that their new political economy is closer to past hegemonic creations than the counter-hegemonic failure.

What is this latest political economy? I will look at the economic practices first and then consider the nature of the Japanese state. Thurow provides a very clear description of the distinctiveness of the new Japanese economics which he terms 'producer economics' to distinguish it from contemporary American-led 'consumer economics'.[109] That is, it is most certainly not a variant of Americanization. Instead of profit-maximizing on behalf of their shareholders, Japanese companies seek to maximize market share. Instead of profits being an end in themselves, in Japan they are a means to a different goal; their corporations are the contemporary empire-builders of this world, given that states no longer have the opportunity to pursue such actions. Enlarging market share is like traditional territorial expansion except economic motive has replaced political motive. Such a strategy can only have worked if accompanied by an enabling culture: Japanese companies are social-builders as well. They have created communities of workers with the promise of lifetime employment and then have used workers' loyalty to ensure investment comes before consumption. Their achievement was remarkable: a relatively poor yet satisfied people in a rich country.[110] Such an outcome in the USA or Europe would be translated into a shareholders' bonanza but not so in Japan. Return on capital is also kept low as profits are ploughed back into the business. This is another remarkable achievement: business groups, not unlike trusts outlawed elsewhere, ensure shareholders get little or no more than they would get from investing in government bonds. The result is a corporate empire-building strategy that appears unique to Japan.

How does the state fit into this power play? Most interpretations see the state as supportive by providing the political and legal framework that prevents workers, consumers, shareholders and foreigners from being obstacles to corporate strategies, which collectively constitute a rigorously pursued national strategy. But it is by no means as simple as that. Van Wolferen refers to Japan as a 'stateless nation'.[111] In search of an 'elusive state', he argues that although Tokyo is the capital of Japan there is no political core, only a diffused pattern of power. When the USA conducts bilateral negotiations with Japan, the meetings are really fictional as inter-governmental discussions because Japan has no responsible central government. Japan is a 'truncated pyramid' with no top and therefore the head of government, the prime minister, does not function as a chief executive.[112] Given the lack of central direction, the popular notion of 'Japan, Inc' is particularly misleading.[113] Rather there is a unified body of political and economic elites who constitute a system of power that overrules the state whenever its government makes 'rash' promises. Thus American pressures to increase Japanese domestic consumption are doomed to failure since the whole party system is premised upon avoiding such electoral competition. Hence the joke that the USA, as champion of the Japanese consumer, is 'Japan's only authentic political opposition party'.[114]

What sort of state is Japan, therefore? Interestingly this weak political structure giving a singular freedom to economic elites looks like an extreme version of the classic hegemonic state. Dutch merchants dominated what some think was not a state at all, British liberals promoted the minimal state and Americans produced the minimal welfare state leaving the question of citizen well-being to their corporations. Although the contemporary Japanese state is different from each of these domestic politics, elements of all three can be glimpsed. Hence we can accept Japanese political distinctiveness but still interpret it in modern world-systems terms. Hans Maull describes Japan, along with Germany, as the new 'civilian powers'.[115] He argues that due to the circumstance of World War II defeat and subsequent incorporation under the American defence umbrella, these two countries have been forced to spawn a new type of international power which concentrates upon non-military means of assuring national security, largely through economic power. In effect this is just like a hegemonic formula (but pursued by non-hegemons) made possible by the uniquely favourable circumstances of international relations provided by the hegemonic Americans. In hindsight, therefore, it is hardly a surprise that forcing two defeated core states to concentrate their national energies on economic growth produced genuine 'economic miracles'. Maull goes on to suggest that these 'new civilian powers' are 'prototypes of a promising future'.[116] In this context we focus again on Japan. Germany's success did not involve a distinctive political economy in the way we have described for Japan. Though taking advantage of the same international situation, the Japanese drew upon a rather different cultural milieu to create more than a 'new civilian power'; they 'made the water flow uphill'.

Does the rise of Japan represent the beginning of a new hegemonic cycle? There is no doubt that, as Thurow reminds us, Japan has caused 'an enormous economic pressure on the rest of the industrial world to change'.[117] Will this be translated into a new hegemony? There are four main reasons why the answer is 'no'. First, there is the simple matter of size. Hegemons have become larger as the world-economy has expanded, but Japan would represent a reversal from the continental scale of the USA back to island-state size. Today, as the other economic powers move towards larger domestic markets, notably the European Community and the North American Free Trade Area, the Japanese have no such arrangement despite the rise of Pacific Rim institutions.

If the next century is to be the 'Pacific century', it is not at all clear that Japan will lead this zone as a base for world hegemony. Certainly there are no signs of Japanese dominance of China, say, in the way the USA dominated Western Europe in mid-20th century. Of course, in the USA's case its path to such dominance was facilitated by world war. This is precisely an option closed to Japan, not just as a civilian power but because, with contemporary armaments, in the nuclear age nobody can have a good war. We can conclude, therefore, that in terms of political processes it is hard to see a Japanese political trajectory to world hegemony.

Second, it is by no means clear that world-wide emulation of Japanese economic practices produces a feasible future in the sense of creating a new world political economy. This relates to the Japanese economic strategy of export-led growth which has been a huge success for climbing the economic hierarchy but can hardly be the collective economic policy of all core states. Britain could pursue such a strategy in the mid-19th century in a much smaller world-economy that was still geographically expanding, but if everyone imitates Japan and raises production accordingly, the question arises as to who does the consuming in such a Japanese-led future. Quite simply, 'to emulate Japan would bring the world trading system to a halt'.[118] Today there is probably more pressure on the Japanese to conform to other economies – that is, increase domestic consumption – than vice versa. Not surprisingly, Mikio Sumiya, in reviewing the argument for Japan as a 'model society of the future', suggests that Japan can only act in that role for 'developing' countries, not for other core countries.[119] In addition, the Japanese economic bubble seems to have been pricked in the 1990s, suggesting structural obstacles to continued economic successes. We can conclude, therefore, that in terms of economic processes it is hard to find a Japanese trajectory to world hegemony.

Third, there is the key question from our hegemonic perspective of whether Japanese ideas can be universalized. Previous hegemons propounded versions of liberalism to convert their interests into world interests. It is not clear how the Japanese could achieve this. Their new political economy reduces the importance of the individual and promotes group behaviour. Above all it promotes the encompassing group, the Japanese nation. Hence the Japanese model would seem to point towards a more divisive future rather than one world under hegemonic guidance. In addition the fact that Japanese culture is so much more nationalist than cosmopolitan means that 'Japan has been reluctant to export its culture en masse'.[120] There is little or no evidence that Japan aspires 'to lead the world by its own vision and designs'.[121] Equally, the rest of the world shows no sign of 'Japanization'. As Koji Taira notes, 'Japan's money is welcome, but its voice is not.'[122] This leads him to conclude: 'It is doubtful that the rest of the world accepts Japanese hegemony as legitimate.'[123] Here we are at the heart of the matter which Deborah Haber sums up as follows:

> Japan is unlikely to see the kind of success that Britain and the US had in propagating their cultures throughout the globe, rendering Japanese cultural hegemony an impossibility.[124]

We can conclude, therefore, that in terms of cultural processes, it is hard to find a Japanese trajectory to world hegemony.

Fourth, and ultimately the most important reason to doubt a future Japanese hegemony, there is the argument that a state trajectory to world hegemony is no longer possible given the nature of the contemporary world-economy. Obviously this relates to all states but is particularly pertinent to Japan as the most likely American successor. This is Haber's argument for 'why "pax nipponica" is impossible'.[125] The world is becoming far too complex for any one country to impose its leadership in the manner of past hegemons. Hence Japan cannot be 'halfway to hegemony' for the simple reason that 'true hegemony is dead'.[126] This is the position taken here. It leads directly on to the question: if not Japanese hegemony, what's next?

Ultra-hegemony?

Adding the prefix 'ultra' to a concept is usually carried out with the intention of implying more than merely its basic meaning of 'beyond'. Rather, it is a device for suggesting an excessive or extreme version of the concept. This is precisely what I intend by coining the term 'ultra-hegemony'. As an excessive version of hegemony, this new concept helps our understanding of an important contradiction introduced in Chapter 1. Although on any quantitative criteria America ranks as the most powerful of the hegemons, Hopkins identifies US hegemony as the demise moment of the modern world-system. This seeming paradox was explained as 'a success too far' – American hegemony taking capital accumulation towards its global limits. In particular the USA has created an increasingly trans-state world that is superseding the orthodox inter-stateness of the modern world-system.[127] This is, as we have already suggested, the fundamental reason why there will be no successor hegemon to the USA. As more and more people and their lives are directly subjected to world market imperatives, hegemony over the capitalist process can only be achieved through an excess of leadership beyond states. Ultra-hegemony is the process that presages system demise.

The idea of ultra-hegemony has been borrowed directly from another debate about the end of capitalism. In the great Marxist arguments over imperialism before 1914, the leading German Social Democratic theorist Karl Kautsky, known affectionately as the 'pope of Marxism', countering the thesis that contemporary internationalization of capitalism made it ripe for revolution, identified a further stage of capitalism he called 'ultra-imperialism'. Rather than emphasizing state imperial rivalries, he interpreted the growing international dimension of economic activities as producing a situation where the inter-penetration of state capitalisms would make major wars impossible. Instead he envisaged international co-operation among the leading capitalist states organizing the world for their mutual benefit as an ultra-imperialism. He obviously was well wide of the mark in 1914, but events since 1945 have shown that a co-operative world capitalism need not be an impossible dream given the prerequisite of hegemonic leadership. The question today is can the necessary degree of economic co-operation survive the demise of American hegemony through the rise of an ultra-hegemony?

What exactly is the process of ultra-hegemony? As with most new ideas, we are better at defining what it is not. World hegemony thus far has operated through the inter-state system. The social groups who have constructed hegemony have done so using their own state's apparatus. In all three cases there was a symbiotic convergence of civil society with the state unleashing an unstoppable power, a new political economy, on to the world scene. It is just such a process that contemporary trans-state processes make impossible. For instance Robert Reich envisages a 21st century in which there will be 'no *national* products or technologies, no national corporations, no national industries' because there 'will no longer be national economies'.[128] He provides one of the best descriptions of contemporary processes leading to ultra-hegemony. We already have an inter-penetration of capitals that makes the national identification of commodities problematic. Consider the all-American car the Pontiac Le Mans. Reich shows that the American producer General Motors only receives about

$4000 of its $10 000 wholesale price; the rest is divided among eight other countries in this order: South Korea, Japan, Germany, Taiwan, Singapore, Britain, Ireland and Barbados.[129] Of course the typical consumer thinks he or she is buying an 'American' car. Not so, says Reich. Any patriotic American concerned for the US trade deficit would do better to buy a Honda rather than a Pontiac Le Mans![130]

Not only is it difficult to imagine a military war between the major powers, it is becoming just as difficult to understand what trade wars can be about in this world of global capitalism. For instance, in one investigation of Japanese dumping in the American market, the US Commerce Department discovered that 'strictly speaking, there was no such thing as a US forklift, or a foreign forklift for that matter'.[131] This was in response to a complaint in 1987 by a US producer, Hyster Company. The Japanese retaliated by making forklifts in the US, and Hyster complained a second time arguing that the rival forklifts were still 'Japanese' because so many parts still came from Japan. Hyster's credibility was undermined, however, because it used more foreign parts in its 'American' forklifts than were to be found in those it claimed to be 'Japanese'.[132] Obviously here the US state is being used in what is effectively a non-national inter-corporate war. The nationality of products today is decided by company accountants in their calculations for tax advantages and other corporate purposes.

Showing that it is no longer possible to use the state to create a hegemony does not tell us for whom hegemony is still a credible strategy or how they might go about achieving it. The 'who' question is relatively easy to answer: as in the past, it is the leading controllers of capital and their helpers but this time in a relatively de-nationalized form. The beginnings of the production of a global class of capital is a crucial outcome of American hegemony. We can see this development in the changing nomenclature of the largest enterprises in the world-economy. As American corporations began to invest heavily in Europe after 1945, they began to be called multinational companies. This meant that they produced in more than one country, but for the vast majority they were still very much American in ownership. As the companies began to develop sophisticated strategies of production across many countries playing one off against another, they soon became known as trans-national corporations. Today few doubt the future lies with global corporations, the largest companies that make 'international alliances' with one another, acting just like states have done in the past. The result is an incredibly complex web of economic linkages with a new 'international management bourgeoisie' at its heart.[133] This corporate elite includes, as well as top managers, the professionals whose services make the global organization possible: including international lawyers, accountants, advertisers and communications and media personnel. Can these constitute a new hegemonic class? Interestingly Leslie Sklair talks of a 'brain drain' from domestic to trans-national enterprises replacing the social mobility that used to target the USA.[134] What of political links? In fact Sklair includes political elites, both top bureaucrats and politicians in his new trans-national class. As political organization has grown larger with such institutions as the European Union, so functionaries who had been 'national' became separated from their 'roots', moving, say, between the IMF to GATT to the EU and so on. Politicians remain state-based but become the new 'compradors', peddling the neo-liberal economic ideology to justify opening their countries to the world market.[135] In case there is too much national resistance, the new 'captains of consciousness' in a global media are always on hand convincing people to replace thoughts about their life by concerns for their 'lifestyle'.[136] This is Americanization become globalization.

Finally, how might this ultra-hegemony be organized spatially across the world? Although we do not hypothesize the complete demise of states, they are clearly losing authority as globalization proceeds apace. Where is the authority being transferred? To corporations, of course; but concretely this is represented by the rise of world cities. Castells and Hall identify 'cities and regions' as 'increasingly becoming critical agents of economic development' as the world's economic geography changes 'fundamentally'.[137] Historically, capital has always been a matter of organization through cities; with the rise of the modern inter-state system many economic functions were transferred to the states. For instance, in the early rise of capitalism in Europe, Braudel identifies 'world-cities' like Venice, Genoa and Antwerp as the financial centres around which the nascent world-economy developed.[138] As we argued in Chapter 1, defence imperatives led to the territorial state replacing the city scale of organization so that Braudel's later world-cities, Amsterdam, London and New York, are world financial centres but as part of the 'national economies' of hegemons. However with the contemporary international guarantees for sovereign boundaries which have been a feature of US hegemony, the defence imperative has been partially neutralized. 'National territory' is no longer a requirement for city success as both Hong Kong and Singapore have illustrated in recent decades.[139] But the major world cities of today remain within territorial states. John Friedmann identifies New York, London and Tokyo as the triple apex of a new global control system.[140] These and other world cities such as Paris, Los Angeles, São Paulo and Singapore, act as the control centres of contemporary global capitalism. With new technology in computers and communications allowing for more centralized and remote control by corporations, these cities have become the nodes in a global network of information. With selected high-tech regions they are set to become, in Castells and Hall's terminology, the 'technopoles of the world' in the 21st century.[141] They are the homes of the global class we described above. This is important because new technology provides the means for decentralization as well as centralization. The latter occurs at the control level of organization since world-cities provide places with a critical mass of global-class people, so necessary for keeping abreast with rapid changes in a globalized world.

The new world hegemony that seems to be emerging, therefore, takes a network rather than a territorial form, but its most important feature is its 'ultra' nature. The modern world-system has always been a highly dynamic historical entity. Globalization implies not only a deepening of its spatial scope, there is the implication that the system is, in some sense, speeding up.[142] Unlike post-hegemonic trauma, we do not seem to have to wait until after the hegemony has passed to experience trauma associated with ultra-hegemony. Where is our world going? Putting it most baldly, is there a sustainable living world after ultra-hegemony?

6 World impasse

Alexander the Great was an extraordinary leader of men and conqueror of lands. In his short life of some 32 years (356–23 BC), he amassed an empire extending from his European home in Macedonia to the Indus Valley in northern India. For Alexander, the conquest of 'India' represented the final subjugation of his realm as King of Asia. One of the famous stories told of this premodern hero is that on completing his lordship of Asia, the still young Alexander knelt down and punched the earth in frustration because there were no new territories to conquer. We may be concerned for the quality of the geographical intelligence he was receiving, but the interesting point from our perspective is the notion of earthly limits to his conquests. World-empires recognize no sovereignty but their own and so lay claim to all the known world. Successful expansion, therefore, entailed territorial conquests, such as those of Alexander, that could continue to the 'ends of the earth'. This is precisely what Alexander achieved in his creation of an extensive Hellenistic world combining Nile, Euphrates and Indus centres of civilization in the fourth century BC.

Territorial limits to system expansion no longer apply. The modern world-system became global in scope, the ultimate territorial limit, about a hundred years ago but this did not bring its expansion to a close. Quite the opposite, in fact: the 20th century has witnessed the greatest growth in the history of the modern world-system. This is a different type of growth: the traditional extensive mode of expansion has given way to an intensive mode. The latter enables growth to proceed *in situ* without conquest. This is what the modern world-system has been doing since global closure. This intensive mode of expansion is achieved by accumulation of capital. All world-systems before 1900 employed a mixture of extensive and intensive expansions with the former particularly rewarded in world-empires resulting in its domination as the means of system growth. In contrast, the balance between extensive and intensive modes of growth is reversed in a world-economy like the modern world-system. This has culminated in the automatic elimination of the extensive mode once global territorial limits were reached. Although formal imperialism had been endemic to European expansion from 1492, territorial conquest was relegated in importance – Marx termed it primitive accumulation – as part of the ceaseless capital accumulation. The massive continued expansion of the capitalist world-economy since 1900 has proven the centrality of intensive capital accumulation as the main motor of change in the modern era.

Thus, there has been no Alexandrian frustration for capitalists as their world continues to expand despite reaching its global territorial limits. This 20th-century outcome is certainly in line with the system's own metatheory of universal progress. In the modern era, we are assured, all obstacles to expansion have, or will be, cleared away to enable humanity to continue on its inevitable forward march. The idea of limits to this progress is anathema to the whole notion of being modern. But that is precisely what I am suggesting by entitling this chapter 'world impasse'. As we described in Chapter 1, we interpret the modern world-system as historical rather than eternal. That is to say, like other world-systems before it, the capitalist world-economy will finally reach its demise phase. Hence we argue that capitalism's intensive expansion is just as vulnerable to material limits as traditional territorial expansion: the idea that 'us moderns' have discovered the secret of eternal expansion is emphatically denied. But that is the only way the system can survive because capitalism *is* growth; the *raison d'être* of the capitalist world-economy is ceaseless capital accumulation. Whereas premodern world-empires could stop expanding and consolidate their position, this is impossible for the capitalist world-economy. Capitalism can never stop; no more accumulation equals no more system. Even the slightest slowdown in expansion creates a crisis of the system. For capitalists to be capitalists, there must always be new worlds to conquer in the sense of devising new products to sell to new markets. More and more production for more and more consumption uses ever more resources. But the earth is a finite world. However ingenious future technology becomes, there are environmental limits to the exploitation of the earth. Hence, because capitalism can never stop, it follows that the earth is ultimately too small for the modern world-system. That is our world impasse.

This argument that our world is moving relentlessly towards its demise is by no means original. At about the time when US high hegemony was ending, the problem of unrestrained growth was discovered, focusing upon massive increases in population. With titles like *The Population Bomb*, a new generation of concerned biologists were warning the public of the unsustainability of contemporary trends.[1] The most famous report was first published in 1972 for the Club of Rome's 'Project on the Predicament of Mankind', entitled simply *The Limits to Growth*.[2] Using the latest dynamic computer-modelling techniques, a world model was developed which allowed different assumptions about future trends to be tested. The resulting variety of outcomes was dwarfed by one overwhelming conclusion: under all reasonable assumptions, we are *en route* to an ecological catastrophe sooner or later. Subsequently, the downturn in the world-economy in the 1970s deflected concern for problems of growth, but they reappeared in the 1980s as more broadly based environmental questions. In 1992 the dynamic modelling exercise that produced the original 'limits' conclusion was repeated with updated information in *Beyond the Limits* to show again that if things continue as they are today we will 'overshoot and collapse' sometime in the next century.[3]

The main achievement of the Club of Rome publications has been to push the question of the sustainability of our world to the forefront of debate about the future. The result has been discussions and arguments over more than two decades, with the Club of Rome and its supporters cast as pessimists and their critics as optimists. The latter have identified many problems with the Club of Rome's complex world model, but whatever the detailed criticism of its various submodels, the thrust of its overall conclusions cannot be dismissed as fanciful.[4] However there is a serious problem with their overall approach: its dire predictions are ultimately fuelled by exponential population increases giving a biological rather than social foundation to the predictions. But 'mankind's predicament' is not due to demographic causes, it is the nature of the system that leads to unsustainability. Capitalism does not appear in the Club of Rome's world model (there is reference to 'capital' but no capitalism); instead we have industrialization as socially benign but environmentally destructive. The key point is that once we interpret our modern world as a capitalist world-economy, we no longer have to choose sides between pessimists and optimists. The 'predicament' is not 'mankind's' in the sense of an inevitable result of historical progress, rather it is the outcome of the particular social system that got us into this situation. Identifying the crisis as 'capitalism's predicament' allows us to be both optimistic and pessimistic – optimistic for the future of humanity while being pessimistic for the future of the current world-system. This is what I have intended by the phrase 'world impasse'. There is a population problem developing today that is threatening the earth, but it is not demographic; it is the increasing 'population' of shopping malls across the world.

The problem is the hegemonic legacy of Americanization. As we described in the last two chapters, this was a promise of development, and therefore affluence, for all. The image of the future that was projected was a world where everybody has the means to consume at the same level as Americans. This is not possible; Americanization is a promise that can't be kept. A brief, critical look at the original case of Americanization, US consumerism during its high hegemony, shows the limitations of this universal model. The first affluent society was built upon much more than exploitation of American land and resources. In its heyday in 1960, the USA with approximately ¹⁄₁₅ of the world's population was using about one-third of the world's resources. This is obviously no basis for general imitation. In fact, one estimate of the carrying capacity of the world, assuming an American standard of living, is 600 million people, a figure passed in 1675 before the USA, let alone the American Dream, was ever thought of.[5] The current world population is 5.4 billion people and rising fast. It is expected to stabilize eventually at between 10 and 15 billion people, depending upon demographic assumptions. Wherever it finishes up, it makes the promise of everybody consuming as if they were members of American middle-class households ever more incredible. Notice that this is not, despite the reference to billions of people, a demographic argument. There are no doubt many global social formations which can sustain 15 billion people, but the capitalist world-economy is not one of them. Imagine China and India with a density of shopping malls the same as in the USA and Canada, and the point should be clear.

The importance of focusing upon the nature of the system can be best illustrated with reference to the role of technology in predictions of the future. Typically, optimists have great faith in the ingenuity of humanity to create the technology to solve all obstacles in the way of progress. In the Club of Rome's work, technology slows down the depletion of resources and therefore postpones social collapse. Hence the debate between the optimists and pessimists can be viewed as a sort of race pitting growth against technology and you choose sides by whether you think technology can keep up with the demands of growth and prevent disaster or vice versa. But there is no race. Technology cannot be an exogenous variable; it is socially created and therefore part of the system. Technology and growth are intrinsically linked together in the capitalist world-economy. That is, after all, the basis for world hegemonic cycles as described in Chapter 3. The prime role of technology in our world is to create new products for new markets – for suburban shoppers, for generals, for doctors, for businesses, for farmers, for bankers – precisely the growth that is relentlessly leading to impasse. Technology within the capitalist world-economy is part of the problem not the solution.

Americanization is sometimes dismissed as a relatively superficial phenomenon, merely McWorld or cocacolarization or everybody wearing blue cowboy trousers. If this were all it amounted to then it could hardly be a threat to the world's ecology, in the way that capital accumulation will finally precipitate world impasse. We argue in this chapter that consumer society represents much more than the contemporary face of capitalism; rather it is the culmination of a tradition of modernity intimately linked to world hegemony. Americanization's popularity based upon its appeal to ordinary people is not totally an invention of the 20th century. We introduce the concept of ordinary modernity in this chapter to describe the way in which the Dutch, British and Americans have built a bourgeois culture in opposition to the 'high' culture of traditional upper strata. This unusual celebration of ordinariness is traced, in the first section, through three rounds of hegemonic artistic inventiveness in which ordinary people, rather than the usual cast of kings and warriors or angels and saints, figure as subjects. It is argued that these new art forms express a particular distinctiveness of the hegemonic states that we have not previously considered. Hence, we return to consider the nature of the hegemons once again but from a more artistic cultural perspective than previously.

The second section deals explicitly with ordinary modernity. We treat it as an aspect of what Fernand Braudel has called material civilization, his 'structures of everyday life', and what Siegfried Giedion terms 'anonymous history'.[6] The latter consists of the 'slow shaping of daily life' which is of 'equal importance to the explosions of history'.[7] Braudel treats the everyday more systematically: in addition to the economic processes of markets and the great organization of international affairs, he argues that there is a third 'layer' of history, the analysis of daily life underpinning the 'higher' levels of human activities. 'Material life', Braudel tells us, 'is made up of people and things' and in his study of the 15th–18th centuries he analyses the everyday lives of ordinary people to provide 'an evaluation of the limits of what was possible in the pre-industrial world'.[8] It is only at this level that you obtain a true measure of a world-system, and we trace the development of ordinary modernity through the evolution of the modern home as a private place for comfortable family life. The wealth derived from economic and political success enabled citizens of the hegemonic states to define a new way of life whose development has been unique to modernity: bourgeois comforts beginning with Dutch merchants and culminating in American suburbia. It is the latter that represents the everyday structure of Americanization and which defines the limits of the modern world-system.

Both Dutch and British hegemonic impasses were finally resolved by a new hegemon restructuring the world-economy and creating a new modernity. However, with no new hegemon following the USA, this process of resolution through inventing another modernity is closed off and American hegemonic impasse becomes world impasse in the wake of American dream becoming world dream. The only resolution that is now possible is the creation of a new world to replace the modern world-system. Going beyond a restructuring requires a total change in material life for a postmodern world-system. In the third section of the chapter we search for signs of such a profound change in the writings of those who understand the coming world impasse. Recognition of the uniqueness of this impasse – a secular vision of the end of the world – began as American high hegemony was coming to a close. In the quarter of a century of contemplation on this momentous question, two contrasting visions of postmodernity, which we identify as ecofascist and deep green, are clearly discernible. Both are described as alternative resolutions to the travails of ordinary modernity. In a brief concluding section, we consider where our story from world hegemony to world impasse has got us.

Hegemonic celebrations of ordinariness

Celebrating the ordinary person in society is historically a very rare cultural trait. The usual celebration is of the great and the transcendent as part of the ideological legitimation of the ruling strata. This is reflected in our language by there being two rather different meanings for the word 'culture'. On the one hand, culture is used in the general sense of describing the norms and practices of a distinctive group of people – we talk of French culture, for instance. On the other hand there is a specific sense of culture as elite practices and tastes – the opera is considered a cultural event, for example. We sometimes refer to this second meaning as 'high culture', which properly expresses its social position. If we refer to a 'cultured man', we do not mean he possesses a culture, since that is assumed to be ubiquitous of all humanity; rather we mean he has the appropriate manners expected of the upper class.

The idea of high culture implies there must be a 'low culture'. This can be a derogatory term of dismissal relating to 'low life' and its unrespectable behaviours but this need not always be the case. In the 19th century the building of nationalist politics involved a re-evaluation of low culture as the true expression of the people. This involved a search for folk culture with romantic reconstructions of peasant costumes, dances, songs and music.[9] There was much invention of tradition in such exercises, but they do represent a celebration of the ordinary in the development of modern politics.[10] They legitimated the state by discovering its nation within its territory. Whatever the ideological purpose the message was clear: in a nation-state people matter because they are the people.

This very modern politics of the ordinary had another important expression which I wish to focus upon here. As well as the general nationalist celebration of the ordinary, there has been a very specific hegemonic celebration relating specifically to the Dutch, the British and Americans. The civil societies of the three hegemonic states have each made contributions to the creative arts that are distinctive in two crucial ways. First, the hegemon's civil society is found to be exceptionally innovative and has created new art forms. These are, respectively, Dutch genre painting, the English novel and American popular cinema. Second, with these new cultural vehicles, the everyday lives of ordinary people have been made a particular focus of attention. These were not the usual developments of high culture but represent new artistic departures expressing the nature of what were unusual and special societies. This was a non-nationalistic portrayal of ordinary people which contributed to the

Plate 22 *Vietnam War Memorial*, Washington, DC. This simple black marble wall, in which the names of all 57 939 Americans killed in the war are inscribed, is the classic monument of ordinary modernity. By eschewing the typical heroic image of war memorials, the wall was unpopular among the political and military establishment but is hugely popular with the public. The dignified and equal identification of each American victim provides an intense emotional image that simply says 'war kills ordinary people'

universalizing of hegemonic ideas that we describe in the next section as ordinary modernity.

Dutch genre paintings

The culture of absolutism is the baroque, European 'high culture' in which an elaborate symbolism glorified church and king.[11] Originating in Italian church architecture intended to replicate heaven on earth, kings soon discovered the power of such cultural artifacts to impress rivals and subjects alike. Louis XIV's magnificent palace at Versailles remains the greatest monument of absolutism. From today's perspective this is 'tourist Europe', the world of magnificent cities and palaces – what Nussbaum has called the 'holy places of European culture'.[12] This grand European style permeated all high culture going beyond architecture to 'classical' music, heroic sculptures and glorious paintings. But there was one country that stayed outside the 'High Tradition': the baroque had little to offer the Dutch. This does not mean a Philistine or 'uncultured' United Provinces, quite the opposite: the Dutch invented a unique anti-baroque style.[13]

The greatest Dutch cultural achievements in the 17th century were in painting, where a totally new style was developed. In contrast to baroque symbolism illustrating a decisive moment in a narrative, Dutch 'genre' painting merely portrayed a scene.[14] It is this 'realism' that marks off Dutch painting as special.[15] As an art, it attempted to mirror the facts of life as they existed by drawing directly on the artist's visual experiences of his surroundings. Unlike the other great 'masters' of the period, Rembrandt did not visit Rome to enhance his artistic sensibilities, a feature he shared with many less esteemed Dutch artists.[16] The result was that, in Fuchs's words, the new realism originated from the 'context of the optimistic contemplation of one's own world'.[17] There could hardly be a greater contrast with baroque painting; instead of glorifying the great, we find a celebration of the ordinary.

It is important to understand the context in which this new art emerged. Gombrich writes of 'a crisis of art' in northern Europe in the wake of the Reformation.[18] Protestant Europe's suspicion of idolatry took away the artist's stock in trade, the devotional picture. Although a few artists were able to find work in the courts of princes as portrait painters 'there was only one Protestant country in Europe where art fully survived the crisis of the Reformation – that was the Netherlands'.[19] Instead of waiting for commissions, artists in the United Provinces painted to sell, thus creating the first art market.[20] In this competitive context, artists specialized in certain types or 'genre' of paintings so as to achieve a reputation in the market-place. As well as portraits, scenes at sea, rural landscapes, domestic scenes and even still-life pictures all became popular. In short, painting became an industry with middle men, the first art dealers, supplying people from a wide range of occupations with a new commodity to consume.

According to Nussbaum, genre artists

> made a vision of the world in the prosaic terms of the new bourgeois, without royalty and without religion, even without more philosophy than a comfortable bourgeois acceptance of solidity and luxury.[21]

We can interpret these paintings at two levels. First, as an attempt at realism, they provide scenes that give a visual insight into Dutch society. From group portraits of satisfied burghers to scenes of ordinary working people, we can view the ruled in the United Provinces when elsewhere we see only the rulers. For instance, Fuchs describes one of Jan Steen's paintings as showing 'an ordinary interior with ordinary people', which is typical of the domestic genre of which Steen was a master.[22] Second, we can interpret the meaning of the painting; why subjects are painted and what it tells about the nature of the society. Among the various genre, one is particularly interesting in this respect: still-life composition which Gombrich calls 'the most "specialized" branch of Dutch painting'.[23] They are interesting for our argument for two reasons. First, as simple paintings of a group of ordinary items, they show us just how far removed Dutch culture was from the art of baroque Europe. In the latter, the subjects of the great paintings were major episodes from the Bible or some equally revered topic. In contrast, the Dutch created masterpieces from the most trivial of subjects. Second, although the subjects may have been trivial, they were not chosen arbitrarily but reflected the new comforts of Dutch bourgeois society. Typically still-lives showed 'beautiful vessels filled with wine and appetizing fruit, or other dainties arranged on lovely china' which were painted to be hung in the dining rooms of Dutch homes as permanent 'reminders of the joys of the

Plate 23 *The Kitchen-maid* (*c*. 1660) by Jan Vermeer (Rijksmuseum, Amsterdam). A classic painting of an ordinary Dutch person carrying out an everyday task. Despite its simplicity, Gombrich (1989, 340) considers it to be 'one of the great masterpieces of all time'

table'.[24] No wonder this genre of paintings sold so well in the new popular art market of 17th-century Netherlands.

The English novel

A very different popular market emerged in 18th-century Britain commonly known as the rise of the reading public.[25] To quote Dr Johnson, Britain became 'a nation of readers' in a new 'age of authors'.[26] In London, alone, the number of printers increased from just 70 in 1724 to 372 by 1802 producing newspapers, magazines, pamphlets and books.[27] One notable feature was the tendency 'for literature to become a primarily feminine pursuit'.[28] This was the result of increasing numbers of middle-class households in which the women of the family had much time on their hands for leisure pursuits. Nobody knows how much the growth of the publications market was due to women, but the development of the novel as a new product suggests that they were important. In any case, the English novel played a role analogous to genre paintings in Britain's celebration of the ordinary.

As a form of fiction, the novel is undoubtedly 'modern': it was an English invention of the 18th century and use of the term 'novel' was only established at the end of that century.[29] Unlike more traditional story telling, the novel aspired to be realistic, and Ian Watt uses this to draw parallels with philosophical realism.[30] The term 'realism' was first used in France in the 1830s with reference to Rembrandt's paintings as imitations of reality. Watt traces modern realism to another Dutch source, the immigrants Descartes and Locke. This triple Dutch connection is quite suggestive. We can interpret the novel as the British cultural invention for articulating the concerns and interests of ordinary people; for instance, Jane Austen teasing her readers on who will marry whom. A crucial point about the novel is that it eschews mythology and legend as traditional sources of stories and instead produces original 'storylines'. Traditional stories drew their audience into an unchanging world of customs, the novel took an individualistic turn and since any individual's experience is always unique, the story is always new. Hence Watt notes, the novel 'is well-named'.[31] Every novel is about particular people in particular circumstances with definite time and place contexts. In short it is a literary vehicle for an ever-changing world which is why it is quintessentially modern, a product of the modern world-system. It reaches its apogee as a cultural influence in Britain during her hegemony in the great era of the Victorian novel. In a remarkable flourishing of an art form, the following great novelists, who were to dominate world literature in the mid-19th century, were all born in England between 1811 and 1819: William Thackeray, Charles Dickens, Anthony Trollope, Charlotte and Emily Brontë, George Eliot and Charles Kingsley.[32] Allen describes their collective contribution thus: 'Sharing the preoccupations of their times rooted in the popular life of their age, they produced an art that was truly national.'[33]

It was only 'national' in the sense that the British nation was middle class. 'It was the respectable who composed the great reading public, and it was for the respectable that the great Victorian novelists wrote.'[34] This idea of respectability was at the heart of English novel writing. It was the way the middle class separated themselves from a dissolute aristocracy on the one hand and an ill-disciplined working class on the other. For instance, by promoting the ideal of the 'domestic woman' over her aristocratic counterpart, Nancy Armstrong argues that a 'modern domesticity' was cast in the role of the 'only haven from the trials of a heartless economic world'.[35] She goes on to link the popularity of the novel and the new female ideal with the 'cultural hegemony' of the rising middle class in England.[36] In general, we can note that the English novel was 'very much a middle class enterprise' because it incorporated bourgeois interests within its plots while generally omitting much else that was happening.[37] The high politics of Napoleon and Wellington are missing from the English novel as are the radical politics of the Luddites. Instead a safe and stable world is provided as the context for the private middle-class lives that make up the story.[38]

Hollywood movies

America's great cultural contribution to the modern world has been in the cinema. Above all it made popular movies. While Europeans developed a reputation for 'high-brow' films that were difficult to understand, Americans produced films for everyone. John Lukacs describes the resulting domination of this medium thus:

> As early as 1925, millions of people in Europe knew the names and faces of American movie stars while they knew not the name of their own prime minister.[39]

In the 1930s Hollywood provided escapism from poverty, with its glittering stars and spectacular films. After being harnessed to the war effort in the early 1940s, the last years of the decade were a time of major changes. Anti-trust legislation ended studio control of outlets and anti-communist witch-hunts eliminated any artistic radicalism. Cinema audiences in the USA peaked in 1946; although the export market remained buoyant, the coming threat of TV was hanging over the industry.[40] The new suburban lifestyle that was growing rapidly in the post-war years favoured the home entertainment TV offered in competition with films shown in cinemas in far away downtown. In the 1950s this problem was overcome by the Hollywood studios through producing for TV: the age of the 'fifty minute featurette' had arrived.[41]

All this resulted in the safe and bland films typifying the 1950s. Although various old film genre dominate critical discussion – westerns, musicals, war, gangsters, horror, science fiction, etc – it is a brand new genre that tells us more about America at this time. Teen films were an invention of the 1950s along with their audience – teenagers. This youth culture was a product of America's affluent society. Ordinary young people constituted a sizeable market for the first time in history and the new consumers were called 'teenagers'. Teenage became equated with 'leisure, pleasure and conspicuous consumption'.[42] Hollywood was only too pleased to cater for this new market with a string of films including rock and roll features, teenage/school love stories and holiday/beach movies. Simple formulas were recycled time and again – in later periods TV would find it difficult to run a season of Elvis Presley films, for instance, because nearly all used the same story. Above all, these films represented the ordinary concerns of youth, adolescent worries that were timeless.

But the stock-in-trade movies of the 1950s hardly qualify as a genre at all. Domestic films – simple comedies and lightweight dramas, some drawn from early successes of TV series – were produced in their hundreds.[43] These are interesting, not for their quality, but for the taken-for-granted world they portray. As John Russell Taylor observes: 'As the fifties progressed, the movies showed American life becoming more secure, cozy and domestic'.[44] This is the same bourgeois domesticity to be found in Dutch genre paintings and the English novel. Quoting Taylor again:

> In the magical sanctuary of the cinema you could have been forgiven for suppos-
> ing that the most important issue in the world was whether Doris Day would
> succeed . . . in preserving her virginity until wedding bells at the final fade-out.[45]

These were stories of ordinary people living comfortable lives – for much of the rest
of the world it was the American dream on cellulose.[46]

Not only did the films change, so did the stars. In the old Hollywood star system,
the leading actors and actresses were promoted by the studio publicity machines to
be demi-gods. In contrast the 1950s have been termed 'the great period of the star-as-
ordinary-person'.[47] The stars came down to earth, as the saying goes, and instead of
being promoted as super human, they were presented to their audiences as 'straightforward, uncomplicated average human beings'.[48] This is a hegemonic self-
confidence in its own ordinariness that we have come across before. In Ann Lloyd's
words: 'stars like Doris Day, Rock Hudson, June Allyson and Gregory Peck insisted
that the everyday was best'.[49] And the everyday was middle-class homelife in
American suburbia.

The most influential portrayal of American middle-class life was probably to be
found in the new medium of entertainment that flourished during US high
hegemony: television. One example was particularly important. The 1950s' American TV show *I Love Lucy* is the most popular programme of all time: it is still played
regularly on TV across the world. What is its appeal? What is its message? The
central character is the key. Looking behind the humour, we find a person who
organizes her life in a rather chaotic manner but is never punished for it. Lucy's
appeal is that she is very ordinary and yet has no real worries about making ends
meet or where the next meal is coming from. All her audience can feel equal or
superior to this scatty American middle-class housewife. If Lucy can do it, it follows
that anybody – the ordinary of the world – can have the good life. *I Love Lucy* can be
interpreted as the limiting case of hegemonic celebration of the ordinary.

Ordinary modernity

To say that modernity has a 'dark side' has become commonplace in the 20th century. In particular, the 'industrialization' of war has created a litany of horror – the
gas warfare of the trenches in World War I, the holocaust and the atomic destruction
of Hiroshima and Nagasaki in World War II, the threat of global nuclear annihilation
in the Cold War – far worse than anything experienced in any other world-system.
No wonder those writing about modernity insist on viewing it as 'a double-edged
phenomenon'.[50] But academic writers are atypical in their reaction to modernity.
Although certainly aware of the horrors, for most people to be modern is considered
a good thing. The idea of something being modern is that it does what it does better
than what it replaces. Although as applied to bombs this has a terrible outcome, for
most of the time its most influential effect has been to create a better life for many
ordinary people. Whether enjoying the good life or cherishing hopes for a good life,
for so many people across the world in the 20th century, it is this idea of progress to
a better future that has made modernity so popular despite its dark side. Advertisers
understand this when they present the commodity they are promoting as 'modern';

unlike academic writers, this profession of scribes interprets being modern as a single-edged sword for good(s).

What is this ordinary modernity? In general we can note that modernity is a very complex, multifaceted concept enabling many different interpretations of its core characteristics. Most commonly its 'rationality' is emphasized, especially in historical arguments: being rational lay behind the scientific revolution of the 17th century, provided the cutting edge for the Enlightenment in the 18th century and created the technology of the 19th century that made universal progress seem so inevitable.[51] Recently Anthony Giddens, with his eye firmly focused on contemporary globalization, has argued that modernity depends upon new relations of trust.[52] All world-systems separate everyday life experiences from important determinants that are system-wide, but the modern world-system deals with this 'disembedding' distinctively. Whereas premodern societies treated 'extra-local' effects in terms of divine providence, under modernity such risks are dealt with through trust in ordered systems of social relations that operate to integrate the local into the system. The contemporary explosion of reliance on 'plastic' money, for instance, is only possible because of widespread trust in the system that operates this banking innovation. Both philosophers and historians arguing for rationality and sociologists and economists arguing for trust are 'top-down' interpretations of modernity that seem far from the ordinary modernity we are seeking. Studying modernity should focus on the fact that our society is self-consciously modern. The popularity of modernity in the 20th century has been crucial, not only for sustaining modernity, but also in influencing the changing nature of modernity. Can we identify a single concept, like rationality and trust, to capture the essence of ordinary modernity? I think we can and offer *comfort* as my candidate as the concept to take on this onerous role.[53]

What can we mean when we elevate the commonplace notion of comfort to be a core concept of modernity? Like rationality and trust, once we begin to look at comfort seriously it becomes a very complex idea. Although basically meaning to make life easy, in practice this can and has been viewed in many different ways. Witold Rybczynski writes of the 'mystery of comfort' because it is impossible to measure it objectively:

> it may be enough to realize that domestic comfort involves a range of attributes – convenience, efficiency, leisure, ease, pleasure, domesticity, intimacy, and privacy – all of which contribute to the experience; common sense will do the rest.[54]

But, of course, this common sense is only common to modern society. In the invention of medieval society as a foil for modernity, this premodern setting may have been romantically enchanting, but it was never viewed as comfortable. Every suburbanite appreciates that her or his life has a degree of comfort unattainable in medieval Europe, even for a king and queen in their (draughty) castle.[55] Knowledge of sumptuous lifestyles in other civilizations, both classical Rome and the great Oriental empires, is part of the modern historical consciousness, but it is understood that these extreme images of comfort were enjoyed by the very few, a very small elite living off the backs of the many. Modern comfort, in contrast, is available to the ordinary man and woman, the descendants of serfs and slaves not kings and emperors. Modernity, therefore, is for ordinary people.

But not all ordinary people: for a majority of people across the world the comfortable life of modernity is a wish rather than a fact. As we have seen, Americanization has led to more and more people in the richer countries of the world, the core of the world-economy, enjoying a degree of affluence reflected in consumption. The latter is not arbitrary buying; a major component of American-style consumption has been to create comfort and convenience. The consequence of Americanization has been, therefore, a trend towards the replacement of the traditional polarization of rich versus poor by poverty being contrasted to comfort.[56] We may all live in a single modern world-economy, but differences in material well-being across countries are popularly understood as defining 'degrees of modernity': it requires a 'comfortable' standard of living to acquire the necessary commodities to live in the 'modern mode'. Most ordinary people from rich countries would never contemplate migrating to a poor country because they would lose their relatively comfortable lifestyles. They may visit as tourists but ensure their comfort by checking into a four-star hotel. There are exceptions: young backpackers see the world on the cheap and thereby sacrifice comfort — but only for a little while since comfort awaits them back home after the great adventure. Thus, even though the peoples of the periphery of the world-economy are tightly integrated into the modern world-system, their struggles for survival are generally not seen as a modern mode of living. However, despite the dominant image of the world divided into a 'world of comfort' and a 'world of struggle' with only the former viewed as modern, everyday struggles for survival are premised upon hopes of achieving comfort, that is becoming modern. This is not evidence for the particular persuasiveness and influence of social scientists' modernization theory, rather it is the result of modernity's ordinary face. Beneficiaries may be a world minority, but they are both very numerous and very ordinary making prospects for 'modernization' in poor countries not appearing to be too far-fetched.

Given that the basis of modernity as comfort is obviously materialist, it follows that we should expect it to be related to hegemony. We charted major linkages between modernity and hegemony in Chapter 1 and here we add to these connections by tracing the development of comfort to the three hegemonic states. Striving for comfort is traditionally sneered at by traditional upper-class elites as vulgar and bourgeois, and they have been right to see it as a threat to their social leadership. Modern comfort is about being middle class and has replaced aristocratic mores by a more popular way of life. And it is the hegemons who have promoted the new bourgeois worlds that have undermined older traditional ways of life.

The final part of this section is a short digression which is necessary to relate our approach to modernity and its aftermath to contemporary work on postmodernism. Although I agree with Giddens that the idea of postmodern is best reserved for a change in social trajectory away from modernity rather than the aesthetic reflection on the nature of modernity of the self-ascribed postmodernists, the particular approach to modernity developed in this section does provide an unusual perspective from which to view this debate. The cultural celebration of the ordinary includes an implicit critique of architectural modernism as a modern *cul-de-sac*, not the end of modernity. Modern architecture is a rare example of something modern and un-popular and can be contrasted with suburbia as modern and popular. We conclude by exploring the idea of post-traditional as a better designation of contemporary social dilemmas than postmodern. Our post-traditional world can be interpreted as high modernity, the culmination of ordinary modernity.

Home, sweet home

Contemporary houses where ordinary people live usually have a hall, a small room behind the front door where the stairs begin and outside clothes are hung. Medieval houses of merchants and the nobility also had halls but these were very large and dominated the whole house. These two house arrangements represent two completely different worlds. The great halls of the past were multiple-use spaces that were essentially public in nature: a place for transacting business, for cooking and eating, for entertainment and for sleeping at night.[57] Today the hall has been reduced to a small transition zone between a private home and a public outside. It is the home's frontier, where we enter and leave, where visitors are dealt with. Although important for providing a home's initial image to the outside world, the hall does not have to be comfortable like other rooms because it is not a place where you are expected to stay for long. If the visitors are friends they may be invited beyond the hall to specialized rooms that are prized for their comfort and convenience – living room or lounge, dining room, kitchen, bathroom and bedrooms. It is this private space of the home that is the essential locus of ordinary modernity.[58]

This modernity as domesticity beyond the hall had to be created and the three hegemons are intimately implicated in the invention of the home and making it comfortable. The modern sense of the word comfort only came into usage in the 18th century but 'there was one place', according to Witold Rybczynski, where 'seventeenth century domestic interior evolved in a way that was arguably unique, and that can be described as having been, at the very least, exemplary'.[59] This place was the United Provinces where economic successes went hand in hand with new cultural behaviours.[60] Dutch merchants were family-oriented and lived in small households with few or no servants.[61] Children were integral to the new family life and, instead of being apprenticed to another household, stayed at home and attended school. In this way the Dutch invented what we understand today as childhood.[62] New town houses were built or converted to adapt to these new practices and therefore eliminated the traditional mix of work with residency. The ground floor was still treated as a public space to entertain visitors but the upper floors were a special family place. Friends allowed access to the upstairs were required to remove their street shoes so as not to disrupt the cleanliness of the home. This boundary between public and private spaces was a new idea which enabled houses to become homes.[63] Here the Dutch could express their personal likes and dislikes to fit individual family needs such as decorating their walls with maps or paintings. A contemporary critic of the Netherlands, Sir William Temple, after noting the propensity for monetary tightness among the Dutch, gives one exception: expenditure on furniture and other commodities for the home.[64] Rybczynski highlights developments in the kitchen.[65] With few servants, the mother of the family ensured this new specialized space was properly equipped for its function and convenient to its user.[66] All in all, the Dutch produced the first modern homes in the world, cozy settings for the family life of ordinary people.

In the 18th century, interior comfort advanced in two forms. In France aristocratic and royal tastes were converted into sumptuous fashions for palaces. In more bourgeois England where the court had little cultural influence, a simpler comfort was developed for the country houses of the middle classes.[67] This Georgian style is a fashion that refuses to become out of date because of its suitability for comfortable homelife. This was the era of Chippendale chairs and the ubiquitous diffusion of the 'Windsor chair', both popular because they were so easy to sit in.[68] English economic successes provided the enabling wealth for new cultural practices related to leisure. The home became the locus of card games, dinner parties, various entertainments such as billiards and dances and, of course, it was where the latest novels were read.[69] Rybczynski thinks it highly relevant that Jane Austen so frequently used the words 'comfort' and 'comfortable' in what he describes as her 'domestic genre of novel writing', focusing on the homelife of England's middle classes.[70] She even coins the phrase 'English comfort' as two words that seemed naturally to go together. In fact it was the English who brought carpets down from the walls to make floors quieter and nicer to walk on. They even introduced wall-to-wall carpeting for the first time.[71] But their main contribution to domestic comfort was to bring furniture out from the walls. It is with the 18th-century English that the arrangement of sofas and easy chairs around the fireplace, the epitome of warm coziness, makes its appearance in the home.[72] It is this 'English taste' that spread through Europe and America to create millions of ordinary homes with their many personal 'knick-knacks' and which became the hallmark of the 'Victorian age'.

It is very interesting that the cultural practices associated with British hegemony are named for a monarch, Queen Victoria. In Chapter 1 we identified British hegemony as the phase of dominium when the capitalist world-economy carried all before it; and here we see this process operating on the domestic front with the leading monarch of the world representing middle-class mores. The 'Victorian age' refers to the set of social values that mark out the bourgeois ordinariness of British civil society. With Victoria's accession to the throne in 1837, the tenor of the court changed to match a new decorum at variance with the old Regency manners. This more sober court was confirmed by Victoria's marriage to Albert whose concern was for new industrial progress rather than traditional aristocratic pursuits.[73] The result was that while remaining the pinnacle of Britain's social class system, the Queen also cultivated a domesticity: Victoria, Albert and their children came to personify the ideal family. In this way they played a vital role in Bagehot's 'dignified' part of the British constitution as described in Chapter 2. He refers to the monarchy as the 'head of morality', which encompasses 'domestic virtues' and even 'domestic excellence'.[74] This was achieved by the royal family being conceived as both special, because it was royal, and 'just like us', because it was a family.[75] 'Victorian values' became a synonym for what were considered ordinary bourgeois qualities: the Queen's devotion to duty was equated with middle-class hard-work, her simple lifestyle without ostentation was seen as middle-class thrift and, although she was constitutionally head of the Anglican Church, her court's probity and good behaviour matched the 'low church' high-minded morals of her middle-ranked subjects. In this way a monarch gave her name to some quite unroyal patterns of behaviour. And not only in Britain: this middle-class culture had a much wider scope than the kingdom Victoria actually ruled. In fact, one of the ironies of the period is that Americans call their

Plate 24 *Emma and Mr Knightley*, a 19th-century illustration by Hugh Thomson for Jane Austen's *Emma*. Emma is helping make her future husband more comfortable in this simple domestic scene. It fits well with the first sentence of the novel where we are informed that Emma lives in 'a comfortable home'

culture in this period 'Victorian America', only two or three generations after freeing themselves from the rule of Victoria's grandfather. In his book *Victorian America*, D. W. Howe admits being embarrassed by the term but uses it because it has become firmly part of the historical lexicon.[76] Such is the cultural dominance of the hegemon.

Even as an icon of domesticity, Victoria's residences were palaces, castles and great houses. Nevertheless, the popular image of the queen, especially in her later years, was a homely one wearing her shawl over her clothes as she drew her chair up to the fire to keep warm. This was a ritual all her subjects engaged in. Although the image is a cosy one, it also indicates limitations of the English home in the 19th century. In fact there is a major 'comfort gap' between 'English comfort' and what we have come to expect as comfort today. Lighting, heating and plumbing lagged behind furniture in the development of the home. For most of the 18th century artificial lighting still came from wax candles. Although new oil lamps appeared by 1800, it was not until the 1840s that gas lighting in homes became popular.[77] But gas lighting was dirty and added to the smoky atmosphere created by poorly fumed fires. There were many inventions to try to make the home more efficient, but they all floundered on one key stumbling block: the lack of access to power in a form small enough for domestic needs.[78] Comfort depended upon servants until the introduction of the electric motor.[79]

The introduction of electricity into the home illustrates well the transition from British to American cultural leadership. The first domestic light bulbs were invented independently in Britain and the USA in 1877 by Joseph Swan and Thomas Edison respectively. But there the similarity ended. In 1880 Swan's invention was used to light up Cragside, the Northumbrian home of Lord Armstrong, the first house to have electric lights.[80] This was exceptional, however. By now social support for such innovation was disappearing in England; Rybczynski writes of 'a curious situation' in England whereby modern conveniences came to be seen as vulgar.[81] In the last chapter we identified such curiosity as symptomatic of Britain's post-hegemonic trauma. In fact Thoresby Hall, a new country house in Nottinghamshire completed as late as 1875, did not even have gas lighting![82] In contrast, by 1882 Edison had laid electric cables in part of New York so that 200 houses were using 5000 Edison bulbs for their lighting.[83] This was the lead the rest of the world followed, and by 1900 major cities throughout America and Europe had electric companies supplying current through underground cables. Once such distribution networks were in place, 'home appliances' could be produced with electric motors finally to extend comfort from domestic leisure to domestic work – what Rybczynski refers to as 'the great American innovation in the home'.[84] At the 1893 Chicago World Fair an 'electric kitchen' was exhibited and very soon a large range of appliances was widely available from such well-known companies as Westinghouse and Hoover.[85] Irons, vacuum cleaners, washing machines, sewing machines, fans, toasters, cookers, hotplates – convenience came to the home, especially the American home. By the middle of the 1920s over 60% of American houses had electricity, constituting more than half the world market.[86] It was this scale of operation that reduced the price of electricity, which stimulated the market for appliances and which used more electricity creating a spiralling market. Hence domesticity was at the forefront of the USA developing the first mass consumption society. With all this convenience basic comfort was never forgotten: it is America that invented the bathroom as a three-fixture space of bath, water closet and hand basin.[87] This ubiquitous place of ordinary luxury illustrates how far modernity has improved the lives of millions of people in the 20th century.

What of the dwelling that housed this new domesticity? Alan Gowans identifies a particular genre of architecture he calls the 'Comfortable House' that was developed in the USA between 1890 and 1930.[88] This was explicitly American in origin: a post-frontier age combined optimism in national progress with personal upward mobility to create a popular demand 'to own your own home'. The result was a very eclectic mix of architectural styles but with one common denominator: comfort at an affordable price. The new market was buttressed by a moral crusade promoting the home as a 'molder of virtue': American President Harding in 1923 referred to the home as the 'apex' of society; more grandly the home was seen as 'a salvation for the whole world' with Frank Lloyd Wright's 'World Citizen' overcoming the problems of modern life in a new comfortable house.[89] An initial key technical development came at the end of the 19th century with the mass prefabrication of houses which led to house buying through mail order.[90] Sears, already selling the new appliances, moved into the housing market with a catalogue entitled *Book of Modern Homes and Building Plans* in 1908.[91] By providing everything except the land and foundations but including finance, Sears and similar suppliers made home ownership more widely available than ever before. Quite simply, in the first decades of the 20th century in the USA, 'a Comfortable House for all' became a realistic goal.[92]

Ordinary modernity as comfort was therefore a product of hegemonic civil societies where wealth was accumulated and distributed widely enough to create new domestic worlds. To a large extent the process was cumulative as bourgeois influence spread throughout the world-economy. But the three hegemonic episodes in this development were very different in their geographies. In particular, the Dutch and the British created new homes in very different locales: small town houses and Georgian country houses respectively. In some ways America's contribution to ordinary modernity represents a geographical compromise with suburbia integrating conveniences of urban life with the atmosphere of country life, but suburbia is much more than a blend of past locales. It represents a distinctive new geographical phenomenon which we may call 'spaces of concentrated comfort'. The Dutch and British contributions to ordinary modernity focused at the level of the house; American suburbia is many such houses in a homogeneous environment of comfort writ large.

Suburbia as concentrated comfort

In strictly geographical terms, the existence of suburbs is as old as urban growth. Indeed, residential growth on the edge of the city was distinctive in premodern urban development, but its characteristics were the opposite to what we associate with suburbs today. Suburbs were for urban outcasts, they were dens of iniquity outside respectable urban society. In contrast the modern suburb oozes respectability. This is a classic example of a modern concept and reality completely subverting its historical antecedent. Suburbia is a special place for family living that takes homes out of a corrupting urban influence and relocates them in new communities with rural settings. The classic modern suburb consists of single family houses in large gardens set back from tree-lined roads. Perhaps the key feature is the front lawn which is a private space that has a public function.[93] Maintained by the homeowner, its effect is a communal one: by separating houses from their road, the sequence of green front lawns converts an urban street into a country lane to produce the ideal suburban landscape.

Although, significantly, American writers believe the modern suburb to be a US invention, Robert Fishman has shown that its origins may be traced back to the growth of 18th-century London.[94] These early high-class suburbs were converted into a general middle-class residential pattern in mid-19th-century Manchester where new wealth was used to move out of the industrial city producing the first example of the now familiar urban structure of working-class inner city and middle-

Plate 25 *Building Modern New Worlds*. Although most well known for their catalogues of consumer goods, Sears was also one of several companies that sold prefabricated houses by mail-order. This 1914 advertisement shows 23 bungalows of 'California architecture' from Sears' *Book of Modern Homes*, ranging in price from $393 to $1407. Such prices made home ownership possible for all with regular employment. The business became a victim of the 1930s' depression

class outer city.[95] The British invented the suburb as an exclusionary zone, therefore. The American contribution was to popularize the idea of the suburb as a goal for every family. This notion of 'suburbs for all' can be found as early as 1868, although it is only with the coming of the 'affluent society' in the 20th century that it achieved widespread credibility.[96] Americans did not eliminate exclusion from suburbia, but they produced gradations of exclusion so that there were different suburbs for different family budgets. This culminated in the 1950s as the decade of greatest suburban growth in US history: the 1960 census recorded an additional 19 million people living in the country's suburbs since 1950.[97]

Large-scale suburbanization began in the late 19th century in both Britain and the USA as a result of improvements in urban transport. The resulting railway and streetcar suburbs created linear patterns of growth in the outer city combined with congestion in the inner city. It is Los Angeles that broke away from this structure and released suburbia to invade all available spaces and hence to dominate the modern city. Fishman designates Los Angeles a 'suburban metropolis', which he views as the climax of suburban history.[98] Although its original growth was by streetcar suburbs like other US cities, by the 1920s Los Angeles already had more automobiles per capita than anywhere else in the world. In addition, as the fastest-growing American city in the first decades of the 20th century, Los Angeles realtors and developers were especially powerful in local politics. The result was the 1926 approval of a massive bond issue to fund a large road network to overcome development constraints.[99] Los Angeles became the city of the automobile, the city that could spread out across the landscape for mile after mile. As a city of suburbs, differentiation was achieved through concentrating more expensive homes on hills looking down on cheaper suburbs: Hollywood stars lived in their mansions in Beverly Hills. But it was still suburbia for all.

But with the building of urban freeways across all American major cities in the early post-World War II years, suburbia becomes the dominant settlement form of the USA. At the other end of the social spectrum from Beverly Hills came the 'Levittowns' of the north-east which brought suburban living to almost anybody with a regular job. The Levitt building company specialized in the mass production of suburbs. Peter Hall describes their methods as based upon 'flow production, division of labour, standardized designs and parts, new materials and tools, maximum use of prefabricated components, easy credit, good marketing'.[100] The latter facilitated mass consumption; people queued for hours to buy their piece of suburbia, and in one development alone 17 000 homes were built and bought.[101] In his survey of 'Levittowners', Herbert Gans finds that their reason for moving to this suburbia was that 'they wanted the good and comfortable life for themselves and their family'.[102] In terms of aspirations, Gans identifies two that stand out: 'comfort and roominess' and 'privacy and freedom of action'.[103] These are quintessentially concepts of ordinary modernity. It is in Levittowns and developments like them that achievements of American hegemony reach the lives of ordinary Americans. Living in suburbs enabled manual workers to identify themselves as middle class in the way we described in Chapter 2: in suburbia the middle class became the universal class.

Initially the suburban route to middle-class comfort was not itself universal. Fishman describes it as an Anglo–American phenomenon in the 19th century, with the middle classes in the rest of Europe and the Americas staying much more loyal to traditional urban residential preferences.[104] But with American hegemony the middle-class suburb has spread to cities across the world. The particular form that suburbs take varies among countries, but the ideal of suburbia as collective comfort remains: people who can afford it move to suburbs for a better family life. Throughout the world, 'however modest each suburban house might be, suburbia represents a collective assertion of class wealth and privilege'.[105] It is the true monument of the modern world, our equivalent to the cathedrals of medieval Europe.

Modern, postmodern and post-traditional

In 1937, just three years before the beginning of the German bombing blitz on London, John Betjeman (later Britain's poet laureate), wrote a poem about a London suburb which began: 'Come, friendly bombs, and fall on Slough'.[106] Although the wording is quite extreme, the sentiment expressed represents a general intellectual fashion of cultural elites in the 20th century. For instance, Herbert Gans has referred to suburbia as 'a much maligned part of America'.[107] The section of the intellectual elite specifically concerned with such matters, modern architects and planners, has provided a legitimation for derision of suburbia although their language has hardly been purely 'technical'. Hall refers to the 'architects' revenge' which involved devising very negative metaphors such as 'octopus', 'lice along a tape worm' and 'disfiguring disease' to describe 'urban sprawl'.[108] This intense hatred of suburbia was the one thing the three most influential architect/planners of the 20th century, Ebenezer Howard from Britain, Frank Lloyd Wright from America and Le Corbusier from Switzerland, agreed upon despite their very different urban prescriptions.[109] In what Peter Hall calls the 'great debate' on suburbia, architects have queued up to condemn the 20th-century American city as representing the death of urbanism as the centre of civilization.[110]

What is happening here? The cultural paradox is that whereas we have identified suburbia as the 20th-century monument to modernity, self-ascribed modern elite experts have invariably condemned it. Part of their problem has been a failure to accommodate to the new, a reaction to the unfamiliar that can afflict all in a modern world-system. This was wonderfully illustrated in 1931 at the Brussels meeting of the Congress International d'Architecture Moderne. This organization had been set up three years earlier to promote new ideas in architecture. For the 1931 conference, maps were prepared of all the world's great cities to the same scale and using standard symbols to denote land uses. But what to do with Los Angeles? Its map was very much larger than any other, and its land uses spread out in patterns that could not be accommodated by the standard symbols. Those attending the conference thought the map anomalous; Los Angeles was viewed, at best, as a puzzle and certainly not the harbinger for future cities.[111]

The degree of hostility to suburbia suggests that the cultural paradox is based upon much more than initial unfamiliarity. Clearly the common use of the idea of modern to describe both condemnations and celebrations of suburbia is the source of some confusion. Given our pluralist position on modernity, this need not be a problem. Modernist architecture and planning is imbued with an ideology of industrialization. When one of their leading number describes a house as 'a machine to live in', he lets the cat out of the bag: we can identify his ideas immediately as a form of modernity derived from Britain's hegemonic restructuring.[112] Hence suburbia and modern architecture represent two very different paths to modernity: one a legacy of 19th-century modernity, the other the locus of 20th century modernity. It is hardly surprising, therefore, that they are not only different, in most respects they are the opposite of each other. However, the failure of the modernist movement has precipitated a critique of the modern which has led on to a widespread contemporary identification of 'postmodernity'. Since our idea of world impasse also leads, inevitably, to a notion of postmodernity, we cannot leave this important debate untouched in this chapter.

The ideas of Le Corbusier, the doyen of modern architecture, are the polar opposite of ordinary modernity. He thought the design of cities 'was too important to be left to citizens'.[113] He was a great admirer of authoritarian leaders because they had the power to raze existing cities to the ground and start anew. In 1933 he published *The Radiant City* which envisaged the modern city as a geometric arrangement of great towers for 'vertical living'.[114] Fortunately Le Corbusier was conspicuously a failure in terms of architectural practice, but what he did build does show the opposite of modernity as comfort. His most famous building is the *Unité d'Habitation* on the outskirts of Marseilles which one of his supporters describes unpromisingly as 'a compact, slab-like building, raised on tapering concrete columns, housing 1,600 people'.[115] 'The problems', so Robert Hughes tells us, 'begin under that slab.'[116] Le Corbusier's criteria of minimum efficiencies led to small apartments supported by collective services for typical family activities like child care, cooking and cleaning. For instance, instead of a personally cooked meal eaten in the family dining room, residents of the *Unité* were expected to eat in the communal atmosphere of a cafetaria on the roof.[117] It is difficult to imagine anything more unlike suburbia. Of course the residents

> soon restored the *machine à habiter* to the true style of suburban France. The flats of the Unité are crammed with plastic chandeliers, imitation Louis XIV *bergères*, and Monoprix ormolu — just the furniture Corbusier struggled against all his life.[118]

The most explicit example of Le Corbusier eschewing comfort itself can be found in student accommodation for the University of Paris. There the design determined that windows could not be opened, resulting in evacuation during the summer months.[119] Although an extreme example, Le Corbusier has been much admired, influential – witness high-rise residential development in post-World War II Europe – and is by no means exceptional as a representative of the art world's modernism: his work is very obviously influenced by Cubism, for example.[120] Most important, we find similar disdain for comfort in modernist interior design with uncomfortable furniture promoted for its aesthetic qualities as if it never had to be used. Forgetting the lessons of Chippendale, modern designers create chairs upon which it is impossible to sit for more than a few minutes.[121] From the perspective of ordinary modernity, such tube and canvas contraptions are far less 'modern' than an 18th-century Windsor chair. Descendants of the latter easily outsell modern-designer chairs today, since they remain popular with ordinary users of chairs.

The postmodern literature is first and foremost, a critique of the modernism we have just briefly described. From our alternative modern position, we are equally critical but without privileging concern for aesthetics that postmodernists share with those they criticize. As an artistic reaction to the absurdities of the modernist movement, postmodernism has been interpreted as the particular cultural expression of late capitalism.[122] As such it does not define a new society as its 'post' appellation implies; rather it is merely a 'phase' in the development of high culture in the modern world-system. So how does this relate to our 'modernity as comfort'? It is not just a matter of 'low' culture, it is all about styles and fashions versus customs and traditions.[123]

Both the modernist movement and its contemporary postmodern critics are ultimately concerned with styles and fashions. These are relatively short-term, or at best medium-term, phenomena that have come and gone in the history of the modern world-system. They are good for temporarily boosting markets but do not have lasting significance. In contrast, ordinary modernity based upon comfort is a long-term feature of the system, a custom that by now warrants the label of a 'modern tradition'. Neither modernists nor postmodernists have anything in their repertoire of ideas that can match the significance of the 'democratization of comfort' of ordinary modernity in the 20th century.[124] Whatever the debates going on in the high cultural realms of architecture, the suburban ideal won the battle of ideas because of 'enough support from ordinary people in the real world to transform the structure of the modern city'.[125] Its power derived from what Fishman calls 'the compelling vision of the modern family' which has relegated professional architecture and planning to a minor bit-part in the story of social change.[126] As a social tradition, ordinary modernity transcends styles and ultimately will dismiss those incompatible with its core character: without comfort, the modernist movement was condemned to irrelevance from its inception.

Postmodernism has come to mean much more than the critique we have outlined above, of course. Postmodernists have identified contemporary changes in society as fundamental social shifts that challenge the intellectual project of modernity stemming from the Enlightenment. In particular, the universalism of modernity is being replaced by a diversity in which differences are central to social life.[127] However, these social changes need not be interpreted as signalling an end to modernity. Here we follow Anthony Giddens in arguing that 'post-traditional' is a preferable descriptor of this situation than postmodern.[128] By post-traditional, he does not mean the elimination of traditions but that traditions have been profoundly altered by the contemporary context in which they are forced to operate. In normal circumstances, traditions prosper when they are taken for granted: 'you don't really have to justify them; they contain their own truth, a ritual truth, asserted as correct by the believer'.[129] Today, two social forces have put traditions on the defensive. First, globalization has meant that cultures throughout the world are confronting one another on an everyday basis. Second, there has been a great expansion in social reflexivity so that individuals make decisions about their behaviour on the basis of considered reflection of options. These two forces combined have produced 'a world of interrogation and dialogue' with which traditions are ill-equipped to cope.[130]

In these circumstances, traditional assertion of ritual truth has come to be called 'fundamentalism', the situation where a given tradition looks inwards and demands purity and looks outward and is potentially violent. Generally the idea of fundamentalism is associated with defence of religion, notably Islam, but Giddens's definition means it applies to defence of traditions in other areas of culture. For instance, nationalism in the form of the paranoid 'patriot' groups in the USA is a classic fundamentalism. Similarly, at the household level, traditional gender roles have been challenged by feminist social critiques so that the angry supporters of a particular devalued 'masculinity', that was until very recently taken for granted, can be termed 'fundamentalists'. We are living in a time of 'thoroughgoing detraditionalization', and much social turmoil can be traced back to this novel circumstance.[131]

Giddens's insightful analysis fits in neatly with our concept of ordinary modernity. Social reflexivity produces 'a world of *clever people*', not more intelligent individuals but more informed and more able to engage in the wider world.[132] This spells doom for the 'experts', purveyors of certified universal knowledge deriving from the Enlightenment project; the authority of teachers, doctors, lawyers, politicians, architects and all other professions is being queried by the public as never before. Instead of interpreting this scepticism of the universal and willingness to consider 'alternative' prescriptions as postmodern diversity, it can be seen as the era of 'high modernity' when modernity's traditional foe, tradition, is being well and truly routed.[133] In this interpretation, the 'clever people' who are defining new social limits are both very modern and very ordinary. Intense social reflexivity can be interpreted as the culmination of ordinary modernity; it is directly related, for instance, to consumption in the increased specialization of retailing demanded by the contemporary shopper.

A post-traditional social order is not necessary good news for the future of modernity. In the past modernity has largely defined itself in terms of its battles with tradition. Tradition is modernity's 'other'; what happens when this disappears? In what Giddens calls 'simple modernity', tradition was confronted and often undermined but only for new traditions to be invented in new rounds of 'culture wars'. The assertive questioning in today's more complex modernity prevents new traditions being created. This, Giddens argues, is severely detrimental to social reproduction.[134] We interpret high modernity as the final modernity in the overall trajectory of our world-system. And the steering mechanism is ordinary modernity. Hence, suburbia is not only the contemporary monument to modernity, it is the omen of world impasse and, therefore, future postmodernities.

Postmodernities

World impasse means that there is no way forward for our world. The development of the modern world-system is coming to an end and there will be a transition to a postmodern world-system. Since we cannot know future worlds, we must think of the postmodern in the plural; the concept can define possible worlds only. Such openness can be misleading. New worlds do not just appear, they are constructed out of the ruins of the old and therefore it follows that clues to the future can be found in the present.

One approach to defining a postmodern world is to revert to using civilizations as possible future units of social organization. Civilizations are viewed as powerful cultural complexes that are deeply ingrained in the peoples they cover. Modernity can be seen as such a cultural complex based upon capitalist imperatives.[135] In fact, in the 19th century it was commonly considered to be simply 'civilization', viewed in the singular, as other civilizations were despatched to history by imperialism. But were they? The idea of civilization is being resurrected as plural phenomena. Although it is true that some civilizations were definitively destroyed, for instance in the Americas, the spread of modern civilization may be culturally quite superficial in some areas, allowing alternative civilizational projects to survive. Hence one future scenario is what Samuel Huntington calls 'the clash of civilizations'.[136] He identifies 'cultural fault-lines' in today's world and suggests that these are pointers to future world politics. Eight world culture regions are identified of which the modern industrial world is just one. Obviously Huntington's projection owes much to contemporary Western concerns for the rise of religious fundamentalisms, conventionally viewed as the threat of Islam. The power of the latter can be easily over emphasized, especially at the global level. The argument about ordinary modernity is that its appeal has been remarkably global in scope. This is not to say that consumerism eliminates indigenous cultural traits but that the latter merge with intrusive modernity to create a myriad of cultural expressions of a 'modern society'. Japan, one of Huntington's cultural regions, is a classic example of a distinctive culture that is, nevertheless, intrinsically capitalist in nature. From the perspective adopted here, Huntington underestimates the power of modernization and the degree of integration in the capitalist world-economy.[137]

There is, however, perhaps a more compelling reason to doubt a future of competing civilizations. Put simply, it betrays a lack of imagination; as a future vision it is curiously backward in orientation. In essence, this exercise recognizes that the materialist ideas of modernity were created in Europe in conflict with religious conceptions of a spiritual universe, and it is proposed that the latter return to centre stage. This is a very modernist view of the future where modernity takes on its traditional foes in seeming perpetuity. There is nothing here to divert us from our alternative interpretation of fundamentalism as part of contemporary high modernity with its post-traditional social order. In short, Huntington's scenario is nothing more than a wish for how the modern world would like to pursue its future, fighting anew battles it won long ago.[138] This failure to suggest anything remotely new by the civilizationalists contrasts markedly with the rise of 'green' scholarship over the last few decades. It is in the writings of environmentalists that we can find the most imaginative thinking about replacement of the modern world-system.

Disparaging all other parties as 'grey', green politicians claim to be pioneering a distinctively new politics.[139] Of course, it is not as simple as this but, nevertheless, there are important strands of green politics that do depart significantly from the modern politics we described in Chapter 2. Their overt concern for ecological processes means that states are problematized as the locus of politics because ecology does not respect state boundaries. This is dealt with in two distinct ways. The first approach is reformist and involves working through or with governments to create international co-operation to tackle environmental problems. The last phrase reveals its instrumentalism; it broadly coincides with what Tim O'Riordan terms technological environmentalism or 'technocentrism'.[140] Its proponents are environmentalists who believe solutions can be found to all environmental problems either through technological advances, for instance finding new energy sources, or by creative economic persuasion, for instance taxing polluters. Their politics is one of permeation so that all governments and opposition political parties are 'greened'. Since they do not recognize the world impasse, we can designate them modernist greens.[141] The second approach is radical and involves challenging or by-passing the state to build alternative ways of life that are compatible with environmental survival. Its supporters often dismiss the first group as 'shallow' greens and identify themselves as 'deep' greens. O'Riordan calls this position ecological environmentalism or 'ecocentrism'. Since its adherents base their ideas on the existence of a world impasse, we can designate them postmodern greens.[142] It is this latter variety of environmental thinking with which we are concerned in the discussion below.

Postmodern environmental thinking is treated in terms of alternative transitions from the modern world-system. Samir Amin has identified two types of transition in historical changes from one world-system to another.[143] In a controlled transition, there is a degree of continuity across systems in terms of the ruling classes. For instance, Immanuel Wallerstein interprets the transition from feudal Europe to the capitalist world-economy as controlled because the same strata of ruling families were in charge in 1650 that were running things in 1450.[144] In contrast, the long transition from the classical world-empire to feudalism in Western Europe exhibited very little continuity in rulers: the Romans were replaced by German leaders from beyond the frontier. Amin calls such a transition 'disintegration'. Since we cannot know if the next transition will be controlled or a disintegration, I consider both possibilities here. For each type of transition the argument is divided into two parts, first concentrating on the conditions for the transition and then outlining a possible new world-system outcome. The putative postmodernities are an eco-fascist world-system and a deep green world-system from controlled transition and disintegration respectively.

Et tu, bourgeoisie?

Given that the world is ultimately too small for ceaseless capital accumulation and that its latest expression as Americanization is in crisis, how might we envisage the demise of the modern world-system? The first point to make is that it will not just simply collapse as its contradictions reach breaking point. What we are dealing with is a social entity with multitudes of people who will respond to changing circumstances as they affect their self-interests. Adaptations and reforms will be the order of the day, but practices pointing towards a completely new system will also emerge. Put crudely we can ask: who will kill capitalism? Which social group will construct anti-capitalist practices that will counter the self-destroying social logic of accumulation? Marx's answer, as we all know, was that this was to be the historic role of the proletariat. Consequently, Marxian politics has been about organizing the working class to carry out its great task. Clearly, after the final collapse of Marxist–Leninism as a world force, the time is ripe to look again at this question.

The big political message from our previous analysis is that most ordinary people, poor and middle class alike, are not enemies of capitalism. Rather, seeing what the system does for those better off than themselves, they want more capitalism. After all, it provides the jobs that enable the consumption that is the good life as defined by Americanization. They may be victims of capitalism at the present time but these circumstances need not define their hopes for the future: today's victims can be tomorrow's consumers. This is why socialists have had so much trouble selling their message as anti-capitalist, especially since the promise of Americanization. Socialists in Western European countries quickly understood this message after 1945 and redefined their goal to reforming the system, a 'fairer capitalism'. Not surprisingly, these have been the best survivors in the crisis of socialism during the world-economy's current stagnation. Revolutionary socialism is long dead. Finally overcoming more than a century of socialist resistance is very good news for the rich of this world — but only in the short and medium term.

Let us turn to the self-interests of those I have called 'the rich'. In individual countries this term conjures up images of the super wealthy but here I use it from a world perspective. The rich are those people living the good life as defined by Americanization. It is these comfortably off people in the USA that John Galbraith has recently dubbed the contented majority of the American electorate.[145] Throughout the other core countries they constitute a large population encompassing, as well as the very wealthy, both the middle class and traditional working people who have achieved middle-class standards of living. These people are the backbone of the system. But what is their self-interest as the system shows signs of reaching its limits? They will come to realize, in David Korten's words, that if things continue unabated: 'the North [ie the rich world] will find that the current Southern experience is a window into its future – not the reverse'.[146] Considering that defining the future is a prime attribute of hegemony, this prediction represents our cultural world 'turned upside down', the ultimate nightmare of the rich and comfortable. It seems to me that while many of the poor of this world still scramble to join in the good life, it is the world strata of rich people who will turn against the system. Quite simply, they have the most to lose from the demise of the system. If capitalism is seen to be unsustainable and if the rich wish to maintain their comfortable lifestyles, they will have no alternative but to invent a new system to further their interests and thereby overthrow a redundant but still environmentally destructive capitalism.

The idea that the ultimate challenge to capitalism will come from the rich seems at first to be quite absurd.[147] All our thinking assumes that capitalism serves the rich, and that is quite correct in the normal working of the system. But here we are concerned with the 'abnormality' of the demise phase of the modern world-system when that service is becoming problematic. Capitalism teaches the rich, not loyalty to its system, but straightforward self-interest. It is this basic lesson that, ironically, will lead those who have gained most from the capitalist world-economy to work to overthrow it. We may wish to call this the greatest double-cross in history – *et tu, bourgeoisie!*

Is there any evidence that such an unlikely outcome can be seen in contemporary politics? Actually there is one particular conflict that pits the rich against capital accumulation. Starting in the 1960s in California, there has been the rise of an 'urban environmentalism' that peaked as a political force in Los Angeles in the 1980s. There are some 16 000 Homeowners Associations in California – Mike Davis calls them the 'trade unions' of the middle class – who have led a slow-growth rebellion against the growth policies of politicians and developers.[148] Groups that had supported economic growth when they were building their 'bourgeois utopias', now turned on their erstwhile development allies to conserve what they had created.[149] Although sometimes referred to as 'sunbelt bolshevism', in fact the key characteristic of this politics has been its localism, an explosion of NIMBY (not in my back yard).[150] In the late 1980s, elections throughout southern California were dominated by slow-growth versus pro-growth conflicts, pitting rich homeowners against capital accumulation. Of course, the rich are only against capital accumulation in their own locality, not against accumulation in general. Obviously their good life depends on capital accumulation elsewhere while they protect their local environment. Nevertheless this is an instance of an anti-accumulation politics that is an important consequence of Americanization. Despite its inherent localism, NIMBY became a rallying cry of the selfish 1980s across the world.[151] By no means limited to California, it can be found in different forms in wealthy suburbs throughout core countries.

In Western Europe environmental politics has spawned Green Parties that have organized to place environmental issues at the top of the political agenda. Although typically split in terms of 'degree of greenness', their influential radical wings are quite explicitly anti-capitalist: they understand that the world is too small for capitalism.[152] Despite much lauding of a 'red–green alliance', these parties have made little headway in replacing traditional working-class socialist radicalism. In fact quite the opposite. The 1989 European Election in Britain is very instructive here. The big surprise was that the British Greens, hitherto with no track record of electoral success comparable to their continental colleagues, received a very respectable 15% of the national vote.[153] Not only did they push the traditional third party in Britain, the Liberals, into fourth place, they became the most popular Green Party in the European Community. What was happening? A quick look at the map of their votes gives us a clue. They received their highest votes in the richer constituencies of the south of England. These were exactly those localities complaining about 'overdevelopment' in the late 1980s' economic mini-boom. Here we have a quite remarkable proportion of the very contented, more than a quarter in some constituencies, willing to vote for a radical environmental programme.[154] The Green Party in this situation had become a vehicle for this rich group's protests against threats to their green and pleasant land.

This contemporary paradox of the rich supporting what is basically an anti-capitalist political party may be a current glimpse of a future politics. This is what we explore in our first foray into the future business below where we extrapolate much more sinister contemporary environmental politics than mass NIMBY. At their 1987 conference, the Los Angeles slow-growth organization Not Yet New York, approved a sweeping social programme including extreme restrictions on immigration and compulsory family planning. As Mike Davis concludes: 'the definitive imposition of slow growth would require the construction of a California Reich'.[155]

An eco-Fascist world-system

What would be the world political outcome of the rich finally becoming truly conservative and rejecting ever-changing capitalism? They would want to conserve their acquired capital while denying capital accumulation to others. The resulting politics of self-interest would require a cover of legitimation, a justification that defines the new politics as a logical and sensible reaction to a world in crisis. Such a position cannot be created out of the blue as and when necessary, it must be built up over time by intellectuals who know what has to be done. It seems to me that the neo-Malthusian school that originated in the 1960s with the 'discovery' of the 'population bomb' looks very much like the precursor of a new politics of the rich. As Edwin Brooks warned at the time, 'eco-catastrophe' can be used as 'a subterfuge of the rich to maintain their dominant status'.[156] The controversial biologist Garrett Hardin may well become the great intellectual hero of the conservationist conservatives of the future: their 'Darwin of the 20th century'.

Hardin is famous for two metaphors that helped frame the agenda for the neo-Malthusians: the tragedy of the commons and the lifeboat ethic.[157] Both ideas are developed via a simple logic based upon a limited world. For the first, Hardin uses the idea of a simple commons on which herders may graze their animals as a right. The problem is that since there is no control over numbers, it is in the interests of every herder to add animals to his herd at the expense of the common good resulting in overgrazing. In this case the system is locked into inevitable catastrophe.[158] The tragedy is one of freedom and Hardin extrapolates this to the whole world in terms of pollution where costs are notoriously not paid by the polluter. So far so good, but Hardin goes on to equate pollution with overpopulation and we soon reach the stage where people become pollutants. For Hardin the main target becomes 'the freedom to breed', which he believes to be 'intolerable'.[159] This brings us to the lifeboat ethic. This metaphor envisages countries as sovereign lifeboats each with a known carrying capacity. People keep falling off the poor lifeboats and attempt to gain access to the rich ones. Should we save them or let them drown? An absolutist ethics of the sanctity of human life would haul all swimmers aboard.[160] The problem is that this results in capsizing the rich lifeboat so that everybody dies.[161] Hardin proposes a relativist ethics whereby 'the morality of an act is determined by the state of the system at the time the act is performed'.[162] This 'situational ethics' allows for the abandonment of drowning swimmers and their overloaded and therefore doomed lifeboats. Extrapolation to the world is obvious: we have an ethical justification for abandoning the Third World.

Martin Bookchin has dubbed such ideas 'eco-Fascism'. This terminology can be justified on several grounds.[163] First, Hardin doubts whether there can be democratic solutions to the problems he considers since voters may accept the wrong policies out of 'humanitarian motives'.[164] Second, Hardin accepts the need for coercion to ensure necessary policies are carried out: he calls it 'mutual coercion'.[165] Third and most damning, the implication of Hardin's logic is nothing less than acceptance of the extermination of millions of people. In the words of one critic: 'Genocide remains genocide, whether advocated in a Munich beer hall in 1920 or in a Texas college auditorium in 1967.'[166]

Genocide is a very emotive term and a very serious accusation that must be precisely specified. If we define genocide as policy for the elimination of targeted people, it is relatively easy to justify applying this term to Hardin's prescriptions. Basically Hardin advocates no food aid to countries that desperately need it. If you provide food, you turn it from a commodity into a 'commons' and the poor will only breed more. As the lobby group 'The Environmental Fund' put it rather meanly in 1977 'improving the nutrition of poor women *increases* their fertility' (emphasis in the original).[167] Such humanitarian gestures are in the long run detrimental; they keep people alive and merely postpone the population catastrophe. The message is that saving lives today only makes things worse tomorrow.[168] A classic case of such genocidal logic appeared recently in the distinguished British medical journal *The Lancet*.[169] Here we find a public-health expert advocating 'mortality control' in poor countries. In particular, reduced infant mortality is no longer seen as a something to be promoted:

measures [such] as oral rehydration should not be introduced on a public health scale, since they increase the man-years of human misery, ultimately from starvation. However the individual doctor must rehydrate his patient. . . . Mother Teresa has reminded us that the world's poorest need our love and compassion – tragically, such programmes may not necessarily be part of that love.[170]

This gives a whole new meaning to 'loving you to death'! It seems 'patients' don't pollute but people, or at least poor people, do. Of course, if we were to be serious about eliminating people as polluters then an efficient death control policy would be to target rich middle-class males like this public-health expert. This is to employ an alternative scientific brief, operations research, where we might use as our objective function reduction of pollution for the lowest number of deaths. Given their consumption of resources, you would need to eliminate only a small number of rich people to replace every hundred poor babies sacrificed. That is a different diabolical politics that seems not to be on any ecological agenda. The message is that we can only save the Earth by killing the poor.

How would this new world-system be organized? Hardin applies his lifeboat metaphor to today's world of competitive states. Extrapolation of it as a future scenario beyond ultra-hegemony requires a little modification. In our metaphor there is just one lifeboat in which the rich are firmly in control with the remainder of the world's people struggling to keep their heads above water in a turbulent sea. In other words, the rich section of the world will be segregated from the remainder. In the rich zone capital accumulation will be ended in a no-growth politics to conserve the good life. Outside in the poor zone, coercion will be the order of the day. Capital accumulation will be prevented here also, but there the similarity ends. Forced sterilization will be necessary but otherwise the people will be effectively abandoned except where they are needed to provide raw materials for the rich. Security will be the main concern and this will have to be organized through a world state operating at the behest of the rich. The world-city hierarchy of ultra-hegemony will have its role transformed. From being control centres of global capital, world-cities will divide into two types. In the rich zone they become the organization centres for the bounty which will continue to be very large – much larger than today after ultra-hegemony – and in the poor zone they will revert to being security centres, garrison towns with functions similar to the old colonial cities. With no capital accumulation or inter-state system, this is the end of capitalism replaced by a postmodern global apartheid which we can call an eco-Fascist world-system. Despite the mammoth discrimination involved, there is a sort of perverse universalism here suitable as a legacy of capitalism's ultra-hegemony. According to relativist ethics, the rich will not be acting out of self-interest; they will be saving the Earth from the irresponsibility and selfishness of the world's poor.

This new universalism would be, of course, the inverse of the humanitarian liberalism which has dominated the political ideologies of the modern world-system. As we showed in Chapter three, hegemons have been deeply implicated in the creation of this ideology: the Dutch through their religious tolerance, the British with their notion of liberal constitutionalism and the Americans with their trumpeting of democracy. To be sure, humanitarian liberalism has acted as a mask to cover up many of the worst excesses of capitalism – slavery, imperialism, contemporary 'friendly tyrants' – but there is a basic core of ideas that have contributed to a better life for millions. Ideals of humanitarian liberalism are generally held by all mainstream political tendencies in the richer countries of the contemporary world-economy. The ideology encompasses a set of ideas that are broadly agreed upon from Christian democrats to Marxist socialists – Garrett Hardin explicitly refers to 'Christian–Marxian ideals' in his critique of humanitarianism.[171] Its major contribution to ordinary modernity has been the concept of equality of opportunity. This is precisely what is denied in the eco-Fascist world-system. The 21st century's putative hero, Garrett Hardin, understands this well. Christian–Marxian appeals to our conscience are prime targets in his work: in a discussion entitled 'Pathogenic effects of conscience', he applies the Nietzschean dictum that 'a bad conscience is a kind of illness'.[172] But the end of modernity does not have to mean an appalling world in which people have no conscience for what they do. There can be a postmodern world in which conscience plays a major part.

Conspicuous asceticism

Delineating possible worlds from a disintegration transition is more difficult than for the outcome of a controlled transition. With less continuity a greater leap of imagination is required. Hence, with eco-Fascism the politics of limits can be reduced to a simple strategy of 'maintain what you can and ditch the rest'. The usual modernist alternatives to Fascism have no such simple projection to a postmodern world. The problem is that the politics of distribution that accompanies any form of socialism or social democracy sits uneasily with a politics of limits. Once the commitment to social justice is applied globally, as it would be with the demise of the states in a postmodern world, redistribution of resources creates a future of shared poverty. It is hard to see how this situation could generate the necessary consensus to avoid massive coercion for its maintenance. As such, daily life for everybody in such a system would not seem very much different from life in the poor zone under eco-Fascism. The luxury of maintaining a conscience is bought at the price of generalized poverty.

Clearly, we are not imagining hard enough. What is required is not just to keep individual consciences but to change the collective world consciousness. A completely new basis for everyday life is required which we can term 'conspicuous asceticism', the nemesis of Americanization built upon conspicuous consumption.[173] As many observers have pointed out, consumerism will continue as a world ideal until another want replaces acquisitive materialism. Given an impending world impasse, I am assuming that any sustainable non-Fascist future will require the development of a popular world view that condemns unnecessary consumption as anti-social behaviour. As such, any 'deviants' will be unable to be positively conspicuous and cannot become role models in the new postmodern world.

Where is perpetual consumerism being contested in today's world? It seems to me that this is occurring in two different, although sometimes overlapping, challenges: by religious teachings and by post-materialist environmentalism. It is the former case that provides superficial credibility for Huntington's clash of civilizations thesis.[174] As spiritual projects, most religions have an ascetic tendency. Equally they have been able to accommodate to wealth acquisition both past and present – material success as a mark of God's favour was well understood in all three hegemonic societies, for example. Hence, while religious leaders have commonly condemned the materialism of Americanization, it has not stemmed the spread of consumerism across the world. But there has been one chink in Americanization's edifice: the Iranian revolution of 1978–9. The Shah and his middle-class supporters were swept away by massive popular support for the radical Islamic message of Ayatollah Khomeini. In the subsequent rewriting of the constitution, this conspicuous ascetic was made religious and political leader for life and Muslim clergy were given supreme power in the new Islamic state. This example of a spiritual rising is important because it encompasses both everyday life and inter-state politics.

The Iranian revolution was as much a political shock as a cultural challenge. Quite simply the new regime refused to play by the rules of the international game like a 'normal' state. Its 'abnormality' was most vividly expressed in the take-over of the US Embassy and in keeping diplomats as hostages. Such flagrant flouting of the diplomatic convention was justified on the grounds of the USA being the 'Great Satan'. The scale of the action, keeping 52 hostages for over a year, and the target, the major power in the world, combined to make this action by Iran's revolutionary guards unprecedented in the history of the modern world-system. It promoted the idea that the new Iran was no respecter of sovereignty and therefore not really a modern state. But Iran remained a state, albeit a revolutionary Islamic state, within the inter-state system, maintaining political links through membership of the United Nations and economic links through membership of the Organization of Petroleum Exporting Countries. In case it needed any reminding of the inter-state system, the Iraqi invasion of 1980 led to a war with over a million casualties. Hence, like previous revolutionary states, Iran found itself playing a conventional inter-state politics that sits uneasily with its professed radicalism. Islam continues to be fragmented into numerous sovereign states in conformity with the nature of modern politics. We might say, therefore, that Khomenei, while certainly an anti-materialist role model, was not a postmodern conspicuous ascetic but rather another of the 20th century's failed revolutionaries.

This leaves post-materialist environmentalists as the most likely source of conspicuous asceticism for a postmodern world. All postmodern greens accept limits to growth, but not all reject social justice to attain their goals like the eco-Fascists. Deep greens reject the idea of organizing life around material values. Whereas eco-Fascists maintain the 'good life' for themselves, deep greens query whether the consumption of goods really does provide a good life. This is a much more fundamental break from the modern, targeting as it does the ordinary modernity that we have argued defines the whole trajectory of the capitalist world-economy through the practices of the civil societies of hegemonic states.

Such a post-materialism is based upon the rejection of two key practices in the reproduction of modernity. First, development is interpreted as dysfunctional since it incorporates a complex of processes that cannot lead to anywhere but disaster. Modern greens talk about 'green development', meaning steering development along environmentally friendly paths, but to deep greens this phrase is a contradiction in terms: development is inherently unfriendly to the environment.[175] Second, the state is viewed as an instrument for growth and is therefore equally dysfunctional. As we argued in Chapter 2, *raison d'état* in the modern world-system is distinguished by its economic imperative resulting in the modern state becoming an 'economic growth machine'. Modern greens talk about 'greening the state', meaning steering government policies towards environmentally friendly ends. To deep greens this is impossible: states are inherently unfriendly to the environment.[176] Hence, post-materialism is anti-development and anti-state.

Post-materialist politics is associated institutionally with elements within the new social movements. As well as the environmental movement there are feminist and peace movements, and smaller regional and communal movements, all of which incorporate non-material goals.[177] Conspicuous by their absence from this radical roll-call are the labour movements whom deep greens consider too closely tied to development concerns and state strategies.[178] New social movements are trans-state in operation, but unlike the elite trans-state organizations, such as the Club of Rome and the Environmental Fund, where top-down neo-Fascist strategies can be promoted, the movements aspire to be bottom-up in orientation. This is in keeping with a philosophy that values self-reliance and personal realization. In fact post-materialism, in so far as it provides a source for a future conspicuous asceticism, will have to be as much a cultural challenge to modernity as a political or economic one. Friberg and Hettne, for instance, describe their deep green arguments as delivering 'a civilizational criticism'.[179] This is very different from Huntington's clash of civilizations; it is asking how there can be a renewed meaning to life after conspicuous consumption.

A deep green world-system

The power of ordinary modernity is to be found in the link it forges between the individual and the collective. We have shown that the mass consumption of the affluent society is made up of millions of distinctive individual decisions – for instance every home is composed of a different mix of commodities that its members have chosen. In a postmodern system that is not dependent on coercion, both personal and social levels of action will have to be changed, but the crucial transformation will be in individual ideas about appropriate behaviour. For one of the foremost thinkers in this area, Arne Naess, this can be understood as moving from concern for 'standard of living' to 'quality of life'.[180] His slogan for a new lifestyle is 'Simple in means, rich in ends' which he explicitly distances from the idea of a 'Spartan' or austere way of life.[181] Naess has no quarrel with people enjoying 'opulence, richness, luxury, affluence' but argues that such conditions must be 'defined in terms of quality of life, not standard of living'.[182] The latter only measures the superficial pleasure of excessive consumption in which personal experiences are narrowly constrained and largely beyond individual control. This is a very limited 'good life' compared to a situation in which individual wants are derived from self-realization so that every good life is a personalized experience. This is not a recipe for self-indulgence: Naess's concept of self-realization is not self-centred but relates to a person's total self-view and his or her place in the world.[183]

This total view Naess calls an 'ecosophy'.[184] Every individual develops his or her own ecosophy based upon understanding gleaned from ecologists and philosophers but also from intuitions and experiences derived from a uniquely rich and satisfying relation to his or her environment. Each ecosophy is, therefore, a world view reflecting a specific consideration of the conditions of life in the ecosphere. This is the ideological path to a deep green world in which every person builds his or her own life as part of a greater 'web of life', the basic premise of ecological thinking that 'all things hang together'. This will only work if individuals feel comfortable with their ecosophy and its meaning for their lifestyle – Naess refers to a 'total world view which you feel at home with'.[185] With reference to our previous terminology for modernity, we may refer to this as ordinary postmodernity. Just like ordinary modernity, or the ordinary Christianity that underlay European feudalism, ordinary postmodernity provides the cultural basis for the everyday lives of people in a world-system. The key difference with ecosophy is that it provides for the individual taking responsibility for decisions about everyday life as they relate to the Earth as a whole.[186]

The appreciation that all things hang together produces a completely new attitude to nature. In the modern world-system the relationship between humanity and the natural world takes many forms of which the four most common are a scientific attitude to understand nature, an aesthetic attitude to love nature, a hedonistic attitude to enjoy nature and a commercial attitude to exploit nature.[187] In a non-coercive postmodern world the attitude to nature is one of respect for its inherent worth. This is incompatible with the modern instrumentalism of viewing nature as a commodity that has only value in terms of human demands. A deep green position is compatible with the three other modern attitudes but is quite distinct from them. Respect for nature means relating to nature on its own terms. All living things have their own meaning for life; they have ends and their living is the means to achieve those ends.[188] Their life, therefore, has worth in its own right. This is the basis of a new morality in which moral subjects – entities with rights – are all living things and moral agents – entities with responsibilities – are human beings.[189] This is in stark contrast to eco-Fascism where human conscience is eliminated. In a deep green world individuals can be said to have 'super consciences'.

Collectively this new morality defines a belief system which is a biocentric world view. The prime element of the system is acceptance of humanity as part of Earth's Community of Life, as Paul Taylor terms it.[190] In this community, survival is not solely dependent on individual action but depends equally on inter-dependencies between living things. Furthermore there is no assumption of the intrinsic superiority of humanity. Since all living things have their own worth relating to their own ends, there are no clear criteria for ranking the importance of lives. To think otherwise is to commit the error of speciesism.[191] The Earth's Community of Life transcends humanity: for instance, the Community existed before humanity and if humanity were to disappear from the scene this would not mean the end of the Community.[192] Like all world views for a world-system, this one claims universality. In fact Taylor refers to the idea of a 'universal Community of Life' as the 'ultimate universality'.[193]

In the previous description of a postmodern world-system, we found that eco-Fascism negates the modern tradition of humanistic liberalism. Deep green postmodernity, in contrast, transcends humanistic liberalism. Obviously, the human individualism at the heart of any liberal practice cannot be sustained, but Robyn Eckersley argues that embeddedness in ecological relationships does not mean the total loss of autonomy for the individual.[194] People are neither 'passive and determined beings' nor 'autonomous and self-determining beings' but retain a relative autonomy. Human psychological and social needs have to be respected like those of other species but without the freedom to dominate. For Eckersley

> each human individual and each human culture [is] just as entitled to live and blossom as any other species, *provided* they do so in a way that is sensitive to the needs of other human individuals, communities, and cultures, and other life-forms generally.[195]

The humanistic ideal of the dignity of the person is not discarded but set into a different context. Although humanism without regard to the rest of nature has grown into an 'ugly and dangerous' ideology for other species, this does not mean that ecocentric living is contrary to humanism *per se*.[196] There is much in the humanist tradition that represents what is best in our species and this should be treasured and developed.[197] In short this is 'emancipation writ large' within which concern for social justice in human communities is a necessary element.[198]

What would this deep green world look like? Given its non-coercive nature, it would complete the process of relegation of the state's importance in ultra-hegemony to its logical conclusion of elimination. Such a post-state condition is, of course, the old anarchist vision and deep green thinkers can be interpreted as heirs of 19th-century anarchism. The latter's promotion of a world of local self-sufficiency in food and most essentials based upon small communities is directly related to the green belief that 'small is beautiful'. But this rural image of the future has to be modified in the light of the ultra-hegemony legacy. The deep greens will not be new settlers on the landscape but will inherit a network of great world-cities in a global hierarchy. This will be the ultimate geographical expression of modern technology centralizing social control. Deep greens will not be anti-technology but will be against the social relations that have led to technology's use as an instrument of control.[199] Global information networks can equally be instruments of decentralization, and in a deep green world this will be automatic. The role of world-cities will be reversed from control centres to service centres, providers of needs that can best be organized collectively in a hierarchy from global city to local centre. This means that the spatial network integrating the social world will survive but much less intensively than during late modernity. Although most needs will be met locally, there will be some trade deriving from specialization where geographical concentration of production is deemed more ecologically sound from a whole world perspective. The result is a world of diversity in which the variety of communities, some local, some connected globally, is a necessary prerequisite to provide the social environment for billions of individual self-realizations. In particular, there will be numerous shades of green within the deep spectrum which will produce the politics of the deep green world-system. 'Anthropocentrists' will resist the biocentrism of the majority and may build their own communities. But one rule will dominate across the whole world-system. Change through new technology will be assessed in terms of the whole biosphere: only 'soft' technology will be allowed so that once again humanity will 'tread lightly on the Earth'.[200]

Beyond hegemony

World hegemony to world impasse has been a very 'big' story with many major themes. For instance we have travelled from a Catholic Christian universalism through a modern progressive universalism to the putative ultimate ecological universalism of the last section. What has made our argument particularly unusual is the mixture of historical interpretation and speculation about the future. By employing what Fernand Braudel termed a *longue durée* approach, we have been able to bring past and future together in the unfolding of a single world-system from its rise in the long 16th century to its demise in what looks likely to be a very long and agonizing 21st century.[201] But however seamless our story, studying the past is very different from trying to understand what the future has in store. Both are rooted in our present concerns, theories and concepts, but with history there is a factual bank which limits withdrawals. That is to say, in dealing with the past we have to tell a story that is consistent with available evidence. We can differ about interpretation of the evidence, what is important and what is not, but all history has to have an empirical grounding in facts. In contrast, there are no facts about the future by definition. All we have are so-called 'lessons of history', an extrapolation of contemporary trends, models of social change and utopian imaginings. Without the discipline of facts there is an exhilarating liberation of ideas about human possibilities, but there is also a responsibility to be extremely modest about the 'understanding' of future worlds.

The two postmodern world-systems we have described above are in no sense predictions. Rather, they are projections of some contemporary ideas which are consistent with our overarching model of the rise and fall of modernity. I have no doubt that neither will come to pass. Reasonable predictions are difficult enough within systems; such predictions between systems are all but impossible. Immanual Wallerstein has expressed this position particularly well: expecting a modern person to predict a postmodern world is like assuming a 14th-century European peasant could foresee our globalized existence.[202] All that we can be sure of is that there are many surprises in store for humanity. World hegemony was a new invention of the modern world-system and we have no reason to assume that, in the future, people will not be equally inventive as they try to grapple with changing conditions. In Chapter 1 we argued for 'the difference hegemony makes', and there will be have to be an invention with an equivalent role to hegemony in the future – let us call it 'complex X'. All we can say is that for complex X to be successful, the fundamental difference it must make is to create global sustainability.

One similarity we have with a 14th-century person is the widespread belief in the end of the world. The medieval Christian world view was of a coming Armageddon when a sinful world would be finally destroyed. Our apocalypse is secular but no less frightening for that. We cannot know there will be a world impasse for the capitalist world-economy but we cannot see a way out of the present trajectory that leads down an environmental *cul-de-sac*. The purpose of our presentation of possible postmodern world-systems, therefore, was to show how contemporary social change may pan out to make us think about what we want from our world-system and its possible successors. We are different from the 14th-century person because we do have a faith in our being able to control our collective future and that is important.[203]

The real problem is that steering a system in a desired direction is something that is only even moderately feasible during the normal, and therefore relatively predictable, workings of a world-system. In fact, this is what hegemons have achieved in constructing new modernities and creating worlds in their own image. But that phase of modernity is over; approaching impasse is much more complex and infinitely more unpredictable. Our whole space and time frameworks for action are disintegrating. Modern politics, for instance, is losing its basic inside/outside spatial frame that is the state. Globalization has meant that crucial decisions and policies affecting our everyday lives are no longer meaningful at the level of the state. What is the purpose of liberal democracy, therefore, if those we elect to government cannot possibly provide what they promise however modest their promises? Alongside this crisis of the territorial state there is a crisis of progress. The basic politics of progress has been that government policies can be devised to ask for contemporary sacrifices to ensure a better future. What if this promise of progress is taken away? We soon get into a new generational politics – do the present occupants of this planet have the right to vote themselves a good life at the expense of unborn future generations who will inherit a dying planet? As past space–time constructions of politics collapse, we enter a very exciting new world but one that is very uncomfortable for the contented.

Notes

Chapter 1

1. Wallerstein (1992, 562)
2. Blaut (1993) provides an excellent critique of this mode of thinking. See also Frank and Gills (1993)
3. Wallerstein (1992)
4. Wallerstein (1979); Taylor (1993a, chapter 1)
5. This example is taken from Peyrefitte (1992)
6. Peyrefitte (1992, 73)
7. Peyrefitte (1992, 88)
8. Peyrefitte (1992, 291)
9. This is the title of Peyrefitte's (1992) book
10. Wilkinson (not dated)
11. Watson (1992, 85)
12. Yates (1975, chapter 1) provides a good discussion of the post-Roman European tradition of empire
13. Elliot (1989, 7)
14. Strayer (1970, 22)
15. Burke (1986); for the changing relationship between cities and states, see Tilly (1990) and Taylor (1995b)
16. Strayer (1970, 24)
17. Luard (1986, 34)
18. The standard source is Dowdall (1923) but it is also thoroughly discussed in Skinner (1978) and chapter 1 of Dyson (1980)
19. Skinner (1978, 358)
20. Skinner (1978, 349)
21. Skinner (1978, 358)
22. James (1984, 2)
23. For a full discussion of this concept, see Taylor (1995a)
24. Rosenberg (1990, 257)
25. Strayer (1970, 83). In his history of modern diplomacy, Anderson (1993, 4) shows that the practice of sending and receiving diplomatic representatives as 'an attribution of sovereignty, a right to which only rulers were entitled' emerged in the 16th century and then only slowly. This 'relative modernity' of the diplomatic network replaced a medieval system when 'all sorts of principals sent diplomatic agents to all sorts of recipients'
26. Sylvan (1987)
27. Coplin (1968); Rosenberg (1990)
28. Herz (1959, 51) calls it the 'great divide'; see also Gottmann (1973) and Watson (1992, 186–9)
29. Holsti (1991, 25)
30. Watson (1992) reviews several such premodern codes, the most impressive being the *Arthashastra* or *Book of the State* which deals with behaviour among states in India during the fourth century BC (pp. 78–83)

31. Wight (1978)
32. Wight (1978, 136)
33. This is a very old idea: Bull and Watson (1984, 1) quote Voltaire's description of 18th-century Europe as 'a commonwealth divided into several states' and Burke's concept of 'the diplomatic republic of Europe'
34. Watson (1992, 14)
35. Wight (1978)
36. Wilkinson (1984, 15–25)
37. Watson (1992)
38. Wight (1978)
39. Chase-Dunn (1990)
40. Wilkinson (1994, 2); Arrighi (1990, 366–7) also explores two meanings of hegemony
41. This remains a common usage and Holsti (1991), for instance, uses the term to describe imperial ventures in early modern Europe. The most developed usage of hegemony in this way is by Watson (1992) where he defines a spectrum of political relations from independence through hegemony and dominium to empire. This is a legitimate use of the term but it is not the concept of hegemony used here
42. Wilkinson (1994, 2)
43. This was developed in his analysis of Italian politics (Hoare and Smith, 1971, 55–60); Bocock (1986, 76) argues that: 'Hegemony, when successfully achieved, is unnoticeable in every day political, cultural and economic life.'
44. Hoare and Smith (1971, 181–2)
45. Bocock (1986)
46. Thompson (1991, 10–11); Lears (1985, 568)
47. Lears (1985, 567)
48. According to Arrighi (1990, 367), 'it is entirely possible that Gramsci used the term metaphorically to clarify relations among social groups through an analogy with relations among states'. In fact, Gramsci employed hegemony with reference to inter-state relations in his discussion of the 'foreigner's party' (the party representing external links) (Hoare and Smith, 1971, 176–7)
49. Kindleberger (1973); Gilpin (1987, 72–80)
50. Arrighi (1990)
51. Gilpin (1987, 73–4) argues, for instance, that the case for Dutch hegemony 'is not a convincing one' partly because the 17th century was the era of mercantilism, a question we deal with in some detail in Chapter 4. For the counter-argument, see Taylor's (1994b) discussion which concurs with John Motley's (1856, 1) famous assessment:

> The rise of the Dutch Republic must even be regarded as one of the leading events of modern times. Without birth of this great commonwealth, the various historical phenomena of the sixteenth and following centuries must have either not existed or have presented themselves under essential modifications

52. These are drawn from Wallerstein (1984, chapter 4)
53. Trevor-Roper (1971, 269–70)
54. Cooper (1970, 34–5)
55. Woolf (1991, 25 and 29)
56. Stokes (1986, 168)
57. Stokes (1986, 164–5)
58. Contemporaries recognized this unusual situation of 'good war'. During the Thirty Years War, an Amsterdam burgomaster described the situation thus:

> It is known to all the world that whereas it is generally the nature of war to ruin the land and people, these countries [the United Provinces] on the contrary have been notably improved thereby' (Murray, 1967, 51)

During the Napoleonic War Viscount Hamilton commented: 'Our commerce has flourished, our wealth has increased, our possessions have multiplied . . . War, the curse of every other nation, has to Great Britain been a comparative blessing' (Harvey, 1978, 322). But this was not, as Harvey later calls it, 'a unique achievement' (p. 334) rather it was one of a triplet of such unusual events

59. This is described very well for the British and American cases by McCormick (1989, chapter 2) and we follow his ideas here
60. Ikenberry (1989, 380) gives the figures for US GNP as $91 billion in 1939, rising to $210 billion in 1945
61. Wallerstein (1984, chapter 4)
62. Wallerstein (1984, 4)
63. Wallerstein (1980, chapter 2) reviews the evidence
64. Nijman (1994)
65. Amsterdam's commercial calendar was organized around the return of the four great fleets which 'fed on and reinforced each other' to create the Dutch world entrepôt (Israel, 1989, 257–8)
66. Braudel (1984, 235–65)
67. Bousquet (1980, 50)
68. Wallerstein (1984, 46). This is usually interpreted in structural language, see especially Chase-Dunn (1989) and Overbeek (1990, 11): 'The cycle of hegemony and decline is not an historical contingency . . . Hegemony and decline are structural characteristics of the world order.'
69. Arrighi (1990 and 1994)
70. Arrighi (1990, 368)
71. Arrighi (1990, 376–85)
72. Taylor (1991a, 83–4)
73. Arrighi (1990, 385–95)
74. Taylor (1991a, 84)
75. Arrighi (1990, 396–403)
76. Taylor (1991a, 84–5)
77. Chase-Dunn (1990)
78. Arrighi (1990, 405) argues that the next struggle for world hegemony has started and takes the form of 'the ongoing crisis of the interstate system and . . . its supersession by suprastatal organizations'
79. Hopkins (1990)
80. Hopkins (1990, 411)
81. He puts it forward 'tentatively' (Hopkins, 1990, 409)
82. See, for instance, Inkeles and Smith's (1974) study entitled *Becoming Modern*
83. Toulmin (1990) has a very good discussion of dating the start of modernity
84. Berman (1988, 15); 'To be modern is to be part of a universe in which, as Marx said, "all that is solid melts into air." '
85. Berman (1988, 5): 'I define modernity as any attempt . . . to get a grip on the modern world.'
86. Woolf (1991, 13) refers to this as 'the administrative project for modernity'
87. Berman (1988, 16–17)
88. Paul Johnson's (1991) treatment of the years 1815 to 1830 as 'the birth of the modern' is, from this interpretation, the birth of the second main modernity. Culler (1985, 74) argues that the use of the word 'modern' in its positive sense was part of the 'spirit of the age' in the first third of the 19th century. Modernity as an intellectual project is traced back to the 18th century Enlightenment (Habermas, 1983; Harvey, 1990). However, according to Lukacs (1993, 282), the word 'modern' changes its meaning from simply 'today's' or 'present' to 'new and enlightened' in the 17th century
89. Hoare and Smith (1971, 182)
90. Hoare and Smith (1971, 161)
91. Wallerstein (1989) has considered France from this perspective

Chapter 2

1. Giddens (1985); Michael Mann (1986) uses a similar metaphor when he refers to society 'caged' by the state. See also Taylor (1994a)

2. In a classic naturalizing statement, J. D. B. Miller (1981, 1) argues that we cannot prove that the 'world of states' is any more 'unnatural' than 'a pride of lions'. But this is to be insensitive to the historical record: 'Far from being natural entities, modern sovereign states are entirely historical artifacts.' (Jackson, 1990, 7; see also Brown, 1981, ix)
3. Taylor (1993a, chapter 4). The fullest discussion of this structure occurs in Walker (1993)
4. This is Basil Davidson's (1993) argument in his *Black Man's Burden*
5. Davidson (1993, 257)
6. Holsti (1991, 93–4); the states under threat were Austria (1742), Prussia (1745), Prussia (1756), Poland (1772), Sweden (1773), European Turkey (1787), Poland (1792) and Poland (1795) although only the last was actually removed from the inter-state system
7. See Ashley (1988) and Walker (1993) for the best critical discussions of this 'trap'
8. The earliest 'peace society' was set up in New York in 1815 with the first in Europe founded a year later in London (Trueblood, 1932, xiii). However Trueblood traces the development of 'the peace idea' back to the 17th century. Here the Dutch jurist Grotius is given pride of place: 'It was as if the suffering spirit of the entire continent had dictated his words' (p. 17). We consider Grotius's role in our story in the next chapter
9. Taylor (1991a)
10. Taylor (1994a)
11. Schama (1987, 62)
12. Duke (1990, 191): '*Bons patriots* conveniently left open the precise geographical location of the *patrie*'
13. Duke (1990, 194)
14. This is described in much detail by deVries (1978)
15. Galbraith (1993, 14)
16. Galbraith (1993, 14)
17. Mackay is quoted by Galbraith (1993, 15)
18. Duke (1990, 175). See also Israel (1995b, chapter 4)
19. Parker (1977, 69) reports the rebels to be 'greatest in the outlying provinces' and provides maps of the various stages of the rebellion. For an interpretation of the geography of the Dutch rebellion, see Taylor (1994b)
20. Parker (1977, 193 and map 5)
21. Schama (1987, 54)
22. For a detailed assessment of the Calvinist contribution, see Gorski (1993) and Israel (1995b, chapter 16)
23. Duke (1990, 194)
24. Rowen (1988, 1) refers to 'old structures adapted to new needs and a new situation'. For a detailed treatment of the political institutions of the United Provinces and how they worked in practice, see Price (1994) and Israel (1995b, chapter 13)
25. Braudel (1984, 193) asks: 'Can the United Provinces be called a state?'
26. Barbour (1963)
27. Rowen (1986, 35); as 'de facto' foreign minister (see p. 62) and as foreign minister see Rowen (1978, 238)
28. Rowen (1978, 141)
29. This is the famous dictum of a contemporary, Peter de la Court, writing in 1665 quoted by Rowen (1978, 176)
30. This is a point made by Zolberg (1986, 88):

> Organizing itself into an oligarchic federation, this mercantile society turned war into a specialized activity, which it entrusted to 'subcontractors' led by the House of Orange-Nassau, applying to it innovations of the same kind that brought about the country's spectacular economic growth in the seventeenth century: that is to say chiefly capitalist-intensive method of investment

31. Hence Ardant's (1975, 193) reference to the 'surprising importance' of the United Provinces which he explains in terms of the rare circumstance for early modern Europe of fiscal ability and political ambition being in balance
32. Parker (1977, 156)
33. Parker (1977, 167)

34. Taylor (1994b)
35. See the text in Kossmann and Mellick (1974): Paragraph IV (p. 167) and Paragraph VII (p. 168)
36. Rowen (1988, 39)
37. This is the oasis of peace that enabled the Dutch to have a 'good war' behind 'the fixed garrison system' of some 21 fortified towns in a defensive ring (Israel, 1995b, 262–7)
38. Rowen (1978, 392); Boogman (1979, 394). See also Peter de la Court's proposal to build a canal to create an effective 'island' of Holland (Wansink, 1971, 143)
39. Braudel (1984, 202) provides a map of the 'fortified island'
40. Barbour (1963, 13)
41. Braudel (1984, 35) argues that Amsterdam was more like Venice than London
42. Braudel (1984, 175)
43. Many of these cities had obtained voting rights as a result of the rebellion against centralization; in Holland such cities rose from six to 18 ('T Hart, 1989, 666–7). See also Wansink (1971)
44. Rowen (1986, 70–1)
45. 'T Hart (1989, 668)
46. 'T Hart (1989, 677) and Wansink (1971)
47. 'T Hart (1989, 672); Israel (1990, 56) provides a good example of Amsterdam, although in alliance with Rotterdam, being defeated over truce negotiations with Spain: 'The unyielding persistence of the war towns through January 1630, led by Haarlem and Leiden, brought the truce moves in the province of Holland finally to a halt.' According to Rowen (1986, 179), Amsterdam did not even act like the leading city due to its 'characteristic reluctance to put broad provincial and national interests ahead of their city's particular rights and needs'. For a detailed discussion of the political relations between the cities of the United Provinces, see Wansink (1971) and Price (1994)
48. Burke (1974, 45–7)
49. Boogman (1979, 398)
50. In 1622 it is estimated that one-third of Amsterdam's population consisted of 'southerners' (Boxer, 1965, 19)
51. The quotation is from a letter, see Braudel (1984, 187) and Boxer (1965, 19)
52. Israel (1989, 33)
53. Israel (1989, 36)
54. Boogman (1979, 402)
55. Wallerstein (1980, 65)
56. Boogman (1978, 55)
57. Boogman (1978, 58) argues that historians have overemphasized the traditional 'continental monarchical' variant of raison d'état at the expense of the Dutch invention of the 'maritime-republican' variant
58. This is from the manuscript 'The True Interest' discussed further below. This quotation is from Rowen's (1972, 212–13) reprinting of the original
59. Braudel (1984, 203)
60. Israel (1982, 1)
61. Parker (1978, 57, 68)
62. Parker (1978, 58)
63. Parker (1978, 72)
64. Luard (1992, chapter 1)
65. Trueblood (1932, 15)
66. Kossmann (1963, 3)
67. Kossmann (1963, 4) refers to the United Provinces as the only 'pacific state' in the world because of its lack of interest in territorial aggrandizement; Boogman (1978, 60; 1979, 401) goes further and finds 'even a tendency for contraction' which Rowen (1978, 253) supports from a contemporary (1669) source: 'This state has enough fortresses and land, even perhaps too many.'
68. See the document reproduced in Rowen (1972, 76)
69. 'In the main, villages, unprotected towns and prosperous, intensively farmed agricultural land on either side was kept, by mutual consent, and through fear of retaliation, safe from harm' (Israel, 1982, 97)

70. Israel (1982, 97): 'The conflict could not have been more unlike that waged simultaneously, nearby in Germany.'
71. Kossmann (1970, 380)
72. Kossmann (1970, 380)
73. Rowen (1978, 253); according to Wilson (1957, 146), 'Her pacificism was not idealistic: it was the pacificism of expediency, even of necessity.'
74. Kossmann (1963, 6) describes the Lydius policy as 'isolationism, pacificism, collective self-glorification'. More generally Boogman (1978, 59) refers to the 'Holland tradition' in foreign policy as 'peace, quiet and commerce'
75. Wilson (1957, 6) refers to the unparalleled extent of Dutch dependence on the outside world so that the state had no choice but to be 'intimately concerned with the maintenance of favourable conditions in the world beyond their boundaries'
76. An 1667 'maxim of state' stated that it was necessary, not only for the Dutch to maintain good bilateral relations with other countries, but to promote good relations between 'all the Governments of Christendom' (Rowen, 1978, 253)
77. Kossmann (1963, 7)
78. Coplin (1968, 19)
79. Gross (1968, 65)
80. This is from the 8th Federalist Paper and is quoted by Herz (1959, 64)
81. Mulier (1987); Kossmann (1960)
82. Rowen (1978, 383–9)
83. Boogman (1978, 64)
84. This is reproduced in Rowen (1972). Published anonymously, it was later ascribed to de Witt but see Rowen (1978, 391). It has been reprinted in full as de la Court (1972)
85. Caton (1988, 233)
86. Caton (1988, 235)
87. Beloff (1954)
88. Rowen, 1972, 202
89. Wallerstein (1989)
90. Wallerstein (1991a, chapter 1)
91. Dyson (1980) shows that terms such as 'realm', 'body politic' and 'commonwealth' are used instead of 'state'
92. Dyson (1980, 37) on no legal concept of state. Nairn (1977, 26) calls it a 'low profile state'
93. Dyson (1980, 43)
94. Nairn (1977, 19)
95. This is Nairn's (1977, 26) description
96. Nairn (1977, 26)
97. The best political interpretation of low and high politics in Britain is by Bulpitt (1986)
98. Nairn (1977, 26)
99. Dyson (1980, 40)
100. This quotation is from *Wealth of Nations* (1776) reproduced in Hall and Ikenberry (1989, 4)
101. Bagehot (1963, 266); elsewhere he writes, 'A Republic has insulated itself beneath the folds of a Monarchy' (p. 94) and 'the appendages of monarchy have been converted into the essence of a republic' (p. 262). Being published in 1867, Bagehot's work was made out of date almost immediately by the Reform Act of that year. Nevertheless the book's longevity has been remarkable: a century later it was still viewed as 'the best introduction available' for understanding British politics (Crossman, 1963, 1). However our interest focuses upon Bagehot's real subject, what Richard Crossman (1963, 1) calls 'the period of classical parliamentary government'. Bagehot (1963, 266) himself thought the 'disguised republic' to be particularly 'suited to such a being as the Englishman in such a century as the nineteenth'
102. Bagehot (1963, 61):

    > first, those which excite and preserve the reverence of the population — the *dignified* parts, if I may so call them; and next, the *efficient* parts — those by which it, in fact, works and rules

103. Bagehot (1963, 82) begins his chapter on the monarchy with the statement: 'The use of the Queen, in a dignified capacity, is incalculable. Without her in England, the present English Government would fail and pass away.'

104. Nairn (1977, 19); he sees it as an intermediate 'midwife' that never became modern (p. 22)
105. The best discussion of early English nationalism is by Newman (1987)
106. Nairn (1988, 163)
107. Johnson (1985, 232)
108. Grainger (1986, 20)
109. Taylor (1991b)
110. Schroeder (1986, 11); Clark (1989, 105)
111. Schroeder (1986)
112. Clark (1989, 93) also uses 1815 to represent a key change in international politics
113. Anderson (1985, 3)
114. Hinsley (1982, 1)
115. Hinsley (1982, 2) refers to 'modernization' of the international system
116. Schroeder (1986, 13) refers to this as Europe 'fenced off from the rest of the world'
117. Bourne (1970, 3)
118. Taylor, (1952, 30–40) quoted by Schroeder (1986, 5)
119. Gough (1990, 167)
120. The full phrase is 'maritime keys to lock up the world' (Gough, 1990, 172)
121. Smith (1981, 60)
122. Gallie (1978, chapter 2)
123. Semmel (1986)
124. Semmel (1986, 6)
125. Semmel (1986, 6)
126. Schroeder (1986, 11)
127. Edward Said (1978, 3) refers to a 'Western style for dominating, restructuring and having authority over the "Orient" '
128. Bartlett (1984)
129. According to Said (1978, 5) the Orient was not found to be 'oriental', it was 'orientalized'. Hence 'Orientalism is premised upon exteriority' (p. 20) and 'the Orientalist is outside the Orient' (p. 21)
130. Said (1978, chapter 2) considers this discipline to be unique due to its geographical definition
131. Chandra (1981)
132. Said (1978, 22): 'that Orientalism makes sense at all depends more on the West than on the Orient'
133. Kabbani (1988, 6)
134. Kabbani (1988, 36)
135. Weinstein (1967)
136. Galbraith (1958, 13) emphasizes its uniqueness:

> Nearly all throughout all history have been very poor. The exception, almost insignificant in the whole span of human existence, has been the last few generations in a comparatively small corner of the world populated by Europeans. Here, and especially in the United States, there has been great and quite unprecedented affluence

See Fossum and Roth (1981, 5–8) for a discussion of the many uses of the 'American Dream'
137. Quoted by Ehrenreich (1989, 20)
138. Fox and Lears (1983, xi)
139. Lukacs (1993, 145)
140. Gramsci wrote this in 1929 (Hoare and Smith, 1971, 316) and went on to refer to a "new culture' and 'new way of life' which are being spread around under the American label" (p. 317)
141. Hoare and Smith (1971, 318)
142. Ehrenreich (1989, 35)
143. Fox and Lears (1983, x)
144. Westbrook (1983)
145. Dyson (1980, 37)

146. Shonfield (1965, 315)
147. Turner (1932)
148. Berry *et al* (1990, iv)
149. Shonfield (1965, 326)
150. Shonfield (1965, 309)
151. Markusen and Yudken (1992)
152. John Gaddis (1987) used the phrase usually associated with the period 1815–1914 as the title of his book on post-1945 international relations
153. Wilson viewed the USA as 'global workshop and banker, umpire and policeman, preacher and teacher' (ie hegemon) (McCormick (1989, 33)
154. Clark (1989, chapter 7)
155. Hinsley (1982, 5)
156. Coplin (1968, 31)
157. Hinsley (1982, 8)
158. Range (1959, 31)
159. Range (1959, 11)
160. Range (1959, 30)
161. Schurmann (1978, 36) provides a discussion of 'Roosevelt's vision of "one world" '
162. Hathaway (1981, 18)
163. US GNP rose from $91 billion in 1939 to $210 billion in 1945 (Ikenberry, 1989, 380)
164. Kolko and Kolko (1972, 2)
165. Kolko and Kolko (1972, 22) call US loans at the end of World War II 'the key vehicle of structural change in the capitalist world'
166. 'American leaders erroneously conceived England as the main barrier to the attainment of their postwar goals' (Kolko and Kolko, 1972, 18)
167. Taylor (1990, chapter 6) describes 'Britain's geoeconomic dilemma'
168. Ikenberry (1989, 384–5) argues that the 'chief political strength of the British (and the Europeans generally), in resisting American designs was their economic weakness'
169. For the 'orthodox versus revisionist' debate, see McCauley (1983)
170. Kennan is credited with introducing the concept of containment to US foreign policy in his anonymous ('Mr X') article in the journal *Foreign Affairs* in 1947 (Gaddis, 1982, 25–6)
171. Isaacson and Thomas (1986, 388)
172. See McCauley (1983, 121–2) for text
173. Isaacson and Thomas (1986, 395)
174. Isaacson and Thomas (1986, 398)
175. Kolko and Kolko (1972, 342)
176. Herz (1959)
177. Clark (1989, chapter 8)
178. Roosevelt originally thought US involvement in World War II would turn it into 'the New Deal War' with the outcome a 'New Deal for the World' (Judis, 1992, 59–60)
179. Adler and Paterson (1970)
180. Kolko and Kolko (1972, 69) describe the change of tactics thus: 'It would not be a transaction, it would be a crusade.'
181. McCauley (1983, 121)
182. Wolfe (1984, 224) describes it as a temporary device that became entrenched in the political culture
183. Adler and Paterson (1970)
184. 'The prewar decade provided an accurate map for the postwar era' (Adler and Paterson, 1970, 1060)
185. Whitaker (1984)
186. Ehrenreich (1989, 5)
187. Halle (1984)
188. Halle (1984, 202)
189. Whitaker (1984)
190. Fox and Lears (1983, ix)
191. Henry Wallace, Roosevelt's vice-president was associated with the global New Deal concept. The Say's Law interpretation is from McCormick (1989, 50)

192. McCormick (1989, 50)
193. McCormick (1989, 48) calls this the 'great trade-off' to get its allies into line – less autonomy for material rewards. Quite simply, 'America had to make a plausible case that its hegemony served systemic interests as well as self interests if others were to defer to it voluntarily' (pp. 48–9)
194. Pipes and Garfinkle (1991, xvi)
195. Miliband and Liebman (1984)

Chapter 3

1. Ehrenreich (1989, 19)
2. McDougall (1985, 407)
3. Friedberg (1988, 27)
4. Hyam (1976, 20); using a slightly different time frame, he goes on to say: 'To have lived in the flow of life . . . as a Briton from 1810 to 1860 was . . . the last, the consummate blessing.'
5. Cotterell (1972, 86)
6. Mokyr (1990, 6)
7. Israel (1989, 357)
8. Wallerstein (1980, 42)
9. Mokyr (1990, chapter 4)
10. Mokyr (1990, 59–60)
11. Mokyr (1990, 60, 62, 68, 69, 70, 71, 74, 105, 179). This list of innovations does not do justice to the Dutch as the leading innovators in agriculture in the 17th century (van Bath, 1960)
12. Wallerstein (1980, 40)
13. Lambert (1985, 196–202); as well as wind power, the Dutch were unique in the quantity of peat they used (de Zeeuw, 1978)
14. In Mokyr's (1990, 68) words: 'Dutch shipbuilding yards were at the center of progress.'
15. Lambert (1985, 283–6)
16. Mokyr (1990, 68)
17. Schama (1987, 42)
18. Lambert (1985)
19. Lambert (1985, 183)
20. Schama (1987, 38)
21. Kain and Baigent (1984, 20)
22. Lambert (1985, 184)
23. Kain and Baigent (1984, 21)
24. Kain and Baigent (1984, 21)
25. Lambert (1985, 210)
26. Lambert (1985, 267)
27. Schama (1987, 39) refers to the 'geographical roots of republicanism'
28. Murray (1967, 3)
29. Beaver (1970); for an historical description of the origins, see Greenhalgh (1988, chapter 1)
30. Jordan (1963, 158–9)
31. Richards (1990, 25); de Cauter (1993) has called it 'the grid of the world'
32. The exhibition was open from 1 May to 11 October and attracted six million visitors to see the wares of 7381 British exhibitors and 6556 foreign exhibitors (Beaver, 1970). In all, 34 countries were represented (Greenhalgh, 1988, 12). See also Gibbs-Smith (1981)
33. Beaver (1970, 270); there was also a model of Liverpool docks including 1600 fully-rigged ships
34. Richards (1990, 24)
35. As *The Times* described it: 'It was felt to be more than what was seen' (Beaver, 1970, 42)
36. Greenhalgh (1988, 12)
37. Richards (1990, 36)
38. Bird (1976); Richards (1990, chapter 4)

39. Bird (1976); Richards (1990, chapter 4)
40. Sorensen (1965, 525)
41. According to Sorensen (1965, 525), a 'second-rate, second-place space effort [was] inconsistent with its role as world leader'
42. McDougall (1985, 362)
43. Sorensen (1965, 524)
44. Sorensen (1965, 525)
45. McDougall (1985, 303); this was to be carried out, as Kennedy saw it, 'in full view of the world' (p. 302)
46. It was on this flight that the famous 'Earthrise' photograph was taken. President Johnson realized the propaganda value and sent copies to every world head of state (including the North Vietnam leader Ho Chi Minh!) (McDougall, 1985, 412)
47. According to Sorensen (1965, 524), Kennedy realized from the first that it was a matter of 'world leadership generally and scientific leadership particularly'
48. Notice the juxtaposition of the national and the universal: Armstrong went on to plant the Stars and Stripes on the surface of the Moon
49. McDougall (1985, 3)
50. McDougall (1985, 3)
51. Haley (1988, 79–80)
52. Haley (1988, 123)
53. 'A new and non-religious ground was needed' (Dunning, 1905, 188)
54. Edwards (1981)
55. Figgis (1916, 222)
56. Figgis (1916, 223)
57. By 'general consent', according to Dunning (1905, 153), he provided 'the foundation of the science of international law'
58. Dunning (1905, 187)
59. Dunning (1905, 188)
60. According to Dunning (1905, 188), his work fitted 'the manifest needs of his time'
61. Edwards (1981, 95–6)
62. Edwards (1981, 82)
63. Edwards (1981, 83–4)
64. Edwards (1981, 95–6)
65. Dunning (1905, 171); he later refers to Grotius producing *ius inter gentes* (p. 189)
66. Figgis (1916, 242)
67. Figgis (1916, 242)
68. According to Figgis (1916, 242), Grotius looked to the new world of 'territorial sovereignty and the equality of the juristic persons (ie states) of International Law'
69. Dunning (1905, 153)
70. Cooper (1970, 5)
71. Bull (1990, 77)
72. Bull (1990, 77). Cooper (1970, 5) suggests Grotius 'may have contributed in some sense to a European community of nations'
73. It was originally written for his employers, the Dutch East India Company, and appeared as a chapter in an unpublished report of 1604–5. Its purpose is summed up by the subtitle of its published form: 'The right of the Dutch to take part in the East India Trade' (Kwiatkowska, 1984)
74. Kwiatkowska (1984, 25)
75. It was, he argued, *res communis* (Kwiatkowska, 1984, 25)
76. The 16th century had been an age of 'closed waters' (Wilson, undated, 44)
77. Reproduced in Rowen (1972, 155)
78. Fielden (1969, 81)
79. Deane (1978, 44)
80. Deane (1978, 44)
81. Blaug (1978, 126) refers to him being 'virtually first' to separate international and intranational trade. The work discussed here is Ricardo's *Essay on the Influence of a Low Price of Corn on the Profit of Stock* published in 1815 (Deane, 1978, 61)

82. In effect Ricardo provided the ammunition for an anti-landowner politics (Deane, 1978, 63)
83. Fielden (1969, 81)
84. This slow process is traced by Fielden (1969)
85. Hobson (1919, 41)
86. Hinde (1987, 172)
87. Hobson (1919, 41–2); the tour was originally planned for health reasons, but Cobden changed it into a political trip after hearing from Sir Roderick Murchison that the Czar would meet him (Hinde, 1987, 170)
88. Hobson (1919, 46)
89. 'Expounding among influential men in many European countries the gospel of Free Trade and Internationalism' (Hobson, 1919, 52)
90. Queen Victoria called it a 'peace festival', for instance (Beaver, 1970, 40)
91. Fielden (1969, 78)
92. Hobson (1919, 245)
93. Hobson (1919, 246)
94. Hobson (1919, 246)
95. Hinde (1987, 289)
96. Hinde (1987, 288); *Punch* ran a cartoon entitled 'Dame Cobden's New Pupil' (p. 290)
97. Hinde (1987, 300)
98. Fielden (1969, 85)
99. Henry Luce was a 'one-world Republican' who supported Roosevelt during World War II. His original writings on this question were published in *Life* magazine and then brought together as a book including comments from critics (Luce, 1941)
100. 'To accept wholeheartedly our duty and opportunity as the most powerful and vital nation in the world (Luce, 1941, 23)
101. Luce (1941, 39)
102. Luce (1941, 26); elsewhere his writing reads like a parody: 'an internationalism of the people, by the people and for the people' (p. 33)
103. This is one of Luce's critics complaining about his 'Anglo-Saxon gift' he shared with British 19th-century statesmen (Luce, 1941, 55)
104. Luce (1941, 56)
105. Touraine (1990, 247)
106. Carr (1939); Morgenthau (1948). These were a reaction to post-World War I idealism in international relations
107. Wightman (1983, 1)
108. Wightman (1983, 1)
109. Wightman (1983, 14)
110. Chekki (1987, 9) describes American sociology as culture-bound and parochial but globally dominant
111. Gouldner (1971, 22–3)
112. Connell (1990, 271)
113. Chekki (1987, 9) refers to 'Its hegemonic influence over several national sociologies'
114. Touraine (1990, 252)
115. Connell (1990, 270)
116. Andreski (1972) remains the best description of this process
117. Bekker (1952, 234)
118. By 1964 Moscoso (1964, v) was writing that: 'International Development had come of age as an academic discipline and profession and national policy.'
119. Black (1964, 7) in an essay entitled 'So hopeful a challenge'
120. Nisbet (1967, 317)
121. Horowitz (1967, 6–8). If followed earlier, smaller exercises: Project Revolt on French Canada and Project Simpatico on Colombian rural politics. For a broad analysis that puts the project within the wider context of the USA's attempt to 'manage political change in the Third World', see Gendzier (1985)
122. Horowitz (1967, 1–3)
123. Horowitz (1967, 4–5)

124. Sahlins (1967, 71). It was organized through the American University which served 'as a sort of camouflage' and took 20% commission on a 'gentleman's agreement' to ask no questions (Horowitz, 1967, 24)
125. The countries finally recommended for study were as follows: 1. 'For Comparative Historical studies' — Argentina, Bolivia, Brazil, Colombia, Cuba, Dominican Republic, El Salvador, Guatemala, Mexico, Paraguay, Peru, Venezuela, Egypt, Iran, Turkey, Korea, Indonesia, Malaysia, Thailand, France, Greece and Nigeria; 2. 'For Survey Research and Other Field Studies' — Bolivia, Colombia, Ecuador, Paraguay, Peru, Venezuela, Iran, Thailand; 3. 'Field Work to Generate Data on "Currently Critical Situations" — Brazil and Argentina (Horowitz (1967, 57)
126. Horowitz (1967, 56–7)
127. Horowitz (1967, 44)
128. Interestingly Horowitz (1967, 11) considers Chile to be an unlikely locale for resisting this work. He thinks the Chileans were unduly worried about the USA instigating an anti-democratic coup. In hindsight, of course, we know their fears were fully justified
129. Laski (1936, 9 and 19); Arblaster (1984) strongly takes this position also. Vincent (1992, 22) perceptively notes that liberalism 'has permeated so deeply into the cultural life of the West that it is difficult to disentangle the partisan from the more objective commentary'
130. Vincent (1992, 23)
131. Manning (1976, 140) represents a good example of this tendency where varieties of liberalism are interpreted as 'an on-going evaluation of changing circumstances' but based upon the same basic principles
132. Hayek (1975, 56), identifies two liberalisms which 'rest on altogether different philosophical foundations'. More specifically, Schultz (1972, x-xi) argues that

> No ideology, in all its political, economic and social dimensions, changed more profoundly than did Victorian liberalism . . . Is not the 'nightwatchman state' the logical opposite of the 'welfare state'? How then can the welfare state be the 'logical corollary' of the nightwatchman state?

133. Manning (1976, 57)
134. Laski (1936, 238) writes of the 'unending battle on two fronts'
135. Boogman (1979, 378)
136. Haley (1988, 77–80) argues that, despite cultural and political similarities, there was no necessary communality of interests because of economic rivalry
137. As two apologists for alliances with such 'not wholly savoury allies' state: 'All things being equal, Americans want to spread their values and domestic moral standards around the globe, and helping tyrants hardly advances that cause' (Pipes and Garfinkle, 1991, xvi)
138. FitzSimmons (1972, 3)
139. The use of the term to mean a political opinion is a 19th-century invention, first employed to describe Spanish rebels in 1820 (Collins, 1957, 3). This initial use was pejorative (Vincent, 1992, 23)
140. Arblaster (1984, 108) calls this the 'whig theory' of liberalism because of its emphasis on a smooth, predictable evolution
141. Arblaster (1984, 108)
142. Coplin (1968)
143. Arblaster (1984, 124); see also Caton (1988, 222–3)
144. Israel (1995b, 569)
145. Israel (1995b, 570)
146. Israel (1995b, 572)
147. Israel (1995b, 578)
148. Israel (1995b, 637)
149. Israel (1995b, 639)
150. Rowen (1972, 209); Peter de la Court's first maxim was 'the Freedom of all sorts of Religions differing from the Reformed' (p. 208). However we should be careful to note the limitations of tolerance even in this most liberal thinker. De la Court accepted the need for a state church which meant excluding dissenting religions from public office

(Israel, 1995b, 639). Both Grotius and Descartes left the United Provinces in periods of intolerance and even during long phases of toleration new ideas had to be carefully presented – see, for example the work of Spinoza (Caton, 1988, 257; Israel, 1995b, 917–21). It is noteworthy that the long careers of the two Dutch leaders associated with toleration, Oldenbarnevelt and de Witt, both ended in political executions. For Caton (1988, 240) this was because 'The times were out of phase, the old and the new sat juxtaposed in sharp antagonism'. Another way of viewing this is to say they were both pioneers, always a dangerous undertaking, at the birth of modernity. For a good discussion of the scope and limitations of toleration in the United Provinces, see Price (1994, chapters I,6 and II,6)

151. Walzer (1992, 169)
152. Nussbaum (1953, 6); see also Israel (1995b, 581–7)
153. Nussbaum (1953, 2)
154. Schultz (1972, ix)
155. Arblaster (1984, 250); according to Bellamy (1992, 9) 'European intellectuals generally regarded Britain as the embodiment of the liberal ideal.'
156. Furley (1969, 147)
157. Horne (1970, 24); Britain's role was to 'teach other nations how to live' (p. 23) because, for liberals, 'the morality of Britain was also becoming the motive force of world progress' (p. 25)
158. Watson (1969, 125) refers to 'the great flexibility of parliamentarianism'
159. Watson (1969, 108)
160. Smith (1981, 34)
161. This was a speech given in 1865 at Birmingham Town Hall which included the lines: 'We may be proud of this, that England is the ancient country of Parliament . . . England is the mother of Parliaments' (Watson, 1969, 101)
162. Fulbright (1966, 13–34)
163. Arblaster (1984, chapter 18)
164. Arblaster (1984, 310)
165. Coleman (1989)
166. Coleman (1989, 9)
167. Coleman (1989, 16 and 139)
168. The fact that this speech was delivered to 15 000 people shows the scale of the operation (Coleman, 1989, 32)
169. Coleman (1989, 50)
170. Coleman (1989, 54) argues that this was 'the basis of almost all the Congress's activity'
171. Bell (1961); despite applying ideology largely to left-wing thought, he claimed 'The perspective I adopt is anti-ideological, but not conservative' (p. 16)
172. Bell (1961, 402)
173. Quoted by Arblaster (1984, 322)
174. FitzSimmons (1972, 8); Kennedy was especially influenced by the idea of non-ideology, Schlesinger (1965, 739) claims 'The president stood for the politics of modernity' and quotes Kennedy in support: 'Liberalism and conservatism are categories of the thirties, and they don't apply anymore.' The obvious policy initiative along these lines was the Peace Corps which was pledged to be 'non-political in world affairs' (Sorensen, 1965, 532)
175. One supporter was explicit on this matter: 'There is no ideological orientation of the project beyond the conviction that the scientific method is useful' (Horowitz, 1967, 39)
176. Ruggie (1983)
177. 'God is an Englishman' is the title of Horne's (1970) book on Englishness but was also popularized by the fiction writer R. F. Delderfield who used the phrase as the title for one of his novels set in the mid-19th century. On watching goods being unloaded at Calais, the hero exclaims, 'God is an Englishman, sure enough' (Sternlicht, 1988, 104). The proof is simple: 'God is decent, fair, just, straightdealing, neat, reticent, orderly, and always a winner. That is, an Englishman' (Delderfield, 1970, 660)
178. Schama (1987, 254)
179. Modelski (1987, chapter 7)
180. Rowen (1978, 253)

Chapter 4

1. Nisbet (1969) shows how this type of social thinking is predicated on a biological meta-phor of growth but then goes on to argue that nobody has ever seen a society 'grow': 'All that we see are the mingled facts of persistence and change' (p. 3)
2. Nisbet (1969, 105)
3. Horne (1970, 214)
4. deVries (1973, 191)
5. Hobsbawm (1967)
6. deVries (1973)
7. deVries (1973, 194–6); see also deVries (1974)
8. Kain and Baigent (1984, 12); deVries (1973, 198–9)
9. deVries (1973, 199)
10. Kain and Baigent (1984, chapter 1)
11. Kain and Baigent (1984, 23)
12. Kain and Baigent (1984, 24)
13. deVries (1973, 200)
14. Smith (1984, 996); see also Israel (1995a)
15. Smith (1984, 1000 and 1002)
16. Smith (1984, 1004–5)
17. Caton (1988, 222)
18. Stearns (1969, 29)
19. Stearns (1969, 12)
20. Stearns (1969, 12–13)
21. Stearns (1969, 7)
22. Horne (1970, 21–2)
23. Robbins (1988, 9)
24. Hinde (1987, 8)
25. Fielden (1969, 77)
26. Briggs (1963, 116); contemporaries visited Manchester to find out 'the truth' about their era (p. 96)
27. These are: 'possible cradle of revolution' (Briggs, 1963, 90); 'cradle of wealth and social disorder' (p. 93); 'cradle of wealth and of new and formative social values' (p. 94) and 'cradle of universal industrialism' (p. 117)
28. Briggs (1963, 115)
29. Briggs (1963, 97)
30. Briggs (1963, 94)
31. Briggs (1963, 125); see also Grampp (1960)
32. Briggs (1963, 96); Anti-Corn Law League people used religious analogies to express this idea – Manchester was sometimes Mecca, sometimes Jerusalem (p. 118)
33. Arblaster (1984, 260)
34. Stearns (1969, 8); 'Forward-looking businessmen or statesmen could hope, did hope, to build new Manchesters' (p. 27)
35. Briggs (1963, 106)
36. Stearns (1969, 27)
37. Vann Woodward (1991, 81)
38. 'One of the words for modernity in Europe is now "Americanization" ' (Horne, 1970, 97)
39. Horne (1970, 214); in a British book written in 1901 entitled *The Americanization of the World*, the author welcomes the new developments across the Atlantic because it is 'but the Anglicanization of the world at one remove' (Vann Woodward (1991, 80)
40. Wallerstein (1984, 72)
41. Galbraith (1958)
42. Lukacs (1965, 223)
43. Lukacs (1965, 221)
44. Ney (1970, 26)
45. Ney (1970, 464)

46. Ney (1970, 64); he even argues that 'When England embraced the Beatles, it embraced America. Their rags to riches story was, in itself, intensely American' (p. 63)
47. Ney (1970, 3)
48. Ney (1970, 4–5); more generally Inkeles and Smith (1974, 3–4) have argued that 'it is impossible for a state to move into the twentieth century if its people continue to live in an earlier era'
49. Quoted by Nisbet (1969, 107); see also Nisbet (1980, 151)
50. Carr (1961, 145)
51. Tsanoff (1971, chapter 3); Nisbet (1980) develops this argument in some detail
52. Clarke (1979, 4)
53. Zerubavel (1992, 72) finds a reference to *Novi orbis* in a letter referring to Columbus's voyage of a year earlier and the following year (1594) he cites an Italian letter referring to *orbo novo*
54. Zerubavel (1992, 76)
55. Zerubavel (1992, 85); his map sold 1000 copies in its year of publication and on it he referred explicitly to 'four parts'. In this he followed Pacheco Periera whose new cosmography of 1505 included a 'fourth part' (p. 79)
56. Zerubavel (1992, 7 and 69)
57. Clarke (1979, 6); he considers these 'terrestrial utopias' as a key link between Christian epic and modern progress
58. Clarke (1979, 6)
59. According to Clarke (1979, 119–20), after the 'discovery' of Australia there was a decline in territorial utopias: 'distance could no longer lend enchantment to the view of faraway nowheres' (p. 122)
60. See Allen's (1992) chapter 3, 'The dominance of the Dutch'; Murray (1967, 110–14); Wilson (undated, 30–4)
61. Murray (1967, 114); 'In the last quarter of the 16th-century Amsterdam became the world publishing centre for maps, atlases, travel books and works on navigation and ship-building' (p. 110)
62. Baker (1955); Mukerji (1983, chapter 3)
63. Porter (1981, 6)
64. The relative decline of the United Provinces in the 18th century created an 'intellectual isolation of the Republic within the European Enlightenment' (Mijnhardt (1992, 212). See also Israel (1995b, chapter 39)
65. Schoffer (1978, 103); Porter (1981, 4)
66. Schama (1981, 55–6); Figgis (1916, 219) has argued that 'The Dutch revolt gathered up the various tendencies against absolutism, made them effective as a practical force and operative in the future'
67. Schama (1981, 56); Voltaire's first experience of 'international society' was as an attaché to the French ambassador to the Netherlands in 1713 at the age of 17 (Aldridge, 1975, 18)
68. The Dutch, according to Schama (1981, 56), enjoyed 'a collective pedigree' as 'an early historical and geographical reference point' of the Enlightenment
69. Schama (1981, 56)
70. This is a phrase used by an English observer in 1665 (Wilson, undated, 22)
71. Haley (1988, 108); Schama (1987, 44)
72. For contemporary derogatory descriptions of the Dutch, see Haley (1988, 107–10)
73. Figgis (1916, 220)
74. Mijnhardt (1992, 192)
75. Kumar (1978, 46)
76. Kumar (1978, 46); Culler (1985, 39) argues that in the 1820s to 1840s 'the spirit of the age' was 'perpetual change' which replaced 18th-century ideas on stages of progress
77. Kumar (1978, 46)
78. Carr (1961, 146–7); Clarke (1979, 7) refers to it as 'the Victorian doctrine of progress'
79. Kochan (1971, 113)
80. Burchill (1966, 7)
81. 'The Exhibition both commemorated the past and annihilated it' (Richards, 1990, 61)
82. Richards (1990, 61); Prince Albert was explicit on this:

> The Exhibition of 1851 is to give us a true test and a living picture of the point of development at which the whole of mankind has arrived ... and a new starting point from which all nations will be able to direct their further exertions (Burchill, 1966, 9)

One contemporary essay devoted to ranking countries' exhibits explicitly compares the English Medieval Court with contemporary India and China (Wornum, 1970)

83. Richards (1990, 29)
84. Carr (1961, chapter 5)
85. Nisbet (1967, 123–4)
86. Hofstadter (1959, 33); in the chapter 'The Vogue of Spencer', Hofstadter describes how his work was considered more advanced than Aristotle, Kant and Hegel with only Newton being considered as comparable in stature (p. 30)
87. Hofstadter (1959, 40)
88. Hofstadter (1959, 48); Galbraith (1958, 57) observes that 'he was accorded a welcome by the faithful befitting a messiah'
89. Hofstadter (1959, 48)
90. In his critique of the Whig school, Herbert Butterfield (1931, 109) argues that 'in Lord Acton, the whig historian reached his highest consciousness'
91. Mathew (1968, 361)
92. Carr (1961, 147)
93. Carr (1961, 152)
94. Butterfield (1931, v and 5) defines Whig history as producing 'a story which is a ratification if not the glorification of the present', requiring the world of the past to be divided into 'friends and enemies of progress'
95. Butterfield (1931, 30)
96. Bury (1920); Carr (1961, 154); Butterfield (1931, 30)
97. Carr (1961, 148 and 176)
98. John Viner (1952, 176), asked the rhetorical question, continuing:

> We want them ... to have some participation in the good material things of this life which we enjoy ... We want the common man and his wife and his children to have not only Coca Cola and chewing gum and ice cream, not only modern plumbing, automobiles, refrigerators, and electric lighting, but also good health and a good diet, good education and good prospects for betterment in life

99. For instance in their book *Becoming Modern*, Inkeles and Smith (1974) survey over 6000 people in six countries: Argentina, Chile, India, Israel, Nigeria and Bangladesh. Respondents were assessed in terms of 12 personal qualities which made them 'more effective in modern society' (pp. 19–24). 76% of all respondents were found to be modern with India having the highest proportion and Argentina the least (pp. 7 and 89)
100. Taylor (1989a)
101. Rostow (1960, 4)
102. Rostow (1960, xii)
103. The subtitle of Rostow's (1960) book is 'A non-communist manifesto'
104. See the discussion by Taylor (1989a, 304–8) on 'The world is not a ladder'
105. The evidence and debates concerning global polarization can be found in Seligson and Passe-Smith (1993)
106. Brookfield (1975, 2) has described it as 'a sort of euphoria' which exhibits 'a sublime confidence'
107. Hoffman (1962)
108. Hoffman (1962, 37)
109. Hoffman (1962, 37)
110. Hoffman (1962, 40)
111. Hoffman (1962, 8)
112. Hoffman (1962, 142) – this is the final sentence of his book
113. This is Wilkinson's (1984) 'duck shoot' we referred to in Chapter 1
114. Ikenberry (1989, 398) considers the USA to have got more than and less than it expected in 1945. He calls this the 'duality of American postwar experience'

115. Wilson (1958, 27–8)
116. Coleman (1969); Wilson (1958, 3) notes that Smith referred to mercantilism as 'the modern system', meaning it was based upon commerce rather than agriculture
117. Coleman (1969)
118. Heckscher (1955)
119. Wilson (1958, 19)
120. Viner (1969, 78)
121. Wilson (1958, 10)
122. Wolfe (1969, 191)
123. Heckscher (1955)
124. The 'conventional apparatus of "mercantilism" was neither appropriate nor necessary' (Wilson, 1958, 21)
125. Rowen (1978, 189)
126. Wallerstein (1980, 43)
127. Wilson (1958, 11)
128. Wilson (1958, 12–13)
129. A famous mercantilist tract of 1677 entitled *England's Improvement by Sea and Land* was quite explicit in this as expressed by its subtitle: 'How to beat the Dutch without actually fighting' (Treasure, 1966, 304)
130. Coleman (1969, 11)
131. Treasure (1966, 304)
132. Treasure (1966, chapter 21) calls his chapter on Colbert, 'Colbert and the Planned Economy'
133. Treasure (1966, 299)
134. Heckscher (1969, 25)
135. Coleman (1969, 104)
136. Coleman (1969, 110)
137. 'Rising exports of manufactured goods announced British industrialisation to the world' (Stearns, 1969, 10)
138. Stearns (1969, 8); the British proved mechanization was profitable by 'the overwhelming example of their success'
139. Stearns (1969, 8)
140. Lukacs (1965, 236)
141. We follow Pollard (1973) and Stearns (1969) who both adopt an approach that transcends country-by-country description
142. Stearns (1969, 14); as early as 1845 Germany had bought 237 locomotives from Britain
143. Pollard (1973, 639) argues that we should view 'the whole of Europe as one single "macro-development area" '. Stearns (1969, 7) suggests a simple spatial model: 'The countries first to industrialise . . . were closest to Britain, geographically or, in the case of the United States, culturally.'
144. Pollard (1973, 640) calls this 'the between argument' with continental industry having 'an intermediate role'
145. Stearns (1969, 14)
146. Stearns (1969, 20)
147. Stearns (1969, 20)
148. Stearns (1969, 15)
149. Stearns (1969, 17)
150. 'Many French industrialists claimed that their British counterparts had a distinctive spirit. They said that the British loved work more than the French did' (Stearns, 1969, 22)
151. O'Sullivan (1988)
152. Brewer (1980, 81–3)
153. Jessop (1982, chapter 2)
154. Winkler (1988, 113–14):

> corporatism could be interpreted as a sub-category of capitalism, a sub-category of socialism, a hybrid, or as a distinct economic system. . . . The argument here is that corporatism is sufficiently different . . . to be considered an economic system in its own right

155. President Teddy Roosevelt called major capitalists of the day 'malefactors of great wealth' (Collier and Horowitz, 1976, 4)
155. Collier and Horowitz (1976, 4)
156. Hogan (1987, 23–9)
157. Hogan (1987, 19)
158. Hogan (1987, 13)
159. Hogan (1987, 3)
160. Winkler (1988)
161. Mee (1984, 249) describes it thus: 'to be young, to be American, were wonderful things in the late forties; to be one of Averell Harriman's aides – or an aide to one of his aides – was transcendental'
162. Mee (1984, 246)
163. Although European governments provided their own plans, they were well aware of the limits of American economic indulgence. Mee (1984, 254) credits the Marshall Plan with producing a 'liberal Europe' instead of a 'socialist Europe'. Price (1955, 406) called it a 'classic campaign' for the free world
164. Hogan (1987, 19)
165. Mee (1984, 250)
166. Mee (1984, 249); 'They were a happy confident lot, all of them strictly can-do' (p. 250)
167. Lukacs (1993, 272–3) provides a very good description in terms of 'the overwhelming influence and prestige of things American': 'American customs, American practices, American music and American popular culture were emulated in the farthest corners of the globe.'
168. Servan-Schreiber (1968)
169. Servan-Schreiber (1968, chapter 1)
170. Of course, some thought this impossible: according to Ney (1970, 10) 'Americans are on top because they are intrinsically different' and 'Americans are the only people who can cope with technological living at the American level' (p. 6). Such thinking produced a remarkable alternative lesson:

> Considering the extraordinary lead enjoyed by American industry in the key sectors of our economy, some economists have asked whether the fastest path to development might not lie in letting Americans manage our industries (Servan-Schreiber, 1968, 27)

171. Servan-Schreiber (1968, 199)
172. Ruggie (1983)
173. Lundestad (1986)
174. Bullock (1983)

Chapter 5

1. Kennedy (1987)
2. Kennedy (1987, 514–35)
3. Kennedy (1987, 520)
4. As part of my duties I had to give the 1992 'Garvin Lecture', which has been published as Taylor (1993b)
5. For an analysis that emphasizes the similarities between British and American experiences, see Stein (1984). Jacob and Mijnhardt (1992, 6) compare contemporary American debates to the Dutch decline debates of the 18th century
6. Seeley (1971, 7)
7. Marsh (1994)
8. Friedberg (1988, 73)
9. Fulbright (1966)
10. Friedberg (1988); Fulbright (1966)
11. Friedberg (1988, 38); Friedman (1991)

12. Taylor (1989b)
13. Stein (1984) refers to this as the 'hegemon's dilemma': by pursuing a liberal trade regime the hegemon, like the rest of the world, gains absolutely but it also suffers decline relative to the rest of the world. For the latter, Stein emphasizes asymmetric trade bargains at the expense of the hegemon (p. 297)
14. Jacob and Mijnhardt (1992, 2); although they do add the caveat 'with the possible exception of Great Britain in the postwar era'. For a full description, see Israel (1995b, Part IV)
15. Kossmann (1992, 19); Price (1974, 211)
16. Kossmann (1992, 31)
17. Schama (1987, 283); Price (1974, 211) defines the 18th century for the Dutch as a 'concept' as much as a chronological period and argues that it 'started around 1670 or 1680'
18. Schama (1987, 283)
19. Kossmann (1992, 319)
20. Price (1974, 215) goes as far as to argue that: 'After 1715 the Republic ceased to play any role of significance in European affairs.'
21. Israel (1989, 346–7)
22. Kossmann (1992, 30); Israel (1989, 370)
23. Israel (1989, 397)
24. Jacob and Mijnhardt (1992, 5); Price (1974, 213)
25. Boxer (1965, 108); Price (1974, 212–4). Huizinga (1968, 103) provides a more poetic description of the process: 'From the hustle and bustle of the seventeenth century, the eighteenth century substituted a way of life that may be compared to dozing in the sunset of a long summer's day.'
26. Boxer (1965, 290)
27. Boxer (1965, chapter 10)
28. Adams (1994, 346)
29. Jacob and Mijnhardt (1992, 5 and 3)
30. Kossmann (1992, 25–9)
31. From 80 medals in 1851 to just 12 in 1867 (Horne, 1970, 214–15). According to Pollard (1989, 117) 'the Paris Exhibition of 1867 . . . shocked large sections of British public opinion'
32. See Coleman's (1973) seminal essay on 'Gentlemen and Players' and Cain and Hopkins (1986 and 1987)
33. Rubinstein (1993, chapter 4)
34. Wiener (1981); for a critique, see Rubinstein (1993)
35. Wiener (1981, 14)
36. Wiener (1981, 14)
37. Wiener (1981, 18)
38. Wiener (1981, 23)
39. Rubinstein (1993, 113) estimates that only about 7% of middle-class boys went to public schools in the late 19th century, but this is a wholly inadequate measure of the educational influence of elite schooling
40. Pollard (1989, 207)
41. Pollard (1989, 197)
42. Pollard (1989, 198)
43. Wiener (1981, 81)
44. Horne (1970, 21–2) terms this the victory of the 'southern metaphor' over the 'northern metaphor' so that Manchester becomes viewed as 'the first American city' (p. 125). See also Briggs (1963, 311–12, 326–30) and Dyos (1971)
45. Fielden (1969, 76)
46. Wiener (1981, 82)
47. Coleman (1973, 96) refers to 'the pursuit of very English non-economic ends'
48. Hynes (1968)
49. Read (1982, chapter 1) asks whether the period was a golden age or a crisis. Despite the 'stress', Tivey (1988, 35–6) believes that, in the period before 1914, Britain still thought of itself as a country that controlled its own destiny: 'Nobody thought that it was seriously constrained by the pressure or hostility of the rest of the world.'

50. Dangerfield (1936)
51. See, for instance, Fabian socialist attitudes to foreign policy and imperialism (MacKensie and MacKensie, 1977)
52. Wiener (1981, 104); or as a popular churchman of the time put it: 'The whole episode that made England the workshop of the world was alien to the spirit and character of the English people' (p. 113)
53. Wiener (1981, 109)
54. Wiener (1981, 142)
55. Wiener (1981, 145)
56. The word 'consumptionism' was coined as a derogatory term (Wiener 1981, 112)
57. Wiener (1981, 113)
58. Horne (1970, 111) refers to it as the 'Cardboard Commonwealth' because 'the function of the Commonwealth was to provide an ersatz assurance'; for Nairn (1977, chapter 1) it is another external mirage to cover economic failure
59. Taylor (1989b, 33). See also Overbeek (1990)
60. According to Horne (1970, 263), 'Britain may now be too small to be a lion, but it is too big to be a pussycat.'
61. Horne (1970, 259)
62. Horne (1970, 7–8)
63. For a summary of this debate see O'Loughlin (1993)
64. Shapiro (1992)
65. Strange (1987); Russett (1985)
66. Strange (1987)
67. Russett (1985)
68. Lukacs (1959); James Fallows (1989, 11) worries 'maybe we'll repeat the pattern of England's decline' and he most certainly does not think 'a second Britain will be enough'
69. Rosecrance (1990, 61)
70. Modelski (1987, 87) argues that Britain's 'bungled colonial war was the shock that stimulated new ideas' which led to 'Britain's golden age'
71. To produce Rosecrance's (1990) 'trading state'
72. See Israel (1989, 293) for a description of the 'disaster of 1672' beyond the war itself
73. Bartlett (1984, 40–6)
74. Judis (1992, 3)
75. Morris (1968, 31); he describes one of the two columns thus

> There were cavalrymen from New South Wales — gigantic soldiers . . . There were Hussars from Canada and Carabiniers from Natal, camel troops from Bikaner and Dyak head-hunters from North Borneo . . . The seventeen officers of the Indian Imperial Service troops were all princes, and the Hong Kong Chinese Police wore conical coolie hats. There were Malays, and the Sinhalese, and Hausas from the Niger and the Gold Coast, Jamaicans in white gaiters . . . British Guiana police in caps . . . Cypriot Zaptiehs [in] fezzes . . . and a jangling squadron of Indian lancers . . . one of the Maoris weighed twenty eight stone . . . London had never seen such a spectacle. (p. 32)

76. Morris (1968, 21–2): 'The nineteenth century had been pre-eminently Britain's century, and the British saw themselves still as top dogs.'
77. Cotterell (1972, 175)
78. Cotterell (1972, 175–6)
79. Murray (1967, 20); Cotterell (1972, 176–7)
80. Price (1974, 75)
81. Price (1974, 131) argues that this was the result of Amsterdam developing an 'urban aristocracy' before other major cities
82. Cotterell, (1972, 177)
83. This was evident before the demise of communism, of course. For instance, Fallows (1989) celebrates American exceptionalism in his book subtitled 'Making America Great Again' in which the 'Introduction' is 'The importance of being abnormal' (pp. 1–12)
84. Wallerstein (1987, 20)
85. Gaddis (1982, chapter 9)

86. Reich (1970, chapter 1)
87. Russett (1985)
88. Ney (1970, 469) understood this a quarter of a century ago: 'it is doubtful whether the decline of America . . . would spell the end of Americanization'
89. Haley (1988, 107)
90. MacKensie and MacKensie (1977, 407); there were many others on the political left who made the same pilgrimage — one American is reported as saying 'I have seen the future and it works' (Nisbet, 1980, 304)
91. MacKensie and MacKensie (1977, 406)
92. MacKensie and MacKensie (1977, 407)
93. MacKensie and MacKensie (1977, 407)
94. Wallerstein (1984, 88–9)
95. See the debate in Chase-Dunn (1982)
96. Frank (1980, chapter 4) proclaims 'Long live transideological enterprise!'
97. Levinson (1980) described hundreds of economic ventures crossing the East–West political divide
98. Brucan (1981, 95)
99. This quotation is from the Preface to the first German Edition of *Das Kapital* where Marx defends his use of English examples to German readers by arguing that England represents the 'classic ground' of the capitalist mode of production (Marx, 1954, 19)
100. Brucan (1981, 100) describes it as planned development for rapid industrialization. Such thinking was by no means limited to communist regimes. Mountjoy (1963, chapter 4) discusses industrialization as the panacea to economic ills up to the 1950s. The general logic was as follows:

> Modern civilization is based on iron and steel and the establishment of iron and steel works is one of the most desired features of planned development, opening the doors to a great range of other industries, particularly those making heavy capital goods (p. 146)

Mountjoy mentions Hungary, Algeria, India, Egypt, Chile and Argentina as countries adopting this policy
101. Brucan (1981, 102)
102. Brucan (1981, 107)
103. This was predicted many years ago by Ney (1970, 22): 'nothing on earth will be able to prevent Russia from becoming like America'
104. Thurow (1992, 247)
105. Wallerstein (1984, chapter 4)
106. Thurow (1992, 113–14)
107. Thurow (1992, 114)
108. van Wolferen (1989, 2); the idea of 'seeing the future' in present-day Japan is sometimes mooted (Fallows, 1989, viii)
109. Thurow (1992, 120); Fallows (1989, 41) calls it 'the anticonsumer social compact'
110. Fallows (1989, 42) describes the low Japanese standard of living despite the high per capita GNP. He comments: 'By American standards it is a strange victory indeed that Japan has won' (p. 41)
111. van Wolferen (1989, 26)
112. van Wolferen (1989, 41)
113. van Wolferen (1989, 44)
114. van Wolferen (1990, 43)
115. Maull (1990)
116. Maull (1990, 92)
117. Thurow (1992, 114)
118. van Wolferen (1989, 2)
119. Sumiya (1991)
120. Haber (1990, 905); she argues that 'Japan's intrinsic motivation' is not to foster a 'cultural hegemony'; see Fallows (1989, 31) for 'Japan's idea that it is separate from the world'
121. Taira (1991, 161)

122. Taira (1991, 160)
123. Taira (1991, 160)
124. Haber (1990, 905)
125. This is the subtitle of her article entitled 'The death of hegemony' (Haber, 1990)
126. Haber (1990, 907)
127. For a discussion of inter-stateness and trans-stateness, see Taylor (1995a)
128. Reich (1991, 3)
129. Reich (1991, 113)
130. Reich (1991, 134)
131. Reich (1991, 115)
132. Reich (1991, 115)
133. Sklair (1991, 62)
134. Sklair (1991, 63)
135. Sklair (1991, 68)
136. Sklair (1991, 76–7)
137. Castells and Hall (1994, 7–8)
138. Braudel (1984)
139. For a discussion of the relationship between world-cities and territorial states, see Taylor (1995b)
140. Friedmann (1986), see also Sassen (1991)
141. Castells and Hall (1994)
142. Arrighi (1990, 405)

Chapter 6

1. Ehrlich (1972)
2. Meadows et al (1974)
3. Meadows et al (1992, chapter 1)
4. The most comprehensive critique is by Cole et al (1973), but I agree with Eckersley (1992, 13) that methodological problems 'have not, by and large, detracted from its essential message'
5. Watt (1982, 144). A world consuming at US levels is what Daly (1977) calls his 'impossibility theorem'
6. Braudel (1981, Introduction); Giedion (1948, 4). I am indebted to Kees van der Pijl for providing initial reference to Giedion's book and pointing out its relevance to my arguments
7. Giedion (1948, 3)
8. Braudel (1981, 31 and 25); James Fallows (1989, 13) makes the same point: 'In the long run, a society's strength depends on the way ordinary people voluntarily behave. Ordinary people matter because there are so many of them.' This is, of course, the basic argument for promoting 'green consumerism' (Ekins, 1992, 156–60)
9. The use of the arts for nationalism in the 19th century is described by Billington (1980)
10. Hobsbawm and Ranger (1983) are the basic source for this process
11. The term 'baroque' was coined by critics of a later period when the classical style was in vogue: it is meant to imply the absurd and grotesque (Gombrich, 1989, 302)
12. Nussbaum (1953, 30)
13. 'Here the Baroque had little appeal' (Levey 1969, 9); Huizinga (1968, 11–2), in particular, emphasizes the anti-baroque position of the Dutch Republic
14. Fuchs (1978, 45–6). The term 'genre' to describe this Dutch school was coined in the late 18th century to mean outside the 'High Tradition' (p. 42). Mukerji (1983, 78) refers to 'the little tradition', an artistic rebellion against 'the Great Tradition'
15. Fuchs (1978, 40–1)
16. Levey (1969, 9) states that Rembrandt was the only major 17th-century artist not to have visited Italy. Fuchs (1978, 43) lists six other major Dutch artists as well as Rembrandt who never visited Italy. One of them was Jan Steen whom Sir Joshua Reynolds called an

'extraordinary man' but who, so Reynolds argued, failed to reach greatness because he lived in Leiden rather than Rome and therefore painted vulgar subjects instead of elevated ones – a typical 'High Tradition' assessment (pp. 42–3)

17. Fuchs (1978, 62)
18. Gombrich (1989, 288)
19. Gombrich (1989, 295)
20. Gombrich (1989, 328); Fuchs (1978, 43). This market was based upon large sales to middle- and lower-class consumers (Price, 1974, 122); there are reports of quite modest households owning 100 or even 200 paintings (p. 134). Of course, the Orange family court favoured baroque painting (Price, 1974, 123–5)
21. Nussbaum (1953, 50); Price (1974, 119) argues that 'the roots of this originality and uniqueness lay in the nature of seventeenth century Dutch society'. In a similar vein, Israel (1995b, 562) states:

> The art and artists of the Golden Age captured the whole of the physical, social, and cultural reality surrounding the Dutch burgher of the day, depicting his own household and civic world, the rural surroundings, and also what surrounded that — the soldiers, on the landward side, and ships and the sea on the other

Paintings of everyday life were not a Dutch monopoly, their Flemish roots led to some similar developments in other Hapsburg territories, but the Dutch were unique in the quantity and variety of production (Mukerji, 1983, 71). One estimate puts the number of paintings in Holland in 1650 at two and a half million (Israel, 1995b, 555)

22. The reference here is to Steen's *The Life of Man* (Fuchs, 1978, 41)
23. Gombrich (1989, 339); in general 'the sheer insignificance of the subject matter' of Dutch painting surprised foreigners (Price, 1974, 127)
24. Gombrich (1989, 339); he concludes in a very modern way: 'Just as trivial words may provide the text for a beautiful song, so trivial objects can make a perfect picture.'
25. Watt (1972, 39) estimates this to have been about 80 000 persons in 1790
26. Watt (1972, 40 and 64)
27. Watt (1972, 40)
28. Watt (1972, 48)
29. Watt (1972, 10)
30. Watt (1972, 10)
31. Watt (1972, 14)
32. Allen (1958, 139)
33. Allen (1958, 145); the 1840s even spawned a 'genre' of Manchester novels (Briggs, 1963, 93)
34. Allen (1958, 145)
35. Armstrong (1987, 8)
36. Armstrong (1987, 9)
37. Tomlinson (1976, 14)
38. 'Writers seem to have concentrated their feelings in private rather than in public discourse' (Tomlinson, 1976, 15)
39. Lukacs (1993, 273)
40. In 1948 Hollywood still enjoyed 'wild success' due to a backlog of demand after the war years: 432 films were produced in a single year (Lloyd, 1986, 204)
41. Lloyd (1986, 230)
42. Lloyd (1986, 244) calls this 'full blooded consumerism'
43. Taylor (1982, 84)
44. Taylor (1982, 84)
45. Taylor (1982, 84)
46. Taylor (1982, 84)
47. Lloyd (1986, 253)
48. Lloyd (1986, 253) goes on to argue that they stood for the idea of normality, the reigning idea of the times
49. Lloyd (1986, 253)
50. Giddens (1990, 7); it is relevant to the argument developed here that intellectual forebodings about modernity in the 20th century have not been shared by most ordinary people; see Nisbet (1980, chapter 8) on the continuing popularity of the idea of progress

51. Toulmin (1990)
52. Giddens (1990, chapter 3)
53. Giedion (1948, 3) in his 'inquiry into the rise of our modern way of life' refers directly to the 'rise of our way of life, of our comfort'
54. Rybczynski (1986, 231); see also Giedion (1948, 260) on 'the changing concept of comfort'
55. 'From today's point of view the Middle Ages had no comfort at all' (Giedion, 1948, 299)
56. Galbraith (1992) implies the same division in his concept of the culture of contentment
57. Rybczynski (1986, 25)
58. Of course, like all modernities, this one is full of contradictions. Allan and Crow (1989, chapter 1) describe home as 'a private place', 'a place of security, control and freedom', and 'a place of creativity and expression'. Clearly, privacy provides opportunities for both freedom and repression. It is, of course, the locus of modern patriarchal relations in the family (Williams, 1987)
59. Rybczynski (1986, 51)
60. Rybczynski (1986, 52) refers to 'the peculiar character of the Dutch social fabric, which was different from that of the rest of Europe'
61. Four or five persons per house (Rybczynski, 1986, 59)
62. 'It was the opinion of more than one contemporary visitor that the Dutch prized three things above all else: first their children, second their homes, and third their gardens' (Rybczynski, 1986, 60)
63. 'This boundary was a new idea . . . a desire to define the home as a separate, special place' (Rybczynski, 1986, 66)
64. Rybczynski (1986, 61); the Dutch were so proud of their houses they had scale models made of them which should not be confused with doll's houses (p. 62)
65. 'The importance accorded the kitchen reflected the central position of the women in the Dutch household' (Rybczynski, 1986, 73)
66. 'The feminization of the home in seventeenth century Holland was one of the most important events in the evolution of the domestic interior' (Rybczynski, 1986, 72)
67. On the limited influence of the British royal family in the 18th century see Colley's (1992, 196–204) discussion of 'a royal culture confined'. By the time of the Great Exhibition in 1851, one contemporary essayist could observe that:

    > While England has been devoting nearly all its efforts to the mere comfort of the million, France has expended its energies, for the most part, over luxuries for the few (Wornum, 1970, VII***)

68. Rybczynski (1986, 115–16) describes the Windsor chair as: 'Inexpensive and practical, well proportioned and gracious, it was the epitome of English comfort and common sense.'
69. 'The home became a place of leisure' (Rybczynski, 1986, 107)
70. Rybczynski (1986, 112)
71. Rybczynski (1986, 116)
72. Rybczynski (1986, 118) refers to this as 'a landmark moment in the evolution of domestic comfort'
73. Thompson (1990, chapters 2 and 3)
74. Bagehot (1963, 85). Horne (1970, 51) defines the 'Victorian metaphor' in terms of morality and conformity and it was definitely 'not heroic'. Briggs (1988) has been able to write a wonderful book on 'Victorian things' as 'ordinary and typical'; he is consciously following in the footsteps of 'collectors' of all manner of everyday things which began in Victorian Britain (p. 29)
75. Nairn (1988) is very good on this process and its history
76. Howe (1976, 3)
77. Rybczynski (1986, 140)
78. Rybczynski (1986, 148)
79. According to Giedion (1948, 515), this was a particular problem for the USA where a paradox was thought to exist between democracy and servants
80. Rybczynski (1986, 150–1)
81. Rybczynski (1986, 143)

82. It also had no bathrooms (Rybczynski, 1986, 143)
83. Rybczynski (1986, 150)
84. Rybczynski (1986, 158). Giedion (1948, 512) refers to this as the 'enfranchisement of the housewife' producing the 'American woman' (ie with no servants) (p. 515)
85. Rybczynski (1986, 153). See also Giedion (1948, Part VI) on 'Mechanization encounters the household'
86. In 1927 there were 17 million homes with electricity in the USA, over three-quarters of which had electric irons and over half vacuum cleaners (Rybczynski, 1986, 153)
87. Rybczynski (1986, 164). See also Giedion (1948, Part VII) on 'The mechanization of the bath'
88. Gowans (1986, xiv)
89. Gowans (1986, 13)
90. Gowans (1986, 48)
91. Gowans (1986, 52); of course stimulating home ownership boosted Sears' mainstream business
92. Gowans (1986, xv)
93. Fishman (1987, 146–7)
94. Fishman (1987, 116)
95. Fishman (1987, chapter 3)
96. Fishman (1987, 129)
97. Hall (1988, 294)
98. Fishman (1987, chapter 6)
99. Fishman (1987, 166)
100. Hall (1988, 295)
101. Hall (1988, 295)
102. Gans (1967, 37)
103. Gans (1967, 39)
104. Fishman (1987, chapter 4) shows how state sponsorship of urban development enabled the European bourgeoisie to find their comfort in the city.
105. Fishman (1987, 4); Gowans (1986, 3) refers to suburbs as 'the greatest declaration of wealth and power of all'
106. The poem is reproduced in Hall (1988, 73)
107. Gans (1967, v)
108. Hall (1988, 79)
109. Fishman (1987, ix)
110. Hall (1988, 297)
111. Fishman (1987, 156) refers to 'the puzzled amazement of European students'
112. Le Corbusier made this statement right at the beginning of his career (Hall, 1988, 206–7)
113. Hall (1988, 207)
114. 'The Corbusian ideal city' is described by Hall (1988, 207–12)
115. Richards (1940, 107); Robert Hughes (1991, 190) refers to 'the extreme monasticism of the Unité' with 'little privacy in this nobly articulated beehive of raw concrete'
116. Hughes (1991, 190)
117. Hall (1988, 210) and see Richards (1940, 153) diagram 'Flats at Marseilles'
118. Hughes (1991, 190)
119. Harvey (1989, 36)
120. Richards (1940, 84)
121. Curiously experts have tried to assimilate comfort to their modernist ideal: 'I think that comfort is a function of whether you think a chair is good-looking or not.' Rybczyynski (1986, 211) refers to such sentiments as charming naïvety about 'the power of art to overcome physical reality'. He also quotes a more honest architect's position:

    > I like [the chairs] in an intellectual way. They aren't awfully comfortable to sit on, although of course you can sit in them for an hour or so without danger of collapse

122. Jameson (1991); Harvey (1989)
123. 'What is needed is a reexamination not of bourgeois styles, but of bourgeois traditions' (Rybczyynski, 1986, 221)

124. Rybczyynski (1986, 220)
125. Fishman (1987, ix)
126. Fishman (1987, x)
127. See debates in Jones et al (1993)
128. Giddens (1994, 83)
129. Giddens (1994, 6)
130. Giddens (1994, 85)
131. Giddens (1994, 84)
132. Giddens (1994, 7)
133. Giddens (1994) does not use the term 'high hegemony' in his discussion of post-tradition but it is a phrase he has used in an earlier discussion of contemporary modernity (Giddens, 1990)
134. Hence his turn to 'philosophic conservatism' (Giddens, 1994, 10)
135. Wallerstein (1991b, chapter 14)
136. Huntington (1993)
137. In the debate that followed Huntington's paper, Ajami (1993) argues this point
138. It can be interpreted as the latest version of Orientalism
139. Eckersley (1992, 8); for a critique of this position, see Pepper (1993, chapter 1)
140. O'Riordan (1981); Pepper (1993, 33–4)
141. Their key concept is sustainable development (Adams, 1990, chapters 2 and 3)
142. O'Riordan (1981); Pepper (1993, 33)
143. Amin (1982)
144. Wallerstein (1984)
145. Galbraith (1992)
146. Korten (1990, 1)
147. The absurdity of the idea is not based upon historical precedence: Nowak (1983) points out that past transitions have been about conflict within the ruling class, not overthrow from below. I am indebted to Andre Gunder Frank for reference to this source
148. Davis (1990, 160)
149. Davis (1990, 169–70)
150. Davis (1990, 156)
151. This was a general recognition that, after all, 'the universalization of the suburban ideal' was impossible (Fishman, 1987, 157)
152. 'I believe that the ecological crisis will bring about the end of capitalism' (Bahro, 1984, 11); see general discussions in Pepper (1993, chapter 5) and Adams (1990, chapter 4)
153. The British Greens obtained 14.9% of the national vote compared with 8.4% for the more established German Greens. The average Green vote across the European Community was 7.7% (Curtice, 1989, Table 3)
154. There were six Euro-constituencies where the Greens came second to the Conservatives: Devon, Dorset East and Hampshire West, Somerset and Dorset West, Surrey West, Sussex West, and the Cotswolds. (In addition they were within a few votes of coming second in two other Euro-constituencies: Sussex East and Wiltshire.) These areas define a broad zone south and west of London in which fears of 'overdevelopment' were a major political issue
155. Davis (1990, 209)
156. Brooks (1974, 126)
157. Hardin's key papers (1977a and b) are reproduced in Hardin and Baden (1977) which is the source I use here although they were originally published in 1968 and 1974 on the commons metaphor and the lifeboat metaphor respectively
158. Hardin (1977a, 19–21)
159. Hardin (1977a, 23)
160. Hardin's (1977b, 263) examples of such ethics are 'the Christian ideal of being "our brother's keeper" ' and 'the Marxist ideal of . . . to each according to his needs'
161. 'Complete justice, complete catastrophe' (Harden (1977b, 263)
162. Hardin (1977a, 22)
163. Pepper (1984, 204–13)
164. Hardin (1977b, 277)

165. Hardin (1977a, 26): 'mutual coercion mutually agreed upon'
166. Quoted by Pepper (1984, 210). For a general discussion of the Fascist roots of green politics, see Bramwell (1989)
167. Pepper (1984, 210)
168. 'Every life saved this year in a poor country diminishes the quality of life for subsequent generations' (Hardin (1977b, 272))
169. King (1990)
170. King (1990, 666–7)
171. Hardin (1977b, 264)
172. Hardin (1977a, 25)
173. My concept is essentially the same as the idea of 'voluntary simplicity' with its credo 'to live simply so others can simply live' (Little, 1995, 132). See also Gregg (1977) and Elgin (1981). I am indebted to Susan Place and Ben Wisner for these references and for pointing out the similarity between the two concepts
174. Huntington (1993)
175. Friberg and Hettne (1985, 231) reject both 'red' and 'blue' developmentalism
176. The nation-state is seen as 'one of the greatest obstacles' by Friberg and Hettne (1985, 237)
177. Friberg and Hettne (1985, 248)
178. Friberg and Hettne (1985, 253)
179. Friberg and Hettne (1985, 218)
180. Naess (1989, 88); he claims to have invented the concept of 'deep ecology' in 1973 (p. 27)
181. Naess (1989, 88)
182. Naess (1989, 88)
183. Naess (1989, 9)
184. Naess (1989, 38) defines ecosophy as 'a philosophical world-view or system inspired by the conditions of life in the ecosphere'
185. Naess (1989, 38)
186. Naess (1989, 80): ' "finding oneself", not in isolation, but in deep connection to all that surrounds'
187. Taylor (1986, 91)
188. Taylor (1986, 45)
189. Taylor (1986, 14–25)
190. Taylor (1986, 101–16)
191. Taylor (1986, 152); elsewhere he refers to 'the principle of species impartiality' (p. 45) and 'the vanity of the claim of human superiority' (p. 113); Eckersley (1992, 56) criticizes the 'ideology of human chauvinism'
192. Taylor (1986, 115); he goes on to suggest the rest of the Community of Life would shout 'a hearty "Good riddance!" ' if our species were to disappear
193. Taylor (1986, 101)
194. Eckersley (1992, 53)
195. Eckersley (1992, 56)
196. Eckersley (1992, 2); this is analysed by David Ehrenfeld (1978) as 'the arrogance of humanism'
197. For instance, the promotion of questioning and criticizing as in scientific endeavour and the subtle understandings of the humanities (Eckersley, 1992, 57)
198. Eckersley (1992, 57)
199. Naess (1989, 95)
200. Naess (1989, 97)
201. Braudel (1981)
202. Wallerstein (1982, 51)
203.
    'We are more aware of historical time than was any previous generation in the history of mankind. This is the outcome of the development of historical consciousness, one of the most important and least recognized developments of the Modern Age' (Lukacs, 1993, 281)

Bibliography

Adams, J. 1994: Trading states, trading places: the role of patrimonialism in early modern Dutch development. *Comparative Studies in Society and History*, 36, 319–55

Adams, W.M. 1990: *Green Development*. London: Routledge

Adler, L. K. and Paterson, T. G. 1970: Red fascism: the merger between Nazi Germany and Soviet Russia in the American image of totalitarianism, 1930s–1950s. *American Historical Review*, 75, 1046–64

Ajami. F. 1993: The Summoning. *Foreign Affairs*, 72 (4), 1–9

Aldridge, A. O. 1975: *Voltaire and the Century of Light*. Princeton, NJ: Princeton University Press

Allan, G. and Crow, G. (eds) 1989: *Home and Family. Creating the Domestic Sphere*. London: Macmillan

Allen, P. 1992: *The Atlas of Atlases*. New York: Abrams

Allen, W. 1958: *The English Novel*. London: Penguin

Amin, S. 1982: Crisis, nationalism and socialism. In S. Amin, G. Arrighi, A.G. Frank and I. Wallerstein, *Dynamics of Global Crisis*. New York: Monthly Review Press

Anderson, M. S. 1985: *The Ascendancy of Europe 1815–1914*. London: Longman

Anderson, M. S. 1993: *The Rise of Modern Diplomacy 1450–1919*. London: Longman

Andreski, S. 1972: *Social Science as Sorcery*. London: Penguin

Arblaster, A. 1984: *The Rise and Decline of Western Liberalism*. Oxford: Blackwell

Ardant, G. 1975: Financial policy and economic infrastructure of modern states and nations. In C. Tilly (ed.), *The Formation of National States in Western Europe*. Princeton, NJ: Princeton University Press

Armstrong, N. 1987: *Desire and Domestic Fiction. A Political History of the Novel*. New York: Oxford University Press

Arrighi, G. 1990: The three hegemonies of historical capitalism. *Review*, 13, 365–408

Arrighi, G. 1994: *The Long Twentieth Century*. London: Verso

Ashley, R. K. 1988: Untying the sovereign state: a double reading of the anarchy problematique. *Millennium*, 17, 227–62

Bagehot, W. 1963: *The English Constitution*. London: Fontana

Bahro, R. 1984: *From Red to Green*. London: Verso

Baker, J. N. L. 1955: The geography of Bernhard Varenius. *Transactions of the Institute of British Geographers*, 21, 51–60

Barbour, V. 1963: *Capitalism in Amsterdam in the Seventeenth Century*. Ann Arbor: University of Michigan Press

Bartlett, C. J. 1969: *The Crystal Palace 1851–1936: a Portrait of Victorian Enterprise*. London: Evelyn

Bartlett, C. J. 1984: *The Global Conflict, 1880–1970*. London: Longman

Bath, B. H. S. van 1960: The rise of intensive husbandry in the Low Countries. In J. S. Bromley and E. H. Kossmann (eds), *Britain and the Netherlands*. London: Chatto and Windus

Beaver, P. 1970: *The Crystal Palace 1851–1936*. London: Evelyn

Bekker, K. 1952: The Point IV Program of the United States. In B. F. Hoselitz (ed.), *The Progress of Underdeveloped Areas*. Chicago: Chicago University Press

Bell, D. 1961: *The End of Ideology*. New York: Free Press

Bellamy, R. 1992: *Liberalism and Modern Society*. Cambridge, UK: Polity
Beloff, M. 1954: *The Age of Absolutism 1660–1815*. London: Hutchinson
Berman, M. 1988: *All that is Solid Melts into Air: the Experience of Modernity*. New York: Penguin
Berry, M., Maude, G. and Schuchalter, J. 1990: *Frontiers of American Political Experience*. Turku: Turan Yliopisto
Billington, J. H. 1980: *Fire in the Minds of Men*. London: Temple Smith
Bird, A. 1976: *Paxton's Palace*. London: Cassell
Black, E. R. 1964: So hopeful a challenge. In G. Hambridge (ed.), *Dynamics of Development*. New York: Praeger
Blaut, J. M. 1993: *The Colonizer's Model of the World*. New York: Guilford
Blaug, M. 1978: *Economic Theory in Retrospect*. Cambridge, UK: Cambridge University Press
Bocock, R. 1986: *Hegemony*. London: Tavistock
Boogman, J. C. 1978: The *raison d'état* politician Johan de Witt. *Low Countries History Yearbook*, 1978, 55–78
Boogman, J. C. 1979: The Union of Utrecht: its genesis and consequences. *Bijdragen Mededlingen Detreffende de Geschiedenis der Nederlanden*, 94, 277–407
Bourne, K. 1970: *The Foreign Policy of Victorian England, 1830–1902*. Oxford: Clarendon
Bousquet, N. 1980: From hegemony to competition: cycles of the core? In T.K. Hopkins and I. Wallerstein (eds), *Processes of the World-System*. Beverly Hills, CA: Sage
Boxer, C. R. 1965: *The Dutch Seaborne Empire 1600–1800*. London: Hutchinson
Bramwell, A. 1989: *Ecology in the Twentieth Century. A History*. New Haven, CT: Yale University Press
Braudel, F. 1981: *The Structures of Everyday Life*. London: Collins
Braudel, F. 1984: *The Perspective of the World*. London: Collins
Brewer, A. 1980: *Marxist Theories of Imperialism*. London: Routledge and Kegan Paul
Briggs, A. 1963: *Victorian Cities*. London: Penguin
Briggs, A. 1988: *Victorian Things*. London: Batsford
Brogan, D. 1966: Introduction. In S. C. Burchill, *Age of Progress*. New York: Time-Life Books
Brookfield, H. C. 1975: *Interdependent Development*. London: Methuen
Brooks, E. 1974: The implications of ecological limits to development in terms of expectations and aspirations in developed and less developed countries. In A. Vann and P. Rogers (eds), *Human Ecology and World Development*. London: Plenum
Brown, P. G. 1981: Introduction. In P. G. Brown and H. Shue (eds), *Boundaries. National Autonomy and its Limits*. Totowa, NJ: Rowman and Littlefield
Brucan, S. 1981: The strategy of development in Eastern Europe. *Review*, 5, 95–112
Bull, H. 1990: The importance of Grotius and the study of International Relations. In H. Bull, B. Kingsbury and A. Roberts (eds), *Hugo Grotius and International Relations*. Oxford: Clarendon
Bull, H. and Watson, A. (eds) 1984: *The Expansion of International Society*. Oxford: Clarendon
Bullock, A. 1983: *Ernest Bevin: Foreign Secretary*. London: Heinemann
Bulpitt, J. 1986: The discipline of the new democracy: Mrs Thatcher's domestic statecraft. *Political Studies*, 34, 95–112
Burchill, S. C. 1966: *Age of Progress*. New York: Time-Life
Burke, P. 1974: *Venice and Amsterdam. A Study of Seventeenth Century Cities*. London: Temple Smith
Burke, P. 1986: The city state. In J. Hall (ed.), *States in History*. Oxford: Blackwell
Bury, J. B.. 1920: *The Idea of Progress*. London: Methuen
Butterfield, H. 1931: *The Whig Interpretation of History*. London: Bell
Cain, P. J. and Hopkins, A. G. 1986: Gentlemanly capitalism and British expansion overseas. I The old colonial system, 1688–1850. *Economic History Review*, 34, 501–25
Cain, P. J. and Hopkins, A. G. 1987: Gentlemanly capitalism and British expansion overseas. II The new imperialism, 1850–1945. *Economic History Review*, 35, 1–26
Carr, E. H. 1939: *The Twenty Years Crisis 1919–1939*. London: Macmillan
Carr, E.H. 1961: *What is History?* London: Macmillan
Castells, M. and Hall, P. 1994: *The Technopoles of the World. The Making of 21st Century Industrial Complexes*. London: Routledge
Caton, H. 1988: *The Politics of Progress*. Gainseville: University of Florida Press
Cauter, de L. 1993: The panoramic ecstasy; on world exhibitions and the disintegration of experience. *Theory, Culture and Society*, 10, 1–23

Chandler, T. and Fox, G. 1974: *3,000 Years of Urban Growth*. New York: Academic Press
Chandra, B. 1981: Karl Marx, his theories of Asian societies and colonial rule. *Review*, 5, 13–94
Chase-Dunn, C. (ed.) 1982: *Socialist States in the World-System*. Beverly Hills, CA: Sage
Chase-Dunn, C. 1989: *Global Formation*. Oxford: Blackwell
Chase-Dunn, C. 1990: World-state formation: historical processes and emergent necessity. *Political Geography Quarterly*, 9, 108–30
Chekki, D. A. 1987: *American Sociological Hegemony*. New York: University Press of America
Chetley, J. 1979: *The Baby Milk Scandal*. London: War on Want
Clark, I. 1989: *The Hierarchy of States. Reform and Resistance in the International Order*. Cambridge, UK: Cambridge University Press
Clarke, I. F. 1979: *The Pattern of Expectation, 1644–2001*. London: Cape
Cole, H. S. D., Freeman, C., Jahoda, M. and Pavitt, K. L. R. 1973: *Thinking about the Future. A Critique of The Limits to Growth*. London: Chatto and Windus
Coleman, D. C. 1969: Editor's introduction. In D. C. Coleman (ed.), *Revisions in Mercantilism*. London: Methuen
Coleman, D. C. 1973: Gentlemen and players. *Economic History Review*, 26, 92–116
Coleman, P. 1989: *The Liberal Conspiracy. The Congress for Cultural Freedom and the Struggle for the Mind of Postwar Europe*. New York: Free Press
Colley, L. 1992: *Britons*. New Haven, CT: Yale University Press
Collier, P. and Horowitz, D. 1976: *The Rockefellers: an American Dynasty*. New York: Holt, Rinehart and Winston
Collins, I. 1957: *Liberalism in Nineteenth Century Europe*. London: History Association
Connell, R. W. 1990: Notes on American sociology and American power. In H. J. Gans (ed.), *Sociology in America*. Newbury Park, CA: Sage
Cooper, J. P. 1970: General introduction. In J. P. Cooper (ed.), *The Decline of Spain and the Thirty Years War 1609–48/59*. Cambridge, UK: Cambridge University Press
Coplin, W. D. 1968: International law and assumptions about the state system. In R. Falk and W. F. Hanrieder (eds), *International Law and Organization*. Philadelphia: Lippincott
Cotterell, G. 1972: *Amsterdam. The Life of a City*. Boston: Little, Brown
de la Court, P. 1972: *The True Interest and Political Maxims of the Republic of Holland*. New York: Arno
Crossman, R. H. S. 1963: Introduction. In W. Bagehot, *The English Constitution*. London: Fontana
Culler, A. D. 1985: *The Victorian Mirror of History*. New Haven, CT: Yale University Press
Curtice, J. 1989: The European election: protest or Green tide? *Electoral Studies*, 8, 217–30
Daly, H. E. 1977: *Steady-state Economics*. New York: Freeman
Dangerfield, G. 1936: *The Strange Death of Liberal England*. London: Constable
Davidson, B. 1993: *The Black Man's Burden*. New York: Times Books
Davis, M. 1990: *City of Quartz*. London: Verso
Deane, P. 1978: *The Evolution of Economic Ideas*. Cambridge, UK: Cambridge University Press
Dearlove, J. and Saunders, P. 1984: *Introduction to British Politics*. Cambridge, UK: Polity
Delderfield, R. F. 1970: *God is an Englishman*. New York: Simon and Schuster
Dowdall, H. C. 1923: The word 'state'. *Law Quarterly Review*, 39, 98–125
Duke, A. 1990: *Reform and Revolt in the Low Countries*. London: Hambledon
Dunning, W. A. 1905: *A History of Political Theories from Luther to Montesquieu*. London: Macmillan
Dyos, H. J. 1971: Greater and greater London. In J. S. Bromley and E. H. Kossmann (eds), *Britain and the Netherlands*. The Hague: Martinus Nijhoff
Dyson, K. H. F. 1980: *The State Tradition in Western Europe*. Oxford: Robertson
Eckersley, R. 1992: *Environmentalism and Political Theory*. London: UCL Press
Edwards, C. S. 1981: *Hugo Grotius. The Miracle of Holland*. Chicago: Nelson Hall
Ehrenfeld, D.W. 1978: *The Arrogance of Humanism*. New York: Oxford University Press
Ehrenreich, B. 1989: *Fear of Falling*. New York: Pantheon
Ehrlich, P. R. 1972: *The Population Bomb*. London: Ballantine
Ekins, P. 1992: *A New World Order*. London: Routledge
Elgin, D. 1981: *Voluntary Simplicity; Toward a Way of Life that is Outwardly Simple*. New York: Morrow

Elliot, J. H. 1989: *Spain and its Empire, 1500–1700*. New Haven, CT: Yale University Press

Fallows, J. 1989: *More Like Us. Making America Great Again*. Boston: Houghton Mifflin

Fielden, K. 1969: The rise and fall of free trade. In C. J. Bartlett (ed.), *Britain Pre-eminent*. London: Macmillan

Figgis, J. N. 1916: *Studies in Political Thought: from Gerson to Grotius*. Cambridge, UK: Cambridge University Press

Fishman, R. 1987: *Bourgeois Utopias. The Rise and Fall of Suburbia*. New York: Basic

FitzSimmons, L. 1972: *The Kennedy Doctrine*. New York: Random House

Fossum, R. H. and Roth, J. K. 1981: *The American Dream*. London: British Association for American Studies

Fox, R. W. and Lears, T. J. J. 1983: Introduction. In R. W. Fox and T. J. J. Lears (eds), *The Culture of Consumption*. New York: Pantheon

Frank, A. G. 1980: *Crisis in the World Economy*. London: Heinemann

Frank, A. G. and Gills, B. K. (eds) 1993: *The World System. Five Hundred Years or Five Thousand?* London: Routledge

Friberg, M. and Hettne, B. 1985: The greening of the world: towards a non-deterministic model of global processes. In H. Addo et al (eds) *Development as Social Transformation*. Sevenoaks, UK: Hodder and Stoughton

Friedberg, A. L. 1988: *The Weary Titan: Britain and the Experience of Relative Decline*. Princeton, NJ: Princeton University Press

Friedman, G. 1991: *The Coming War with Japan*. New York: St Martin's Press

Friedmann, J. 1986: The world city hypothesis. *Development and Change*, 17, 69–83

Fuchs, R.H. 1978: *Dutch Painting*. London: Thames and Hudson

Fulbright, J.W. 1966: *The Arrogance of Power*. London: Cape

Furley, O. 1969: The humanitarian impact. In C. J. Bartlett (ed.), *Britain Pre-eminent*. London: Macmillan

Gaddis, J. L. 1982: *Strategies of Containment*. New York: Oxford University Press

Gaddis, J. L. 1987: *The Long Peace*. New York: Oxford University Press

Galbraith, J. K. 1958: *The Affluent Society*. London: Penguin

Galbraith, J. K. 1992: *The Culture of Contentment*. Boston: Houghton Mifflin

Galbraith, J. K. 1993: *A Short History of Financial Euphoria*. New York: Whittle

Gallie, W. B. 1978: *Philosophers of Peace and War*. Cambridge, UK: Cambridge University Press

Gans, H. J. 1967: *The Levittowners*. London: Penguin

Gendzier, I. L. 1985: *Managing Political Change. Social Scientists and the Third World*. Boulder, Co: Westview

Gibbs-Smith, C. H. 1981: *The Great Exhibition of 1851*. London: HMSO

Giddens, A. 1985: *The Nation-State and Violence*. Cambridge, UK: Polity

Giddens, A. 1990: *The Consequencies of Modernity*. Cambridge, UK: Polity

Giddens, A. 1994: *Beyond Left and Right. The Future of Radical Politics*. Cambridge, UK: Polity

Giedion, S. 1948: *Mechanization takes Command: a Contribution to Anonymous History*. New York: Oxford University Press

Gilpin, R. 1987: *The Political Economy of International Relations*. Princeton, NJ: Princeton University Press

Gombrich, E. H. 1989: *The Story of Art*. Oxford: Phaidon

Gorski, P. S. 1993: The Protestant ethic revisited: disciplinary revolution and state formation in Holland and Prussia. *American Journal of Sociology*, 99, 265–316

Gottmann J. 1973: *The Significance of Territory*. Charlottesville, VA: University Press of Virginia

Gough, B. M. 1990: *Pax Britannica*: peace, force and world power. *Round Table*, 314, 167–88

Gouldner, A. W. 1971: *The Coming Crisis of Western Sociology*. New York: Basic Books

Gowans, A. 1986: *The Comfortable House. North American Suburban Architecture 1890–1930*. Cambridge, MA: MIT Press

Grainger, J. H. 1986: *Patriotism. Britain 1900–39*. London: Routledge and Kegan Paul

Grampp, W. D. 1960: *The Manchester School of Economics*. Stanford, CA: Stanford University Press

Greenhalgh, P. 1988: *Ephemeral Vistas*. Manchester, UK: Manchester University Press

Gregg, R. 1977: Voluntary simplicity. *CoEvolution Quarterly*, Summer, 20–7

Gross, L. 1968: The Peace of Westphalia, 1648–1948. In R. A. Falk and W. F. Hanrieder (eds), *International Law and Organization*. Philadelphia: Lippincott

Haber, D. L. 1990: The death of hegemony. Why 'Pax Nipponica' is impossible. *Asian Survey*, 30, 892–907

Habermas, J. 1983: Modernity: an incomplete project. In H. Foster (ed.), *The Anti-Aesthetic: Essays on Postmodern Culture*. Port Townsend, WA: Bay Press

Haley, K. H. D. 1988: *The British and the Dutch*. London: George Philip

Hall, J. A. and Ikenberry, G. J. 1989: *The State*. Cambridge, UK: Polity

Hall, P. 1988: *Cities of Tomorrow*. Oxford: Blackwell

Halle, D. 1984: *America's Working Man*. Chicago: Chicago University Press

Hardin, G. 1977a: The tragedy of the commons. In G. Hardin and J. Baden (eds), *Managing the Commons*. San Francisco: Freeman, 16–30

Hardin, G. 1977b: Living on a lifeboat. In G. Hardin and J. Baden (eds), *Managing the Commons*. San Francisco: Freeman, 261–79

Harvey, A. D. 1978: *Britain in the Early Nineteenth Century*. London: Batsford

Harvey, D. 1989: *The Condition of Postmodernity*. Oxford: Blackwell

Hathaway, R. M. 1981: *Ambiguous Partnership: Britain and America, 1944–1947*. New York: Columbia University Press

Hayek, F. A. 1975: Liberalism. In A. de Crespigny and J. Cronin (eds), *Ideologies of Politics*. London: Oxford University Press

Heckscher, E. F. 1955: *Mercantilism* (second edition). London: George Allen and Unwin

Heckscher, E. F. 1969: *Mercantilism*. In D. C. Coleman (ed.), *Revisions in Mercantilism*. London: Methuen

Herz, J. H. 1959: *International Politics in the Atomic Age*. New York: Columbia University Press

Hinde, W. 1987: *Richard Cobden. A Victorian Outsider*. New Haven, CT: Yale University Press

Hinsley, F. H. 1982: The rise and fall of the modern international system. *Review of International Studies*, 8, 1–8

Hoare, Q. and Smith, G. N. (eds) 1971: *Selections from the Prison Notebooks of Antonio Gramsci*. London: Lawrence and Wishart

Hobsbawm, E. H. 1967: The crisis of the seventeenth century. In T. Aston (ed.), *Crisis in Europe, 1560–1660*. New York: Doubleday

Hobsbawm, E. and Ranger, T. (eds) 1983: *The Invention of Tradition*. Cambridge, UK: Cambridge University Press

Hobson, J. A. 1919: *Richard Cobden. The International Man*. London: Ernest Benn

Hoffman, P. G. 1962: *World without Want*. Westport, CT: Greenwood

Hofstadter, R. 1959: *Social Darwinism in American Thought*. New York: Braziller

Hogan, M. J. 1987: *The Marshall Plan. America, Britain and the Reconstruction of Western Europe, 1947–1952*. Cambridge, UK: Cambridge University Press

Holsti, K. J. 1991: *Peace and War: Armed Conflicts and International Order 1648–1989*. Cambridge, UK: Cambridge University Press

Hopkins, T. K. 1990: A note on the concept of hegemony. *Review*, 13, 409–12

Horne, D. 1970: *God is an Englishman*. Sydney: Angus and Robertson

Horowitz, I. L. 1967: The rise and fall of Project Camelot. In I. L. Horowitz (ed.), *The Rise and Fall of Project Camelot*. Cambridge, MA: MIT Press

Howe, D. W. 1976: Victorian culture in America. In D. W. Howe (ed.), *Victorian America*. Philadelphia: University of Pennsylvania Press

Hughes, R. 1991: *The Shock of the New* (second edition). London: Thames and Hudson

Huizinga, J. H. 1968: *Dutch Civilization in the Seventeenth Century and Other Essays*. London: Collins

Huntington, S. P. 1993: The clash of civilizations. *Foreign affairs*. 72(3) 22–49

Hyam, R. 1976: *Britain's Imperial Century 1815–1914*. London: Batsford

Hynes, S. 1968: *The Edwardian Turn of Mind*. Princeton, NJ: Princeton University Press

Ikenberry, G. J. 1989: Rethinking the origins of American hegemony. *Political Studies Quarterly*, 104, 375–400

Inkeles, A. and Smith, D. H. 1974: *Becoming Modern*. Cambridge, MA: Harvard University Press

Isaacson, W. and Thomas, E. 1986: *The Wise Men. Six Friends and the World They Made*. London: Faber and Faber

Israel, J. I. 1982: *The Dutch Republic and the Hispanic World, 1606–1661*. Oxford, UK: Clarendon

Israel, J. I. 1989: *Dutch Primacy in World Trade, 1585–1740.* Oxford: Clarendon
Israel, J. I. 1990: *Empires and Entrepots.* London: Hambledon
Israel, J. I. 1995a: Innovation in Dutch cities. *History Today,* 45(3), 14–20
Israel, J. I. 1995b: *The Dutch Republic. Its Rise, Greatness and Fall 1477–1806.* Oxford: Clarendon
    Press
Jackson, R. H. 1990: *Quasi-states: Sovereignty, International Relations and the Third World.*
    Cambridge, UK: Cambridge University Press
Jacob, M. C. and Mijnhardt W. W. 1992: Introduction. In M. C. Jacob and W. W. Mijnhardt
    (eds), *The Dutch Republic in the Eighteenth Century.* Ithaca, NY: Cornell University Press
James, A. 1984: Sovereignty: ground rule or gibberish? *Review of International Studies,* 10, 1–18
Jameson, F. 1991: *Postmodernism, or the Cultural Logic of Late Capitalism.* Durham, NC: Duke
    University Press
Jessop, B. 1982: *The Capitalist State.* Oxford: Robertson
Johnson, R. W. 1985: *The Politics of Recession.* London: Macmillan
Johnson, P. 1991: *The Birth of the Modern. World Society 1815–1830.* London: Weidenfeld and
    Nicolson
Jones, J. P., Natter, W. and Schatzki, T. R. (eds) 1993: *Postmodern Contentions.* New York:
    Guilford
Jordan, R. F. 1963: Sir Joseph Paxton. In P. Ferriday (ed.), *Victorian Architecture.* London:
    Jonathan Cape
Judis, J. B. 1992: *Grand Illusion.* New York: Farrar, Straus and Giroux
Kabbani, R. 1988: *Europe's Myth of the Orient.* London: Pandora
Kain, R. J. P. and Baigent, E. 1984: *The Cadastral Map in the Service of the State.* Chicago: Chicago
    University Press
Kennedy, P. 1987: *The Rise and Fall of the Great Powers.* New York: Random House
Kindleberger, C. P. 1973: *The World in Depression, 1929–1939.* Berkeley, CA: University of
    California Press
King, M. 1990: Health is a sustainable state. *The Lancet,* 336, September 15, 664–7
Kochan, L. 1971: *Acton on History.* London: Kennikat
Kolko. J. and Kolko, G. 1972: *The Limits of Power.* New York: Harper and Row
Korten, D. C. 1990: *Getting to the 21st Century.* West Hartford, CT: Kumarian
Kossmann, E. H. 1960: The development of Dutch political theory in the seventeenth century.
    In J. S. Bromley and E. H. Kossmann (eds), *Britain and the Netherlands.* London: Chatto and
    Windus
Kossmann, E. H. 1963: *In Praise of the Dutch Republic: Some Seventeenth Century Attitudes.*
    London: University College
Kossmann, E. H. 1970: The Low Countries. In J. P. Cooper (ed.), *The Decline of Spain and the
    Thirty Years War. 1609–1648/59.* Cambridge UK: Cambridge University Press
Kossmann, E. H. 1992: The Dutch Republic in the eighteenth century. In M. C. Jacob and W. W.
    Mijnhardt (eds), *The Dutch Republic in the Eighteenth Century.* Ithaca, NY: Cornell University
    Press
Kossmann, E. H. and Mellick, A. F. (eds) 1974: *Texts Concerning the Revolt of the Netherlands.*
    Cambridge, UK: Cambridge University Press
Kumar, K. 1978: *Prophecy and Progress.* London: Allen Lane
Kwiatkowska, B. 1984: Hugo Grotius and the freedom of the seas. In J. L. M. Elders et al (eds)
    Hugo Grotius: 1583–1983. Assen: Van Gorcum
Lambert, A. M. 1985: *The Making of the Dutch Landscape.* London: Academic Press
Laski, H. J. 1936: *The Rise of European Liberalism.* London: George Allen and Unwin
Lears, T. J. J. 1985: The concept of cultural hegemony: problems and possibilities. *American
    Historical Review,* 90, 567–93
Levey, M. 1969: *The Dolphin History of Painting.The Seventeenth and Eighteenth Centuries.* Lon-
    don: Thames and Hudson
Levinson, C. 1980: *Vodka Cola.* Horsham, UK: Biblios
Little, M. 1995: The liberation of development. *GeoJournal,* 35, 123–35
Lloyd, A. 1986: *The Illustrated History of the Cinema.* London: Orbis
Loth, W. 1988: *The Division of the World.* London: Routledge
Luard, E. 1986: *War in International Society.* Baltimore: Johns Hopkins University Press

Luard, E. 1992: *The Balance of Power*. London: Macmillan

Luce, H. R. 1941: *The American Century*. New York: Farrar and Rinehart

Lukacs, J. A. 1959: A second Holland is not enough. *Encounter*, 12, May, 59–63

Lukacs, J. 1965: *Decline and Rise of Europe*. Westport, CT: Greenwood

Lukacs, J. 1993: *The End of the Twentieth Century and the End of the Modern Age*. New York: Ticknor and Fields

Lundestad, G. 1986: Empire by invitation? The United States and Western Europe, 1945–1952. *Journal of Peace Research*, 23, 261–77

McCauley, M. 1983: *The Origins of the Cold War*. London: Longman

McCormick, T. J. 1989: *America's Half Century*. Baltimore: Johns Hopkins University Press

McDougall, W. A. 1985: *The Heavens and the Earth*. New York: Basic

MacKensie, N. and MacKensie, J. 1977: *The Fabians*. New York: Simon and Schuster

Madison, A. 1982: *Phases of Capitalist Development*. New York: Oxford University Press

Mann, M. 1986: *The Sources of Social Power* (Volume 1). Cambridge, UK: Cambridge University Press

Manning, D. J. 1976: *Liberalism*. London: Dent

Markusen, A. and Yudken, J. 1992: *Dismantling the Cold War Economy*. New York: BasicBooks

Marsh, P. T. 1994: *Joseph Chamberlain. Entrepreneur in Politics*. New Haven, CT: Yale University Press

Marx, K. 1954: *Capital*. London: Lawrence and Wishart

Mathew, D. 1968: *Lord Acton and his Times*. Montgomery: University of Alabama Press

Maull, H. W. 1990: Germany and Japan: the new civilian powers. *Foreign Affairs*, 69(5), 91–106

Meadows, D. H., Meadows, D. L. and Randers, J. 1992: *Beyond the Limits*. Post Mills, VT: Chelsea Green

Meadows, D. H., Meadows, D. L., Randers, J. and Behrens III, W. W. 1974: *The Limits to Growth*. London: Pan

Mee, C. L. 1984: *The Marshall Plan. The Launching of Pax Americana*. New York: Simon and Schuster

Mijnhardt, W. W. 1992: The Dutch Enlightenment: humanism, nationalism and decline. In M. C. Jacob and W. W. Mijnhardt (eds), *The Dutch Republic in the Eighteenth Century*. Ithaca, NY: Cornell University Press

Miller, J. D. B. 1981: *The World of States*. London: Croom Helm

Miliband, R. and Liebman, M. 1984: Reflections on anti-communism. *Socialist Register 1984*, 1–22

Modelski, G. 1987: *Long Cycles of World Politics*. London: Macmillan

Mokyr, J. 1990: *The Lever of Riches. Technological Creativity and Economic Progress*. New York: Oxford University Press

Morgenthau, H. J. 1948: *Politics among Nations*. New York: Knopf

Morris, J. 1968: *Pax Britannica*. London: Faber and Faber

Moscoso, T. 1964: Foreword. In G. Hambridge (ed.), *Dynamics of Development*. New York: Praeger

Motley, J. L. 1856: *The Rise of the Dutch Republic*. London: Swan Sonnerschein

Mountjoy, A. B. 1963: *Industrialization and Underdeveloped Countries*. London: Hutchinson

Mukerji, C. 1983: *From Graven Images. Patterns of Modern Materialism*. New York: Columbia University Press

Mulier, E. H. 1987: The language of seventeenth century republicans in the United Provinces: Dutch or European? In A. Pagden (ed.), *The Languages of Political Theory in Early-Modern Europe*, Cambridge, UK: Cambridge University Press

Murray, J. L. 1967: *Amsterdam in the Age of Rembrandt*. Norman, OK: University of Oklahoma Press

Naess, A. 1989: *Ecology, Community and Lifestyle*. Cambridge, UK: Cambridge University Press

Nairn, T. 1977: *The Break-up of Britain*. London: New Left Books

Nairn, T. 1988: *The Enchanted Glass: Britain and its Monarchy*. London: Radius

Newman, G. 1987: *The Rise of English Nationalism. A Cultural History 1740–1830*. New York: St Martin's

Ney, J. 1970: *The European Surrender. A Descriptive Study of the American Social and Economic Conquest*. Boston: Little, Brown

Nijman, J. 1994: The VOC and the expansion of the world-system. *Political Geography*, 13, 211–27

Nisbet, R. A. 1967: Project Camelot and the science of man. In I. L. Horowitz (ed.), *The Rise and Fall of Project Camelot*. Cambridge, MA: MIT Press

Nisbet, R. A. 1969: *Social Change and History*. New York: Oxford University Press

Nisbet, R. A. 1980: *History of the Idea of Progress*. New York: Basic Books

Nowak. L. 1983: *Property and Power. Towards a Non-Marxian Historical Materialism*. Dordrecht: Reidel

Nussbaum, F. L. 1953: *The Triumph of Science and Reason*. New York: Harper and Row

O'Loughlin, J. 1993: Fact or fiction? The evidence for the thesis of US relative decline, 1966–1991. In C. H. Williams (ed.), *The Political Geography of the New World Order*. London: Belhaven

O'Riordan, T. 1981: *Environmentalism*. London: Pion

O'Sullivan, N. 1988: The political theory of neo-corporatism. In A. Cox and N. O'Sullivan (eds), *The Corporate State*. Aldershot, UK: Elgar

Overbeek, H. 1990: *Global Capitalism and National Decline*. London: Unwin Hyman

Parker, G. 1977: *The Dutch Revolt*. Ithaca, NY: Cornell University Press

Parker, G. 1978: The Dutch Revolt and the polarization of international politics. In G. Parker and L. M. Smith (eds), *The General Crisis of the Seventeenth Century*. London: Routledge and Kegan Paul

Pepper, D. 1984: *The Roots of Modern Environmentalism*. London: Croom Helm

Pepper, D. 1993: *Eco-Socialism*. London: Routledge

Peyrefitte, A. 1992: *The Immobile Empire*. New York: Knopf

Pipes, D. and Garfinkle, A. (eds) 1991: *Friendly Tyrants: an American Dilemma*. London: Macmillan

Pollard, S. 1973: Industrialization and the European economy. *Economic History Review* (series 2), 26, 636–48

Pollard, S. 1989: *Britain's Prime and Britain's Decline. The British Economy 1870–1914*. London: Arnold

Porter, R. 1981: The Enlightenment in England. In R. Porter and M. Teich (eds), *The Enlightenment in National Context*. Cambridge, UK: Cambridge University Press

Price, H. B. 1955: *The Marshall Plan and its Meaning*. Ithaca, NY: Cornell University Press

Price, J. L. 1974: *Culture and Society in the Dutch Republic in the Seventeenth Century*. London: Batsford

Price, J. L. 1994: *Holland and the Dutch Republic in the Seventeenth Century*. Oxford: Clarendon

Range, W. 1959: *Franklin D. Roosevelt's World Order*. Athens, GA: University of Georgia Press

Read, D. 1982: Introduction: Crisis or Golden Age? In D. Read (ed.), *Edwardian England*. New Brunswick, NJ: Rutgers University Press

Reich, C. A. 1970: *The Greening of America*. New York: Random House

Reich, R. B. 1991: *The Work of Nations*. New York: Knopf

Richards, J. M. 1940: *An Introduction to Modern Architecture*. London: Penguin

Richards, T. 1990: *The Commodity Culture of Victorian England*. Stanford, CA: Stanford University Press

Robbins, K. 1988: *Nineteenth Century Britain. Integration and Diversity*. Oxford: Clarendon

Rosenberg, J. 1990: A non-realist theory of sovereignty? Giddens' 'The Nation-State and Violence'. *Millenium*, 19, 249–59

Rosecrance, R. 1990: *America's Economic Resurgence*. New York: Harper and Row

Rostow, W. W. 1960: *The Stages of Economic Growth*. Cambridge, UK: Cambridge University Press

Rowen, H. H. (ed.) 1972: *The Low Countries in Early Modern Times: Selected Documents*. New York: Walker

Rowen, H. H. 1978: *John de Witt, Grand Pensionary of Holland, 1625–1672*. Princeton, NJ: Princeton University Press

Rowen, H. H. 1986: *John de Witt: Statesman of the 'True Freedom'*. Cambridge, UK: Cambridge University Press

Rowen, H. H. 1988: *The Princes of Orange. The Stadholders in the Dutch Republic*. Cambridge, UK: Cambridge University Press

Rubinstein, W. D. 1993: *Capitalism, Culture and Decline in Britain 1750–1990*. London: Routledge

Ruggie, J. 1983: Continuity and transformation in the world polity. *World Politics*, 35, 261–85

Russett, B. 1985: The mysterious case of vanishing hegemony. *International Organization*, 39, 207–31

Rybczynski, W. 1986: *Home. A Short History of an Idea*. London: Penguin

Sahlins, M. 1967: The established order: do not fold, spindle or mutilate. In I. L. Horowitz (ed.), *The Rise and Fall of Project Camelot*. Cambridge, MA: MIT Press

Said, E. W. 1978: *Orientalism*. New York: Pantheon

Sassen, S. 1991: *The Global City*. Princeton, NJ: Princeton University Press

Schama, S. 1981: The Enlightenment in the Netherlands. In R. Porter and M. Teich (eds), *The Enlightenment in National Context*. Cambridge, UK: Cambridge University Press

Schama, S. 1987: *The Embarrassment of Riches*. London: Collins

Schlesinger, A. M. 1965: *A Thousand Days: John F. Kennedy in the White House*. Boston: Houghton Mifflin

Schoffer, I. 1978: Did Holland's Golden Age coincide with a period of crisis? In G. Parker and L. M. Smith (eds), *The General Crisis of the Seventeenth Century*. London: Routledge and Kegan Paul

Schroeder, P. W. 1986: The nineteenth century international system: changes in structure. *World Politics*, 39, 1–26

Schultz, H. J. 1972: *English Liberalism and the State*. Lexington, MA: Heath

Schurmann, F. 1978: Selections from *The Logic of World Power*. In C. S. Maier (ed) *The Origins of the Cold War and Contemporary Europe*. New York: New Viewpoints

Seely, J. R. 1971: *The Expansion of England*. Chicago: Chicago University Press

Seligson, M. A. and Passe-Smith, J. T. (eds) 1993: *Development and Underdevelopment. The Political Economy of Inequality*. Boulder, CO: Lynne Rienner

Semmel, B. 1986: *Liberalism and Naval Strategy*. London: Allen and Unwin

Servan-Schreiber, J-J. 1968: *The American Challenge*. London: Hamish Hamilton

Shapiro, A. L. 1992: *We're Number One*. New York: Vintage

Shonfield, A. 1965: *Modern Capitalism*. London: Oxford University Press

Skinner, Q. 1978: *The Foundation of Modern Political Thought* (Volume 2). Cambridge, UK: Cambridge University Press

Sklair, L. 1991: *Sociology of the Global System*. New York: Harvester-Wheatsheaf

Small, M. and Singer, J. D. 1982: *Resort to Arms*. Beverly Hills, CA: Sage

Smith, T. 1981: *The Pattern of Imperialism*. Cambridge, UK: Cambridge University Press

Smith, W. D. 1984: The function of commercial centres in the modernization of European capitalism: Amsterdam as an information exchange in the seventeenth century. *Journal of Economic History*, 44, 985–1005

Sorensen, T. C. 1965: *Kennedy*. New York: Harper and Row

Stearns, P. N. 1969: Britain and the spread of the industrial revolution. In C. J. Bartlett (ed.), *Britain Pre-eminent*. London: Macmillan

Stein, A. A. 1984: The hegemon's dilemma: GB, the US, and the international economic order. *International Organization*, 38, 95–110

Sternlicht, S. 1988: *R. F. Delderfield*. Boston: Twayne

Stokes, G. 1986: *Hitler and the Quest for World Domination*. Lemington Spa, UK: Berg

Strange, S. 1987: The persistent myth of lost hegemony. *International Organization*, 41, 551–74

Strayer, J. R. 1970: *On the Medieval Origins of the Modern State*. Princeton, NJ: Princeton University Press

Sumiya, M. 1991: Japan: model society for the future. *Annals, AAPSS*, 513, 139–49

Sylvan, D. J. 1987: Did Florence have a foreign policy? Paper presented to the American Political Science Association Conference, 1987.

Taira, K. 1991: Japan, an imminent hegemon? *Annals, AAPSS*, 513, 151–63

Taylor, A. J. P. 1952: *Rumours of War*. London: Hamilton

Taylor, J. R. 1982: A little light relief. In D. Robinson (ed.), *Movies of the Fifties*. London: Orbis

Taylor, P. J. 1989a: The error of developmentalism in human geography. In D. Gregory and R. Walford (eds), *Horizons in Human Geography*. London: Macmillan

Taylor, P. J. 1989b: Britain's changing role in the world-economy. *Review*, 13, 33–48

Taylor, P. J. 1990: *Britain and the Cold War*. London: Pinter

Taylor, P. J. 1991a: If Cold War is the problem, is hot war the solution? In N. Kliot and S. Waterman (eds), *Political Geography of Conflict and Peace*. London: Belhaven

Taylor, P. J. 1991b: The English and their Englishness: 'a curiously mysterious, elusive and little understood people'. *Scottish Geographical Magazine*, 107, 146–61

Taylor, P. J. 1993a *Political Geography: World-Economy, Nation-State and Locality*. London: Longman

Taylor, P. J. 1993b: The last of the hegemons: British impasse, American impasse, world impasse. *Southeastern Geographer*, 33, 1–23

Taylor, P. J. 1993c: States in world-systems analysis: massaging a creative tension. In R. Palan and B. Gills (eds), *Transcending the State-Global Divide*. Boulder, CO: Rienner

Taylor, P. J. 1994a: The state as container: territoriality in the modern world-system. *Progress in Human Geography*, 18, 151–62

Taylor, P. J. 1994b: Ten years that shook the world? The United Provinces as the first hegemonic state. *Sociological Perspectives*, 37, 25–46

Taylor, P. J. 1995a: Beyond containers: inter-nationality, inter-stateness, inter-territoriality. *Progress in Human Geography*, 19, 1–22

Taylor, P. J. 1995b: States and world cities: the rise and fall of their mutuality. In P. Knox and P. J. Taylor (eds), *World Cities in a World-System*. Cambridge, UK: Cambridge University Press

Taylor, P. W. 1986: *Respect for Nature. A Theory of Environmental Ethics*. Princeton, NJ: Princeton University Press

Temperley, H. 1976: Anglo-American images. In H. C. Allen and R. Thompson (eds), *Contrast and Connection*. London: Bell

'T Hart, M. 1989: Cities and statemaking in the Dutch Republic, 1580–1680. *Theory and Society*, 18, 663–87

'T Hart, M. 1993: *The Making of a Bourgeois State*. Manchester, UK: Manchester University Press

Thompson, D. 1990: *Queen Victoria. Gender and Power*. London: Virago

Thompson, E. P. 1991: *Customs in Common*. London: Merlin

Thurow, L. 1992: *Head to Head. The Coming Economic Battle among Japan, Europe and America*. New York: Morrow

Tilly, C. 1985: Connecting domestic and international conflicts, past and present. In U. Literbacher and M. D. Ward (eds), *Dynamic Models of International Conflict*. Boulder, CO: Rienner

Tilly, C. 1990: *Coersion, Capital and European States AD 990–1990*. Oxford, UK: Blackwell

Tivey, L. 1988: *Interpretations of British Politics. The Image and the System*. London: Harvester-Wheatsheaf

Tomlinson, T. B. 1976: *The English Middle Class Novel*. London: Macmillan

Touraine, A. 1990: American sociology viewed from abroad. In H. J. Gans (ed.), *Sociology in America*. Newbury Park, CA: Sage

Toulmin, S. 1990: *Cosmopolis. The Hidden Agenda of Modernity*. New York: Free Press

Treasure, G. R. R. 1966: *Seventeenth Century France*. London: Rivingtons

Trevor-Roper, H. 1971: Spain and Europe, 1598–1621. In J. P. Cooper (ed.), *The Decline of Spain and the Thirty Years War, 1609–1648/59*. Cambridge, UK: Cambridge University Press

Trueblood, B. F. 1932: *The Development of the Peace Idea*. Boston: Plimpton

Tsanoff, R. A. 1971: *Civilization and Progress*. Lexington, KY: University Press of Kentucky

Turner, F. J. 1932: *The Significance of Sections in American History*. New York: Holt

Vann Woodward, C. 1991: *The Old World's New World*. New York: Oxford University Press

Vincent, A. 1992: *Modern Political Ideologies*. Oxford: Blackwell

Viner, J. 1952: America's aims and the progress of underdeveloped countries. In B. F. Hoselitz (ed.), *The Progress of Underdeveloped Areas*. Chicago: Chicago University Press

Viner, J. 1969: Power and plenty as objects of foreign policy in the seventeenth and eighteenth centuries. In D. C. Coleman (ed) *Revisions in Mercantilism*. London: Methuen

Vries, J. de 1973: On the modernity of the Dutch Republic. *Journal of Economic History*, 33, 191–202

Vries, J. de 1974: *The Dutch Rural Economy in the Golden Age 1500–1700*. New Haven, CT: Yale University Press

Vries, J. de 1978: Barges and capitalism. Passenger transportation in the Dutch economy, 1632–1839, *A.A.G. Brijdragen*, 21, 33–398

Walker, R. B. J. 1993: *Inside/Outside: International Relations as Political Theory*. Cambridge, UK: Cambridge University Press

Wallerstein, I. 1979: *The Capitalist World-Economy*. Cambridge, UK: Cambridge University Press

Wallerstein, I. 1980: *The Modern World-System II*. New York: Academic

Wallerstein, I. 1984: *The Politics of the World-Economy*. Cambridge, UK: Cambridge University Press

Wallerstein, I. 1987: The United States and the world 'crisis'. In T. Boswell and A. Bergesen (eds), *America's Changing Role in the World-System*. New York: Praeger

Wallerstein, I. 1989: France: a special case? A world-systems perspective. In E. D. Genovese and L. Hochberg (eds), *Geographic Perspectives in History*. Oxford: Blackwell

Wallerstein, I. 1991a: *Unthinking Social Science*. Cambridge, UK: Polity

Wallerstein, I. 1991b: *Geopolitics and Geoculture*. Cambridge, UK: Cambridge University Press

Wallerstein, I. 1992: The West, capitalism, and the modern world-system. *Review*, 15, 561–619

Walzer, M. 1992: The new tribalism. *Dissent*, Spring, 164–71

Wansink, H. 1971: Holland and six allies: the Republic of the Seven United Provinces. In J. S. Bromley and E. H. Kossmann (eds), *Britain and the Netherlands* (Volume IV). The Hague: Martinus Nijhoff

Watson. A. 1992: *The Evolution of International Society*. London: Routledge

Watson, D. R. 1969: The British Parliamentary system and the growth of constitutional government in Western Europe. In C. J. Bartlett (ed.), *Britain Pre-eminent*. London: Macmillan

Watt, I. 1972: *The Rise of the Novel*. London: Penguin

Watt, K. E. F. 1982: *Understanding the Environment*. Boston: Allyn and Bacon

Westbrook, R. 1983: Politics as consumption: managing the modern American election. In R. W. Fox and T. J. J. Lears (eds), *The Culture of Consumption*. New York: Pantheon

Whitaker, R. 1984: Fighting the Cold War on the home front: America, Britain, Australia and Canada. *Socialist Register 1984*, 23–67

Weinstein, J. 1967: *The Decline of Socialism in America, 1912–1925*. New York: Monthly Review Press

Wiener, M. J. 1981: *English Culture and the Decline of the Industrial Spirit, 1850–1980*. Cambridge, UK: Cambridge University Press

Wight, M. 1978: *Power Politics*. Leicester, UK: Leicester University Press

Wightman, D. 1983: *American Academics and the Rationalization of American Power*. Birmingham, UK: Institute for Advanced Research in the Humanities, University of Birmingham, Occasional Paper No. 8

Wilkinson, D. not dated: States systems: pathology and survival. Los Angeles: UCLA, Department of Politics

Wilkinson, D. 1984: Kinematics of world systems. Los Angeles: UCLA, Department of Politics

Wilkinson, D. 1994: Reconceiving hegemony. Conference paper, International Studies Convention, Washington, DC

Williams, P. 1987: Constituting class and gender: a social history of the home. In N. Thrift and P. Williams (eds), *Class and Space. The Making of Urban Society*. London: Routledge and Kegan Paul

Wilson, C. not dated: *Holland and Britain*. London: Collins

Wilson, C. 1957: *Profit and Power. A Study of England and the Dutch Wars*. London: Longman Green

Wilson, C. 1958: *Mercantilism*. London: Historical Association

Wilson, C. 1976: *The Transformation of Europe, 1558–1648*. London: Weidenfeld and Nicolson

Winkler, J. T. 1988: Corporatism. In A. Cox and N. O'Sullivan (eds), *The Corporate State*. Aldershot, UK: Elgar

Wolfe, A. 1984: The irony of anti-communism: ideology and interest in post-war American foreign policy. *Socialist Register 1984*, 214–29

Wolfe, M. 1969: French views on wealth and taxes from the middle ages to the old regime. In D. C. Coleman (ed) *Revisions in Mercantilism*. London: Methuen

Wolferen, K. van 1989: *The Enigma of Japanese Power. People and Politics in a Stateless Nation*. New York: Knopf

Wolferen, K. van 1990: The Japan problem revisited. *Foreign Affairs*, 69, 41–55

Woolf, S. 1991: *Napoleon's Integration of Europe*. London: Routledge

Wornum, R. N. 1970: The exhibition as a lesson in taste. In *The Art-Journal Illustrated Catalogue. The Industry of all Nations 1851*. Newton Abbot, UK: David and Charles Reprints

Yates, F. A. 1975: *Astrea. The Imperial Theme in the Sixteenth Century*. London: Routledge and Kegan Paul

Zeeuw, J. W. de 1978: Peat and the Dutch Golden Age, *A.A.G. Bijdragen*, 21, 3–32

Zerubavel, E. 1992: *Terra Cognita. The Mental Discovery of America*. New Brunswick, NJ: Rutgers University Press

Zolberg, R. 1986: Strategic interactions and the formation of modern states: France and England. In A. Kazancigil (ed.), *The State in Global Perspective*. Aldershot, UK: Gower

Index

DATE DUE

GAYLORD			PRINTED IN U.S.A.